THE
Old Farmer's Almanac

CALCULATED ON A NEW AND IMPROVED PLAN FOR THE YEAR OF OUR LORD

2000

BEING LEAP YEAR AND (UNTIL JULY 4) 224TH YEAR OF AMERICAN INDEPENDE

Fitted for Boston and the New England states, with special corrections
calculations to answer for all the United States.

Containing, besides the large number of Astronomical Calculations and the Farm
for every month in the year, a variety of

New, Useful, and Entertaining Matter.

Established in 1792
by Robert B. Thomas

What's past is prologue.

– William Shakespeare

ORIGINAL WOOD ENGRAVING BY RANDY MILLER

Cover T.M. registered
in U.S. Patent Office

Copyright 1999 by Yankee Publishing Incorporated
ISSN 0078-4516

Library of Congress
Card No. 56-29681

Address all editorial correspondence to
THE OLD FARMER'S ALMANAC, DUBLIN, NH 03444

Contents

Weather

44

Forecast Methods

134

General U.S. Forecast

135

Map of U.S. Regions

136-155

Regional Forecasts

1. New England 136
2. Greater New York–
   New Jersey 137
3. Middle Atlantic Coast   138
4. Piedmont & Southeast
   Coast 140
5. Florida 141
6. Upstate New York 142
7. Greater Ohio Valley . . 144
8. Deep South 145
9. Chicago & Southern
   Great Lakes 146
10. Northern Great Plains–
    Great Lakes 148
11. Central Great Plains . . 149
12. Texas–Oklahoma 150
13. Rocky Mountains 152
14. Desert Southwest 153
15. Pacific Northwest 154
16. California 155

Features

6 Consumer
Tastes
and
Trends
for 2000

page 6

56 Relax!
Maybe It's
Not the Millennium
After All

88 Best Sky Sights of
the Next Century —
Guaranteed!

page 92

92 So You Want
to Make a Time
Capsule?

102 A Poultry Primer
for the Year 2000

108 The Most
Important
Inventions of the
Past 2,000 Years

112 How to Become
a Prophet

126 Remembering
Galveston's
Night of
Agony

156 12
Garden
Myths
and Why
They're
Wrong

160 Be Honest: Do You
Know What pH Is?

page 156

A Special Report

116

The
State of
Romance
in the Year
2000

(continued on page 4)

12 Great Reasons to Own a Mantis Tiller

1. Weighs just 20 pounds. Mantis is a joy to use. It starts easily, turns on a dime, lifts nimbly over plants and fences.

2. Tills like nothing else. Mantis bites down a full 10" deep, churns tough soil into crumby loam, prepares seedbeds in no time.

3. Has patented "serpentine" tines. Our **patented** tine teeth spin at up to 240 RPM – twice as fast as others. Cuts through tough soil and vegetation like a chain saw through wood!

4. Weeds faster than hand tools. Reverse its tines and Mantis is a precision power weeder. Weeds an average garden in 20 minutes.

5. Digs planting furrows. With the optional Planter/Furrower, Mantis digs deep or shallow furrows for planting. Builds raised beds, too!

6. Cuts neat borders. Use the optional Border Edger to cut crisp edges for flower beds, walkways, around shrubs and trees.

7. Dethatches your lawn. Thatch on your lawn prevents water and nutrients from reaching the roots. The optional Dethatcher quickly removes thatch.

8. Aerates your lawn, too. For a lush, healthy carpet, the optional Aerator slices thousands of tine slits in your lawn's surface.

9. Trims bushes and hedges! Only Mantis has an optional 24" or 30" trimmer bar to prune and trim your shrubbery and small trees.

10. The Mantis Promise. Try any product that you buy directly from Mantis with **NO RISK!** If you're not completely satisfied, send it back to us within one year for a complete, no hassle refund.

11. Warranties. The entire tiller is warranted for two full years. The tines are guaranteed forever against breakage.

12. Fun to use. The Mantis Tiller/Cultivator is so much fun to use gardeners everywhere love their Mantis tillers.

For FREE details, call

TOLL FREE 1-800-366-6268

(continued from page 2)

Contents

page 230

172 Palms and Portents

176 Home Remedies for Your Pets

182 Who Was Leif Eriksson?

190 Five Stories from the Hall of Fame

198 Mr. Smith's Maddening Mind-Manglers

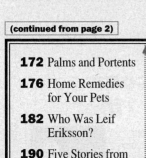

page 176

200 Favorite Foods for Family Reunions

210 Sharing My Best Apple Recipes

220 That Scandalous Dance Called the Waltz

224 The (Sickening) Secrets of Winning an Eating Contest

230 The Greatest Bargains of the Last 100 Years

254 Thinking a Little Too Big: Four Ideas That Didn't Change the World

259 Horseshoeing: Still a Ringer of a Career

262 Anecdotes and Pleasantries

273
A Reference Compendium

Astronomical Data

39

How to Use This Almanac

Aphelion, Earth at 42
Calendar Pages 60-87
Calendars, 1999-2001 . . . 272
Chronological Cycles 42
Conjunctions . . . 42, 50, 61-87
Day, Length of 40, 60-86
Daylight Saving Time
. . . . 39, 70, 82
Earthquakes 43
Eclipses. 52
Eras. 42
Glossary 46
Key Letters
. . . . 40, 50, 54, 60-86, 234
Meteor Showers 52
Moon:
  Age 41, 60-86
  Astronomical Place
  . . . . 41, 60-86
  Full, 2000-2004. 52
  Phases of 60-86
  Rise and Set 60-86
Perihelion, Earth at 42
Planets:
  Rise and Set 50
  Symbols for 42
Seasons 39, 42
Stars, Bright 54
Sun:
  Declination 40, 60-86
  Rise and Set 60-86
  Sundials 40
  Sun Fast 40, 60-86
Tides:
  Boston. 41, 60-87
  Corrections 240
  Glossary 239
Time Corrections 234
Twilight, Length of 239

Charts, Tables, and Miscellany

Astrology:
  Gardening by Moon's
    Sign. 167
  Moon's Place 167
  Timetable 169
  Zodiac 170
Classified Advertising . . 249
Contests:
  Essay 217
  Recipe 216
Fishing, Best Days for . . . 30
Foreword, To Patrons. . . . 34
Frosts and Growing
  Seasons 166

Gestation and Mating Table 270
Holidays for 2000 44
How Old Is Your Dog?. . 180
Makeshift Measures . . . 229
Outdoor Planting Table. . 164
Puzzles, Mathematical. . 198
  Answers to 228
Religious Observances
  . . . . 42, 44, 61-87
Table of Measures 268
What People Fish for Most
  (freshwater). 30
When Will the Moon
  Rise Today?. 90

As writer **Jamie Kageleiry** talked to futurists, trend-watchers, experts, and researchers in fields ranging from cooking to demographics, she noticed some themes for the beginning of the new century:

- **Simplicity and quality ("casual luxe")**
- **Nostalgia (boomers turn toward their past)**
- **Glowing color (orange, celestial blue)**
- **Sense of community (family, ethnic, and regional bonds)**

Watch for these trends in the pages that follow and in the year to come.

Fashion and Style

"Celestial blue and wasabi green are the millennium colors. We are likely to see a move toward vibrant colors such as orange in the post-millennium period."

– Anne Marshall and Diana Holman, partners in WomanTrend, Washington, D.C.

COLORS FOR CLOTHES. Gray will still be fairly ubiquitous through winter for women, but men's fashions will be darker, with flashes of rich hues. Come spring 2000, look for "natural neutrals" such as khaki, flax, sand, and olive drab. Whites will be popular, and **reds** (hooray! the whole spectrum, from orange to lavender). And, as always, green can't miss — everything from aqua to chartreuse.

The millennium celebration will influence fashion this fall and winter, with lots of glitter, shine, taffeta, brocade, and beading for the holidays.

"If you sum up this time in fashion, it's casual luxe."

– Michael Kors, named women's-wear designer of the year by the Council of Fashion Designers of America

Look for two big trends in women's fashion:

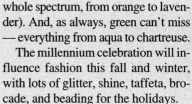

VERY FEMININE. Florals, sheers, soft-washed linens, embroidery, peasant blouses, and still lots of cashmere. Hems will stay just above the knee, or down around the ankle.

UTILITARIAN. Cargo pockets and drawstrings will continue; high-tech fabrics and shiny finishes (like nylon) will be popular. A combination of the two trends is a trend unto itself — wearing a pretty beaded twin set with cargo pants.

(c o n t i n u e d)

Now! Join The National Arbor Day Foundation and Get

FREE TREES
10 Flowering Trees

The Arbor Day Foundation, a nonprofit organization, will give ten free flowering trees to members contributing $10.

The ten trees are 2 White Flowering Dogwoods, 2 Flowering Crabapples, 2 Golden Raintrees, 2 Washington Hawthorns, and 2 American Redbuds, or other trees selected for growing in your area.

Members also receive the Foundation's newsletter, *Arbor Day*, and *The Tree Book* with tree planting and care information. Your six to twelve inch trees are guaranteed to grow and come postpaid with easy planting instructions. Trees ship Feb. through May in the spring or

Oct. through mid-Dec. in the fall. **Join today, and plant your Trees for America!**

The National Arbor Day Foundation®
www.arborday.org

"In accessories, I'm seeing a lot of what I call 'utility bags' — taking the backpack to the next level. Carryalls are now strapped to the torso, such as over the chest or around the waist. Finally someone is realizing how much STUFF we all carry around!"

– Aimee Marchand, designer at Liz Claiborne

OTHER ACCESSORY NEWS. Stay away from giant sunglasses and eyeglasses. "The coolest people choose horizontal rectangles and other geometric shapes that just cover the eyes," reports *The New York Times*.

BLUE JEANS FOREVER. Watch for vintage and novelty denims with distressing, rips, and embroidery: "Think hippy denim," says Ms. Marchand.

Men's styles show "rural hardiness" — modern clothes that exude nonchalance: pajama-like trousers topped with cashmere crewnecks, and three-button jackets left open. Lots of brawny ribbed sweaters, cargo pants, and patch pockets.

One exception: More and more men are wearing French cuffs — the ones you roll up and fasten with cuff links.

Hot Collectibles

HOLLYWOOD MEMORABILIA. As baby boomers age and become affluent, they may long to relive their youth — say, by purchasing a movie prop or celebrity possession. Anything owned by Walt Disney, Howard Hughes, Clara Bow, or Marilyn Monroe commands a high price, particularly cigarette cases: Marilyn Monroe's fetched $9,500. More typical is Sammy Davis Jr.'s engraved sterling case, which went for $795.

BARBIE. Nostalgic boomers are behind this collecting trend, too. Some people are willing to pay up to $7,000 (for a rare, mint-condition brunette Barbie). A blonde Barbie from 1959, still in the box, recently went for $5,000.

ANTIQUE TACKLE. Old fishing rods, lures, and gear can reel in big bucks. At a recent British auction, in fact, a reel fetched a record $10,450 and an empty lure box went for $1,650.

GENTLEMEN, START YOUR ENGINES. Old pistons and connecting rods from famous race cars are now fetching over $50 apiece — or more if they are broken, burned, or scarred in some way that tells a story.

The Home Front

COLORS. The push this year will be toward blue, as well as shades of purple, from pink to aubergine. Yellow may also enjoy an uptrend. Orange and terra cotta will accent earthy browns.

One of the big trends in furniture (desks, bureaus, tables, chair frames) is brushed aluminum, steel, and brass. Dark woods will also be popular. Upholstery will feature menswear looks like flannel and denim. Sofa beds will show new sophistication — sleek lines,

(c o n t i n u e d)

DR® FIELD and BRUSH MOWER

— Works like a tractor-drawn brushcutter... but in a walk-behind version that's more maneuverable and much less expensive!

• **CLEARS & MAINTAINS** meadows, pastures, roadsides, fences, wooded and rough non-lawn areas with ease. Mows nearly an acre per hour!

• **CUTS** tall grass, weeds, brush, brambles, sumac — even tough saplings up to 1" thick!

• Plus **CHOPS/MULCHES** most everything it cuts; leaves NO TANGLE of material to trip over or to pick up like hand-held brushcutters and sicklebar mowers.

• **POWERFUL** with up to **15.0 HP**…yet so easy to use thanks to SELF-POWERED WHEELS…POWER REVERSE… and easy turning DIFFERENTIAL. 4 SPEEDS let you zip through grass, weeds, brambles…then c-r-e-e-p into tough brush without reducing power or blade speed.

• *TRANSFORMS* neglected, overgrown areas into beautiful park-like settings!

NEW 15 HP V-Twin!

Made in USA

CALL TOLL FREE 1(800) 520-2525

Too awkward!

Too tiring!

So, *WHY MESS* with a tractor powered brushcutter that's too awkward to maneuver around obstacles and trees you want to save… OR with an under-powered hand-held brushcutter that's so slow and tiring to use?

Please call or write for FREE DETAIL of the Amazing DR® FIELD and BRUSH MOWER!

YES! Please rush complete FREE DETAILS of the **DR® FIELD and BRUSH MOWER** including prices and specifications of Manual and ELECTRIC-STARTING Models and "Off-Season" Savings now in effect.

Name _____

Address _____

City _____ State ____ ZIP _____

To: **COUNTRY HOME PRODUCTS®**
Dept. 5295F, Meigs Road, P.O. Box 25
Vergennes, Vermont 05491
Visit us at: www.drfieldbrush.com

©1999 CHP, Inc.

total comfort, simple conversion.

As more and more of us **work at home,** watch for office furniture that looks pleasing and homelike yet meets the requirements of work.

BUTLERS. As Americans get more affluent (and busy), butlering is back. "Household manager" might be a better description for someone who will buy the family groceries, take care of pets, run errands, cook — basically all the things a wife used to do before she started running corporations (or just running).

Hot Commodities in 2000

YO-YOS. Factories can't keep up with orders — but you can always go to Tiffany's for a sterling silver one.

HULA HOOPS. Great exercise, and pure nostalgia for boomers.

CHAMPAGNE. Supply is up; demand is up more.

"There is, and will be, a lot of interest in making animal habitats that will invite creatures into our yards — birds and butterflies. Nectar-rich flowers such as those found on trumpet vines will attract hummingbirds. Other birds will go for a variety of berry-producing shrubs and trees."

– Philadelphia landscape designer Alysse Einbender

ORANGE FLOWERS, both annuals and perennials from pansies to marigolds to rhododendrons, are sparking garden borders and beds. Exotic cannas, callas, celosias, and other striking plants favored 100 years ago will enjoy renewed popularity.

Eating In and Eating Out

More chefs are heading in the direction of a new ideal: **simplicity.** Complex "fusion" cooking will take a backseat to meals that provide the diner with the essence of one or two flavors. For example, a chicken dish may be just that — a perfectly roasted chicken.

Simple doesn't mean bland. There is a huge move, both in restaurants and at home, toward spicy, piquant flavors. Our growing population of foreign-born people has enriched our cuisine with intense, exotic flavors, and in many families everyone from toddler to grandfather eats curries and chilies. Another factor: that aging baby boomer. Taste buds age, too, and demand more boldness and intensity.

Melinda Davis, of the futurist think tank The Next Group, calls this trend **"Luxe Populi"** — the desire for high-quality meals that are doable in real life. This might explain the resurgence of **pressure cookers:** Sales have grown 1,000 percent at one retailer. They let you make good, old-fashioned food in a fraction of the normal cooking time.

Potatoes will be popular in restaurants

(c o n t i n u e d)

and at home. Look for the 'Yukon Gold' variety, which has a buttery hue.

Tapioca is enjoying popularity among chefs, not as a sweet pudding dessert, but as a thickener or base for sauces.

> *"Marketers will finally wake up to the fact that men do a substantial amount of American meal preparation, and advertising will begin to reflect this. . . . The sudden huge*

> *upswing in home food-gardening prompted by fears of Y2K problems will rapidly subside, but at least some of those who switched from purely ornamental to mixed food and flower gardens will continue to grow vegetables and herbs. . . . 'Organic' and 'natural' will continue their meteoric rise in popularity."*
>
> – Leslie Land, *Yankee* Magazine food editor and *New York Times* columnist

If simplicity is too boring, you can always buy **food that glows in the dark**. A company called Prolume has patented a "self-illuminating extract made from bioluminescent creatures." That means you mix a dollop of jellyfish, glowworm, or firefly into your cake frosting (or beer, or tapioca pudding), turn out the lights, and impress your dinner guests. The stuff is "believed" to be safe to ingest.

FYI. In 1960, the average household devoted 64 days worth of income to its annual food bill; by 1999, it took only 40 days to pay the tab.

Good for You

FIDGETING. We all know people like this: They eat whatever they want and never gain an ounce. How do they do it? Researchers at the Mayo Clinic fed 16 people an extra 1,000 calories a day for eight weeks and told them to refrain from strenuous exercise. Some people (the "lucky ones," they called them) worked off the extra calories simply by fidgeting — bouncing a leg while sitting, tapping a pencil. Don't think that you can start a wiggle-worm regimen and shed pounds, though. It appears that you have to come by it naturally.

ALL THE USUAL SUSPECTS: Soy, green tea, carrots, coffee, ketchup, and chocolate. Did we say coffee? The final word on coffee changes every day, but even though we knew that a double cappuccino was bad for sleeping, it has many upsides: It increases the effects of painkillers, decreases the risk of cirrhosis of the liver, may aid in treating asthma, and has even been shown to have anticancer effects.

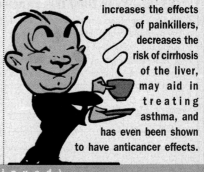

(c o n t i n u e d)

It Takes Guts To Call This "The Best Tiller On Earth"...

Compare for yourself and see - BCS makes the toughest tiller you can buy!

• **Built-in Versatility** - BCS Tillers can run all of these attachments:
18-26" Tiller
30-45" Sickle Bar Mower
20-28" Snow Thrower
40" Power Sweeper
20-30" Brush Mower
38" Lawn Mower

• **Adjustable, Anti-vibe Handles** drop for easy turning, swing aside and rotate 180° to accommodate front and rear-drive attachments.

• **Automotive-style Clutch** means no belts to slip, no chains to break, no pulleys to adjust - ever!

• **All-gear Drive Transmission** featuring precision cut heat-treated steel (not powdered metal gears) and heat-treated hardened shaft (not cold-rolled shaft) for extra durability.

• **No-Time-Limit Warranty** * - includes shafts, gears, case, bearings - even seals! Provides years of protection at no extra cost! *Transmission only

Sickle Bar Mower   *Snow Thrower*   *Power Sweeper*   *Chipper/Shredder*   *Brush Mower*

WAIT — KETCHUP? That's right. Fresh and processed tomatoes (and sauces and soups) are red because they contain lycopene, which apparently can significantly lower cancer risk.

AND CHOCOLATE? We know it's a balm for *l'affaires du coeur,* but here's some sweet news: A recent Harvard University study found that people who consume a few chunks of chocolate a month live longer than those who swear off sweets. However (here's the bad news) — some experts are predicting a looming **chocolate shortage,** due to damage to cocoa trees by a fungus and also by recent El Niño weather.

Don't forget about **cranberries** and **blueberries:** Both are high in antioxidants (blueberries are the champs), and both help ward off urinary tract infections. Please pass the blueberry pie!

TESTOSTERONE. We know it makes men men, but testosterone (which women have in small doses, too) has gotten a bum rap over the years. Recent studies have failed to prove that testosterone causes aggression. In fact, it can generate confidence and a sense of well-being.

ROOTING FOR THE WINNING TEAM. Turns out that testosterone levels in men go up 20 percent in the fans of winning teams and down an equal amount for the losing fans. Psychologist Paul Bernhardt says it is due to a physiological effect called "basking in reflected glory."

Pet News

BAD, BAD DOG. It happens when you leave them alone — they bark, they rip things up, they chew your shoes, and they piddle (at the least) on your rugs. They're not just being naughty: It's because they have "separation anxiety" from being left alone. Never fear — the Food and Drug Administration has just approved a drug called Clomicalm, which eases dogs' psyches.

HEIRDALE LUCK. Baby boomers worry about their pets outliving them and how they will be cared for. So Fluffy and Fido are being figured into estate planning. Owners in some states can donate a set amount of money per pet to a local SPCA so that the pets can be housed in a "life-care cottage" with human caretakers to watch over them.

FLYBALL is the "fastest growing sport in the dog world," reports *The Washington Post.* Flyball is a relay race involving two teams of four dogs. Popularity in Canada and the United States has soared, and there are now 300 registered clubs in the North American Flyball Association, involving 7,000 dogs whose owners, like soccer moms, transport them from match to match.

(c o n t i n u e d)

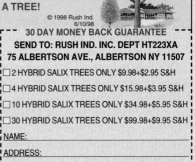

The Difference Between Men and Women, 2000

TASTE. Women have **better taste.** No, we're not talking loud ties — it's in the taste buds themselves. According to Dr. Linda Bartoshuk, who studies sensory processes and nutrition at Yale University Medical School, about 35 percent of women, but only 15 percent of men, are what she calls "supertasters," possessing unusually dense clusters of taste buds.

FIGHTING. A University of Utah researcher found that husbands and wives have different trigger points for arguments. Husbands get angry if their competence or dominance is threatened. Wives react to  accusations involving personal relations or compassion. One thing in common: Frequent fights raise blood pressure and encourage heart disease in both genders.

PHONE TIME. Men spend less than 25 minutes a day on the line at home; women spend 40 minutes.

BLINKING. Women **blink** nearly twice as often as men do. Or was that *wink*?

Good News

A SIGH OF RELIEF FROM WORKING MOMS. University of Massachusetts psychologist Elizabeth Harvey evaluated more than 6,000 children of all races, between the ages of 3 and 12, and compared those whose mothers didn't work at all for the first three years of their babies' lives with those whose mothers did. She found that a mother's working has no adverse effects on children's behavior, mental development, or self-esteem. "Harvey's study suggests that the number of hours spent away from home is not as important as the quality of parenting," says Lindsay Chase-Lansdale, an associate professor of human development at the University of Chicago.

ANOTHER MYTH BITES THE DUST. Sex after menopause? Women lose interest, the theory goes. A recent survey found, however, that a majority of women aged 50 to 65 say their sexual desire and pleasure are just as great as before menopause.

THE RETURN OF THE CONDOR. Fourteen years ago, the last nesting female condor in the wild died in California. Biologists brought the entire species into zoos for safekeeping, training the baby condors to avoid the world's evils — houses, people, power lines. Fifty condors now fly free in California and Arizona. Their further survival will hinge on how well the regal birds can adapt to the wild, learning to hunt, mate, and raise their young on their own.

(c o n t i n u e d   o n   p a g e   2 0)

Bad News

RING, RING, RING. In a survey of 1,000 households across the nation, eight of ten adults reported getting at least three unwanted phone calls at home every day.

A RISING TIDE . . . doesn't raise every boat, even in our buoyant economy. A study by Sheldon Danziger of the University of Michigan shows that college graduates have benefited disproportionately from the surging economy, compared with high-school graduates. In 1978, college graduates earned only 15 percent more than high-school grads; today, the differential is 50 percent.

A ROSE ISN'T A ROSE . . . if you're getting on in years and roses start to smell like, well, nothing. Older people have a higher threshold for noticing a smell, have a shorter time before a smell fades, and are less able to identify a smell.

High Tech

SMART KITCHENS. Now your refrigerator can make your grocery list for you. Electrolux has teamed up with software company ICL to create a prototype of a refrigerator equipped with a touch screen and bar-code scanner. Just swipe your nearly empty container of milk past the scanner and the "Screenfridge" will enter "milk" directly into a Web shopping list. The touch screen will allow you to handle your E-mail, pay bills, and shop from the Internet.

SMARTER ATMS. These cash dis-pensers will soon be able to sell other paper items, such as tickets for airplanes, trains, concerts, and sports events, all with choice of seating. In-bank ATMs will soon be able to open new accounts and handle car loans.

NOT ONLY WHEN, BUT WHERE. The new Global Positioning System Watch from Casio gives you a constant readout of your latitude and longitude, courtesy of its link to satellites.

Why Didn't We Think of That Before?

HOLD-EVERYTHING GOLF HAT. Ralph Lizio of Massachusetts has patented a golf hat made with special stretch pockets for sunglasses, tees, a ball marker, and possibly even a cigar on the brim.

DIET ALTERNATIVE. When your favorite pants no longer fit, instead of shrinking yourself, get the **Easy-Fit Waistband Stretcher** and expand the pants. Simply wet the garment and insert the Easy-Fit, ratcheting it to the desired width.

SELF-SHEARING SHEEP. An Australian company, Bioclip, will market a protein injection that causes sheep to shed their fleece in about a week. It has already been tested successfully on more than 15,000 sheep. The wool begins to grow back within 24 hours.

(c o n t i n u e d)

POTHOLE PANACEA. A California inventor has come up with the Rapid Road Repair Vehicle, a bus filled with computers, scanners, and tanks of epoxy cement, which can rumble down paved roads, filling every pothole and crack in its path.

DON'T THROW OUT THAT OLD VCR! If you think your older model VCR, suffering from the Y2K problem, can't be used for programmed recording after 1999, here's a cheap (in fact, free) solution: Set the machine to 1972. The days of the week have the same dates as in 2000.

Weirdness

The *Fortean Times* of London, which tracks reports of weird happenings, says weirdness was up 4.1 percent last year, making it the weirdest year yet. The "paranormal" category saw the biggest increase — 8 percent — as soothsayers published their millennial pre-

dictions, and cult, UFO, and poltergeist activity rose. A couple of weird events:

A lightning strike in the Democratic Republic of the Congo killed all 11 members of one soccer team while leaving the opposing team in the match untouched, leading to accusations of witchcraft.

A woman who bet regularly in the Rhode Island and Massachusetts state lotteries saw both sets of her numbers come up, but each in the opposite state. Weird, eh?

Demographica

"The two major demographic trends are the growth of the minority population and the glut of boomers getting old — aging boomers on the cusp of retirement."

– Jill Kershchenbaum, features editor,
American Demographics magazine

AGING AMERICANS ARE HEALTHIER THAN EVER, and high-adventure travel is booming for those over 55. States a *New York Times* article, "Many older people, even octogenarians, can be found riding elephants in India, horseback-riding in Costa Rica, and bungee-jumping in New Zealand."

If you make it to age 80, you have a better chance of **living to 100** than you had at age 70, according to the *University of California, Berkeley Wellness Letter.*

The United States now has **31 million teenagers.** Thirteen percent have their own credit cards, and another 13 percent have a card in their parents' names. More teens have part-time jobs than ever before. The result: a huge market for retailers, as witness the apparel catalogs appealing to younger teens.

To determine the exact population of the United States at any given moment — perhaps the stroke of midnight on January 1 (if you have nothing better to do) — go to **www.census .gov/main/www/popclock.html.**

(c o n t i n u e d)

Here's to Your Health

Lyme disease may soon have a formidable enemy. The FDA has recently approved the first vaccine, LYMErix, against the tick-borne illness. So far it hasn't been approved for use in children.

The New England Journal of Medicine recently reported that a sonogram of carotid arteries in the neck will be a great screening tool to assess **risk for heart attack or stroke** in older people. The test should be available within a year or so.

There's a new fix for **myopia**. Corrective eye implants, called Intacs, can actually correct mild nearsightedness. They're inserted in about ten minutes in an ophthalmologist's office. Think of them as permanent contact lenses. Companies are racing to develop other types of implants.

So Long, Farewell, Adios . . .

TOMBS OF UNKNOWN SOLDIERS. Science has outrun a military tradition that dates back to the Civil War. Because genetic testing can now identify human remains, the Pentagon (which takes DNA samples from new enlistees) has decided it will not place new remains in the Tomb of the Unknowns at Arlington National Cemetery.

WILLY LOMAN, or the Fuller Brush Man, or the Avon Lady. . . . Internet commerce and telemarketing have rendered door-to-door sales nearly obsolete.

THE AGE OF OIL. Oil will "inevitably lose its position as the world's dominant source of energy and cede market share to cleaner fuels," Mike Bowlin, CEO of Atlantic Richfield Company, said recently.

THE ALL-AMERICAN LAYER CAKE. Decades of cake mixes and bakery cakes with inch-thick disgusting frosting have lowered the status of this satisfying dessert. But this is one trend we at *The Old Farmer's Almanac* are resisting. We are going straight to the kitchen to bake a homemade chocolate cake from our mother's favorite recipe. It is, after all, our patriotic duty. To enter your favorite cake recipe in our contest, see page 217.

(c o n t i n u e d)

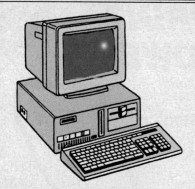

Manners for the Millennium

E-MAIL ETIQUETTE. It's everyone's worst nightmare: You write a chatty E-mail message to a friend, perhaps gossiping about your boss or a cute guy in the office. The friend never gets it, but your boss, or the cute guy, does. Wrong address! What to do if you are on the receiving end of one of these misdirected mails? Miss Manners, never one to miss a trend, weighs in with two-part advice: "The first part is very easy to do, and the second is extremely difficult. The first is to send the E-mail where it belongs, or back where it came from. The difficult part is to pretend you didn't read it. If you know the people, that includes not acting on the information, or pretending you don't know it." We wonder, what is the proper thing for the sender to do? Apologize? Explain? Pretend it never happened?

Trends in Agriculture

"Of alternative enterprises, I think the herbal and medicinal market will hold the most promise in the future."

– Bob Hamblen, Colorado State University Extension Agent

There's a huge future for farmers growing **"nutraceuticals"** or **"pharmafoodicals"** — foods with added benefits. Foods made with soy protein, for instance, have been found to lower blood cholesterol, so soybean products will be bred to contain higher levels of this healthful nutrient.

NO MORE SMELLY CHICKEN COOPS. Scientists have discovered that feeding poultry a diet that is 3 percent garlic powder reduces the odor of their waste (and may lower the cholesterol in their eggs); the chicken coops smell like garlic instead of smelling . . . bad.

WOMEN ARE INVOLVED IN FARMING as never before, as new equipment and technology lessen the need for brute strength on a farm, and as markets explode for such niche items as cashmere wool from goats, specialty goat's- and sheep's-milk cheeses, fresh herbs, and duck pâté.

"TAME GAME" such as elk, pheasants, and domestic deer will be increasingly found on Canadian and American farms. Venison has gained in popularity as a meat, and red-deer antlers are being used for arthritis and menopause relief, as well as for an aphrodisiac.

POTATO VACCINE. Loma Linda University has developed a potato that contains an antigen for cholera. A million people a year die of the disease, and if eating a raw potato is all it takes to

(c o n t i n u e d)

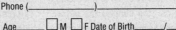

immunize them, the incidence of the disease could be drastically reduced.

The Mood

If the 20th century was epitomized by mass production, the 21st century is shaping up to be the century of **"mass customization."** Technology has become so sophisticated (and affordable) that most products and services will be tailored to your particular location, body shape, tastes, and hobbies. Some clothing retailers are offering to scan your body and make clothes — jeans, suits, dresses — that fit you perfectly.

The combination of busy lives and high expectations manifests itself in many ways. Increasingly, we hire people to walk our dogs, choose our clothes, build our decks, clean our houses. Many two-earner families are choosing to **spend time with their kids** instead

of on housework or running errands. Even matchmakers are busier than ever — in large cities they charge $10,000 to lonely clients who can't waste time dating incompatible people.

Where we can, we use technology to support simplicity. Quality of life is increasingly being defined as "the simpler the better," notwithstanding the complicated wiring that our lives seem to require (and desire).

Researchers have documented a **growing satisfaction with marriage** and relationships — 72 percent of middle-aged respondents rated their marriages very good to excellent. And some sociologists have noted that as trust in public institutions such as the Presidency and the Olympics falls, people turn to family and friends for comfort and kinship.

"Regionalism" is popular again. This shows up in many ways:

■ Sociologists have noted that people increasingly are refusing to change their ethnic-sounding names, and are reclaiming the old Gaelic or Polish spellings and pronunciations.

■ Broadcasters are less apt to kill their native southern or Brooklyn accents in order to sound more blandly professional.

■ Colleges are offering studies in regional culture, such as "Study of Southern Culture" and "Appalachian Regional Studies." Conserving our unique "provincial" tastes, smells, sounds, and cultures is a nice counterpoint to the Internet's "global village" and the fast-food joint on every corner in any American town. □□

2000

Best Fishing Days, 2000

(and other fishing lore from the files of *The Old Farmer's Almanac*)

Probably the best fishing times are when the ocean tides are restless before their turn and in the first hour of ebbing. All fish in all waters — salt and fresh — feed most heavily at those times.

The best temperatures for fish species vary widely, of course, and are chiefly important if you are going to have your own fishpond. The best temperatures for brook trout are 45° to 65° F. Brown trout and rainbow trout are more tolerant of higher temperatures. Smallmouth black bass do best in cool water. Horned pout take what they find.

Most of us go fishing when we can get time off, not because it is the best time. But there *are* best times:

■ One hour before and one hour after high tides, and one hour before and one hour after low tides. (The times of high tides are given on pages 60-86 and corrected for your locality on pages 240-241. Inland, the times for high tides correspond with the times the Moon is due south. Low tides are halfway between high tides.)

■ During "the morning rise" (after sunup for a spell) and "the evening rise" (just before sundown and the hour or so after).

■ When the barometer is steady or on the rise. (But, of course, even in a three-day driving northeaster, the fish aren't going to give up feeding. Their hunger clock keeps right on working, and the smart fisherman will find something they want.)

■ When there is a hatch of flies — caddis flies or mayflies, commonly. (The fisherman will have to match the hatching flies with *his* fly, or go fishless.)

■ When the breeze is from a westerly quarter rather than from the north or east.

■ When the water is still or rippled, rather than during a wind.

■ Starting on the day the Moon is new and continuing through the day it is full.

Moon Between New & Full, 2000

- January 6-20
- February 5-19
- March 6-19
- April 4-18
- May 4-18
- June 2-16
- July 1-16
- July 30-August 15
- August 29-September 13
- September 27-October 13
- October 27-November 11
- November 25-December 11
- December 25-31

What People Fish for Most (freshwater)

Bass	35%
Trout	18%
Catfish	11%
All species	9%
Bream	6%
Crappie	6%
Carp/muskie/panfish/ pike/shad/steelhead/ striper	5%
Walleye	5%
Perch	3%
Salmon	2%

– courtesy American Sportfishing Association

From Resperin Corporation

Rene M. Caisse, RN.
Original Herbal Formula

World Renowned Since 1922

- Traditional Herbal Medicine

- 100% Premium Quality Herbs

- Non-Toxic, Drug Free

- Approved for use in Canada and for export by Health Canada

- GMP & HPB Approved Production Facilities

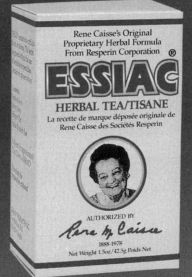

AVAILABLE WORLDWIDE FROM:

- Healthcare Practitioners

- Pharmacies

- Health and Nutrition Centres

Natural - Safe - Effective

Rene M. Caisse Cancer Research Institute
P.O. Box 23155, Ottawa, Ont., Canada K2A 4E2
Tel.: (613)729-9111 • Fax: (613)729-9555

Limited Edition. Hand-Painted Bas-Relief Sculpture.
Honoring The Most Famous Baseball Player Of All Time.

He was the best-loved baseball player ever. "The Sultan of Swat," whose homers made the game America's national pastime! And now you can round the bases and touch 'em all by acquiring a collector knife that Babe Ruth himself would surely have carried and enjoyed.

The real wood handle, crafted to resemble his bat, bears a *hand-painted sculpture of* "The Bambino" beltin' one out. The bolster, accented with *24 karat gold*, features a green enameled "baseball diamond" plus his uniform number – 3. At his feet is a baseball richly accented with 24 karat gold that bears his signature. His name and his lifetime total of 714 major league home runs appear on the blade crafted of tempered stainless steel.

A minted medal, set into the reverse of the handle, bears the emblem of Franklin Mint Collector Knives.

Officially authorized by the Family of Babe Ruth and CMG Worldwide, Inc. Edition *forever limited to just 45 casting days*. With padded and zippered case. Just $37.50. Available only from The Franklin Mint, Franklin Center, PA 19091-0001. **SATISFACTION GUARANTEED.** If you wish to return any Franklin Mint Collector Knives purchase, you may do so within 30 days of your receipt of that purchase for replacement, credit or refund.

A new look, a new sound, and several age-old things you can count on . . .

The year on the cover of this 208th edition of *The Old Farmer's Almanac* not only looks different but sounds different. *Very* different. Two thousand. There's not a single nine in there — for the first time since 1888.

We're aware that there are some people who maintain that neither the third millennium nor the 21st century begins this year. Most of them are adamant that any celebration should start with the year 2001, and they offer mathematical proof. We have no argument with them. If you accept the traditional starting point, they're absolutely correct. (But before you decide for certain, read "Dennis the Short and the Dating Game" on page 58.)

No one can dispute, however, that the new sound and the new look not only to this year, 2000, but to all the years of the forthcoming centuries, will begin at precisely the stroke of midnight, 1999. Surely that, in itself, is worth celebrating. (What about 2001? Well, we should celebrate then, too — but for a different reason.)

This Almanac, begun in 1792, has already been through two century changes. In fact, the 21st century will be the fourth century in which we have existed! But the turn of the century went unremarked in the 1800 and 1801 editions. Instead, editor and founder Robert B. Thomas concentrated on such things as ridding one's property of barberry bushes and suggesting that the safest place to be during a thunderstorm is "within a few feet of your horse which, being more elevated, will receive the shock in preference."

His inclusion of certain dates in the Almanac had nothing to do with the change of centuries. To him, the vacation dates of Harvard, Dartmouth, Providence College, and "Williamstown" College were of far greater interest to his readers. That and a nice recipe for onion sauce, consisting of a lot of butter, a little salt, "and a gill of sweet cream."

Finally, he advised his readers not to allow "young and inexperienced drivers" to take out their horses "harnessed in a pleasure sleigh." In effect, he was saying, "We all know how irresponsible youngsters are these days."

In the 1901 edition, Horace Ware, of Boston, who'd taken over as the seventh editor the year before, wrote, "We now give hearty greetings to our readers at the opening of the Twentieth Century." (Obviously, he wasn't of a mind to question the starting point of the first millennium.) He included college vacation dates, too. But by 1901, the list was up to 82 institutions of higher learning, including the original four. He devoted several pages to carriage fares in Boston and around the Northeast, and the usual advice on a variety of subjects. For instance, he urged his turn-of-the-century readers, if they felt at all ill, to avoid hot bread, biscuits, tea, strong coffee, seasoning, and all fried foods. He also suggested that the reason Goliath was so astonished when David hit him with a stone was because "such a thing had never entered his head before." This, apparently, was funny at the *last* change of centuries.

Now we are about to finally grow out of our "teens." What are we going to be when we grow up? The changes we've experienced in the past 100 years have

(continued on page 36)

Sand, cat-hairs, dust and dust-mites...
Nothing gets by the 8-lb. ORECK XL®!

The favorite vacuum of thousands of hotels and more than 1 million professional and private users. Now you can use this powerful vacuum to clean your home better than ever before.

Exclusive Filter System assures hypo-allergenic cleaning. Ideal for those who suffer from dust-related or allergic discomforts. There's virtually no after dust. Its ingenious top-fill action carries the litter up through the handle and deposits it on the inside top of the bag. Yesterday's dirt can't seep out. And the metal tube top-fill performance works without hoses to crack, leak or break.

The lightest full-size vacuum available. It weighs just 8 pounds. So stairs are a snap. It's super-powerful, with amazing cleaning power: the fast, double helical brushes revolve at an incredible 6,500 times a minute.

ORECK's Helping Hand® handle is orthopedically designed on the principles of ergonomics. To put it simply: no need to squeeze your hand or bend your wrist. A godsend for people with hand or wrist problems.

Exclusive New Microsweep® gets bare floors super clean, without any hoses, attachments or adjustments.

A full 10-year Guarantee against breakage or burnout of the housing PLUS a full 3-year Warranty on the Xtended Life motor. We'll let you try the ORECK XL in your home for 30 days Free. If you don't love it, you don't keep it.

FREE with purchase

Super Compact Canister

The 5-lb. dynamo you've seen on TV. The motor's so powerful it lifts a 16-lb. bowling ball! Hand-holdable and comfortable. Cleans under refrigerators... car seats... books...

ceilings... even typewriter, computer and piano keys. With 8 accessories. Yours FREE when you purchase an ORECK XL upright. Offer limited, so act now.

FOR 30-DAY TRIAL OR FREE INFORMATION CALL NOW TOLL-FREE
1-800-286-8900
and ask for Ext. 82002 No salesperson will visit.

Nothing gets by an
ORECK®

Oreck Direct, LLC.
100 Plantation Road, New Orleans, LA 70123

A1-NC

been mind-boggling. Whereas Editor Ware marveled at the "spread of civilization," today we are equally amazed at the spread of the World Wide Web. What do you suppose we'll be marveling at 100 years from now? What will be *important*?

Well, we at the Almanac can predict some things with certainty. For instance, on Friday, January 1, of the year 2100, the people living in Boston, Massachusetts, will enjoy nine hours and ten minutes of daylight. The Sun will set that day at 4:23 P.M., EST. On Monday, January 25, 2100, the Moon will be full at 9:50 P.M., EST. You can *count* on it.

And nine months later, about the middle of September 2100, the 308th consecutive annual edition of this publication will appear, God willing, everywhere throughout the United States and Canada. Perhaps it will be beamed electronically throughout the entire solar system, for heaven's sake.

The Almanac will be brand new, as each edition has always been. On the other hand, like this changing world of ours, and like you and me as we live out our allotted years, it will be fundamentally the same in all the important ways.

You can count on that, too.

J.D.H., June 1999

However, it is by our works and not our words that we would be judged. These, we hope, will sustain us in the humble though proud station we have so long held in the name of

Your obedient servant,

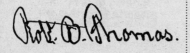

THE 2000 EDITION OF

The Old Farmer's Almanac

Established in 1792 and published every year thereafter

Robert B. Thomas (1766-1846), *Founder*

EDITOR (*12th since 1792*): Judson D. Hale Sr.
MANAGING EDITOR: Susan Peery
EXECUTIVE EDITOR: Tim Clark
ART DIRECTOR: Margo Letourneau
COPY EDITOR: Ellen Bingham
ASSISTANT MANAGING EDITOR: Mare-Anne Jarvela
SENIOR ASSOCIATE EDITOR: Debra Keller
RESEARCH EDITOR: Randy Miller
SENIOR CONSULTING EDITOR: Mary Sheldon
INTERNET EDITOR: Christine Halvorson
ASTRONOMER: Dr. George Greenstein
SOLAR PROGNOSTICATOR: Dr. Richard Head
WEATHER PROGNOSTICATOR: Michael A. Steinberg
WEATHER GRAPHICS AND CONSULTATION: Accu-Weather, Inc.
ARCHIVIST: Lorna Trowbridge
CONTRIBUTING EDITORS: Bob Berman, *Astronomy;*
Castle Freeman Jr., *Farmer's Calendar*
PRODUCTION DIRECTOR: Susan Gross
PAGE PRODUCTION MANAGER: David Ziarnowski
SENIOR PRODUCTION ARTISTS: Lucille Rines, Rachel Kipka
PRODUCTION ASSISTANT: Brian Jenkins
CREATIVE DIRECTOR, ON-LINE: Stephen O. Muskie
INTERNET PRODUCTION ASSISTANT: Lisa Traffie

GROUP PUBLISHER: John Pierce
PUBLISHER (*23rd since 1792*): Sherin Wight
ADMINISTRATIVE ASSISTANT: Sarah Duffy
ADVERTISING PRODUCTION/CLASSIFIED: Donna Stone
MAIL-ORDER MARKETING MANAGER: Susan Way
DIRECT SALES MANAGER: Cindy Schlosser

ADVERTISING MARKETING REPRESENTATIVES
General and Mail-Order Advertising
Northeast & West: Robert Bernbach
Phone: 914-769-0051 • Fax: 914-769-0691
Midwest: Tom Rickert
Phone: 612-835-0506 • Fax: 612-835-0709
South: Dan Waxman
Phone: 207-871-9376 • Fax: 207-879-0453
Michigan (General only): Ed Fisher
Phone: 248-540-0948 • Fax: 248-540-0905

NEWSSTAND CIRCULATION: P.S.C.S.
DISTRIBUTION: Curtis Circulation Company

EDITORIAL, ADVERTISING, AND PUBLISHING OFFICES
P.O. Box 520, Dublin, NH 03444
Phone: 603-563-8111 • Fax: 603-563-8252
Web site: www.almanac.com

YANKEE PUBLISHING INC., MAIN ST., DUBLIN, NH 03444

Joseph B. Meagher, *President;* Judson D. Hale Sr., *Senior Vice President;* Brian Piani,*Vice President* and *Chief Financial Officer;* Jody Bugbee, John Pierce, Joe Timko, and Sherin Wight, *Vice Presidents*.

The Old Farmer's Almanac publications are available at special discounts for bulk purchases for sales promotions or premiums. Contact At-a-Glance Group, 800-333-1125.

"HOW TO MAKE YOUR COMPUTER AS EASY TO USE AS YOUR TELEPHONE ..."

By Webmaster Raymond Steinbacher, and the research staff at Green Tree Press, Inc.

"How come it's so easy for Grannie?"

Are you frustrated by your computer? Is it about as "user-*un*friendly" as it can be?

Well, here's great news!

Green Tree Press - with the assistance of Webmaster Raymond Steinbacher - has developed a unique new computer-training course designed *specifically for beginners!*

Whether you're a complete novice or a person with limited computer experience, *this is the course you've been waiting for!*

Here's why...

☑ It begins with the assumption that you know nothing about computers. None of the terminology. Nothing.

☑ Every lesson ... every step ... is explained in *plain* English. There's no confusing computer jargon. No technical language.

☑ Every step is sequential. You simply can't make a mistake because every step is self-correcting.

☑ It's easy! And it's fun! You'll be amazed at how quickly you're learning.

You'll receive your printed course on large 8 1/2" x 11" pages with a sturdy Bristol cover. So it's exceptionally easy to read. And, everything is fully illustrated with drawings and photographs. So you not only *read — you actually see — each step.*

It comes to you complete. Ready to use. And we're so confident you'll complete the program successfully, we *unconditionally guarantee your results or your money back!*

It will take you about 2 - 3 hours — start to finish.

You'll learn how to navigate through Windows 95™ or Windows 98™ just like a pro ... master basic desktop publishing ... create your own files and spread sheets.

• You'll be able to recognize all the various parts of your computer ... and how each part functions.

• You'll understand the "world wide web" ... "the internet". You'll learn how to go *anywhere* in the world! Instantly!

• You'll discover how to acquire new software absolutely FREE.

• You'll discover how to bypass busy signals and get onto the Internet in a matter of seconds.

• You'll learn a *secret* way to stop receiving junk E-mail.

• You'll learn how to create and send messages to people around the world — even if you *don't type!*

• You'll learn to do financial planning, develop a workable budget ...even do payroll and employment records.

• You'll discover how to acquire and install the best antivirus program in the world — FREE!

• You'll learn how to send clear, colorful family photos around the world — FREE!

• You'll learn how to FULLY protect your computer from lightning and power surges (ordinary power strips don't do the job)!

• You'll learn a secret way to get FREE stereo FM and AM stations from around the *world* and have them play on your sound system — *while you're on line!*

• You'll discover a way to make your modem dial twice as fast as it does now — FREE.

• You'll be able to create files ... short cuts ... address books – even create your own posters and greeting cards!

• You'll be able to *talk* to anyone in the *world* — FREE — for up to 15 minutes (*no* long distance charges.)

• You'll discover how you can save hundreds of dollars by using your computer as a fax machine.

• And much, much more ...

Here are some comments from a few of our customers ...

"... the course is GREAT!! Why can't those computer companies make their instructions *one tenth* as good as your course?"

Sgt. Frank Gorchak, New Mexico

"... a lot better than those "dummies" books and a whale of a lot easier to understand, too. I learned the entire Windows segment in just 38 minutes."

George Roddy, New York

"... I'm a homemaker and grandma. I purchased your program out of self defense because the grandkids know all about computers. Now *I'm* on the internet playing trivia games with several other ladies in Scotland!! ... you made it so easy."

Margaret Hunter, Ohio

MONEY-BACK GUARANTEE

Try the course in your own home for 60 days. If you're not absolutely delighted with the results you achieve, simply return it, at any time, for a FULL REFUND. No conditions. No questions asked. That is our 100% unconditional guarantee.

You're welcome to *try* the course in your own home. If you're not *absolutely* delighted with the results you achieve, simply return it *at any time,* for a full refund. No conditions. No questions asked. That is our 100% guarantee.

To order, simply print your name and address on a piece of paper, enclose your check or money order for $12.95 (plus $3.00 shipping/handling). Send it to Green Tree Press Computer Course, Dept. 364, 3603 West 12th Street, Erie, PA 16505. Or, charge it to Visa, MasterCard or Discover. Please enclose your account number and expiration date. We normally ship within 48 hours.

1999 G.T.P.

How to Use This Almanac

Anywhere in the U.S.A.

■ The calendar pages **(60-87)** are the heart of *The Old Farmer's Almanac*. They present astronomical data and sky sightings for the entire year and are what make this book a true almanac, a "calendar of the heavens." In essence,  these pages are unchanged since 1792, when Robert B. Thomas published his first edition. The long columns of numbers and symbols reveal all of Nature's precision, rhythm, and glory — an astronomical look at the year 2000.

– Beth Krommes

Please note: All times given in this edition of the Almanac are for Boston, Massachusetts, and are in Eastern Standard Time (EST), except from 2:00 A.M., April 2, until 2:00 A.M., October 29, when Eastern Daylight Time (EDT) is given. Key Letters (A-E) are provided so that readers can calculate times for their own localities. The following four pages provide detailed explanations.

Seasons of the Year

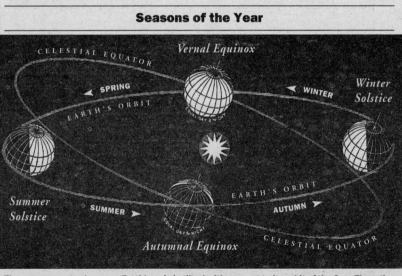

The seasons occur because Earth's axis is tilted with respect to its orbit of the Sun. Thus, the hemispheres take turns reaching their maximum tilt toward the Sun, which occurs at the solstices. The equinoxes mark the intersection of Earth's orbit with the plane of the celestial equator, when the hemispheres equally face the Sun.

....

■ The Web site for *The Old Farmer's Almanac*, **www.almanac.com,** has complete astronomical information for any location in the United States and Canada, as well as tide predictions for thousands of miles of coastline. Weather forecasts, history, advice, gardening tips, puzzles, and recipes are also available on-line. There's even a "black hole" in the corner of the home page.

(c o n t i n u e d   o n   n e x t   p a g e)

The Left-Hand Calendar Pages

(Pages 60-86)

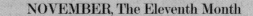

1999   NOVEMBER, The Eleventh Month

Saturn reaches opposition on the 6th. It is now brighter than it has been for two

...gnitude -0.2 among the skimpy stars of Aries. It now ...hout the night. Starting at midnight on the night of ...eor shower peaks and could put on an awesome display. The Moon stands near Jupiter on the 20th and near Saturn on the 21st. Mercury reappears low in the east before dawn on the 25th. Soon after nightfall on the 28th, Mars and Neptune are very close, affording telescope users an unusually good opportunity to locate the eighth planet.

● New Moon	7th day	22nd hour	53rd minute
☽ First Quarter	16th day	4th hour	3rd minute
○ Full Moon	23rd day	2nd hour	4th minute
☾ Last Quarter	...day	...ur	8t... ...ut...

Times are given in Eastern Standard Time.

For an explanation of this page, see page 40; for values of Key Letters, see page 234.

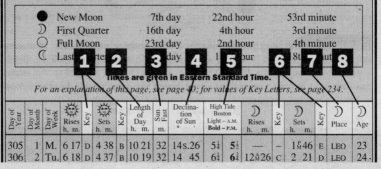

Day of Year	Day of Month	Day of Week	☀ Rises h. m.	Key	☀ Sets h. m.	Key	Length of Day h. m.	Sun Fast m.	Declination of Sun ° ′	High Tide Boston Light – A.M. Bold – P.M.	☽ Rises h. m.	Key	☽ Sets h. m.	Key	Place	Age
305	1	M.	6 17	D	4 38	B	10 21	32	14s.26	5¼ 5¾	—	–	1¾46	E	LEO	23
306	2	Tu.	6 18	D	4 37	B	10 19	32	14 45	6¼ 6¼	12¾26	C	2 21	D	LEO	24.

1 Use these two Key Letter columns to calculate the sunrise/sunset times for localities other than Boston. Each sunrise/sunset time is assigned a Key Letter whose value in minutes is given in the **Time Corrections table on page 234.** Simply find your city, or the city nearest you, in the table, and add or subtract those minutes to Boston's sunrise or sunset time.

EXAMPLE:

■ To find the time of sunrise in Des Moines, Iowa, on November 1, 1999:

Sunrise, Boston, with Key Letter D (above)	6:17 A.M., EST
Value of Key Letter D for Des Moines (p. 235)	+ 28 minutes
Sunrise, Des Moines	6:45 A.M., CST

Use the same procedure to determine the time of sunset.

2 This column gives the amount of time the Sun will be above the horizon in Boston each day. To determine the length of day for your city, first calculate the sunrise and sunset times for your locality, following the procedure outlined in #1; next, convert the time of sunset to 24-hour clock time by adding 12 hours; then subtract the time of sunrise.

EXAMPLE:

Sunset, Cairo, Illinois, Nov. 1	4:58
Convert to 24-hour clock time	+ 12:00
	16:58
Subtract sunrise, Cairo, Nov. 1	– 6:21
Length of day, Cairo, Nov. 1 (10 hr., 37 min.)	10:37

3 The Sun Fast column is designed to change sundial time to clock time in Boston. A sundial reads natural, or Sun, time, which is neither Standard nor Daylight time except by coincidence. From a sundial reading, simply subtract the minutes given in the Sun Fast column to get Boston clock time, and use Key Letter C in the **Time Corrections table on page 234** to convert the time to your city.

E X A M P L E :

■ To change sundial time into clock time in Boston, or Butte, Montana, on November 1, 1999:

Sundial reading, Nov. 1 (Boston or Butte)	12:00 noon
Subtract Sun Fast (p. 40)	− 32 minutes
Clock time, Boston	11:28 A.M., EST
Use Key Letter C for Butte (p. 234)	+ 45 minutes
Clock time, Butte	12:13 P.M., MST

4 This column gives the degrees and minutes of the Sun from the celestial equator at noon, EST or EDT.

5 The High Tide column gives the times of daily high tides in Boston. For example, on November 1, the first high tide occurs at 5:15 A.M. and the second occurs at 5:30 P.M. (A dash under High Tide indicates that high water occurs on or after midnight and so is recorded on the next day.) Figures for calculating high tide times and heights for localities other than Boston are given in the **Tide Corrections table on page 240.**

6 Use these two Key Letter columns to calculate the moonrise/moonset times for localities other than Boston. (A dash indicates that moonrise/moonset occurs on or after midnight and so is recorded on the next day.) Use the same procedure as explained in #1 for calculating your moonrise/moonset time, then factor in an additional correction based on longitude (see table below). For the longitude of your city, **see page 234.**

Longitude of city	Correction minutes
58° – 76°	0
77° – 89°	+1
90° – 102°	+2
103° – 115°	+3
116° – 127°	+4
128° – 141°	+5
142° – 155°	+6

E X A M P L E :

■ To determine the time of moonrise in Flagstaff, Arizona, on November 2, 1999:

Moonrise, Boston, with Key Letter C (p. 40)	12:26 A.M., EST
Value of Key Letter C for Flagstaff (p. 235)	+ 42 minutes
Correction for Flagstaff longitude 111° 39'	+ 3 minutes
Moonrise, Flagstaff	1:11 A.M., MST

Use the same procedure to determine the time of moonset.

– Beth Krommes

7 The Moon's place is its *astronomical,* or *actual,* placement in the heavens. (This should not be confused with the Moon's *astrological* place in the zodiac, as explained **on page 170.**) All calculations in this Almanac are based on astronomy, not astrology, except for the information **on pages 167-170.**

In addition to the 12 constellations of the astronomical zodiac, five other abbreviations may appear in this column: Auriga **(AUR),** a northern constellation between Perseus and Gemini; Cetus **(CET),** which lies south of the zodiac, just south of Pisces and Aries; Ophiuchus **(OPH),** a constellation primarily north of the zodiac but with a small corner between Scorpius and Sagittarius; Orion **(ORI),** a constellation whose northern limit first reaches the zodiac between Taurus and Gemini; and Sextans **(SEX),** which lies south of the zodiac except for a corner that just touches it near Leo.

8 The last column gives the Moon's age, which is the number of days since the previous new Moon. (The average length of the lunar month is 29.53 days.)

(c o n t i n u e d   o n   n e x t   p a g e)

The Right-Hand Calendar Pages

(Pages 61-87)

■ Throughout the Right-Hand Calendar Pages are groups of symbols that represent notable celestial events. The symbols and names of the principal planets and aspects are:

☉	**Sun**	♆	**Neptune**
○●☾	**Moon**	♇	**Pluto**
☿	**Mercury**	☌	**Conjunction (on the same celestial longitude)**
♀	**Venus**		
⊕	**Earth**		
♂	**Mars**	☊	**Ascending node**
♃	**Jupiter**	☋	**Descending node**
♄	**Saturn**	☍	**Opposition, or 180 degrees apart**
⛢	**Uranus**		

For example, ☌♀☾ next to November 3, 1999 (see opposite page), means that a conjunction (☌) of Venus (♀) and the Moon (☾) occurs on that date, when they are aligned along the same celestial longitude and appear to be closest together in the sky.

– Beth Krommes

The Seasons of 1999-2000

Fall 1999	**Sept. 23, 7:31 A.M., EDT**
Winter 1999	**Dec. 22, 2:44 A.M., EST**
Spring 2000	**Mar. 20, 2:35 A.M., EST**
Summer 2000	**June 20, 9:48 P.M., EDT**
Fall 2000	**Sept. 22, 1:27 P.M., EDT**
Winter 2000	**Dec. 21, 8:37 A.M., EST**

Earth at Perihelion and Aphelion 2000

■ Earth will be at perihelion on January 3, 2000, when it will be 91,400,005 miles from the Sun. Earth will be at aphelion on July 3, 2000, when it will be 94,512,258 miles from the Sun.

Movable Feasts and Fasts for 2000

Septuagesima Sunday	**Feb. 20**
Shrove Tuesday	**Mar. 7**
Ash Wednesday	**Mar. 8**
Palm Sunday	**Apr. 16**
Good Friday	**Apr. 21**
Easter Day	**Apr. 23**
Rogation Sunday	**May 28**
Ascension Day	**June 1**
Whitsunday-Pentecost	**June 11**
Trinity Sunday	**June 18**
Corpus Christi	**June 22**
1st Sunday in Advent	**Dec. 3**

Chronological Cycles for 2000

Dominical Letter	**B/A**
Epact	**24**
Golden Number (Lunar Cycle)	**6**
Roman Indiction	**8**
Solar Cycle	**21**
Year of Julian Period	**6713**

Era	**Year**	**Begins**
Byzantine	**7509**	**Sept. 14**
Jewish (A.M.)*	**5761**	**Sept. 29**
Chinese (Lunar) (Dragon)	**4698**	**Feb. 5**
Roman (A.U.C.)	**2753**	**Jan. 14**
Nabonassar	**2749**	**Apr. 23**
Japanese	**2660**	**Jan. 1**
Grecian (Seleucidae)	**2312**	**Sept. 14 (or Oct. 14)**
Indian (Saka)	**1922**	**Mar. 21**
Diocletian	**1717**	**Sept. 11**
Islamic (Hegira)*	**1421**	**Apr. 5**

***Year begins at sunset.**

Sample Right-Hand Calendar Page (from November 1999, page 61)

■ Day of the month.

■ Day of the week.

■ Conjunction of Venus and the Moon.

■ The Moon is on the celestial equator.

■ The bold letter in this column is the Dominical Letter, a traditional ecclesiastical designation for Sunday. For 1999 it was C because the first Sunday of the year fell on the third day of January. The letter for 2000, a leap year, is B through February, then it reverts to A.

■ 24th Sunday after Pentecost. (Sundays and special holy days generally appear in this typeface.)

■ St. Leo the Great was elected Bishop of Rome in A.D. 440. By interceding with Attila, he prevented the city's massacre by invading Huns. (Certain religious feasts and civil holidays appear in this typeface.)

■ First high tide at Boston is 8.6 feet; second high tide is 9.1 feet.

■ Weather prediction rhyme. **(For detailed regional forecasts, see pages 134-155.)**

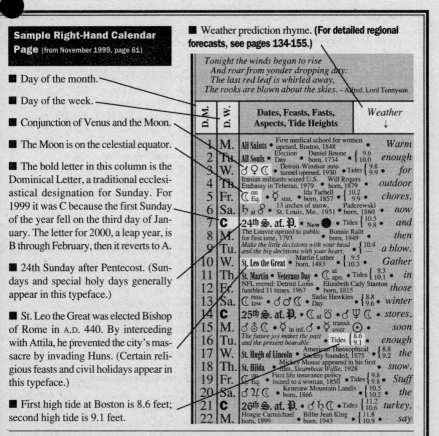

Tonight the winds began to rise
And roar from yonder dropping day:
The last red leaf is whirled away,
The rooks are blown about the skies. – Alfred, Lord Tennyson

D.M.	D.W.	Dates, Feasts, Fasts, Aspects, Tide Heights	Weather ↓
1	M.	**All Saints** • First medical school for women opened, Boston, 1848 •	*Warm*
2	Tu.	**All Souls** • Election Day • Daniel Boone born, 1734 • { 9.6 / 10.0	*enough*
3	W.	☌ ♀ ☾ • Detroit-Windsor auto tunnel opened, 1930 • Tides { 9.8 / 9.9 •	*for*
4	Th.	Iranian militants seized U.S. Embassy in Teheran, 1979 • Will Rogers born, 1879 •	*outdoor*
5	Fr.	☾ on Eq. • ☿ stat. • Ida Tarbell born, 1857 • { 10.2 / 9.9 •	*chores,*
6	Sa.	♄ at ☍ • 13 inches of snow, St. Louis, Mo., 1951 • Paderewski born, 1860 •	*now*
7	**C**	**24th 𝕾. af. 𝕻.** • New ● • Tides { 10.5 / 9.8 •	*and*
8	M.	The Louvre opened to public for first time, 1793 • Bonnie Raitt born, 1949 •	*then*
9	Tu.	*Make the little decisions with your head and the big decisions with your heart.* • { 10.4 / —	*a blow.*
10	W.	**St. Leo the Great** • Martin Luther born, 1483 • { 9.5 / 10.3 •	*Gather*
11	Th.	**St. Martin** • **Veterans Day** • ☾ at apo. • Tides { 9.3 / 10.1 •	*in*
12	Fr.	NFL record: Detroit Lions fumbled 11 times, 1967 • Elizabeth Cady Stanton born, 1815	*those*
13	Sa.	☾ runs low • ☌ ♂ ☾ • Sadie Hawkins Day • { 8.8 / 9.6 •	*winter*
14	**C**	**25th 𝕾. af. 𝕻.** • ☾ at ☊ • ☌ ♆ ☾ •	*stores,*
15	M.	☌ ♅ ☾ • ☿ in inf. ☌ • ☿ transit over ☉ •	*soon*
16	Tu.	*The future joy makes the past and the present bearable.* • Tides { 8.6 / 9.1 •	*enough*
17	W.	**St. Hugh of Lincoln** • American Theosophical Society founded, 1875 • { 8.8 / 9.2	*the*
18	Th.	**St. Hilda** • Mickey Mouse appeared in his first film, *Steamboat Willie*, 1928 •	*snow.*
19	Fr.	☾ on Eq. • First life insurance policy issued to a woman, 1850 • Tides { 9.8 / 9.8 •	*Stuff*
20	Sa.	☌ ♃ ☾ • Kenesaw Mountain Landis born, 1866 • { 10.5 / 10.2 •	*the*
21	**C**	**26th 𝕾. af. 𝕻.** • ☌ ♄ ☾ • Tides { 11.2 / 10.6	*turkey,*
22	M.	Hoagie Carmichael born, 1899 • Billie Jean King born, 1943 • { 11.8 / 10.9 •	*say*

For a more complete explanation of terms used throughout the Almanac, see Glossary, page 46.

Predicting Earthquakes

■ Note the dates, in the **Right-Hand Calendar Pages,** when the Moon (☾) rides high or runs low. The date of the high begins the most likely five-day period of earthquakes in the Northern Hemisphere; the date of the low indicates a similar five-day period in the Southern Hemisphere. Also noted twice each month are the days when the Moon is on the celestial equator (☾ on Eq.), indicating likely two-day earthquake periods in both hemispheres.

– Beth Krommes

More Astronomical Data for 2000

Bright Stars .... page 54
Eclipses .... page 52
Full-Moon Dates 2000-2004 .... page 52
Principal Meteor Showers .... page 52
The Twilight Zone .... page 239
The Visible Planets (Venus, Mars, Jupiter, Saturn, and Mercury) .... page 50

Holidays and Observances, 2000

A selected list of commemorative days, with federal holidays denoted by *.

Jan.   **1** New Year's Day*
Jan. **17** Martin Luther King Jr.'s
Birthday *(observed)**
Feb.   **2** Groundhog Day; Guadalupe-
Hidalgo Treaty Day *(N.Mex.)*
Feb. **12** Abraham Lincoln's Birthday
Feb. **14** Valentine's Day
Feb. **15** Susan B. Anthony's Birthday
(Fla., Wis.)
Feb. **21** Presidents Day*
Feb. **22** George Washington's Birthday
Mar.   **2** Texas Independence Day
Mar.   **7** Town Meeting Day *(Vt.)*;
Mardi Gras *(Baldwin & Mobile
Counties, Ala.; La.)*
Mar. **15** Andrew Jackson Day *(Tenn.)*
Mar. **17** St. Patrick's Day; Evacuation
Day *(Suffolk Co., Mass.)*
Apr.   **2** Pascua Florida Day
Apr. **13** Thomas Jefferson's Birthday
Apr. **17** Patriots Day *(Maine, Mass.)*
Apr. **28** National Arbor Day
May   **1** May Day
May   **8** Truman Day *(Mo.)*
May **14** Mother's Day
May **20** Armed Forces Day
May **22** Victoria Day *(Canada)*
May **29** Memorial Day *(observed)**
June   **1** Statehood Day *(Tenn.)*
June   **5** World Environment Day
June 11 King Kamehameha I Day *(Hawaii)*
June 14 Flag Day
June 17 Bunker Hill Day *(Suffolk Co., Mass.)*
June 18 Father's Day
June 19 Emancipation Day *(Tex.)*
June 20 West Virginia Day
July   **1** Canada Day
July   **4** Independence Day*

July 24 Pioneer Day *(Utah)*
Aug.   **7** Colorado Day
Aug. 14 Victory Day *(R.I.)*
Aug. 16 Bennington Battle Day *(Vt.)*
Aug. 26 Women's Equality Day
Sept.   **4** Labor Day*
Sept.   **9** Admission Day *(Calif.)*
Oct.   **9** Leif Eriksson Day; Columbus
Day *(observed)**; Thanksgiving
Day *(Canada);* Native Americans
Day *(S.Dak.)*
Oct. 18 Alaska Day
Oct. 31 Halloween; Nevada Day
Nov.   **4** Will Rogers Day *(Okla.)*
Nov.   **7** Election Day
Nov. 11 Veterans Day*
Nov. 19 Discovery Day *(Puerto Rico)*
Nov. 23 Thanksgiving Day*
Nov. 24 Acadian Day *(La.)*
Dec. 10 Wyoming Day
Dec. 25 Christmas Day*
Dec. 26 Boxing Day *(Canada)*

Religious Observances

Epiphany	**Jan. 6**
Ash Wednesday	**Mar. 8**
Islamic New Year	**Apr. 6**
Palm Sunday	**Apr. 16**
First day of Passover	**Apr. 20**
Good Friday	**Apr. 21**
Easter Day	**Apr. 23**
Orthodox Easter	**Apr. 30**
Whitsunday-Pentecost	**June 11**
Rosh Hashanah	**Sept. 30**
Yom Kippur	**Oct. 9**
First day of Ramadan	**Nov. 27**
First day of Chanukah	**Dec. 22**
Christmas Day	**Dec. 25**

How the Almanac Weather Forecasts Are Made

■ We derive our weather forecasts from a secret formula devised by the founder of this Almanac in 1792, enhanced by the most modern scientific calculations based on solar activity and current meteorological data. We believe that nothing in the universe occurs haphazardly but that there is a cause-and-effect pattern to all phenomena, thus making long-range weather forecasts possible. However, neither we nor anyone else has as yet gained sufficient insight into the mysteries of the universe to predict weather with anything resembling total accuracy.

Glossary

Aphelion (Aph.): The point in a planet's orbit that is farthest from the Sun.

Apogee (Apo.): The point in the Moon's orbit that is farthest from Earth.

Celestial Sphere: An imaginary sphere projected into space that represents the entire sky, with an observer on Earth at its center. All celestial bodies other than Earth are imagined as being on its inside surface.

Conjunction: When two celestial bodies reach the same celestial longitude or right ascension, approximately corresponding to their closest apparent approach in the sky. (Dates for conjunction are given in the Right-Hand Calendar Pages 61-87; sky sightings of closely aligned bodies are given in the descriptive text at the top of the Left-Hand Calendar Pages 60-86). **Inf. – Inferior:** A conjunction in which Mercury or Venus is between the Sun and Earth. **Sup. – Superior:** A conjunction in which the Sun is between a planet and Earth.

Declination: The celestial latitude of an object in the sky, measured in degrees north or south of the celestial equator; analogous to latitude on Earth. The Almanac gives the Sun's declination at noon EST or EDT.

Dominical Letter: Used to denote the Sundays in the ecclesiastical calendar in a given year, determined by the date on which the first Sunday of that year falls. If Jan. 1 is a Sunday, the letter is A; if Jan. 2 is a Sunday, the letter is B; and so on to G. In a leap year, the letter applies through February and then takes the preceding letter.

Eclipse, Lunar: The full Moon enters the shadow of Earth, which cuts off all or part of the Moon's light. **Total:** The Moon passes completely through the umbra (central dark part) of Earth's shadow. **Partial:** Only part of the Moon passes through the umbra. **Penumbral:** The Moon passes through only the penumbra (area of partial darkness surrounding the umbra).

Eclipse, Solar: Earth enters the shadow of the new Moon, which cuts off all or part of the Sun's light. **Total:** Earth passes through the umbra (central dark part) of the Moon's shadow, resulting in totality for observers within a narrow band on Earth. **Annular:** The Moon appears silhouetted against the Sun, with a ring of sunlight showing around it. **Partial:** The Moon blocks only part of the Sun.

Ecliptic: The *apparent* annual path of the Sun around the celestial sphere. The plane of the ecliptic is tipped $23.5°$ from the celestial equator.

Elongation: The difference in degrees between the celestial longitudes of a planet and the Sun. **Greatest Elongation (Gr. Elong.):** The greatest apparent distance of a planet from the Sun, as seen from Earth.

Epact: A number from 1 to 30 that indicates the Moon's age on Jan. 1 at Greenwich, England; used for determining the date of Easter.

Equator, Celestial (Eq.): The circle around the celestial sphere that is halfway between the celestial poles. It can be thought of as the plane of Earth's equator projected out onto the sphere.

Equinox, Autumnal: The Sun appears to cross the celestial equator from north to south. **Vernal:** The Sun appears to cross the celestial equator from south to north.

Evening Star: A planet that is above the western horizon at sunset and less than $180°$ east of the Sun in right ascension.

Golden Number: A number in the 19-year cycle of the Moon, used for determining the date of Easter. (The Moon repeats its phases approximately every 19 solar years.) Add 1 to any given year and divide the result by 19; the remainder is the Golden Number. When there is no remainder, the Golden Number is 19.

Julian Period: A period of 7,980 years beginning Jan. 1, 4713 B.C. Devised in 1583 by Joseph Scaliger, it provides a chronological basis for the study of ancient history. To find the Julian year, add 4,713 to any year.

(continued on page 48)

Moon on Equator: The Moon is on the celestial equator.

Moon Rides High/Runs Low: The Moon is highest above or farthest below the celestial equator.

Moonrise/Moonset: The Moon's rising above or descending below the horizon.

Moon's Phases: The continually changing states in the Moon's appearance, caused by the different angles at which it is illuminated by the Sun. **First Quarter:** The right half of the Moon is illuminated, as seen from the Northern Hemisphere. **Full:** The Sun and the Moon are in opposition; the entire disk of the Moon is illuminated as viewed from Earth. **Last Quarter:** The left half of the Moon is illuminated, as seen from the Northern Hemisphere. **New:** The Sun and the Moon are in conjunction; the entire disk of the Moon is darkened as viewed from Earth.

Moon's Place, Astronomical: The actual position of the Moon within the constellations on the celestial sphere. **Astrological:** The position of the Moon within the astrological zodiac according to calculations made over 2,000 years ago. Because of precession of the equinoxes and other factors, this is not the Moon's actual position in the sky.

Morning Star: A planet that is above the eastern horizon at sunrise and less than 180° west of the Sun in right ascension.

Node, Ascending/Descending: Either of the two points where a body's orbit intersects the ecliptic. The body is moving from south to north of the ecliptic at the ascending node, and from north to south at the descending node. (An imaginary line through Earth that connects the Moon's nodes also aligns with an Earth-Sun line just twice a year, roughly six months apart; at these times, a new or full Moon that occurs when the Moon is at or near one of its nodes will result in an eclipse.)

Occultation (Occn.): The eclipse of a star or planet by the Moon or another planet.

Opposition: The Moon or a planet appears on the opposite side of the sky from the Sun (elongation 180°).

Perigee (Perig.): The point in the Moon's orbit that is closest to Earth.

Perihelion (Perih.): The point in a planet's orbit that is closest to the Sun.

Precession: The slowly changing position of the stars and equinoxes in the sky resulting from variations in the orientation of Earth's axis.

Right Ascension (R.A.): The celestial longitude of an object in the sky, measured eastward along the celestial equator in hours of time from the vernal equinox; analogous to longitude on Earth.

Roman Indiction: A number in a 15-year cycle, established Jan. 1, A.D. 313, as a fiscal term. Add 3 to any given year in the Christian era and divide by 15; the remainder is the Roman Indiction. When there is no remainder, the Roman Indiction is 15.

Solar Cycle: A period of 28 years in the Julian calendar, at the end of which the days of the month return to the same days of the week.

Solstice, Summer: The Sun reaches its greatest declination (23.5°) north of the celestial equator. **Winter:** The Sun reaches its greatest declination (23.5°) south of the celestial equator.

Stationary (Stat.): The apparent halted movement, as it reaches opposition, of a planet against the background of the stars, shortly before it appears to move backward (retrograde motion).

Sun Fast/Slow: The difference between a sundial reading and clock time.

Sunrise/Sunset: The visible rising and setting of the Sun's upper limb across the unobstructed horizon of an observer whose eyes are 15 feet above ground level.

Twilight: The period of time between full darkness (when the Sun is 18° below the horizon) and either sunrise or sunset. Twilight is classified as **astronomical**, when the Sun is between 18° and 12° below the horizon; **nautical**, when the Sun is between 12° and 6° below the horizon; and **civil**, when the Sun is less than 6° below the horizon.

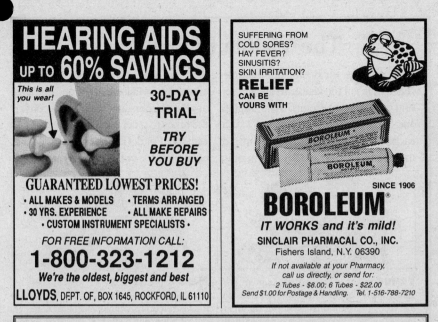
For information on advertising in *The Old Farmer's Almanac* and its Companion publications, call Donna Stone at 800-729-9265, ext. 214.

The Visible Planets, 2000

■ Listed here for Boston are the times (EST/EDT) of the visible rising and setting of the planets Venus, Mars, Jupiter, and Saturn on the 1st, 11th, and 21st of each month. The approximate times of their visible rising and setting on other days can be found by interpolation. The capital letters that appear beside the times are Key Letters and are used to convert the times to other localities **(see pages 40 and 234)**. For definitions of morning and evening stars, see the **Glossary on page 46.**

Venus never achieves its maximum brilliance at any time in 2000, being at its best for the year during the first month in the frosty predawn eastern sky. It spends spring and early summer lost behind the Sun's glare. Although it emerges during late summer as an evening star very low in the west at dusk, it doesn't become eye-catching until autumn, when it gradually gains altitude in the southwest, where it stays until year's end. Venus is in conjunction with Mercury on March 14 and April 28.

Mars experiences an "off" year in 2000, remaining on the far side of the Sun for the entire year. It offers striking meetings, however, with Jupiter and Saturn at nightfall in late March and early April, when the trio is nicely up in the west. After that, it slips behind the Sun and remains a dim curiosity only for those willing to gaze eastward in the predawn hours. Mars is in conjunction with Jupiter on April 6, with Saturn on April 16, and with Mercury on May 19 and August 10.

Boldface — P.M.				Lightface — A.M.			
Jan. 1....... rise 4:09 D	July 1 ...... set 8:49 E	Jan. 1....... set 8:18 B	July 1 ...... rise 5:09 A
Jan. 11..... rise 4:30 E	July 11 ..... set 8:54 E	Jan. 11..... set 8:19 B	July 11 ..... rise 5:01 A
Jan. 21..... rise 4:49 E	July 21 ..... set 8:54 E	Jan. 21..... set 8:20 B	July 21 ..... rise 4:54 A
Feb. 1 ...... rise 5:05 E	Aug. 1..... set 8:48 D	Feb. 1 ...... set 8:20 C	Aug. 1 ..... rise 4:47 A
Feb. 11 .... rise 5:14 E	Aug. 11 ... set 8:38 D	Feb. 11 .... set 8:21 C	Aug. 11 ... rise 4:41 A
Feb. 21 .... rise 5:18 E	Aug. 21 ... set 8:26 C	Feb. 21 .... set 8:20 C	Aug. 21 ... rise 4:35 A
Mar. 1 ..... rise 5:18 D	Sept. 1..... set 8:12 C	Mar. 1 ..... set 8:20 C	Sept. 1..... rise 4:29 B
Mar. 11 ... rise 5:13 D	Sept. 11... set 7:58 B	Mar. 11 ... set 8:19 D	Sept. 11... rise 4:22 B
Mar. 21 ... rise 5:05 D	Sept. 21... set 7:45 B	Mar. 21 ... set 8:18 D	Sept. 21... rise 4:16 B
Apr. 1...... rise 4:53 C	Oct. 1 ...... set 7:34 B	Apr. 1...... set 8:17 D	Oct. 1 ...... rise 4:09 B
Apr. 11.... rise 5:41 C	Oct. 11 .... set 7:26 A	Apr. 11.... set 9:15 D	Oct. 11 .... rise 4:02 B
Apr. 21.... rise 5:30 B	Oct. 21 .... set 7:22 A	Apr. 21.... set 9:13 E	Oct. 21 .... rise 3:55 B
May 1...... rise 5:19 B	Nov. 1..... set 6:25 A	May 1...... set 9:11 E	Nov. 1..... rise 2:46 C
May 11.... rise 5:10 B	Nov. 11.... set 6:33 A	May 11.... set 9:07 E	Nov. 11.... rise 2:38 C
May 21.... rise 5:04 A	Nov. 21.... set 6:48 A	May 21.... set 9:03 E	Nov. 21.... rise 2:30 C
June 1...... rise 5:03 A	Dec. 1...... set 7:07 A	June 1...... set 8:56 E	Dec. 1...... rise 2:22 C
June 11.... rise 5:08 A	Dec. 11.... set 7:28 A	June 11.... set 8:48 E	Dec. 11.... rise 2:13 D
June 21.... set 8:38 E	Dec. 21.... set 7:50 A	June 21.... set 8:39 E	Dec. 21.... rise 2:05 D
	Dec. 31.... set 8:11 B		Dec. 31.... rise 1:55 D

Mercury, on the distant side of its orbit from us, achieves "minus" magnitudes that would make it eye-catching were it not for its eternal proximity to the Sun and closeness to the horizon. The year offers two opportunities when it is maximally high above the horizon. The first comes from June 1 to 10, when Mercury sits above the western horizon in evening twilight. As a morning star in the east just before dawn, it can be glimpsed easily by insomniacs from November 7 to 21.

DO NOT CONFUSE 1) Mars, Jupiter, and Saturn as they hover near each other during the last week of March and first half of April. Jupiter is the brightest and Mars the dimmest of the trio. **2)** Mercury with Mars, low in eastern predawn twilight on August 10 and 11. Mercury is brighter than Mars and less orange. **3)** Mars with Regulus, Leo's brightest star, very near each other from September 16 to 18. Mars is orange, Regulus blue. **4)** Mars with Spica, Virgo's brightest star, somewhat near each other from December 12 to 18. Again, Mars is orange, Spica blue.

Jupiter has a fabulous year, rising higher in the sky than it has all decade. It starts the year in Pisces, crosses into Aries in February, and vanishes into the Sun's glare in late April. Jupiter re-emerges in the predawn eastern sky in June. It ascends and brightens during the summer and fall, attains maximum brilliance during its out-all-night opposition on November 27, and remains dazzling through December. Jupiter is in conjunction with Mars on April 6 and with Saturn on May 31.

Saturn is brighter and higher this year than anytime since 1975. January finds it nicely visible in the west at nightfall, in Aries. Slowly lowering each evening, Saturn slips behind the Sun's glare in late April, moves into Taurus, and returns to sight low in June's predawn eastern sky. Appearing higher at each successive dawn, Saturn remains perfectly placed for observation through December. Saturn is in conjunction with Mars on April 16 and with Jupiter on May 31.

Boldface — P.M.	Lightface — A.M.		
Jan. 1....... set 1:13 D	July 1 ...... rise 2:40 A	Jan. 1....... set 2:28 D	July 1 ...... rise 2:35 A
Jan. 11..... set 12:37 D	July 11 .... rise 2:07 A	Jan. 11..... set 1:48 D	July 11 .... rise 1:59 A
Jan. 21..... set 12:02 D	July 21 .... rise 1:34 A	Jan. 21..... set 1:10 D	July 21 .... rise 1:22 A
Feb. 1 ...... set 11:23 D	Aug. 1 ..... rise 12:58 A	Feb. 1 ..... set 12:28 D	Aug. 1 ..... rise 12:42 A
Feb. 11..... set 10:51 D	Aug. 11 ... rise 12:23 A	Feb. 11 .... set 11:48 D	Aug. 11 ... rise 12:05 A
Feb. 21..... set 10:20 D	Aug. 21 ... rise 11:49 A	Feb. 21 .... set 11:12 D	Aug. 21 ... rise 11:27 A
Mar. 1 ..... set 9:53 D	Sept. 1..... rise 11:10 A	Mar. 1 ..... set 10:40 D	Sept. 1 .... rise 10:45 A
Mar. 11 ... set 9:24 D	Sept. 11.... rise 10:33 A	Mar. 11 ... set 10:05 D	Sept. 11 ... rise 10:06 A
Mar. 21 ... set 8:56 D	Sept. 21.... rise 9:51 A	Mar. 21 ... set 9:31 D	Sept. 21 ... rise 9:23 A
Apr. 1...... set 8:25 D	Oct. 1 ...... rise 9:12 A	Apr. 1...... set 8:54 D	Oct. 1 ...... rise 8:43 A
Apr. 11.... set 8:58 D	Oct. 11 .... rise 8:32 A	Apr. 11.... set 9:21 D	Oct. 11 .... rise 8:02 A
Apr. 21.... set 8:31 D	Oct. 21 .... rise 7:51 A	Apr. 21.... set 8:48 D	Oct. 21 .... rise 7:21 A
May 1...... set 8:03 D	Nov. 1 ..... rise 6:04 A	May 1 ...... set 8:15 D	Nov. 1 ..... rise 5:36 A
May 11.... set 7:36 D	Nov. 11 ... rise 5:21 A	May 11.... set 7:42 D	Nov. 11 ... rise 4:54 A
May 21.... rise 4:53 A	Nov. 21 ... rise 4:37 A	May 21.... rise 5:01 A	Nov. 21 ... set 6:33 D
June 1...... rise 4:17 A	Dec. 1 ..... set 6:40 E	June 1...... rise 4:22 A	Dec. 1 ..... set 5:49 D
June 11.... rise 3:45 A	Dec. 11 ... set 5:54 E	June 11.... rise 3:47 A	Dec. 11.... set 5:06 D
June 21.... rise 3:13 A	Dec. 21.... set 5:09 E	June 21.... rise 3:11 A	Dec. 21.... set 4:24 D
	Dec. 31.... set 4:25 E		Dec. 31.... set 3:42 D

Eclipses, 2000

■ There will be six eclipses in 2000, four of the Sun and two of the Moon. The solar eclipses of February 5 and July 1 will not be visible in the United States or Canada. (A partial solar eclipse requires eye protection to be safely viewed.)

1. Total eclipse of the Moon, January 20-21. The beginning of the umbral phase will be visible throughout North America. The end will be visible in North America and Hawaii. The Moon enters penumbra on January 20 at 9:03 P.M., EST (6:03 P.M., PST); totality begins at 11:05 P.M., EST (8:05 P.M., PST), and ends on the 21st at 12:22 A.M., EST (9:22 P.M., PST, on the 20th); the Moon leaves penumbra on the 21st at 2:24 A.M., EST (11:24 P.M., PST, on the 20th).

2. Total eclipse of the Moon, July 16. Only the beginning of the umbral phase will be visible in the western United States and Hawaii, southern Alaska, and western Canada. The end will be visible only in Hawaii. The umbral phase begins at 4:57 A.M., PDT, and ends at 8:54 A.M., PDT.

3. Partial eclipse of the Sun, July 30. This eclipse will be visible in western North America. Throughout the western United States, the eclipse will begin in the late afternoon. In Alaska, the eclipse will begin about 6:00 P.M., ADT, and last about 90 minutes.

4. Partial eclipse of the Sun, December 25. This eclipse will be visible throughout all of North America except Alaska. In the East, the eclipse will begin shortly after 11:00 A.M., EST, and end shortly after 2:00 P.M. EST. In the central region, it will begin about 9:30 A.M., CST, and end about noon, CST. In the West, it will begin around 8:00 A.M., PST, and end around 9:00 A.M., PST.

Full-Moon Dates

	2000	2001	2002	2003	2004
Jan.	20	9	28	18	7
Feb.	19	8	27	16	6
Mar.	19	9	28	18	6
Apr.	18 *	7	26	16	5
May	18	7	26	15	4
June	16	5	24	14	3
July	16	5	24	13	2&31
Aug.	15	4	22	12	29
Sept.	13	2	21	10	28
Oct.	13	2	21	10	27
Nov.	11	1&30	19	8	26
Dec.	11	30	19	8	26

Principal Meteor Showers

Shower	Best Hour (EST/EDT)	Point of Origin	Date of Maximum*	Approx. Peak Rate (/hr.)**	Associated Comet
Quadrantid	5 A.M.	N	Jan. 4	80	—
Lyrid	5 A.M.	S	Apr. 22	12	Thatcher
Eta Aquarid	5 A.M.	SE	May 4	20	Halley
Delta Aquarid	3 A.M.	S	July 30	10	—
Perseid	5 A.M.	NE	Aug. 11-13	75	Swift-Tuttle
Draconid	10 P.M.	NW	Oct. 9	10	Giacobini-Zinner
Orionid	5 A.M.	S	Oct. 21-22	25	Halley
Taurid	Midnight	S	Nov. 9	6	Encke
Leonid	5 A.M.	S	Nov. 18	20	Tempel-Tuttle
Andromedid	10 P.M.	S	Nov. 25-27	5	Biela
Geminid	2 A.M.	NE	Dec. 14	65	—
Ursid	5 A.M.	N	Dec. 22	12	Tuttle

* **Date of actual maximum occurrence may vary by one or two days in either direction.**

** **The number of sporadic meteors seen per hour on clear nights is about six. The visibility of showers depends on how bright the Moon is on the night of the shower.**

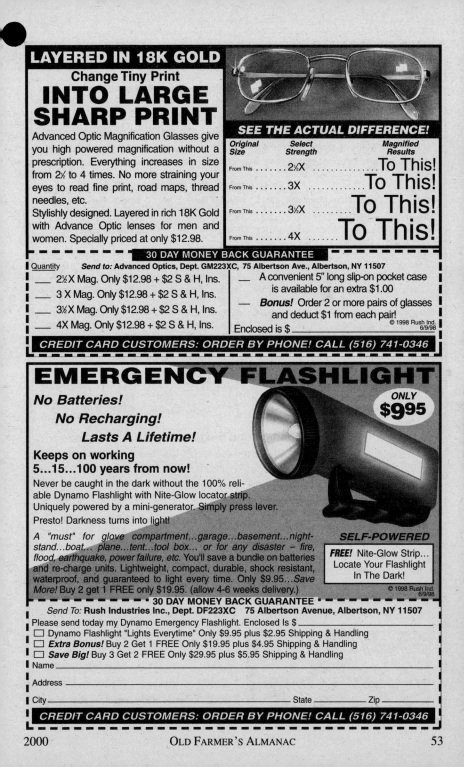

Bright Stars, 2000

■ The upper table shows the time (EST or EDT) that each star transits the meridian (i.e., lies directly above the horizon's south point) at Boston, and the star's altitude above that point at transit on the dates shown. The time of transit on any other date differs from that of the nearest date listed by approximately four minutes for each day. To find the time of the star's transit for a location other than Boston, convert the time at Boston using Key Letter C for that location. (See footnote.)

Star	Constellation	Magnitude	Jan. 1	Mar. 1	May 1	July 1	Sept. 1	Nov. 1	Altitude (degrees)
Altair	Aquila	0.8	**12:51**	8:56	5:56	1:56	**9:48**	**4:48**	56.3
Deneb	Cygnus	1.3	**1:42**	9:46	6:47	2:47	**10:39**	**5:39**	92.8
Fomalhaut	Psc. Aus.	1.2	**3:57**	**12:01**	9:01	5:01	12:54	**7:54**	17.8
Algol	Perseus	2.2	**8:08**	**4:12**	**1:12**	9:12	5:08	12:08	88.5
Aldebaran	Taurus	0.9	**9:35**	**5:39**	**2:39**	10:39	6:36	1:36	64.1
Rigel	Orion	0.1	**10:13**	**6:17**	**3:18**	11:18	7:14	2:14	39.4
Capella	Auriga	0.1	**10:15**	**6:19**	**3:19**	11:19	7:16	2:16	93.6
Bellatrix	Orion	1.6	**10:24**	**6:28**	**3:28**	11:28	7:25	2:25	54.0
Betelgeuse	Orion	var. 0.4	**10:54**	**6:58**	**3:58**	11:58	7:55	2:55	55.0
Sirius	Can. Maj.	−1.4	**11:44**	**7:48**	**4:48**	**12:48**	8:44	3:44	31.0
Procyon	Can. Min.	0.4	12:41	**8:42**	**5:42**	**1:42**	9:38	4:38	52.9
Pollux	Gemini	1.2	12:47	**8:48**	**5:48**	**1:48**	9:44	4:44	75.7
Regulus	Leo	1.4	3:10	**11:11**	**8:11**	**4:11**	**12:07**	7:07	59.7
Spica	Virgo	var. 1.0	6:27	2:31	**11:27**	**7:27**	**3:23**	10:24	36.6
Arcturus	Bootes	−0.1	7:18	3:22	12:18	**8:18**	**4:14**	11:14	66.9
Antares	Scorpius	var. 0.9	9:30	5:34	2:35	**10:31**	**6:27**	**1:27**	21.3
Vega	Lyra	0.0	11:38	7:42	4:42	12:38	**8:35**	**3:35**	86.4

Time of Transit (EST/EDT) Boldface – P.M. Lightface – A.M.

Risings and Settings

■ To find the times of the star's rising and setting at Boston on any date, apply the interval shown to the time of the star's transit on that date. Subtract the interval for the star's rising; add it for its setting. To find the times for a location other than Boston, convert the times at Boston using the Key Letter shown. (See footnote.) The directions in which the stars rise and set, shown for Boston, are generally useful throughout the United States. Deneb, Algol, Capella, and Vega are circumpolar stars— this means that they do not appear to rise or set but stay above the horizon.

Star	Interval (h. m.)	Rising Key	Rising Dir.	Setting Key	Setting Dir.
Altair	6:36	B	EbN	E	WbN
Fomalhaut	3:59	E	SE	D	SW
Aldebaran	7:06	B	ENE	D	WNW
Rigel	5:33	D	EbS	B	WbS
Bellatrix	6:27	B	EbN	D	WbN
Betelgeuse	6:31	B	EbN	D	WbN
Sirius	5:00	D	ESE	B	WSW
Procyon	6:23	B	EbN	D	WbN
Pollux	8:01	A	NE	E	NW
Regulus	6:49	B	EbN	D	WbN
Spica	5:23	D	EbS	B	WbS
Arcturus	7:19	A	ENE	E	WNW
Antares	4:17	E	SEbE	A	SWbW

NOTE: The values of Key Letters are given in the Time Corrections table (page 234).

– Beth Krommes

Nervous about the year 2000? Maybe you'd like to hook up with a different numbering system altogether. For instance, at noon on January 1, 2000, Julian Day 2,451,545 begins. And a few days later comes Lunation 953.

t's been 40 generations since anybody who uses our calendar has experienced a four-digit change, so the millennium hoopla is not surprising. What we're celebrating, though, is nothing of nature, but a simple round number in an arbitrary, man-made numbering system. Even the starting point at Year One is now known not to mark the birth of Jesus, which appears to have happened a few years earlier. (See "Dennis the Short and the Dating Game," page 58.) Moreover, the world brims with other calendar systems in which, depending on whom you ask, it's actually the year 7509 (Byzantine), 5761 (Jewish), 2660 (Japanese), 1421 (Islamic), and so on.

We can also look at *other* numbering schemes — not cultural or religious in character, but ones that actually connect with events of nature, to give the year 2000 some perspective. We don't have to search too hard: We ourselves employ many dating and numbering systems that are used routinely in various sciences, especially astronomy. Some of them have been around since ancient times.

SAROS CYCLE

☆ The Babylonians, for example, perspicaciously noticed that the cycle of lunar and solar eclipses repeated every 18 years and 11⅓ days, and they called this interval a saros. It happens because of the remarkable fact that three separate lunar cycles (the Moon's period of phases of 29.53 days; the Moon's close-approach-to-Earth cycle of 27.55 days; and the Moon's return to its alignment with the Earth-Sun plane every 27.21 days) all come together after one saros interval; the saros is the common denominator of all three periods. So here is a *real* interval, a tangible one invented by nature, with the dramatic and influential consequence of producing total solar eclipses.

Astronomers number these saros cycles and have discovered

BY BOB BERMAN

MILLENNIUM AFTER ALL

that after every three (an interval of 54 years and 1 month), eclipses even return to the same part of the globe, creating a natural pattern that can be experienced in a human lifetime.

LUNATION CYCLE

☆ Astronomers number other celestial apparitions, too. Beautifully thin crescent Moons have been pleasurably noted throughout history, but not many people know or care that astronomers keep tabs on each lunation, or period of time between each new Moon. (The new Moon of January 6, 2000, marks lunation number 953.) Heads up for Moon-worshippers: Get ready to toast the arrival of lunation number 1,000 just three years from now.

JULIAN DAYS

☆ Astronomers, being compulsive numbering freaks, even assign a numeral to each *day*. (Try, for instance, to determine precisely how many days ago you were born, figur-

ing in all manner of irregular months and leap years.) When astronomers want to determine the time elapsed between any two celestial events, they simplify such tasks by using Julian Days, which begin at noon. The numbering system starts on January 1, 4713 B.C., so that at noon on January 1, 2000, it's the start of Julian Day 2,451,545 — which probably won't inspire the popping of too many champagne corks. Nor will fireworks be seen when the Julian Day system reaches a round number like 2.5 million. (Don't hold your breath — it's still 132 years away.)

CARBON-14

☆ Carbon-14, inhaled into our lungs with every breath, breaks down to a form of nitrogen at such a steady rate that it can precisely date the age of anything organic, such as bone or ancient clothing made from cotton. In 5,730 years, exactly 50 percent of a given sample will have changed to ni-

trogen. This, for example, is how the Shroud of Turin controversy was finally decisively settled, when the religious relic was found to date from medieval times rather than being two millennia old.

VENUS

☆ Some celestial cycles are strikingly visible without the slightest need for a telescope, but are still unknown to nearly everyone. Take the variable prominence of Venus, the brightest "star" in the heavens and the planet closest to Earth. As an evening star, Venus rises high for northern hemisphere observers only when it swings to the eastern edge of its orbit in the springtime, reaching its steepest angle from the horizon. This happened in the first months of 1999 and produced a truly beautiful, dazzling apparition (as well as a few UFO reports).

When will that eye-catching event recur? Venus makes 13 orbits of the Sun in almost exactly the same time that our own Earth goes around eight times, so it returns to the same part of our sky, at the same season, after eight years. The great Evening Star apparition of 1999 will replay itself in 2007. Nobody has yet decided to number these eight-year rhythms.

We could go on. There are short cycles like the Sun's 11-year storm periodicity, with its powerful earthly influences of temperature changes, gulf-stream shifts, and auroral displays, and there is the much longer but more dramatic 13,000-year period in which Earth's spin-axis points in opposite directions, stirring up major climatic upheavals. There's almost no end to the numbering systems, whether physical, natural, religious, or arbitrary, that call out to be celebrated this or any other year. But will anyone set off fireworks or pop a champagne cork for most of them? No chance. After this year, you might as well save your next toast for the year 3000. The present vintage should be fairly valuable by then.

Dennis the Short and the Dating Game, or Why We Think It's A.D. 2000

 ionysius Exiguus (whose name can roughly be translated as Dennis the Short, or perhaps the Humble) was born in what is now Romania in about the year A.D. 470, six years before the last Caesar was deposed. After taking his vows as a monk, he was sent to Alexandria in Egypt, where he studied chronology.

Years later, Dennis turned to a task set by Pope John I: Revise the entire calendar that had been in use since the time of Julius Caesar, five centuries earlier, in which years were numbered from the legendary founding of Rome in 1280 A.U.C. (i.e., *ab urbe condita*, meaning "from the city's founding"). Dennis did some calculations and announced that the birth of Christ had occurred in 754 A.U.C., which Dennis renamed *anno Domini* (or "year of the Lord") 1. He figured that the year he was living in was A.D. 525. He never bothered to number the years before Christ's birth, giving his calendar a fresh start with a defining Christian event.

We know now that Dennis was slightly off — most probably by four years, judging from known events. After several centuries, his new system had replaced A.U.C. and other local dating schemes across Europe and the Mediterranean world. In A.D. 731, the writings of the Northumbrian monk Bede, known as the Venerable Bede, popularized anno Domini in Anglo-Saxon England. Bede contributed the B.C. system for the years before Jesus' birth but forgot to stick a zero between A.D. 1 and 1 B.C., giving credence to the argument that the new millennium does not start until the first day of 2001. By the year 1000, most of Europe was dating by Dennis the Short's system.

Dionysius Exiguus died in Italy in A.D. 545, at about 75 years of age. Today, nearly every country uses his count for their civil calendars, calling it the Common Era rather than the Christian Era.

– *Andrew Rothovius*

□ □

🖥 **Spinning the Web:** Go to **www.almanac.com** and click on **Article Links 2000** for Web sites related to this article. – *The Editors*

Saturn reaches opposition on the 6th. It is now brighter than it has been for two decades, shining at an impressive magnitude -0.2 among the skimpy stars of Aries. It now rises at sunset and is visible throughout the night. Starting at midnight on the night of the 17th-18th, the erratic Leonid meteor shower peaks and could put on an awesome display. The Moon stands near Jupiter on the 20th and near Saturn on the 21st. Mercury reappears low in the east before dawn on the 25th. Soon after nightfall on the 28th, Mars and Neptune are very close, affording telescope users an unusually good opportunity to locate the eighth planet.

● New Moon	7th day	22nd hour	53rd minute
☽ First Quarter	16th day	4th hour	3rd minute
○ Full Moon	23rd day	2nd hour	4th minute
☾ Last Quarter	29th day	18th hour	18th minute

Times are given in Eastern Standard Time.

For an explanation of this page, see page 40; for values of Key Letters, see page 234.

Day of Year	Day of Month	Day of Week	☼ Rises h. m.	Key	☼ Sets h. m.	Key	Length of Day h. m.	Sun Fast m.	Declination of Sun °	High Tide Boston Light – A.M. **Bold – P.M.**	☽ Rises h. m.	Key	☽ Sets h. m.	Key	☽ Place	☽ Age
305	1	M.	6 17	D	4 38	B	10 21	32	14s.26	5¼ 5½	—	–	1ᴹ46ᴾ	E	LEO	23
306	2	Tu.	6 18	D	4 37	B	10 19	32	14 45	6¼ 6¾	12ᴹ26	C	2 21	D	LEO	24
307	3	W.	6 20	D	4 35	B	10 15	32	15 04	7½ 7¾	1 31	C	2 51	D	LEO	25
308	4	Th.	6 21	D	4 34	B	10 13	32	15 22	8¼ 8¾	2 34	D	3 19	D	VIR	26
309	5	Fr.	6 22	D	4 33	B	10 11	32	15 41	9 9½	3 36	D	3 47	C	VIR	27
310	6	Sa.	6 23	D	4 32	B	10 09	32	15 59	9¾ 10¼	4 37	D	4 14	C	VIR	28
311	7	**C**	6 25	D	4 31	B	10 06	32	16 17	10½ 11	5 37	E	4 42	B	VIR	0
312	8	M.	6 26	D	4 30	A	10 04	32	16 34	11 11½	6 36	E	5 13	B	LIB	1
313	9	Tu.	6 27	D	4 28	A	10 01	32	16 52	11¾ —	7 35	E	5 46	B	LIB	2
314	10	W.	6 28	D	4 27	A	9 59	32	17 09	12¼ 12¼	8 31	E	6 24	B	OPH	3
315	11	Th.	6 30	D	4 26	A	9 56	32	17 26	12¾ 1	9 26	E	7 06	B	OPH	4
316	12	Fr.	6 31	D	4 25	A	9 54	32	17 42	1½ 1¾	10 17	E	7 52	B	SAG	5
317	13	Sa.	6 32	D	4 24	A	9 52	31	17 58	2¼ 2½	11 04	E	8 44	B	SAG	6
318	14	**C**	6 33	D	4 23	A	9 50	31	18 14	3 3¼	11ᴹ46	E	9 40	B	SAG	7
319	15	M.	6 35	D	4 23	A	9 48	31	18 29	4 4	12ᴹ25ᴾ	E	10 39	B	CAP	8
320	16	Tu.	6 36	D	4 22	A	9 46	31	18 44	4¾ 5	1 00	D	11ᴹ41ᴾ	B	CAP	9
321	17	W.	6 37	D	4 21	A	9 44	31	18 59	5¾ 5¾	1 32	D	—	–	AQU	10
322	18	Th.	6 38	D	4 20	A	9 42	31	19 13	6½ 6¾	2 03	D	12ᴹ46	C	AQU	11
323	19	Fr.	6 39	D	4 19	A	9 40	30	19 27	7¼ 7¾	2 34	D	1 53	D	PSC	12
324	20	Sa.	6 41	D	4 18	A	9 37	30	19 41	8¼ 8½	3 06	C	3 03	D	CET	13
325	21	**C**	6 42	D	4 18	A	9 36	30	19 55	9 9½	3 40	C	4 16	E	PSC	14
326	22	M.	6 43	D	4 17	A	9 34	30	20 08	9¾ 10¼	4 19	B	5 31	E	ARI	15
327	23	Tu.	6 44	D	4 16	A	9 32	29	20 20	10½ 11¼	5 04	B	6 47	E	TAU	16
328	24	W.	6 45	D	4 16	A	9 31	29	20 33	11½ —	5 56	B	8 02	E	TAU	17
329	25	Th.	6 47	D	4 15	A	9 28	29	20 44	12 12¼	6 55	B	9 11	E	ORI	18
330	26	Fr.	6 48	D	4 15	A	9 27	29	20 56	1 1¼	8 00	B	10 12	E	GEM	19
331	27	Sa.	6 49	E	4 14	A	9 25	28	21 07	1¾ 2	9 08	B	11 04	E	CAN	20
332	28	**C**	6 50	E	4 14	A	9 24	28	21 18	2¾ 3	10 16	C	11ᴹ47	E	CAN	21
333	29	M.	6 51	E	4 13	A	9 22	28	21 29	3¾ 4	11ᴹ23ᴾ	C	12ᴹ24ᴾ	D	LEO	22
334	30	Tu.	6 52	E	4 13	A	9 21	27	21s.39	5 5¼	—	–	12ᴹ56ᴾ	D	LEO	23

NOVEMBER hath 30 days. 1999

Tonight the winds began to rise
And roar from yonder dropping day:
The last red leaf is whirled away,
The rooks are blown about the skies. – Alfred, Lord Tennyson

D. M.	D. W.	Dates, Feasts, Fasts, Aspects, Tide Heights	Weather ↓
1	M.	All Saints • First medical school for women opened, Boston, 1848 •	Warm
2	Tu.	All Souls • Election Day • Daniel Boone born, 1734 • { 9.6 / 10.0	enough
3	W.	☌ ♀ ☾ • Detroit-Windsor auto tunnel opened, 1930 • Tides { 9.8 / 9.9 •	for
4	Th.	Iranian militants seized U.S. Embassy in Teheran, 1979 • Will Rogers born, 1879 •	outdoor
5	Fr.	☾ on Eq. • ☿ stat. • Ida Tarbell born, 1857 • { 10.2 / 9.9 •	chores,
6	Sa.	♄ at ☍ • 13 inches of snow, St. Louis, Mo., 1951 • Paderewski born, 1860 •	now
7	C	24th S. af. P. • New ● • Tides { 10.5 / 9.8 •	and
8	M.	The Louvre opened to public for first time, 1793 • Bonnie Raitt born, 1949 •	then
9	Tu.	*Make the little decisions with your head and the big decisions with your heart.* • { 10.4 / —	a blow.
10	W.	St. Leo the Great • Martin Luther born, 1483 • { 9.5 / 10.3 •	Gather
11	Th.	St. Martin • Veterans Day • ☾ at apo. • Tides { 9.3 / 10.1 •	in
12	Fr.	NFL record: Detroit Lions fumbled 11 times, 1967 • Elizabeth Cady Stanton born, 1815	those
13	Sa.	☾ runs low • ☌ ♂ ☾ • Sadie Hawkins Day • { 8.8 / 9.6 •	winter
14	C	25th S. af. P. • ☾ at ☋ • ☌ ♆ ☾ •	stores,
15	M.	☌ ♅ ☾ • ☿ in inf. ☌ • ☿ transit over ☉ •	soon
16	Tu.	*The future joy makes the past and the present bearable.* • Tides { 8.6 / 9.1 •	enough
17	W.	St. Hugh of Lincoln • American Theosophical Society founded, 1875 • { 8.8 / 9.2	the
18	Th.	St. Hilda • Mickey Mouse appeared in his first film, *Steamboat Willie*, 1928 •	snow.
19	Fr.	☾ on Eq. • First life insurance policy issued to a woman, 1850 • Tides { 9.8 / 9.8 •	Stuff
20	Sa.	☌ ♃ ☾ • Kenesaw Mountain Landis born, 1866 • { 10.5 / 10.2 •	the
21	C	26th S. af. P. • ☌ ♄ ☾ • Tides { 11.2 / 10.6	turkey,
22	M.	Hoagie Carmichael born, 1899 • Billie Jean King born, 1943 • { 11.8 / 10.9 •	say
23	Tu.	St. Clement • Full Beaver ○ • ☾ at perig. • { 12.2 / 11.0 •	the
24	W.	☿ stat. • Lee Harvey Oswald shot and killed, 1963 • { 12.5 / — •	blessing,
25	Th.	Thanksgiving • Andrew Carnegie born, 1835 • Upton Sinclair died, 1968 •	pass
26	Fr.	☾ rides high • Ford roadsters on sale for $260, 1925 • Tides { 10.8 / 12.1 •	the
27	Sa.	☾ at ☊ • *It doesn't do any good to buy expensive tools if you can never find them.*	sage
28	C	1st S. in Advent • ☌ ♂ ♆ • Tides { 10.2 / 11.0 •	and
29	M.	First Army-Navy football game, 1890 (Navy 24 - Army 0) • Tides { 9.9 / 10.4 •	onion
30	Tu.	St. Andrew • -45° F, Pokegama Dam, Minn., 1896 •	dressing.

You can't depend on your eyes when your imagination is out of focus. – Mark Twain

Farmer's Calendar

■ Nobody is certain why children so love dinosaurs. Perhaps dinosaurs represent what children somehow believe, or wish, their parents were: large, strong, dumb, and conveniently extinct. However that may be, there's no doubt about the affinity of kids for the tyrannosaurs, triceratops, and the rest. If you want to get caught up on dinosaurs, ask a bright ten-year-old. But don't expect a quick lesson. There has been a good deal of activity in the dinosaur market in recent years. Dinosaurs aren't as easy as they were.

Once dinosaurs were safe and settled. You had the enormous, placid ones with long necks that went on all fours and ate plants. You had the scary, upright ones that ate the former. You had the dinosaurs that swam and the dinosaurs that flew. All were big, slow, and dull — and in those days that was about it.

Today things are more complicated. Now we have dinosaurs that were small and speedy, social, perhaps warm-blooded, and even intelligent in a wild, foxy way. As old fossils are reexamined and new ones are dug up, it develops that the more we know about dinosaurs, the more there is to know.

Why does science always do this to us? You would think that as the science of a field accumulated, it would eventually produce a simpler, more permanent understanding. In fact, the opposite happens: Increasing science makes a subject more complex, provisional, and undecided. That's good news for you if you write signs for museums, but it's frustrating for the rest of us.

1999 DECEMBER, The Twelfth Month

The Moon and Venus keep company on the 4th, while Mercury hovers between Venus and the eastern predawn horizon during the first week. The tiny planet floats to the upper right of the waning crescent Moon on the 6th. On the 12th, the first two hours after nightfall bring a very tight conjunction of the Moon, Mars, and Uranus in the southwest. Mars and Uranus are especially close on the 14th, a superb chance for binocular users to observe the seventh planet. The 22nd offers a rare combination of winter solstice (at 2:44 A.M., EST), full Moon, and lunar perigee, when the Moon reaches its closest approach of 1999, ending the year with a flourish.

●	New Moon	7th day	17th hour	32nd minute
☽	First Quarter	15th day	19th hour	50th minute
○	Full Moon	22nd day	12th hour	31st minute
☾	Last Quarter	29th day	9th hour	4th minute

Times are given in Eastern Standard Time.

For an explanation of this page, see page 40; for values of Key Letters, see page 234.

Day of Year	Day of Month	Day of Week	☼ Rises h. m.	Key	☼ Sets h. m.	Key	Length of Day h. m.	Sun Fast m.	Declination of Sun ° '	High Tide Boston Light – A.M. Bold – P.M.		☽ Rises h. m.	Key	☽ Sets h. m.	Key	☽ Place	☽ Age
335	1	W.	6 53	E	4 13	A	9 20	27	21s.48	6	**6¼**	12 A.M. 27	D	1 P.M. 25	D	VIR	24
336	2	Th.	6 54	E	4 12	A	9 18	27	21 57	7	**7¼**	1 29	D	1 52	C	VIR	25
337	3	Fr.	6 55	E	4 12	A	9 17	26	22 06	7¾	**8¼**	2 30	D	2 19	C	VIR	26
338	4	Sa.	6 56	E	4 12	A	9 16	26	22 14	8¾	**9**	3 30	E	2 46	C	VIR	27
339	5	**C**	6 57	E	4 12	A	9 15	25	22 21	9¼	**9¾**	4 29	E	3 15	B	LIB	28
340	6	M.	6 58	E	4 12	A	9 14	25	22 29	10	**10½**	5 28	E	3 47	B	LIB	29
341	7	Tu.	6 59	E	4 12	A	9 13	25	22 36	10¾	**11¼**	6 25	E	4 23	B	OPH	0
342	8	W.	7 00	E	4 11	A	9 11	24	22 42	11¼	**11¾**	7 21	E	5 03	B	OPH	1
343	9	Th.	7 01	E	4 11	A	9 10	24	22 49	**12**	—	8 13	E	5 48	B	SAG	2
344	10	Fr.	7 02	E	4 12	A	9 10	23	22 54	12½	**12½**	9 02	E	6 38	B	SAG	3
345	11	Sa.	7 03	E	4 12	A	9 09	23	22 59	1¼	**1¼**	9 46	E	7 33	B	SAG	4
346	12	**C**	7 04	E	4 12	A	9 08	22	23 04	1¾	**2**	10 26	E	8 30	B	CAP	5
347	13	M.	7 05	E	4 12	A	9 07	22	23 08	2½	**2¾**	11 01	E	9 30	C	CAP	6
348	14	Tu.	7 05	E	4 12	A	9 07	21	23 12	3¼	**3½**	11 A.M. 34	D	10 33	C	AQU	7
349	15	W.	7 06	E	4 12	A	9 06	21	23 16	4	**4¼**	12 P.M. 04	D	11 P.M. 37	C	AQU	8
350	16	Th.	7 07	E	4 13	A	9 06	20	23 19	5	**5¼**	12 33	D	—	–	AQU	9
351	17	Fr.	7 08	E	4 13	A	9 05	20	23 21	5¾	**6¼**	1 03	C	12 A.M. 43	D	CET	10
352	18	Sa.	7 08	E	4 13	A	9 05	19	23 23	6¾	**7¼**	1 35	C	1 51	D	PSC	11
353	19	**C**	7 09	E	4 14	A	9 05	19	23 24	7½	**8**	2 10	B	3 03	E	CET	12
354	20	M.	7 09	E	4 14	A	9 05	18	23 25	8½	**9**	2 50	B	4 17	E	TAU	13
355	21	Tu.	7 10	E	4 14	A	9 04	18	23 25	9¼	**10**	3 38	B	5 32	E	TAU	14
356	22	W.	7 10	E	4 14	A	9 04	17	23 25	10¼	**10¾**	4 33	B	6 46	E	TAU	15
357	23	Th.	7 11	E	4 15	A	9 04	17	23 25	11	**11¾**	5 37	B	7 53	E	GEM	16
358	24	Fr.	7 11	E	4 16	A	9 05	16	23 25	**12**	—	6 46	B	8 51	E	GEM	17
359	25	Sa.	7 12	E	4 17	A	9 05	16	23 23	12¾	**12¾**	7 57	B	9 41	E	CAN	18
360	26	**C**	7 12	E	4 17	A	9 05	15	23 21	1½	**1¾**	9 07	C	10 22	E	LEO	19
361	27	M.	7 12	E	4 18	A	9 06	15	23 19	2½	**2¾**	10 15	C	10 57	D	LEO	20
362	28	Tu.	7 13	E	4 19	A	9 06	14	23 16	3½	**3¾**	11 P.M. 20	C	11 28	D	LEO	21
363	29	W.	7 13	E	4 19	A	9 06	14	23 13	4½	**4¾**	—	–	11 A.M. 56	D	VIR	22
364	30	Th.	7 13	E	4 20	A	9 07	14	23 09	5¼	**5¾**	12 A.M. 22	D	12 P.M. 23	C	VIR	23
365	31	Fr.	7 13	E	4 21	A	9 08	13	23s.05	6¼	**6¾**	1 A.M. 23	D	12 P.M. 50	C	VIR	24

DECEMBER hath 31 days. 1999

We've had some pleasant rambles,
And merry Christmas gambols,
And roses with our brambles,
Adieu, old year, adieu! – George Lunt

D. M.	D. W.	Dates, Feasts, Fasts, Aspects, Tide Heights	*Weather* ↓
1	W.	Rosa Parks refused to give up her bus seat, Montgomery, Ala., 1955 • Tides 9.7 / 9.6 •	*Pack*
2	Th.	☾ on Eq. • ☌ ♇ ☉ • ☿ Gr. Elong (20° W.) • Maria Callas born, 1923 •	*the*
3	Fr.	☌ ♀ ☾ • First successful human heart transplant, 1967 • Tides 9.9 / 9.3	*malls*
4	Sa.	First day of Chanukah • 70° F, Boston, Mass., 1982 • Tides 10.0 / 9.3	*with*
5	C	2nd S. in Advent • ☌ ☿ ☾ • 10.2 / 9.3 •	*hours*
6	M.	St. Nicholas • First issue of *Ladies' Home Journal* published, 1883 •	*of*
7	Tu.	St. Ambrose • New ● • Pearl Harbor attacked, 1941 • 10.3 / 9.2	*folly.*
8	W.	☾ at apo. • Reagan and Gorbachev signed the INF treaty, 1987 • 10.3 / 9.2 •	*Get*
9	Th.	*If December be changeable and mild, the whole winter will remain a child.* • 10.2 / — •	*ready*
10	Fr.	☾ runs low • First Nobel Prizes awarded, 1901 • Alfred Nobel died, 1896 • 9.1 / 10.1	*for*
11	Sa.	☾ at ☋ • ☌ ♆ ☾ • King Edward VIII abdicated, 1936 • 9.0 / 10.0 •	*a*
12	C	3rd S. in Advent • ☌ ♂ ☾ • ☌ ♅ ☾ •	*storm,*
13	M.	St. Lucy • The "Mona Lisa," missing for 2 years, was recovered and returned to the Louvre, 1913 •	*by*
14	Tu.	☌ ♂ ♅ • Halcyon Days • Nostradamus born, 1503 • 8.8 / 9.4 •	*golly!*
15	W.	Ember Day • *Gone with the Wind* premiered at Loew's Grand Theatre in Atlanta, Ga., 1939 •	*Even*
16	Th.	*From error to error, one discovers the entire truth.* • Tides 9.2 / 9.2 •	*Santa*
17	Fr.	☾ on Eq. • Ember Day • William Lyon Mackenzie King born, 1874 •	*loses*
18	Sa.	☌ ♃ ☾ • Ember Day • Divorce became legal in Italy, 1970 •	*focus*
19	C	4th S. in Advent • ☌ ♄ ☾ • Tides 10.7 / 9.9 •	*in*
20	M.	Bus boycott ended, Montgomery, Ala., 1956 • Sacagawea died, 1812 • 11.3 / 10.2 •	*pre-*
21	Tu.	St. Thomas • ♃ stat. • Beware the Pogonip. •	*millennial*
22	W.	**Winter Solstice** • ☾ at perig. • **Full Long Nights** ○ • 12.3 / 10.7	*hocus*
23	Th.	☾ rides high • Bell Labs announced the invention of the transistor, 1947 •	*pocus.*
24	Fr.	☾ at ☊ • Kit Carson born, 1809 • Howard Hughes born, 1905 • 12.4 / —	*Snow*
25	Sa.	Christmas Day • *Peace on Earth, Goodwill to men.* •	*descends*
26	C	1st S. af. Ch. • **Boxing Day (Canada)** • Tides 10.5 / 11.5	*as the*
27	M.	St. John • St. Stephen • Marlene Dietrich born, 1901 •	*century*
28	Tu.	Holy Innocents • William Semple patented chewing gum, 1869 • 10.0 / 10.2	*ends:*
29	W.	☾ on Eq. • Massacre at Wounded Knee, S.D., 1890 • Tides 9.8 / 9.6 •	*Ready!*
30	Th.	First color TV sets on sale, 1953 • Simon Guggenheim born, 1867 • 9.6 / 9.1 •	*Set!*
31	Fr.	*Fill your life with experiences, not excuses.* • 9.5 / 8.8 •	*Oh-oh-oh!*

Farmer's Calendar

■ If you want to know what the future has in store in any field, you ask those especially concerned. Is your interest sports? Ask a player. Is it loan rates? Ask a banker. Is it elections? Ask someone who has to run for office. Skip the experts and find a witness whose own life will be affected by the course of events you're inquiring about; find someone on the ground, so to speak.

This principle, no more than common sense, is part of the reason people hang stubbornly onto folk weather lore in a scientific age in which that lore ought to be obsolete. Most of us, no doubt, get our weather forecasts from TV and radio — that is, from broadcasters who pass on the conclusions of meteorologists. We have confidence in these scientific forecasts for the best possible reason: We have found them to be generally accurate. Nevertheless, the prescientific indicators of weather — the acorns, groundhogs, woolly bear caterpillars, and so on — are not forgotten. Though they survive mainly as humor, they do survive.

Why don't we let the old weather signs go, at last, and put all our faith in meteorology? Because meteorology isn't on the ground. Those likable, people on the TV, even the scientists whose findings they report, aren't concerned with the weather the way a deer mouse, say, is. If the former get it wrong, they may have to find a job in Sioux Falls. But for them, that's the worst thing that happens. The deer mouse has a different stake. If he underestimates the winter to come and fails to provide in his nest, he starves.

JANUARY, The First Month

The year begins with symmetry: All three bright outer planets (Mars, Jupiter, and Saturn) hang conspicuously in the southwest at nightfall, while both inner planets (Mercury and Venus) lurk in the east in morning twilight. Earth is closest to the Sun (perihelion) on the 3rd, at a distance of 91,400,005 miles. In the early morning hours of the 4th, the Quadrantid meteors cascade in a favorable moonless sky. The crescent Moon is near Mars on the 10th, Jupiter on the 14th, and Saturn on the 15th. The year's only total lunar eclipse for the entire mainland United States and Canada occurs on the 20th, when the Moon enters Earth's dark umbral shadow at 10:01 P.M., EST, with totality beginning at 11:05 P.M.

●	New Moon	6th day	13th hour	14th minute
☽	First Quarter	14th day	8th hour	34th minute
○	Full Moon	20th day	23rd hour	40th minute
☾	Last Quarter	28th day	2nd hour	57th minute

Times are given in Eastern Standard Time.

For an explanation of this page, see page 40; for values of Key Letters, see page 234.

Day of Year	Day of Month	Day of Week	☼ Rises h. m.	Key	☼ Sets h. m.	Key	Length of Day h. m.	Sun Fast m.	Declination of Sun ° '	High Tide Boston Light – A.M.	**Bold – P.M.**	☽ Rises h. m.	Key	☽ Sets h. m.	Key	☽ Place	☽ Age
1	1	Sa.	7 13	E	4 22	A	9 09	13	23s.01	7¼	**7¾**	2 A.M. 22	E	1 P.M. 19	B	LIB	25
2	2	**B**	7 14	E	4 23	A	9 09	12	22 55	8	**8¾**	3 21	E	1 49	B	LIB	26
3	3	M.	7 14	E	4 24	A	9 10	12	22 50	8¾	**9½**	4 19	E	2 23	B	SCO	27
4	4	Tu.	7 14	E	4 25	A	9 11	11	22 44	9½	**10¼**	5 15	E	3 02	B	OPH	28
5	5	W.	7 14	E	4 25	A	9 11	11	22 37	10¼	**10¾**	6 09	E	3 45	B	SAG	29
6	6	Th.	7 14	E	4 26	A	9 12	10	22 31	11	**11½**	6 59	E	4 34	B	SAG	0
7	7	Fr.	7 13	E	4 27	A	9 14	10	22 23	11½	—	7 45	E	5 27	B	SAG	1
8	8	Sa.	7 13	E	4 28	A	9 15	9	22 16	12	**12¼**	8 27	E	6 24	B	CAP	2
9	9	**B**	7 13	E	4 30	A	9 17	9	22 07	12¾	**12¾**	9 04	E	7 24	B	CAP	3
10	10	M.	7 13	E	4 31	A	9 18	9	21 58	1½	**1½**	9 37	D	8 25	C	AQU	4
11	11	Tu.	7 13	E	4 32	A	9 19	8	21 49	2	**2¼**	10 08	D	9 28	C	AQU	5
12	12	W.	7 12	E	4 33	A	9 21	8	21 40	2¾	**3**	10 37	D	10 32	D	AQU	6
13	13	Th.	7 12	E	4 34	A	9 22	7	21 30	3½	**3¾**	11 05	D	11 P.M. 38	D	CET	7
14	14	Fr.	7 12	E	4 35	A	9 23	7	21 20	4¼	**4¾**	11 A.M. 35	C	—	–	PSC	8
15	15	Sa.	7 11	E	4 36	A	9 25	7	21 09	5¼	**5¾**	12 P.M. 07	C	12 A.M. 45	E	CET	9
16	16	**B**	7 11	E	4 37	A	9 26	6	20 58	6¼	**6¾**	12 43	B	1 55	E	ARI	10
17	17	M.	7 10	E	4 39	A	9 29	6	20 46	7	**7¾**	1 25	B	3 07	E	TAU	11
18	18	Tu.	7 10	E	4 40	A	9 30	6	20 34	8	**8¾**	2 14	B	4 20	E	TAU	12
19	19	W.	7 09	E	4 41	A	9 32	5	20 22	9	**9¾**	3 13	B	5 29	E	ORI	13
20	20	Th.	7 08	E	4 42	A	9 34	5	20 09	10	**10¾**	4 19	B	6 32	E	GEM	14
21	21	Fr.	7 08	E	4 43	A	9 35	5	19 56	10¾	**11½**	5 30	B	7 27	E	CAN	15
22	22	Sa.	7 07	E	4 45	A	9 38	4	19 43	11¾	—	6 43	B	8 13	E	CAN	16
23	23	**B**	7 06	D	4 46	A	9 40	4	19 29	12½	**12½**	7 54	C	8 52	D	LEO	17
24	24	M.	7 06	D	4 47	A	9 41	4	19 15	1¼	**1½**	9 02	D	9 26	D	LEO	18
25	25	Tu.	7 05	D	4 48	A	9 43	4	19 00	2	**2¼**	10 08	D	9 56	D	VIR	19
26	26	W.	7 04	D	4 50	A	9 46	3	18 45	3	**3¼**	11 P.M. 11	D	10 25	C	VIR	20
27	27	Th.	7 03	D	4 51	A	9 48	3	18 30	3¾	**4¼**	—	–	10 52	C	VIR	21
28	28	Fr.	7 02	D	4 52	A	9 50	3	18 14	4¾	**5¼**	12 A.M. 12	E	11 21	B	LIB	22
29	29	Sa.	7 01	D	4 54	A	9 53	3	17 58	5½	**6¼**	1 12	E	11 A.M. 51	B	LIB	23
30	30	**B**	7 00	D	4 55	A	9 55	2	17 42	6½	**7¼**	2 11	E	12 P.M. 24	B	SCO	24
31	31	M.	6 59	D	4 56	A	9 57	2	17s.25	7½	**8**	3 A.M. 08	E	1 P.M. 00	B	OPH	25

JANUARY hath 31 days. 2000

. . . January is here,
With eyes that keenly glow —
A frost-mailed warrior striding
A shadowy steed of snow. – Edgar Fawcett

D. M.	D. W.	Dates, Feasts, Fasts, Aspects, Tide Heights	*Weather* ↓
1	Sa.	New Year's Day • Circumcision • Tides {9.6 8.7 •	*White*
2	B	2nd S. af. Ch. • ☌ ♀ ☾ • Isaac Asimov born, 1920	*2day*
3	M.	⊕ at perihelion • Ground broken for Brooklyn Bridge, 1870 • {9.8 8.7 •	*for*
4	Tu.	St. Elizabeth Seton • ☾ at apo. • Louis Braille born, 1809 •	*Y2K.*
5	W.	Twelfth Night • *Work is the greatest thing in the world, so always save some for tomorrow.* •	*Ten*
6	Th.	Epiphany • New ● • ☾ runs low • {10.2 9.0 •	*below,*
7	Fr.	St. Distaff's Day • *Partly work and partly play, Must ye on St. Distaff's Day.* • {10.2 —	*the*
8	Sa.	☾ at ☋ • ☌ ♆ ☾ • Elvis Presley born, 1935 • {9.0 10.2 •	*snow*
9	B	1st S. af. Ep. • ☌ ♅ ☾ • {9.0 10.1	*squeaking;*
10	M.	☌ ♂ ☾ • Plough Monday • League of Nations formed, 1920 • {9.1 10.0	*far*
11	Tu.	*To be born a gentleman is an accident, to die one is an achievement.* • Tides {9.1 9.9	*too*
12	W.	♄ stat. • Hattie W. Caraway (D., Ark.) became first woman elected to U.S. Senate, 1932 •	*brisk*
13	Th.	St. Hilary • ☾ on Eq. • Hubert H. Humphrey died, 1978 • {9.4 9.5 •	*to*
14	Fr.	☌ ♃ ☾ • Propitious day for birth of women. • Treaty of Paris ratified, 1784 •	*risk*
15	Sa.	☌ ♄ ☾ • ☿ in sup. ☌ • Tides {9.8 9.2 •	*streaking.*
16	B	2nd S. af. Ep. • Arturo Toscanini died, 1957 • {10.2 9.2	*Milder*
17	M.	Martin Luther King Jr.'s Birthday • Benjamin Franklin born, 1706 •	
18	Tu.	White bear from Greenland exhibited in Boston, 1733 • Daniel Webster born, 1782 • {11.1 9.7	*now*
19	W.	☾ at perig. • Paul Cézanne born, 1839 • Tides {11.5 10.0	*but hardly*
20	Th.	St. Fabian • Full Wolf ○ • Eclipse ☾ • ☾ rides high • {11.9 10.3	
21	Fr.	St. Agnes • ☾ at ☊ • -32° F, Hainesville, New Jersey, 1994 •	*torrid;*
22	Sa.	St. Vincent • Queen Victoria died, 1901 • Tides {12.0 — •	*look up*
23	B	3rd S. af. Ep. • 20th Amendment ratified, 1933 •	*synonyms*
24	M.	☌ ♆ ☉ • First canned beer sold, Richmond, Virginia, 1935 • {10.5 11.3 •	*for*
25	Tu.	Conversion of Paul • Hudson River frozen solid, 1821 •	*"horrid."*
26	W.	Sts. Timothy & Titus • ☾ on Eq. • Wayne Gretzky born, 1961 •	*The*
27	Th.	Mozart born, 1756 • *Love, love, love, that is the soul of genius.* – Mozart • {9.8 9.3	*teeth-*
28	Fr.	St. Thomas Aquinas • Sarah McLachlan born, 1968 •	*chattering*
29	Sa.	Queen Liliuokalani ascended to Hawaiian throne, 1891 • Thomas Paine born, 1737 • {9.3 8.4	*is*
30	B	4th S. af. Ep. • Orville Wright died, 1948 • {9.2 8.2	*record-*
31	M.	☾ at apo. • First McDonald's in Soviet Union opened, 1990 •	*shattering.*

Farmer's Calendar

■ Everybody who shovels a lot of snow knows you must get to work when the snow is still new-fallen and before it has had time to settle and become hard and heavy. You can't always do your shoveling promptly, however; sometimes the snow gets ahead of you by hours or days. Then shoveling becomes a different kind of work from what it ought to be.

I remember one year sometime back, when I allowed myself to get behind the snow curve, pretty badly behind it. I found I had other things to do that winter than shovel snow — I forget what. By the time I got to work with the shovel, 10 or 12 inches of snow lay before me, snow well packed by the wind and by its own weight.

I set to work. The shoveling, I discovered, was both harder and easier than more-timely shoveling would have been. It was harder because the snow was heavy. It was easier because the snow was compact. Rather than move a shovelful of loose, light snow, half of which would pour off the shovel and back into my way, I would thrust the shovel under and lift out a neat block of snow, an elephant's sugar cube. I'd set it down beside the path, dig again, lift out another block, set it down, dig. . . . *This isn't shoveling,* I thought, *this is mining*. Somehow, that idea seemed to lighten my shovel. In the end, I did a bigger and a better job than I would have under normal circumstances. This kind of endless job like snow shoveling is tricky work: The closer you attend to the task, the harder you make it, the easier it is.

2000 FEBRUARY, The Second Month

A last hurrah for sinking, dimming Venus occurs on the 2nd, with a worthwhile, strikingly close predawn meeting with the crescent Moon. An even thinner crescent hangs above Mercury low in evening twilight on the 6th. On the 5th, an impulsive trip to Antarctica would reward an observer with a partial solar eclipse. The Moon is near Mars on the 8th, Jupiter on the 10th, and Saturn on the 11th, all around dinnertime. From February 9 to 19, Mercury hangs low in the west but is visible without difficulty in evening twilight. All the planets now stand on the far side of their orbits, beyond the Sun in the southern sky, with solitary Earth holding the fort on this side of the solar system.

● New Moon	5th day	8th hour	3rd minute
☽ First Quarter	12th day	18th hour	21st minute
○ Full Moon	19th day	11th hour	27th minute
☾ Last Quarter	26th day	22nd hour	53rd minute

Times are given in Eastern Standard Time.

For an explanation of this page, see page 40; for values of Key Letters, see page 234.

Day of Year	Day of Month	Day of Week	☼ Rises h. m.	Key	☼ Sets h. m.	Key	Length of Day h. m.	Sun Fast m.	Declination of Sun ° '	High Tide Boston Light – A.M.	Bold – P.M.	☽ Rises h. m.	Key	☽ Sets h. m.	Key	☽ Place	☽ Age
32	1	Tu.	6 58	D	4 58	A	10 00	2	17s.08	8¼	**9**	4 A.M. 02	E	1 P.M. 42	B	SAG	26
33	2	W.	6 57	D	4 59	A	10 02	2	16 51	9	**9¾**	4 54	E	2 28	B	SAG	27
34	3	Th.	6 56	D	5 00	A	10 04	2	16 34	9¾	**10½**	5 42	E	3 20	B	SAG	28
35	4	Fr.	6 55	D	5 01	A	10 06	2	16 16	10½	**11**	6 25	E	4 16	B	CAP	29
36	5	Sa.	6 54	D	5 03	A	10 09	2	15 59	11¼	**11¾**	7 04	E	5 16	B	CAP	0
37	6	**B**	6 53	D	5 04	A	10 11	2	15 40	11¾	—	7 39	E	6 18	C	CAP	1
38	7	M.	6 52	D	5 05	A	10 13	2	15 22	12¼	**12½**	8 11	D	7 21	C	AQU	2
39	8	Tu.	6 51	D	5 07	B	10 16	1	15 03	1	**1**	8 40	D	8 25	D	AQU	3
40	9	W.	6 49	D	5 08	B	10 19	1	14 43	1½	**1¾**	9 09	D	9 30	D	PSC	4
41	10	Th.	6 48	D	5 09	B	10 21	1	14 24	2¼	**2½**	9 38	C	10 37	D	CET	5
42	11	Fr.	6 47	D	5 11	B	10 24	1	14 04	3	**3½**	10 09	C	11 P.M. 45	D	PSC	6
43	12	Sa.	6 46	D	5 12	B	10 26	1	13 45	3¾	**4¼**	10 42	B	—	–	ARI	7
44	13	**B**	6 44	D	5 13	B	10 29	1	13 25	4¾	**5¼**	11 A.M. 20	B	12 A.M. 54	E	TAU	8
45	14	M.	6 43	D	5 14	B	10 31	1	13 04	5¾	**6¼**	12 P.M. 05	B	2 04	E	TAU	9
46	15	Tu.	6 42	D	5 16	B	10 34	1	12 44	6¾	**7½**	12 58	B	3 12	E	ORI	10
47	16	W.	6 40	D	5 17	B	10 37	1	12 24	7¾	**8½**	1 58	B	4 15	E	GEM	11
48	17	Th.	6 39	D	5 18	B	10 39	2	12 03	8¾	**9½**	3 06	B	5 13	E	GEM	12
49	18	Fr.	6 37	D	5 20	B	10 43	2	11 42	9¾	**10½**	4 17	B	6 02	E	CAN	13
50	19	Sa.	6 36	D	5 21	B	10 45	2	11 21	10¾	**11¼**	5 29	C	6 44	E	LEO	14
51	20	**B**	6 34	D	5 22	B	10 48	2	10 59	11½	—	6 39	D	7 21	D	LEO	15
52	21	M.	6 33	D	5 23	B	10 50	2	10 37	12	**12¼**	7 48	D	7 53	D	VIR	16
53	22	Tu.	6 31	D	5 25	B	10 54	2	10 16	12¾	**1¼**	8 54	D	8 23	D	VIR	17
54	23	W.	6 30	D	5 26	B	10 56	2	9 54	1½	**2**	9 57	D	8 51	C	VIR	18
55	24	Th.	6 28	D	5 27	B	10 59	2	9 32	2¼	**2¾**	10 P.M. 59	E	9 20	C	VIR	19
56	25	Fr.	6 27	D	5 28	B	11 01	2	9 09	3¼	**3½**	—	–	9 50	B	LIB	20
57	26	Sa.	6 25	D	5 30	B	11 05	3	8 47	4	**4½**	12 A.M. 00	E	10 22	B	LIB	21
58	27	**B**	6 24	D	5 31	B	11 07	3	8 24	4¾	**5½**	12 58	E	10 57	B	OPH	22
59	28	M.	6 22	D	5 32	B	11 10	3	8 02	5¾	**6½**	1 54	E	11 A.M. 37	B	OPH	23
60	29	Tu.	6 21	D	5 33	B	11 12	3	7s.39	6¾	**7½**	2 A.M. 47	E	12 P.M. 21	B	SAG	24

FEBRUARY hath 29 days. 2000

Poor robin redbreast,
Look where he comes;
Let him in to feel your fire,
And toss him of your crumbs. – Christina G. Rossetti

D. M.	D. W.	Dates, Feasts, Fasts, Aspects, Tide Heights	Weather ↓
1	Tu.	St. Brigid • Langston Hughes born, 1902 • {9.4 / 8.3 •	*Groundhogs*
2	W.	Candlemas • Groundhog Day • ☾ runs low • ☌♀☾ • {9.6 / 8.5	
3	Th.	15th Amendment ratified, 1870 • Horace Greeley born, 1811 • Tides {9.8 / 8.8	*better*
4	Fr.	☾ at ☋ • Auspicious day for marriage and repair of ships. • {10.0 / 9.0	*stay*
5	Sa.	St. Agatha • New ● • Eclipse ☉ • {10.2 / 9.2	*indoors*
6	**B**	**5th S. af. Ep.** • ☌♅☉ • ☌☿☾ •	*when*
7	M.	French dancer Mme. Francisquy Hutin introduced ballet to the U.S., 1827 • Tides {9.4 / 10.4	*that*
8	Tu.	☌♂☾ • College of William and Mary chartered, 1693 •	*nor'east*
9	W.	☾ on Eq. • *Be what you would seem to be.* • Alice Walker born, 1944 •	*lion*
10	Th.	☌♃☾ • 25th Amendment ratified, 1967 • Tides {9.9 / 9.9 •	*roars.*
11	Fr.	☌♄☾ • Nelson Mandela released from prison, 1990 • {10.0 / 9.6	*Setting*
12	Sa.	Abraham Lincoln born, 1809 • NAACP founded, 1909 • Tides {10.1 / 9.3	*up*
13	**B**	**6th S. af. Ep.** • Grant Wood born, 1892 •	*evaporators*
14	M.	St. Valentine • **Sts. Cyril & Methodius** • ☿ Gr. Elong. (18° E.) • {10.3 / 9.0	*may*
15	Tu.	*Happiness is like perfume: you can't give it away without getting a little on yourself.* •	*require a*
16	W.	☾ rides high • ☾ at perig. • -59° F at Pokegama Dam, Minnesota, 1903 • {10.8 / 9.4	
17	Th.	☾ at ☊ • Winter's back breaks. • Red Barber born, 1908 • {11.1 / 9.8	*pair*
18	Fr.	Elm Farm Ollie became first dairy cow to fly in an airplane, 1930 • Tides {11.4 / 10.2	*of*
19	Sa.	**Full Snow** ○ • Nicolaus Copernicus born, 1473 • {11.6 / 10.5 •	*waders.*
20	**B**	**Septuagesima** • ☿ stat. • Tides {11.6 / —	*Rookies*
21	M.	Presidents Day • Lucy Hobbs became first woman graduate of dental school, 1866	*sing*
22	Tu.	☾ on Eq. • ☌♀♆ • George Washington born, 1732 • {10.7 / 11.0 •	*of*
23	W.	Wrecking crews began to demolish Ebbets Field, home of the Brooklyn Dodgers, 1960	*spring*
24	Th.	St. Matthias • Winslow Homer born, 1836 • {10.2 / 9.8 •	*training —*
25	Fr.	16th Amendment, authorizing a U.S. income tax, went into effect, 1913 • Tides {9.9 / 9.2 •	*vets*
26	Sa.	*Honesty in little things is not a little thing.* • Grand Teton National Park established, 1929 •	*get set*
27	**B**	**Sexagesima** • 22nd Amendment ratified, 1950 • Tides {9.2 / 8.2 •	*for*
28	M.	☾ at apo. • *There is no one luckier than he who thinks himself so.* • {9.0 / 8.0	*snow,*
29	Tu.	Astronomers at Univ. of Cambridge, England, announced discovery of first pulsar, 1968 •	*raining.*

The only place outside Heaven where you can be safe from all the dangers and perturbations of love is Hell. – C. S. Lewis

Farmer's Calendar

■ There are hunters, and then there are killers; it's a question of true purpose as opposed to mere appearance, however convincing. At this house lives a little dog of the dachshund breed, red in color, low slung, spirited rather than clever. Hunting is his passion and his life. He sits in a window, commanding a view of the bird feeder in front of the house. He's waiting for one of the fat gray squirrels who live in the woods nearby to approach the feeder. When one does, our hunter jumps straight up in the air, whirls about three times, and lands running. He leaps from his post, barking and howling, and races through the workroom, through the parlor, and to the back door, where he is let out. Now baying and bellowing even more loudly, mad for the chase, he gallops around the house to the feeder. There he finds, of course, exactly nothing; the squirrel is long gone. The dog is crestfallen. He returns to the house, to his window, and runs the sequence all over again. To watch him, you would certainly think he wanted to catch that squirrel.

But does he? No. If he did, he would learn from the three cats who also live here. They know squirrels are not killed by clamor and pursuit but by self-control. You stake out the feeder and you wait. You don't move a muscle, you don't make a sound. That is how you get squirrel for lunch. The Keystone Cops routine that the dog goes through will never, never fetch a squirrel. Still, you can't really fault him. His way of hunting suits him, as the cats' way would not. The squirrels prefer it as well, I imagine.

March 3 brings a compact bunching of the Moon, Uranus, Venus, and Neptune low in the predawn twilight. Horizon haze and brightening skies should make this sight too challenging for all but telescope users with oceanically flat horizons. Just as difficult to view is a close meeting between Venus and Mercury from the 13th to the 16th, when they are just above the eastern horizon at the start of morning twilight. However, a beautiful eye-catching union of Jupiter, Saturn, and the Moon occurs in the west at nightfall on the 9th, with dimmer Mars just below the trio. By month's end, Mars, Jupiter, and Saturn arrive impressively close together. The vernal equinox occurs at 2:35 A.M., EST, on the 20th.

●	New Moon	6th day	0 hour	17th minute
☽	First Quarter	13th day	1st hour	59th minute
○	Full Moon	19th day	23rd hour	44th minute
☾	Last Quarter	27th day	19th hour	21st minute

Times are given in Eastern Standard Time.

For an explanation of this page, see page 40; for values of Key Letters, see page 234.

Day of Year	Day of Month	Day of Week	☼ Rises h. m.	Key	☼ Sets h. m.	Key	Length of Day h. m.	Sun Fast m.	Declination of Sun ° '	High Tide Boston Light – A.M. **Bold** – P.M.		☽ Rises h. m.	Key	☽ Sets h. m.	Key	☽ Place	☽ Age
61	1	W.	6 19	D	5 35	B	11 16	3	7 s. 16	7¾	**8¼**	3ᴀ36	E	1ᴘ11	B	SAG	25
62	2	Th.	6 17	D	5 36	B	11 19	3	6 53	8½	**9¼**	4 21	E	2 06	B	SAG	26
63	3	Fr.	6 16	D	5 37	B	11 21	4	6 30	9¼	**9¾**	5 02	E	3 04	B	CAP	27
64	4	Sa.	6 14	D	5 38	B	11 24	4	6 07	10	**10½**	5 38	E	4 06	B	CAP	28
65	5	**A**	6 12	D	5 39	B	11 27	4	5 44	10¾	**11¼**	6 11	D	5 10	C	AQU	29
66	6	M.	6 11	D	5 41	B	11 30	4	5 20	11¼	**11¾**	6 42	D	6 15	D	AQU	0
67	7	Tu.	6 09	D	5 42	B	11 33	5	4 57	**12**	—	7 11	D	7 21	D	PSC	1
68	8	W.	6 07	D	5 43	B	11 36	5	4 34	12½	**12¾**	7 41	C	8 28	D	CET	2
69	9	Th.	6 06	D	5 44	B	11 38	5	4 11	1	**1½**	8 11	C	9 37	E	PSC	3
70	10	Fr.	6 04	D	5 45	B	11 41	5	3 47	1¾	**2¼**	8 44	B	10 46	E	CET	4
71	11	Sa.	6 02	C	5 46	B	11 44	6	3 24	2½	**3**	9 20	B	11ʀ56	E	TAU	5
72	12	**A**	6 01	C	5 48	B	11 47	6	3 00	3½	**4**	10 02	B	—	–	TAU	6
73	13	M.	5 59	C	5 49	B	11 50	6	2 36	4¼	**5**	10 51	B	1ᴀ04	E	TAU	7
74	14	Tu.	5 57	C	5 50	B	11 53	6	2 13	5¼	**6¼**	11ᴍ48	B	2 08	E	GEM	8
75	15	W.	5 56	C	5 51	B	11 55	7	1 49	6½	**7¼**	12ᴘ51	B	3 05	E	GEM	9
76	16	Th.	5 54	C	5 52	B	11 58	7	1 25	7½	**8¼**	1 59	B	3 56	E	CAN	10
77	17	Fr.	5 52	C	5 53	B	12 01	7	1 02	8½	**9¼**	3 09	C	4 39	E	LEO	11
78	18	Sa.	5 50	C	5 55	B	12 05	7	0 38	9½	**10¼**	4 19	C	5 17	D	LEO	12
79	19	**A**	5 49	C	5 56	C	12 07	8	0 s.13	10½	**11**	5 28	D	5 50	D	LEO	13
80	20	M.	5 47	C	5 57	C	12 10	8	0 N.09	11¼	**11¾**	6 35	D	6 20	D	VIR	14
81	21	Tu.	5 45	C	5 58	C	12 13	8	0 33	**12**	—	7 40	D	6 49	C	VIR	15
82	22	W.	5 43	C	5 59	C	12 16	9	0 57	12½	**12¾**	8 44	E	7 18	C	VIR	16
83	23	Th.	5 42	C	6 00	C	12 18	9	1 20	1	**1½**	9 46	E	7 47	B	LIB	17
84	24	Fr.	5 40	C	6 01	C	12 21	9	1 44	1¾	**2¼**	10 46	E	8 19	B	LIB	18
85	25	Sa.	5 38	C	6 03	C	12 25	10	2 07	2½	**3**	11ᴘ44	E	8 53	B	SCO	19
86	26	**A**	5 36	C	6 04	C	12 28	10	2 31	3¼	**3¾**	—	–	9 31	B	OPH	20
87	27	M.	5 35	C	6 05	C	12 30	10	2 54	4	**4¾**	12ᴀ39	E	10 14	B	SAG	21
88	28	Tu.	5 33	C	6 06	C	12 33	10	3 17	5	**5¾**	1 30	E	11 01	B	SAG	22
89	29	W.	5 31	C	6 07	C	12 36	11	3 41	6	**6¾**	2 16	E	11ʀ54	B	SAG	23
90	30	Th.	5 30	C	6 08	C	12 38	11	4 04	7	**7¾**	2 58	E	12ʀ51	B	CAP	24
91	31	Fr.	5 28	B	6 09	C	12 41	11	4 N.27	7¾	**8½**	3ᴀ36	E	1ʀ51	B	CAP	25

MARCH hath 31 days. 2000

Would you think it? Spring has come.
Winter's paid his passage home;
Packed his ice-box — gone — half way
To the Arctic Pole, they say. – Christopher Cranch

D. M.	D. W.	Dates, Feasts, Fasts, Aspects, Tide Heights	Weather ↓
1	W.	St. David • ☾ runs low • ☿ in inf. ☌ • {9.0 8.2 •	Maple
2	Th.	St. Chad • ☾ at ☋ • ☌ ♆ ☾ • Tides {9.3 8.5	buds
3	F.	☌ ♀ ♅ • ☌ ♅ ☾ • ☌ ♀ ☾ • Tides {9.6 8.8 •	are
4	Sa.	*People* magazine launched its first issue, 1974 • Antonio Vivaldi born, 1678 •	turn-
5	A	**Quinquagesima** • "Boston Massacre," 1770 • {10.2 9.6	ing
6	M.	New ● • *There is no need to fear the wind if your haystacks are tied down.* •	pink.
7	Tu.	St. Perpetua • Shrove Tuesday • ☾ on Eq. • {10.6 —	Merc-
8	W.	**Ash Wednesday** • ☌ ♂ ☾ • Tides {10.3 10.6	ury
9	Th.	☌ ♃ ☾ • Amerigo Vespucci born, 1451 • Tides {10.5 10.4	begins
10	Fr.	☌ ♄ ☾ • Kim Campbell, first woman prime minister of Canada, born, 1947 • {10.6 10.2	to
11	Sa.	*Lose an hour in the morning and you'll be all day hunting for it.* • Tides {10.6 9.8 •	sink.
12	A	**1st S. in Lent** • Great Blizzard of 1988 • Tides {10.5 9.4	Snow
13	M.	**Pure Monday** • ☿ stat. • Sir William Herschel discovered Uranus, 1781 •	this
14	Tu.	☾ rides high • ☌ ☿ ♀ • ☾ at perig. • Tides {10.3 9.0 •	late
15	W.	Ember Day • ☾ at ☊ • Beware the Ides of March. • {10.3 9.1 •	can't
16	Th.	♇ stat. • First U.S. black newspaper founded, 1827 • Tides {10.4 9.4	last,
17	Fr.	St. Patrick • Ember Day • Over 18 inches snow, Memphis, Tenn., 1892 •	you
18	Sa.	Ember Day • *Work with the rising Sun, rest with the setting Sun.* • Tides {10.9 10.3	think
19	A	**2nd S. in Lent** • Sunday of Orthodoxy • Full Worm ○ •	
20	M.	St. Joseph • **Vernal Equinox** • ☾ on Eq. • {11.1 10.8 •	(reaching
21	Tu.	"Alvin's Harmonica," by The Chipmunks, was among the musical chart toppers, 1959 • {10.9 —	for
22	W.	First patent for a laser granted, 1960 • Andrew Lloyd Webber born, 1948 • {10.8 10.6	a
23	Th.	Patrick Henry delivered his famous "liberty" speech, Richmond, Va., 1775 • {10.6 10.1 •	good
24	Fr.	*A good laugh and a long sleep are the best cures in the doctor's book.* • Tides {10.3 9.6	stiff
25	Sa.	Annunciation • James A. Lovell Jr. born, 1928 • {10.0 9.1 •	drink).
26	A	**3rd S. in Lent** • Sandra Day O'Connor born, 1930 •	Months
27	M.	☾ at apo. • First Japanese cherry trees planted along the Potomac, 1912 • {9.2 8.2	like
28	Tu.	☾ runs low • ☿ Gr. Elong. (28° W.) • 90° F, Baltimore, Maryland, 1989 • {8.9 8.0	this
29	W.	☾ at ☋ • *If you wait until all conditions are perfect before you act, you'll never act.* •	one
30	Th.	☌ ♆ ☾ • Hyman Lipman patented first pencil with eraser top, 1858 •	really
31	Fr.	☌ ♅ ☾ • Newfoundland became tenth province of Canada, 1949 • {9.1 8.7	stink.

Farmer's Calendar

■ The New England town meeting, held in early March, is supposed to exemplify Democracy in its purest form. Here the men and women whose lives are daily affected by the policies of the township meet to debate their own government and to vote its acts up or down by direct ballot, face-to-face with the town officials who are themselves subject to election at the same momentous assembly. Nowhere else in the world, we are assured, is self-government to be found in a form so intimate, so forthright.

I think I begin to understand why town meeting democracy is unique to New England. Few elsewhere are strong enough to stand it. Pure democracy is difficult. You must tend to it. Above all, you must concentrate. I am not of New England by birth or descent, and I confess that the work is a stretch for me. At one town meeting a few years ago, for example, I found on the agenda for the day an item something like the following: "To see if the Town will stop discontinuing the giving up of certain unused roadways." Say *what?* The measure was voted in before I had even begun to figure out what it meant. You don't meet a quadruple negative every day; but at town meeting, they are common coin. I came out of the town hall with my head spinning.

Spectators of Democracy may have the best of it, after all. They come to these parts from across the land to drink coffee, eat doughnuts, and see a free people govern themselves, a business that may be more fun to watch than it is to do.

APRIL, The Fourth Month

April's first week finds dim Mars and brilliant Jupiter crowded close together in fading evening twilight, with medium-bright Saturn just above them. The crescent Moon joins the party on the 6th (just to Saturn's left), but an unobstructed horizon will soon be needed to see this whole planetary menagerie; hovering just 12 degrees above the horizon (little more than the width of a clenched fist at arm's length) at the middle of evening twilight, it is sinking each evening. By month's end, this group — and Orion to its left — has fallen into the bright skyline, as ever-later nightfalls bring down the curtain on the theater of the western sky. Daylight Saving Time begins at 2:00 A.M. on the 2nd.

● New Moon	4th day	14th hour	12th minute
☽ First Quarter	11th day	9th hour	30th minute
○ Full Moon	18th day	13th hour	41st minute
☾ Last Quarter	26th day	15th hour	30th minute

After 2:00 A.M. on April 2, Eastern Daylight Time (EDT) is given.

For an explanation of this page, see page 40; for values of Key Letters, see page 234.

Day of Year	Day of Month	Day of Week	☀ Rises h. m.	Key	☀ Sets h. m.	Key	Length of Day h. m.	Sun Fast m.	Declination of Sun ° '	High Tide Boston Light – A.M. Bold – P.M.	☽ Rises h. m.	Key	☽ Sets h. m.	Key	Place	☽ Age
92	1	Sa.	5 26	B	6 10	C	12 44	12	4 N.50	8¾ 9¼	4 ᴿᴹ10	E	2 ᴿᴹ53	C	AQU	26
93	2	**A**	6 24	B	7 12	C	12 48	12	5 14	10½ 11	5 41	D	4 58	D	AQU	27
94	3	M.	6 23	B	7 13	C	12 50	12	5 37	11¼ 11½	6 11	D	6 05	D	AQU	28
95	4	Tu.	6 21	B	7 14	D	12 53	13	5 59	12 —	6 40	D	7 13	D	CET	0
96	5	W.	6 19	B	7 15	D	12 56	13	6 22	12¼ 12½	7 11	C	8 23	E	PSC	1
97	6	Th.	6 18	B	7 16	D	12 58	13	6 45	1 1¼	7 43	C	9 35	E	CET	2
98	7	Fr.	6 16	B	7 17	D	13 01	13	7 07	1½ 2	8 19	B	10 46	E	ARI	3
99	8	Sa.	6 14	B	7 18	D	13 04	14	7 30	2¼ 3	9 00	B	11 ᴿᴹ57	E	TAU	4
100	9	**A**	6 13	B	7 20	D	13 07	14	7 52	3¼ 3¾	9 47	B	—	—	TAU	5
101	10	M.	6 11	B	7 21	D	13 10	14	8 14	4 4¾	10 42	B	1 ᴬᴹ03	E	ORI	6
102	11	Tu.	6 09	B	7 22	D	13 13	15	8 36	5 5¾	11 ᴿᴹ43	B	2 03	E	GEM	7
103	12	W.	6 08	B	7 23	D	13 15	15	8 58	6¼ 7	12 ᴿᴹ49	B	2 55	E	CAN	8
104	13	Th.	6 06	B	7 24	D	13 18	15	9 19	7¼ 8	1 57	C	3 39	E	CAN	9
105	14	Fr.	6 04	B	7 25	D	13 21	15	9 41	8½ 9	3 06	C	4 18	E	LEO	10
106	15	Sa.	6 03	B	7 26	D	13 23	16	10 02	9½ 10	4 14	D	4 51	D	LEO	11
107	16	**A**	6 01	B	7 27	D	13 26	16	10 23	10¼ 10¾	5 20	D	5 21	D	VIR	12
108	17	M.	6 00	B	7 29	D	13 29	16	10 44	11¼ 11½	6 26	D	5 50	C	VIR	13
109	18	Tu.	5 58	B	7 30	D	13 32	16	11 05	12 —	7 29	E	6 18	C	VIR	14
110	19	W.	5 56	B	7 31	D	13 35	16	11 26	12¼ 12¾	8 32	E	6 46	B	VIR	15
111	20	Th.	5 55	B	7 32	D	13 37	17	11 47	1 1½	9 34	E	7 17	B	LIB	16
112	21	Fr.	5 53	B	7 33	D	13 40	17	12 07	1½ 2	10 33	E	7 49	B	LIB	17
113	22	Sa.	5 52	B	7 34	D	13 42	17	12 28	2¼ 2¾	11 ᴿᴹ30	E	8 26	B	OPH	18
114	23	**A**	5 50	B	7 35	D	13 45	17	12 47	3 3½	—	—	9 07	B	SAG	19
115	24	M.	5 49	B	7 36	D	13 47	17	13 07	3¾ 4¼	12 ᴬᴹ23	E	9 53	A	SAG	20
116	25	Tu.	5 47	B	7 38	D	13 51	18	13 27	4½ 5¼	1 11	E	10 43	A	SAG	21
117	26	W.	5 46	B	7 39	D	13 53	18	13 46	5¼ 6	1 55	E	11 ᴬᴹ38	A	CAP	22
118	27	Th.	5 44	B	7 40	D	13 56	18	14 05	6¼ 7	2 34	E	12 ᴿᴹ36	B	CAP	23
119	28	Fr.	5 43	B	7 41	D	13 58	18	14 23	7¼ 8	3 08	E	1 37	C	CAP	24
120	29	Sa.	5 42	B	7 42	D	14 00	18	14 42	8 8¾	3 40	D	2 40	C	AQU	25
121	30	**A**	5 40	B	7 43	D	14 03	18	15 N.00	9 9½	4 ᴬᴹ10	D	3 ᴿᴹ45	D	AQU	26

APRIL hath 30 days. 2000

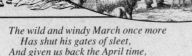

The wild and windy March once more
Has shut his gates of sleet,
And given us back the April time,
So fickle and so sweet. – Alice Cary

D. M.	D. W.	Dates, Feasts, Fasts, Aspects, Tide Heights	*Weather* ↓
1	Sa.	St. Hugh of Grenoble • All Fools • Lon Chaney born, 1883 •	*Now,*
2	**A**	4th S. in Lent • Daylight Saving Time begins, 2:00 A.M. • ☌ ☿ ☾ •	
3	M.	St. Richard of Chichester • ☌ ♀ ☾ • { 10.2 10.2	*oh my!*
4	Tu.	☾ on Eq. • New ● • Maya Angelou born, 1928 • { 10.5 — •	*A sky*
5	W.	Pocahontas married John Rolfe, 1614 • Pop Warner born, 1871 • Tides { 10.7 10.7	*that's*
6	Th.	☌ ♂ ☾ • ☌ ♃ ☾ • ☌ ♄ ☾ • ☌ ♂ ♃ •	
7	Fr.	*A rainbow in spring indicates fair weather for twenty-four hours.* • { 11.3 10.6	*pleasin' —*
8	Sa.	☾ at perig. • Mississippi's poll tax outlawed, 1966 • { 11.3 10.3 •	*showers,*
9	**A**	5th S. in Lent • *Work is not the curse, but drudgery is.* •	*sure,*
10	M.	Walter Hunt patented first safety pin, 1849 • Joseph Pulitzer born, 1847 • Tides { 10.9 9.6	*but*
11	Tu.	☾ at ☊ • ☾ rides high • 95° F, Sacramento, California, 1988 •	*that's*
12	W.	Highest velocity natural wind ever recorded, 231 mph, Mount Washington, N.H., 1934	*no reason*
13	Th.	Thomas Jefferson born, 1743 • First major-league baseball strike ended, 1972 • { 10.1 9.3	*to*
14	Fr.	Noah Webster published first American English dictionary, 1828 • { 10.1 9.7 •	*deplore*
15	Sa.	*In levying taxes and in shearing sheep, it is well to stop when you get down to the skin.* • { 10.3 10.1 •	*this*
16	**A**	Palm Sunday • ☌ ♂ ♄ • Tides { 10.4 10.4	*floral*
17	M.	☾ on Eq. • Bay of Pigs invasion launched, 1961 • Tides { 10.5 10.7 •	*season.*
18	Tu.	Full Egg ○ • Canadian Constitution Act signed by Queen Elizabeth II, 1982 •	*Rain's*
19	W.	Branch Davidian compound burned, 1993 • Explosion on the USS *Iowa*, 1989 • { 10.8 10.3	*not*
20	Th.	First day of Passover • Wisconsin Territory established, 1836 •	*done,*
21	Fr.	Good Friday • Founding of Rome, 753 B.C. • Tides { 10.6 9.7	*still,*
22	Sa.	First Earth Day observed, 1970 • Oklahoma Land Rush, 1889 • Tides { 10.4 9.4	*none is*
23	**A**	Easter • *Late Easter, long, cold spring.* • { 10.0 9.0 •	*freezin' —*
24	M.	☾ runs low • ☾ at apo. • Robert B. Thomas born, 1766 •	*break a*
25	Tu.	☾ at ☋ • Hubble Space Telescope deployed, 1990 • { 9.4 8.4 •	*sweat*
26	W.	☌ ♆ ☾ • Frederick Law Olmsted born, 1822 • Tides { 9.1 8.3	*and*
27	Th.	☾ ♅ ☾ • Coretta Scott King born, 1927 • Samuel Morse born, 1791 •	*get*
28	Fr.	☌ ☿ ♀ • *It is good practice to leave a few things unsaid.* • { 8.9 8.6 •	*your*
29	Sa.	Duke Ellington born, 1899 • Riots erupted in Los Angeles, 1992 • { 9.1 9.0	*peas in!*
30	**A**	1st S. af. Easter • Orthodox Easter • Tides { 9.4 9.6	

Everything should be made as simple as possible, but not simpler. – Albert Einstein

Farmer's Calendar

■ Before other trees have even begun to properly put on their leaves, the shadbush blooms in the woods and along rivers and streams. Its sparse, dainty flower clusters, which hang like scraps of lace from the bare branches, are one of the earliest signs of spring in the North, and so they lift the heart. There is a sadness about the shadbush bloom, however, to those who know its story, for the tree is a kind of widow.

Shadbush is a small tree whose delicate flowers look a little like cherry blossoms, only thinner and less abundant. So early does this tree bring forth its blossoms that the first settlers noticed their appearance around the time the shad began to run. Shad are a foot-long silvery fish that look like a herring and live like a salmon, leaving the sea each spring to swim up rivers to reproduce. They were an essential item of food to the New England colonists and their successors, for whom the shad run might mean deliverance from starvation at the end of a long winter. Hence their name for the pretty little tree whose bloom coincided with the shad's annual return.

Now, of course, the rivers are dammed and otherwise developed and can hardly be negotiated by seagoing fish. The shad are gone, or pretty much so. The shadbush, however, remains along riverbanks, where it goes on flowering every spring to welcome a return that won't take place. The tree and the fish, like sundered lovers in an old tale, continue in their devotion though they are divided.

MAY, The Fifth Month

Every naked-eye planet now lies behind the Sun in an invisible grouping confined within a mere 26-degree diameter. (On the night of the 3rd-4th, even the new Moon invisibly lines up with this compact cluster.) The physical influence of such an assembly is minuscule. Thanks to the long distances and small masses of the planets, the tidal increase in Earth's oceans is less than 1/300 inch. On the 17th, the five-planet conference attains its minimal diameter: 19 degrees. By month's end, Jupiter passes close to Saturn in the rarest of the naked-eye conjunctions (occurring once every 20 years), but this event is obscured by morning twilight. On the 28th, Mercury stands low in the west shortly after sunset.

●	New Moon	4th day	0 hour	12th minute
☽	First Quarter	10th day	16th hour	0 minute
○	Full Moon	18th day	3rd hour	34th minute
☾	Last Quarter	26th day	7th hour	55th minute

Times are given in Eastern Daylight Time.

For an explanation of this page, see page 40; for values of Key Letters, see page 234.

Day of Year	Day of Month	Day of Week	☼ Rises h. m.	Key	☼ Sets h. m.	Key	Length of Day h. m.	Sun Fast m.	Declination of Sun ° '	High Tide Boston Light – A.M.	Bold – P.M.	☽ Rises h. m.	Key	☽ Sets h. m.	Key	☽ Place	☽ Age
122	1	M.	5 39	B	7 44	D	14 05	19	15N.18	9¾	**10¼**	4 A.M. 39	D	4 P.M. 52	D	PSC	27
123	2	Tu.	5 38	B	7 45	D	14 07	19	15 36	10½	**11**	5 08	C	6 02	E	CET	28
124	3	W.	5 36	A	7 46	D	14 10	19	15 54	11½	**11¾**	5 40	C	7 14	E	PSC	29
125	4	Th.	5 35	A	7 48	D	14 13	19	16 11	**12¼**	—	6 14	B	8 28	E	ARI	0
126	5	Fr.	5 34	A	7 49	D	14 15	19	16 29	12½	**1**	6 53	B	9 42	E	TAU	1
127	6	Sa.	5 32	A	7 50	D	14 18	19	16 45	1¼	**1¾**	7 39	B	10 52	E	TAU	2
128	7	**A**	5 31	A	7 51	D	14 20	19	17 02	2	**2¾**	8 33	B	11 P.M. 57	E	ORI	3
129	8	M.	5 30	A	7 52	D	14 22	19	17 18	3	**3½**	9 34	B	—	–	GEM	4
130	9	Tu.	5 29	A	7 53	D	14 24	19	17 34	3¾	**4½**	10 40	B	12 A.M. 53	E	CAN	5
131	10	W.	5 28	A	7 54	D	14 26	19	17 49	4¾	**5¾**	11 A.M. 49	B	1 41	E	CAN	6
132	11	Th.	5 27	A	7 55	D	14 28	19	18 04	6	**6¾**	12 P.M. 58	C	2 21	E	LEO	7
133	12	Fr.	5 26	A	7 56	D	14 30	19	18 19	7	**7¾**	2 06	C	2 55	D	LEO	8
134	13	Sa.	5 24	A	7 57	D	14 33	19	18 34	8¼	**8¾**	3 12	D	3 26	D	VIR	9
135	14	**A**	5 23	A	7 58	E	14 35	19	18 48	9¼	**9¾**	4 16	D	3 54	C	VIR	10
136	15	M.	5 22	A	7 59	E	14 37	19	19 02	10	**10½**	5 19	D	4 21	C	VIR	11
137	16	Tu.	5 21	A	8 00	E	14 39	19	19 16	11	**11¼**	6 22	E	4 49	C	VIR	12
138	17	W.	5 20	A	8 01	E	14 41	19	19 30	11¾	**11¾**	7 24	E	5 18	B	LIB	13
139	18	Th.	5 20	A	8 02	E	14 42	19	19 43	**12¼**	—	8 24	E	5 49	B	LIB	14
140	19	Fr.	5 19	A	8 03	E	14 44	19	19 56	12½	**1**	9 22	E	6 24	B	OPH	15
141	20	Sa.	5 18	A	8 04	E	14 46	19	20 08	1	**1¾**	10 17	E	7 03	A	OPH	16
142	21	**A**	5 17	A	8 05	E	14 48	19	20 20	1¾	**2½**	11 07	E	7 46	B	SAG	17
143	22	M.	5 16	A	8 06	E	14 50	19	20 32	2½	**3**	11 P.M. 52	E	8 35	B	SAG	18
144	23	Tu.	5 15	A	8 07	E	14 52	19	20 43	3¼	**3¾**	—	–	9 28	B	SAG	19
145	24	W.	5 15	A	8 08	E	14 53	19	20 54	4	**4¾**	12 A.M. 33	E	10 25	B	CAP	20
146	25	Th.	5 14	A	8 09	E	14 55	19	21 05	4¾	**5½**	1 09	E	11 A.M. 24	B	CAP	21
147	26	Fr.	5 13	A	8 10	E	14 57	19	21 15	5½	**6¼**	1 41	E	12 P.M. 25	C	AQU	22
148	27	Sa.	5 13	A	8 11	E	14 58	19	21 25	6½	**7**	2 10	D	1 28	C	AQU	23
149	28	**A**	5 12	A	8 12	E	15 00	18	21 35	7½	**8**	2 39	D	2 32	D	PSC	24
150	29	M.	5 11	A	8 12	E	15 01	18	21 44	8¼	**8¾**	3 07	D	3 39	D	CET	25
151	30	Tu.	5 11	A	8 13	E	15 02	18	21 53	9¼	**9½**	3 36	C	4 49	E	PSC	26
152	31	W.	5 10	A	8 14	E	15 04	18	22N.01	10	**10¼**	4 A.M. 08	B	6 P.M. 02	E	CET	27

MAY hath 31 days. 2000

Month of little hands with daisies,
Lovers' love, and poets' praises;
O thou merry month complete,
May, thy very name is sweet! – Leigh Hunt

D. M.	D. W.	Dates, Feasts, Fasts, Aspects, Tide Heights	*Weather* ↓
1	M.	Sts. Philip & James • May Day • ☾ on Eq. • { 9.8 10.2	*Out we*
2	Tu.	King James Bible published, 1611 • Dr. Benjamin Spock born, 1903 •	*stagger,*
3	W.	Invention of the Cross • *CBS Evening News* premiered, 1948 • Tides { 10.5 11.3	*pale*
4	Th.	New ● • *It's always a lot easier to react than it is to think.* • { 10.7 — •	*and*
5	Fr.	☌ ♂ ☾ • AMA founded, 1847 • Stock Market crashed, 1893 •	*lumpy,*
6	Sa.	☾ at perig. • *Hindenburg* exploded and burst into flames, 1937 • { 11.9 10.7	*light-*
7	A	**2nd S. af. Easter** • Tides { 11.9 10.4 •	*deprived,*
8	M.	Julian of Norwich • ☾ at ☊ • ☾ rides high • ☌ ♃ ☉ •	
9	Tu.	St. Gregory of Nazianzus • ☿ in sup. ☌ • { 11.2 9.8	*and*
10	W.	☌ ♄ ☉ • 96° F, Jamestown, N.D., 1987 • 21° F, Aurora, Ill., 1966 •	*mud-*
11	Th.	Three • Irving Berlin born, 1888 • Salvador Dali born, 1904 • { 10.3 9.6 •	*time*
12	Fr.	Chilly • *Every difference of opinion is not a difference of principle.* •	*grumpy,*
13	Sa.	Saints • Ludwig M. Wolf patented sewing machine lamp, 1873 • { 9.9 10.0 •	*like a*
14	A	**3rd S. af. Easter** • ☾ on Eq. • Tides { 9.8 10.2	*bear*
15	M.	Ellen Church became first airline flight attendant, 1930 • Tides { 9.8 10.4 •	*done*
16	Tu.	*The art of being wise is the art of knowing what to overlook.* • Tides { 9.8 10.6 •	*hiber-*
17	W.	Brown vs. Board of Education decision, 1954 • N.Y. Stock Exchange established, 1792	*nating,*
18	Th.	Full Flower ○ • Reggie Jackson born, 1946 • Tides { 9.7 — •	*hungry*
19	Fr.	St. Dunstan • ☌ ☿ ♂ • Boys' Clubs founded, 1906 • { 10.6 9.5	*and*
20	Sa.	Christopher Columbus died, 1506 • Jimmy Stewart born, 1908 • { 10.5 9.4	*antici-*
21	A	**4th S. af. Easter** • Lindbergh landed in Paris, 1927 •	*pating.*
22	M.	Victoria Day (Canada) • ☾ at ☋ • ☾ runs low • ☾ at apo. • { 10.1 9.0	
23	Tu.	☌ ♆ ☾ • *Time makes more converts than reason.* •	*Blinking in*
24	W.	Anti-Saloon League founded, Oberlin, Ohio, 1893 • Queen Victoria born, 1819 • { 9.6 8.6	*the*
25	Th.	St. Bede • ☌ ♅ ☾ • ♅ stat. • Tides { 9.3 8.6 •	*gentle*
26	Fr.	St. Augustine of Canterbury • Sally Ride born, 1951 • { 9.1 8.7 •	*sun,*
27	Sa.	Richard Gurley Drew patented adhesive cellophane tape, 1930 • Vincent Price born, 1911 •	*we*
28	A	**Rogation S.** • Dionne quints born, 1934 • Tides { 9.2 9.5	*realize*
29	M.	Memorial Day • ☾ on Eq. • JFK born, 1917 • Tides { 9.4 10.0	*that*
30	Tu.	First U.S. daily newspaper published, 1783 • Gale Sayers born, 1943 •	*winter's*
31	W.	Visit. of Mary • ☌ ♃ ♄ • Joe Namath born, 1943 • { 10.0 11.2	*done.*

Farmer's Calendar

■ The pert and peppery young radish is the garden's quick fix, its instant hit of bliss. For the most part, the vegetable patch is the strict theater of delayed gratification: If you want its rewards, you must plan and plant and weed and hoe and generally tend to business for weeks, for months. Radishes are on the fast track.

Normally, I plant radishes around the last week in April, dropping the seeds into a carelessly made row that's less soil than still-frigid mud. Hardly a promising venue, you would say. A bean seed planted in those conditions, for example, would never be heard from again. Radishes, however, are riding the express. Within days, their tops are out of the ground. In a week, or a little more, you're eating them — a fat two weeks from dirt to dinner. Maybe in the tropics, they've got growables with moves like that, but around here, the radish looks like the easiest money going.

And a lucky thing, too, for by the time the radishes pay off, their winter-weary growers are about busted, coming off six or seven months of vegetables that have been ridden long and hard from Florida and California and taste like dishwater. We need something sharp that tastes of the earth, and we need it not next week or the week after but right now. Only radishes afford that essential spring tonic. Only they can jump-start the gardener into the new season. I begin to eat my radishes when they're about the size of a dime. That's too soon, but I don't care. Let the longer, fuller crops take their time; with them, I promise I'll be all patience. Now I can't wait.

As the month progresses, the rare conjunction of Jupiter and Saturn can be glimpsed low in the east just before sunrise. Both giant worlds have now stepped nearly simultaneously across the dotted line from Aries into Taurus, where they'll remain for the rest of the year. June 3 finds Mercury just above the thin crescent Moon, low in evening twilight. That tiny, dense planet remains easily visible each evening until the 10th, some 10 degrees above the western horizon as twilight starts to fade. The summer solstice occurs on the 20th, at 9:48 P.M., EDT, the date of the Sun's highest noontime elevation (though it does not stand straight overhead anywhere in the mainland United States or Canada).

● New Moon	2nd day	8th hour	14th minute
☽ First Quarter	8th day	23rd hour	29th minute
○ Full Moon	16th day	18th hour	27th minute
☾ Last Quarter	24th day	21st hour	0 minute

Times are given in Eastern Daylight Time.

For an explanation of this page, see page 40; for values of Key Letters, see page 234.

Day of Year	Day of Month	Day of Week	☼ Rises h. m.	Key	☼ Sets h. m.	Key	Length of Day h. m.	Sun Fast m.	Declination of Sun ° '	High Tide Boston Light – A.M. **Bold – P.M.**		☽ Rises h. m.	Key	☽ Sets h. m.	Key	☽ Place	☽ Age
153	1	Th.	5 10	A	8 15	E	15 05	18	22 N.09	11	11¼	4 ᴹ 45	B	7 ᴹ 17	E	TAU	28
154	2	Fr.	5 09	A	8 16	E	15 07	18	22 16	11¾	—	5 28	B	8 31	E	TAU	0
155	3	Sa.	5 09	A	8 16	E	15 07	18	22 23	12	12¾	6 19	B	9 41	E	TAU	1
156	4	**A**	5 09	A	8 17	E	15 08	17	22 30	12¾	1½	7 18	B	10 44	E	GEM	2
157	5	M.	5 08	A	8 17	E	15 09	17	22 37	1¾	2½	8 25	B	11 ᴹ 37	E	GEM	3
158	6	Tu.	5 08	A	8 18	E	15 10	17	22 44	2¾	3½	9 35	B	—	–	CAN	4
159	7	W.	5 08	A	8 19	E	15 11	17	22 49	3½	4¼	10 47	B	12 ᴬ 21	D	LEO	5
160	8	Th.	5 08	A	8 20	E	15 12	17	22 54	4½	5¼	11 ᴬ 56	C	12 58	D	LEO	6
161	9	Fr.	5 07	A	8 20	E	15 13	17	22 59	5¾	6½	1 ᴹ 04	D	1 30	D	LEO	7
162	10	Sa.	5 07	A	8 21	E	15 14	16	23 03	6¾	7½	2 09	D	1 59	D	VIR	8
163	11	**A**	5 07	A	8 21	E	15 14	16	23 07	7¾	8¼	3 13	D	2 26	C	VIR	9
164	12	M.	5 07	A	8 22	E	15 15	16	23 11	8¾	9¼	4 15	E	2 53	C	VIR	10
165	13	Tu.	5 07	A	8 22	E	15 15	16	23 15	9¾	**10**	5 16	E	3 21	B	LIB	11
166	14	W.	5 07	A	8 23	E	15 16	15	23 18	10½	10¾	6 16	E	3 51	B	LIB	12
167	15	Th.	5 07	A	8 23	E	15 16	15	23 20	11¼	11½	7 15	E	4 24	B	SCO	13
168	16	Fr.	5 07	A	8 23	E	15 16	15	23 22	**12**	—	8 11	E	5 01	B	OPH	14
169	17	Sa.	5 07	A	8 24	E	15 17	15	23 23	12	12¾	9 03	E	5 43	B	SAG	15
170	18	**A**	5 07	A	8 24	E	15 17	15	23 24	12¾	1¼	9 50	E	6 30	B	SAG	16
171	19	M.	5 07	A	8 24	E	15 17	14	23 25	1¼	**2**	10 33	E	7 22	B	SAG	17
172	20	Tu.	5 07	A	8 24	E	15 17	14	23 25	2	2¾	11 10	E	8 17	B	CAP	18
173	21	W.	5 07	A	8 25	E	15 18	14	23 25	2¾	3¼	11 ᴹ 43	E	9 15	B	CAP.	19
174	22	Th.	5 08	A	8 25	E	15 17	13	23 25	3½	**4**	—	–	10 15	C	AQU	20
175	23	Fr.	5 08	A	8 25	E	15 17	13	23 25	4¼	4¾	12 ᴬ 13	D	11 ᴬ 16	C	AQU	21
176	24	Sa.	5 08	A	8 25	E	15 17	13	23 23	5	5½	12 41	D	12 ᴹ 18	D	AQU	22
177	25	**A**	5 09	A	8 25	E	15 16	13	23 21	5¾	6½	1 08	D	1 23	D	CET	23
178	26	M.	5 09	A	8 25	E	15 16	13	23 19	6¾	7¼	1 36	C	2 29	D	PSC	24
179	27	Tu.	5 09	A	8 25	E	15 16	13	23 16	7¾	**8**	2 06	B	3 39	E	CET	25
180	28	W.	5 10	A	8 25	E	15 15	12	23 13	8¾	9	2 39	B	4 51	E	ARI	26
181	29	Th.	5 10	A	8 25	E	15 15	12	23 10	9½	9¾	3 17	B	6 05	E	TAU	27
182	30	Fr.	5 11	A	8 25	E	15 14	12	23 N.07	10½	10¾	4 ᴹ 03	B	7 ᴹ 17	E	TAU	28

Roses smile in their white content,
Roses blush in their crimson bliss,
As the vagrant breezes, wooing them,
Ruffle their petals with careless kiss. – Henry Hewlett

D. M.	D. W.	Dates, Feasts, Fasts, Aspects, Tide Heights	*Weather* ↓
1	Th.	Ascension • ☌ ♄ ☾ • ☌ ♃ ☾ • ♇ at ☍ • { 10.3 / 11.7	
2	Fr.	New ● • Thunderstorms with wind gusts to 120 mph, Fitchburg, Mass., 1989	*Spring*
3	Sa.	☾ at perig. • Ayatollah Khomeini died, 1989 • Tides { 12.1 / 10.6	*tides*
4	A	1st S. af. Asc. • ☾ rides high • ☌ ☿ ☾ •	*bring*
5	M.	St. Boniface • ☾ at ☊ • Bill Moyers born, 1934 • { 12.2 / 10.5	*a mess*
6	Tu.	YMCA founded, London, 1844 • Dalai Lama born, 1935 • Tides { 11.9 / 10.4 •	*of*
7	W.	Sony Corp. introduced the Betamax format VCR, 1975 • Tides { 11.4 / 10.2 •	*pogies.*
8	Th.	Orthodox Ascension • Barbara Bush born, 1925 • Tides { 10.9 / 10.0 •	*Hot*
9	Fr.	Shavuot • ☿ Gr. Elong. (24° E.) • Cole Porter born, 1891 • { 10.3 / 9.9	*enough*
10	Sa.	☾ on Eq. • Laszlo Biro patented the ballpoint pen, 1943 • Tides { 9.9 / 10.0 •	*to*
11	A	Whit S. • Pentecost • ♀ in sup. ☌ • { 9.5 / 10.1	*hit*
12	M.	*Never ask a lady her age, her weight, or what's in her purse.* • { 9.4 / 10.2	*the beaches.*
13	Tu.	Medgar Evers assassinated, 1963 • Red Grange born, 1903 • { 9.3 / 10.2 •	*Golfers*
14	W.	St. Basil • Ember Day • Harriet Beecher Stowe born, 1811 •	*swing*
15	Th.	King John set his seal to the Magna Carta, 1215 • Arkansas became 25th state, 1836 • { 9.2 / 10.3	*for*
16	Fr.	Full Strawberry ○ • Ember Day • Total solar eclipse seen Calif. to Mass., 1806	*pars*
17	Sa.	Ember Day • Igor Stravinsky born, 1882 • John Wesley born, 1703 • { 10.4 / 9.1 •	*and*
18	A	Trinity • Orthodox Pentecost • ☾ runs low • ☾ at apo. •	
19	M.	☾ at ☋ • 107° F at Valentine, Nebraska, 1989 • Tides { 10.2 / 9.0	*bogies.*
20	Tu.	Summer Solstice • ☌ ♆ ☾ • Lillian Hellman born, 1905 •	*Grads*
21	W.	☌ ♅ ☾ • Hurricane Agnes hit the eastern seaboard, 1972 • { 9.9 / 8.9	*must sit*
22	Th.	Corpus Christi • ☿ stat. • George Vancouver born, 1757	*through*
23	Fr.	Midsummer Eve • *One cannot clap with one hand only.* • { 9.5 / 9.0 •	*lengthy*
24	Sa.	Nativ. John the Baptist • Tides { 9.4 / 9.2 •	*speeches.*
25	A	2st S. af. P. • Orthodox All Saints • ☾ on Eq. • { 9.3 / 9.5	
26	M.	CN Tower, world's tallest freestanding structure, opened, Toronto, 1976 • { 9.2 / 9.9	*Surfers*
27	Tu.	Heien Keller born, 1880 • *One can never consent to creep when one feels an impulse to soar.*	*rave —*
28	W.	St. Irenaeus • ☌ ♄ ☾ • ☌ ♃ ☾ • { 9.5 / 10.9	*catch*
29	Th.	Sts. Peter & Paul • Charles Dumas broke 7-foot barrier in high jump, 1956 • { 9.8 / 11.4	*the*
30	Fr.	*Gone with the Wind* published, 1936 • 26th Amendment ratified, 1971 •	*heat wave!*

One doesn't have to get anywhere in a marriage. It's not a public conveyance. – Iris Murdoch

Farmer's Calendar

■ The past couple of years have seen a considerable influx into this vicinity of that staple of southern animal lore, the opossum. Opossums have established themselves this far north, and they seem to increase. Whether or not moving to Vermont will prove to have been a good idea from the point of view of the opossums, there's no doubt it's a break for feature writers, for they get to figure out what these opossums mean. When human families in Florida, say, tire of the nice weather and move up here, nobody thinks anything about it; but when opossums do the same, it must mean something.

The opossum is an unprepossessing gray creature that looks like a cross between a rat and a Jack Russell terrier. It's poorly fitted for long, deep winters, hence the debate on the significance of the oppossum's advent in the North. Must it not mean a general warming trend? If opossums are among us, and if they can't stand the cold, doesn't it follow that our winters will turn milder to accommodate them?

So runs the theory of the opossum as climate predictor. But consider what the facts we really know allow us to predict, and what they don't: Opossums are warm-winter animals. Opossums are here. It follows that the past few winters have been relatively mild. So they have. As for the future, we can infer that our recent opossum population presages — what? Either more mild winters or a bunch of frozen opossums, no more. You might say the opossum allows us to predict the past.

JULY, The Seventh Month

Earth reaches its most distant point from the Sun (aphelion) on the 3rd, at 94,512,258 miles. Before the fireworks on the 4th, notice the crescent Moon very close to Leo's bright blue star, Regulus. Meanwhile, the Jupiter/Saturn duo becomes more obvious as it rises higher each day just before dawn. The Moon joins the pair on the 26th; then, reduced to a very thin crescent, it floats above Mercury on the 29th in morning twilight. A total lunar eclipse will be visible from Hawaii on the 16th; its beginnings can be glimpsed only from the westernmost states, with an umbral onset at 4:57 A.M., PDT.

●	New Moon	1st day	15th hour	20th minute
☽	First Quarter	8th day	8th hour	53rd minute
○	Full Moon	16th day	9th hour	55th minute
☾	Last Quarter	24th day	7th hour	2nd minute
●	New Moon	30th day	22nd hour	25th minute

Times are given in Eastern Daylight Time.

For an explanation of this page, see page 40; for values of Key Letters, see page 234.

Day of Year	Day of Month	Day of Week	☼ Rises h. m.	Key	☼ Sets h. m.	Key	Length of Day h. m.	Sun Fast m.	Declination of Sun ° '	High Tide Boston Light – A.M.	Bold – P.M.	☽ Rises h. m.	Key	☽ Sets h. m.	Key	☽ Place	☽ Age
183	1	Sa.	5 11	A	8 25	E	15 14	12	23N.03	11½	**11¾**	4 A.M. 58	B	8 P.M. 25	E	GEM	0
184	2	**A**	5 12	A	8 25	E	15 13	12	22 58	**12¼**	—	6 02	B	9 24	E	GEM	1
185	3	M.	5 12	A	8 24	E	15 12	11	22 53	12½	**1¼**	7 13	B	10 14	E	CAN	2
186	4	Tu.	5 13	A	8 24	E	15 11	11	22 48	1½	**2¼**	8 27	C	10 56	E	CAN	3
187	5	W.	5 14	A	8 24	E	15 10	11	22 42	2½	**3**	9 40	C	11 P.M. 31	D	LEO	4
188	6	Th.	5 14	A	8 23	E	15 09	11	22 36	3¼	**4**	10 51	C	—	–	LEO	5
189	7	Fr.	5 15	A	8 23	E	15 08	11	22 29	4¼	**5**	11 A.M. 59	D	12 A.M. 02	D	VIR	6
190	8	Sa.	5 16	A	8 23	E	15 07	11	22 23	5¼	**6**	1 P.M. 04	D	12 30	C	VIR	7
191	9	**A**	5 16	A	8 22	E	15 06	10	22 15	6¼	**6¾**	2 07	D	12 58	C	VIR	8
192	10	M.	5 17	A	8 22	E	15 05	10	22 07	7¼	**7¾**	3 09	E	1 25	C	LIB	9
193	11	Tu.	5 18	A	8 21	E	15 03	10	21 59	8¼	**8¾**	4 10	E	1 54	B	LIB	10
194	12	W.	5 19	A	8 21	E	15 02	10	21 51	9¼	**9½**	5 09	E	2 26	B	SCO	11
195	13	Th.	5 19	A	8 20	E	15 01	10	21 42	10	**10¼**	6 06	E	3 02	B	OPH	12
196	14	Fr.	5 20	A	8 20	E	15 00	10	21 32	11	**11**	6 59	E	3 42	B	SAG	13
197	15	Sa.	5 21	A	8 19	E	14 58	10	21 23	11½	**11¾**	7 48	E	4 27	B	SAG	14
198	16	**A**	5 22	A	8 18	E	14 56	10	21 13	**12¼**	—	8 32	E	5 17	B	SAG	15
199	17	M.	5 23	A	8 18	E	14 55	9	21 03	12¼	**1**	9 11	E	6 11	B	CAP	16
200	18	Tu.	5 24	A	8 17	E	14 53	9	20 52	1	**1½**	9 45	E	7 09	B	CAP	17
201	19	W.	5 24	A	8 16	E	14 52	9	20 42	1¾	**2¼**	10 16	E	8 08	C	AQU	18
202	20	Th.	5 25	A	8 15	E	14 50	9	20 30	2¼	**2¾**	10 45	D	9 09	C	AQU	19
203	21	Fr.	5 26	A	8 14	E	14 48	9	20 18	3	**3½**	11 12	D	10 10	D	AQU	20
204	22	Sa.	5 27	A	8 14	E	14 47	9	20 06	3¾	**4¼**	11 P.M. 39	C	11 A.M. 13	D	PSC	21
205	23	**A**	5 28	A	8 13	E	14 45	9	19 54	4½	**5**	—	–	12 P.M. 17	D	CET	22
206	24	M.	5 29	A	8 12	E	14 43	9	19 41	5¼	**5¾**	12 A.M. 06	C	1 23	E	PSC	23
207	25	Tu.	5 30	A	8 11	D	14 41	9	19 28	6¼	**6¾**	12 37	C	2 32	E	ARI	24
208	26	W.	5 31	A	8 10	D	14 39	9	19 15	7¼	**7½**	1 11	B	3 43	E	TAU	25
209	27	Th.	5 32	A	8 09	D	14 37	9	19 01	8¼	**8½**	1 52	B	4 54	E	TAU	26
210	28	Fr.	5 33	A	8 08	D	14 35	9	18 48	9¼	**9½**	2 41	B	6 03	E	TAU	27
211	29	Sa.	5 34	A	8 07	D	14 33	9	18 33	10¼	**10½**	3 40	B	7 06	E	GEM	28
212	30	**A**	5 35	A	8 06	D	14 31	9	18 19	11¼	**11¼**	4 47	B	8 01	E	GEM	0
213	31	M.	5 36	A	8 04	D	14 28	9	18N.04	**12**	—	6 A.M. 00	B	8 P.M. 47	E	CAN	1

JULY hath 31 days. 2000

Raised are the dripping oars,
Silent the boat! the lake,
Lovely and soft as a dream,
Swims in the sheen of the moon. – Matthew Arnold

D. M.	D. W.	Dates, Feasts, Fasts, Aspects, Tide Heights	*Weather* ↓
1	Sa.	**Canada Day** • Eclipse ☉ • New ● • ☾ at perig. • { 10.3 12.2 •	
2	**A**	**3rd S. af. P.** • ☾ at ☊ • ☾ rides high •	*Nature*
3	M.	⊕ at aphelion • Dog Days begin. • Tides { 12.3 10.7 •	*trumps*
4	Tu.	**Independence Day** • Abigail Van Buren and Ann Landers born, 1918 • { 12.2 10.7	*the*
5	W.	Rod Lauer became first person to win four Wimbledon titles, 1969 • { 11.9 10.6 •	*fireworks*
6	Th.	☿ in inf. ☌ • First major-league All-Star baseball game, 1933 •	*maker;*
7	Fr.	☾ on Eq. • St. Louis pitcher Dizzy Dean broke his toe during All-Star game, 1937 •	*thunder*
8	Sa.	*The secret of patience: do something else in the meantime.* • Tides { 10.2 10.1	*thumps*
9	**A**	**4th S. af. P.** • 14th Amendment ratified, 1868 • { 9.6 10.0	*on every*
10	M.	134° F, Death Valley, California — highest recorded temperature for North America, 1913 •	*acre.*
11	Tu.	John Quincy Adams born, 1767 • E. B. White born, 1899 • Tides { 8.9 9.9 •	*Hazy,*
12	W.	Minimum wage of $.40 an hour established, 1933 • Andrew Wyeth born, 1917 •	*hot,*
13	Th.	*It's all right letting yourself go, as long as you can get yourself back.* • Tides { 8.7 10.0 •	*and*
14	Fr.	Bastille Day • Cornscateous air is everywhere. • Tides { 8.8 10.1 •	*humerd,*
15	Sa.	**St. Swithin** • ☾ runs low • ☾ at apo. • Tides { 8.9 10.2 •	*it's*
16	**A**	**5th S. af. P.** • ☾ at ☋ • Full Thunder ○ • Eclipse ☾	
17	M.	☿ stat. • ☌ ♆ ☾ • Lucie Arnaz born, 1951 •	*rumored.*
18	Tu.	☌ ♅ ☾ • Baseball-size hail, Kimball, Nebr., 1988 • Tides { 10.2 9.1	*Cooling*
19	W.	United Airlines Flight 232 crashed, Sioux City, Iowa, 1989 • Tides { 10.2 9.2 •	*burst*
20	Th.	*The whole point about getting things done is knowing what to leave undone.* • Tides { 10.1 9.3	*of*
21	Fr.	Marshall McLuhan born, 1911 • Tides { 9.9 9.4 •	*precipitation,*
22	Sa.	**St. Mary Magdalene** • ☾ on Eq. • Gregor Mendel born, 1822 •	*then*
23	**A**	**6th S. af. P.** • "Rock Around the Clock" topped the charts, 1955 • { 9.5 9.7	*it's*
24	M.	Richard M. Hoe patented the rotary-type printing press, 1847 • Tides { 9.4 9.9 •	*back to*
25	Tu.	**St. James** • *Andrea Doria* sank, 1956 • { 9.3 10.2 •	*perspiration.*
26	W.	**St. Ann** • ☌ ♄ ☾ • ☌ ♃ ☾ • { 9.2 10.5 •	*I do not*
27	Th.	☿ Gr. Elong. (20° W.) • ♆ at ☍ • Tides { 9.4 11.0	*embellish:*
28	Fr.	Jacqueline Kennedy Onassis born, 1929 • Tides { 9.6 11.4 •	*hot?*
29	Sa.	**Sts. Mary & Martha** • ☾ at ☊ • ☾ rides high • Occn. ☿ ☾ •	
30	**A**	**7th S. af. P.** • ☾ at perig. • New ● • Eclipse ☉ •	
31	M.	*To know when to be generous and when firm — this is wisdom.* • { 10.6 —	*It's hellish!*

Farmer's Calendar

■ Somebody had seen a big turtle down the hill, so my youngest and I went to look. We found it, all right, a snapping turtle, much the biggest one I have ever seen. The turtle was crossing a dirt road, but when we approached, it stopped. Here, we found, was a serious piece of reptile life altogether.

The turtle must have been two feet long, about half shell, half body. It was the color of mud. The shell was small in proportion to the whole animal, whose legs, neck, and tail seemed to bulge out of it, giving the turtle a muscle-bound look, like that of a professional wrestler. Its neck was long, its head as big as my fist. When the turtle saw us, it craned its neck and thrust its head at us. It had hot, mad little eyes like the eyes of a dangerous dog. It opened its jaws wide and seemed to menace us with them. A big one of these turtles, I remembered hearing, can amputate a finger with one bite. Having seen this specimen, I have no doubt about that at all.

"What are you going to do with it?" my youngest asked. "Not a blessed thing," I replied.

To me, the mystery was what this turtle, a wholly aquatic species, was doing where we found it. I have since read that female snappers may wander far from water to lay their eggs, and I guess that's the answer. But there's no water I know about within a couple of miles that could sink a turtle the size of the one we found. Wherever the thing was bound, though, I imagine it got there. Not many would have offered to stop it.

AUGUST, The Eighth Month

A nearly full Moon will ruin the Perseid meteors from the 11th to 13th. Venus remains a viewing challenge, low in the hazy western horizon after sunset. With the evening skies thus forlorn, all the action moves to the predawn heavens, where Mars, Jupiter, and Saturn, still on the far side of the Sun, climb away from the Sun's glare. The Moon meets Jupiter and Saturn on the 23rd, the two planets now nicely up in the east by dawn. Meanwhile, dim Mars creeps up from the eastern horizon at daybreak, difficult to see just above the Moon on the 28th. Jupiter widens the gap with Saturn while plodding further into Taurus; the two will not align again until the start of the third decade of the century.

☽ First Quarter	6th day	21st hour	2nd minute
○ Full Moon	15th day	1st hour	13th minute
☾ Last Quarter	22nd day	14th hour	51st minute
● New Moon	29th day	6th hour	19th minute

Times are given in Eastern Daylight Time.

For an explanation of this page, see page 40; for values of Key Letters, see page 234.

Day of Year	Day of Month	Day of Week	☀ Rises h. m.	Key	☀ Sets h. m.	Key	Length of Day h. m.	Sun Fast m.	Declination of Sun °	High Tide Boston Light — A.M. **Bold** – P.M.		☽ Rises h. m.	Key	☽ Sets h. m.	Key	Place	☽ Age
214	1	Tu.	5 37	A	8 03	D	14 26	9	17 N.48	12¼	**1**	7ᴀ16	C	9ᴘ26	E	LEO	2
215	2	W.	5 38	A	8 02	D	14 24	9	17 33	1¼	**1¾**	8 30	C	10 00	D	LEO	3
216	3	Th.	5 39	A	8 01	D	14 22	9	17 17	2	**2¾**	9 41	D	10 30	D	VIR	4
217	4	Fr.	5 40	A	8 00	D	14 20	10	17 01	3	**3½**	10 50	D	10 59	C	VIR	5
218	5	Sa.	5 41	A	7 58	D	14 17	10	16 44	4	**4½**	11ᴀ56	D	11 27	B	VIR	6
219	6	**A**	5 42	A	7 57	D	14 15	10	16 28	4¾	**5¼**	1ᴘ00	E	11ᴘ56	B	VIR	7
220	7	M.	5 43	A	7 56	D	14 13	10	16 11	5¾	**6¼**	2 02	E	—	—	LIB	8
221	8	Tu.	5 44	A	7 54	D	14 10	10	15 54	6¾	**7¼**	3 02	E	12ᴀ27	D	LIB	9
222	9	W.	5 45	A	7 53	D	14 08	10	15 37	7¾	**8**	4 00	E	1 02	D	OPH	10
223	10	Th.	5 46	A	7 52	D	14 06	10	15 19	8¾	**9**	4 54	E	1 40	B	SAG	11
224	11	Fr.	5 47	A	7 50	D	14 03	10	15 01	9¾	**9¾**	5 45	E	2 23	B	SAG	12
225	12	Sa.	5 49	A	7 49	D	14 00	11	14 43	10½	**10½**	6 30	E	3 12	B	SAG	13
226	13	**A**	5 50	A	7 48	D	13 58	11	14 25	11¼	**11¼**	7 11	E	4 05	B	CAP	14
227	14	M.	5 51	B	7 46	D	13 55	11	14 06	11¾	—	7 47	E	5 02	B	CAP	15
228	15	Tu.	5 52	B	7 45	D	13 53	11	13 47	12	**12½**	8 19	D	6 01	B	CAP	16
229	16	W.	5 53	B	7 43	D	13 50	11	13 28	12½	**1**	8 48	D	7 02	C	AQU	17
230	17	Th.	5 54	B	7 42	D	13 48	12	13 09	1¼	**1¾**	9 16	D	8 04	C	AQU	18
231	18	Fr.	5 55	B	7 40	D	13 45	12	12 50	1¾	**2¼**	9 43	C	9 06	D	PSC	19
232	19	Sa.	5 56	B	7 39	D	13 43	12	12 30	2½	**3**	10 10	C	10 10	D	CET	20
233	20	**A**	5 57	B	7 37	D	13 40	12	12 10	3¼	**3¾**	10 39	C	11ᴀ15	D	PSC	21
234	21	M.	5 58	B	7 36	D	13 38	12	11 50	4	**4½**	11 11	B	12ᴘ21	E	CET	22
235	22	Tu.	5 59	B	7 34	D	13 35	13	11 30	5	**5¼**	11ᴘ48	B	1 30	E	TAU	23
236	23	W.	6 00	B	7 32	D	13 32	13	11 10	5¾	**6¼**	—	—	2 39	E	TAU	24
237	24	Th.	6 01	B	7 31	D	13 30	13	10 49	6¾	**7¼**	12ᴀ32	B	3 47	E	TAU	25
238	25	Fr.	6 02	B	7 29	D	13 27	14	10 29	8	**8¼**	1 25	B	4 51	E	GEM	26
239	26	Sa.	6 03	B	7 28	D	13 25	14	10 08	9	**9¼**	2 26	B	5 48	E	GEM	27
240	27	**A**	6 04	B	7 26	D	13 22	14	9 47	10	**10¼**	3 35	B	6 37	E	CAN	28
241	28	M.	6 05	B	7 24	D	13 19	14	9 26	10¾	**11¼**	4 49	C	7 19	E	LEO	29
242	29	Tu.	6 07	B	7 23	D	13 16	15	9 04	11¾	—	6 04	C	7 55	D	LEO	0
243	30	W.	6 08	B	7 21	D	13 13	15	8 43	12	**12½**	7 18	C	8 27	D	LEO	1
244	31	Th.	6 09	B	7 19	D	13 10	15	8 N.21	1	**1½**	8ᴀ29	D	8ᴘ57	C	VIR	2

AUGUST hath 31 days. 2000

Buttercups nodded and said "Goodbye!"
Clover and daisy went off together,
But the fragrant water lilies lie
Yet moored in the golden August weather. – Celia Thaxter

D. M.	D. W.	Dates, Feasts, Fasts, Aspects, Tide Heights	Weather ↓
1	Tu.	**Lammas Day** • Anne Frank wrote last entry in her diary, 1944 • Tides {12.2 10.8 •	A
2	W.	Brooklyn Dodgers and St. Louis Cardinals used a yellow baseball as a test, 1938 •	Boston
3	Th.	Ernie Pyle born, 1900 • John T. Scopes born, 1900 • Tides {11.7 10.8 •	boy
4	Fr.	☾ on Eq. • 112° F at Moorefield, W.Va., set new state record, 1930 • {11.2 10.7 •	would
5	Sa.	*Always hold your head up, but keep your nose at a friendly level.* • Tides {10.6 10.4 •	say
6	**A**	**8th S. af. P.** • **Transfiguration** • Tides {9.9 10.1 •	we
7	M.	*Explorer VI* transmitted first picture of Earth from space, 1959 • Tides {9.3 9.8 •	swelt-
8	Tu.	**St. Dominic** • Mount Mitchell, N.C., was U.S. cold spot with 35° F, 1989 • {8.8 9.6	ah,
9	W.	President Nixon's resignation took effect, 1974 • Nagasaki bombed, 1945 • {8.5 9.5	or
10	Th.	**St. Laurence** • ☌☿♂ • Herbert Hoover born, 1874 • {8.4 9.6	that
11	Fr.	**St. Clare** • ⛢ at ☍ • ☾ at apo. • Dog Days end. •	camp-
12	Sa.	☾ at ☋ • ☾ runs low • Thomas Bewick born, 1753 • {8.6 9.9 •	ahs
13	**A**	**9th S. af. P.** • ☌♆☾ • Fidel Castro born, 1927 •	need
14	M.	☌⛢☾ • Congress approved the Social Security Act, 1935 • Tides {9.1 —	some
15	Tu.	**Assumption** • **Full Sturgeon** ○ • Edna Ferber born, 1887 •	shelt-
16	W.	Babe Ruth died, 1948 • Elvis Presley died, 1977 • Bela Lugosi died, 1956 • {10.3 9.4 •	ah.
17	Th.	Cat Nights begin. • Hurricane Camille crashed into Mississippi coast, 1969 • {10.3 9.6	He'd
18	Fr.	☾ on Eq. • Virginia Dare became first English child born in the New World, 1587 •	claim
19	Sa.	*It is sometimes necessary to play the fool to avoid being deceived by clever men.* • {10.1 9.9 •	he's
20	**A**	**10th S. af. P.** • Benjamin Harrison born, 1833 • {9.9 10.0	living
21	M.	☿ in sup. ☌ • Wilt Chamberlain born, 1936 • Tides {9.7 10.1 •	in
22	Tu.	☌♄☾ • ♇ stat. • Carl Yastrzemski born, 1939 • Tides {9.4 10.2	a
23	W.	☌♃☾ • Rudolph Valentino died, 1926 • Tides {9.2 10.3 •	smelt-
24	Th.	**St. Bartholomew** • Mount Vesuvius erupted, A.D. 79 • Tides {9.2 10.5 •	ah,
25	Fr.	*Just remember — when you think all is lost, the future remains.* • Liberation of Paris, 1944 •	hot
26	Sa.	☾ at ☊ • ☾ rides high • Krakatoa erupted, 1883 • {9.5 11.2	enough,
27	**A**	**11th S. af. P.** • ☾ at perig. • ☌♂☾ • {9.9 11.5	he'd
28	M.	**St. Augustine of Hippo** • Elizabeth Ann Seton born, 1774 •	swear,
29	Tu.	New ● • *What we see depends mainly on what we look for.* • Tides {10.7 —	to
30	W.	☌♀☾ • The B&O Railroad discontinued horsepowered locomotives, 1830 • {11.9 11.0	melt
31	Th.	☾ on Eq. • Major earthquake hit Charleston, S.C.; felt up to 800 miles away, 1886 •	yah.

Farmer's Calendar

■ In the summer evening, I heard a whippoorwill, I thought — that peculiar triple phrase, too often repeated, that occupies the half-heard edges of the country evening with the noise of peepers and crickets. Hearing it, I realized I hadn't heard a whippoorwill around here in years. Had they gone away? Were they now back?

The whippoorwill is an odd-looking bird, like a small, more streamlined owl, the size of a robin, brown, soft-feathered, with a flat, whiskered head that looks to be about three quarters beak. It's strictly nocturnal so you aren't apt to see one. That's all right, though, for you don't need to see the whippoorwill. You can hear it.

You can hear it, maybe, more than you'd like. The whippoorwill's call consists of three syllables: TEE-too-TEE. It isn't a loud call, and it isn't especially musical, but it's the only call the whippoorwill has, and so he makes the most of it through repetition. The whippoorwill utters its call over and over and over, to such exasperating effect that the call is famous as the bird itself is not. One book I consulted said the whippoorwill's call has been counted through 400 repetitions — presumably by an ornithologist now safely under lock and key. If you have heard this call and paid any attention to it, you know its overpowering monotony.

And so it is with mixed feelings that I find evidence that the whippoorwill has returned to this hillside, for several years whippoorwill-free. I thought the local whippoorwills had bored themselves to death.

SEPTEMBER, The Ninth Month

Pumpkin-colored Mars is now a bit higher when morning twilight begins. From the 16th to 18th, it skims close to the blue star Regulus, the pair about 10 degrees above the horizon at the murky start of morning twilight. On the 29th, the crescent Moon again meets Venus very low in the bright evening twilight. This month, only Jupiter and Saturn are conspicuous, both now rising around midnight and beginning their retrograde motion as Earth starts to catch up to them from behind. Although Saturn, its rings nearly fully "open," looks very bright at magnitude 0, Jupiter is ten times more brilliant, the sky's brightest "star" from midnight to dawn. Autumn begins with the equinox on the 22nd, at 1:27 P.M., EDT.

☽	First Quarter	5th day	12th hour	27th minute
○	Full Moon	13th day	15th hour	37th minute
☾	Last Quarter	20th day	21st hour	28th minute
●	New Moon	27th day	15th hour	53rd minute

Times are given in Eastern Daylight Time.

For an explanation of this page, see page 40; for values of Key Letters, see page 234.

Day of Year	Day of Month	Day of Week	☼ Rises h. m.	Key	☼ Sets h. m.	Key	Length of Day h. m.	Sun Fast m.	Declination of Sun ° '	High Tide Boston Light – A.M.	Bold – P.M.	☽ Rises h. m.	Key	☽ Sets h. m.	Key	☽ Place	☽ Age
245	1	Fr.	6 10	B	7 18	D	13 08	16	7N. 59	1¾	**2¼**	9 A.M. 38	D	9 P.M. 26	C	VIR	3
246	2	Sa.	6 11	B	7 16	D	13 05	16	7 37	2½	**3**	10 45	D	9 55	B	VIR	4
247	3	**A**	6 12	B	7 14	D	13 02	16	7 15	3½	**3¾**	11 A.M. 49	E	10 26	B	LIB	5
248	4	M.	6 13	B	7 12	D	12 59	17	6 53	4¼	**4¾**	12 P.M. 51	E	10 59	B	LIB	6
249	5	Tu.	6 14	B	7 11	D	12 57	17	6 30	5¼	**5½**	1 51	E	11 P.M. 37	B	OPH	7
250	6	W.	6 15	B	7 09	D	12 54	17	6 08	6¼	**6½**	2 48	E	—	–	OPH	8
251	7	Th.	6 16	B	7 07	D	12 51	18	5 46	7¼	**7½**	3 40	E	12 A.M. 19	B	SAG	9
252	8	Fr.	6 17	B	7 06	C	12 49	18	5 23	8¼	**8½**	4 27	E	1 05	B	SAG	10
253	9	Sa.	6 18	B	7 04	C	12 46	18	5 00	9	**9¼**	5 09	E	1 57	B	SAG	11
254	10	**A**	6 19	B	7 02	C	12 43	19	4 37	10	**10**	5 47	E	2 53	B	CAP	12
255	11	M.	6 20	B	7 00	C	12 40	19	4 15	10½	**10¾**	6 20	E	3 52	B	CAP	13
256	12	Tu.	6 21	B	6 58	C	12 37	19	3 52	11¼	**11½**	6 51	D	4 52	C	AQU	14
257	13	W.	6 22	B	6 57	C	12 35	20	3 29	**12**	—	7 19	D	5 55	C	AQU	15
258	14	Th.	6 23	B	6 55	C	12 32	20	3 06	12	**12½**	7 46	D	6 58	D	PSC	16
259	15	Fr.	6 24	B	6 53	C	12 29	20	2 43	12¾	**1**	8 13	C	8 02	D	CET	17
260	16	Sa.	6 26	B	6 51	C	12 25	21	2 20	1½	**1¾**	8 41	C	9 07	D	PSC	18
261	17	**A**	6 27	B	6 50	C	12 23	21	1 56	2	**2½**	9 12	B	10 14	E	CET	19
262	18	M.	6 28	B	6 48	C	12 20	21	1 33	2¾	**3**	9 48	B	11 A.M. 22	E	ARI	20
263	19	Tu.	6 29	C	6 46	C	12 17	22	1 10	3¾	**4**	10 29	B	12 P.M. 31	E	TAU	21
264	20	W.	6 30	C	6 44	C	12 14	22	0 47	4½	**4¾**	11 P.M. 17	B	1 39	E	TAU	22
265	21	Th.	6 31	C	6 43	C	12 12	23	0 23	5½	**5¾**	—	–	2 42	E	GEM	23
266	22	Fr.	6 32	C	6 41	C	12 09	23	0N. 00	6½	**7**	12 A.M. 14	B	3 40	E	GEM	24
267	23	Sa.	6 33	C	6 39	C	12 06	23	0S. 23	7¾	**8**	1 19	B	4 31	E	CAN	25
268	24	**A**	6 34	C	6 37	C	12 03	24	0 46	8¾	**9**	2 29	B	5 14	E	CAN	26
269	25	M.	6 35	C	6 36	C	12 01	24	1 09	9¾	**10**	3 42	C	5 51	E	LEO	27
270	26	Tu.	6 36	C	6 34	C	11 58	24	1 33	10½	**11**	4 55	C	6 24	D	LEO	28
271	27	W.	6 37	C	6 32	B	11 55	25	1 56	11½	**11¾**	6 07	D	6 54	D	VIR	0
272	28	Th.	6 38	C	6 30	B	11 52	25	2 19	**12¼**	—	7 17	D	7 23	C	VIR	1
273	29	Fr.	6 39	C	6 28	B	11 49	25	2 43	12½	**1**	8 26	D	7 52	B	VIR	2
274	30	Sa.	6 41	C	6 27	B	11 46	26	3S. 06	1½	**1¾**	9 A.M. 32	E	8 P.M. 23	B	LIB	3

The mellow moon, the changing leaves,
The earlier setting sun,
Proclaim at last, my merry boys,
The harvest-time begun. – Charles G. Eastman

Farmer's Calendar

■ The small brown butterfly called the common wood nymph (*Cercyonis pegala*) turns up after midsummer. You have seen it: Its wings are the color of milk chocolate, with an elongated patch of yellow in their top outer corners; in that patch two dark eyespots; less conspicuous eyespots at the bottoms of the hind wings.

Despite its name, I seldom see this butterfly in the thick, shadowy woods of my bailiwick. Here it frequents the sunny forest edges, old fields, mowings, roadsides, and gardens. It's a low flyer, poking around among the grasses at knee height or below, but it's fast and it has a dancing, zigzag flight that must make it a hard butterfly to catch.

Fortunately, you don't have to catch the common wood nymph. It's one of the few butterflies that seem unafraid of people — seem almost to like them. I don't mean it will jump up in your lap and lick your face. Sure, if you chase a wood nymph or try to capture it, it will fly away. But left alone, this butterfly is curiously companionable. It flies just ahead of you, or just behind, or to the side as you walk down a country road; you're out for a walk, and so is the butterfly. I have known one of these butterflies to join me as I worked in the garden. It circled about among the rows, never more than a yard away, as if to watch what I was doing and maybe lend a hand. It even lit on my knee for a moment. I had the idea it enjoyed my company, and I felt the same way, although it must be said that as a weeder of carrots, the affable wood nymph isn't at its most useful.

D.M.	D.W.	Dates, Feasts, Fasts, Aspects, Tide Heights	Weather ↓
1	Fr.	*Do not confine your children to your own learning, for they were born in another time.* ●	*Cooler*
2	Sa.	38° F, Elkins, 110° F, Medford, W.Va., 1987 ● Oregon, 1988 ● Tides { 10.9 / 10.7	*for*
3	**A**	12th �>. af. ℣. ● Treaty of Paris signed, 1783 ● Tides { 10.2 / 10.4	*the*
4	M.	**Labor Day** ● Henry Hudson discovered island of Manhattan, 1609 { 9.6 / 10.0	*back-*
5	Tu.	First Continental Congress assembled, Philadelphia, 1774 ● Darryl F. Zanuck born, 1902	*to-*
6	W.	President William McKinley shot and mortally wounded, 1901 ● { 8.6 / 9.3	*schooler.*
7	Th.	Grandma Moses born, 1860 Queen Elizabeth I born, 1533 ● { 8.3 / 9.2	*Cloudy*
8	Fr.	ℂ at ☍ ● ℂ runs low ● ℂ at apo. ● Patsy Cline born, 1932 ● { 8.3 / 9.3	*and*
9	Sa.	♂ ♉ ℂ ● California became 31st state, 1850 ● { 8.5 / 9.5	*drizzlish.*
10	**A**	13th �>. af. ℣. ● ♂ ♁ ℂ ● Roger Maris born, 1934	*then*
11	M.	**St. Cyprian of Carthage** ● Tom Landry born, 1924 ● { 9.0 / 10.0	*right*
12	Tu.	♄ stat. ● Episcopal bishops voted to remove *obey* from the marriage ceremony, 1922 ●	*back*
13	W.	**Full Harvest** ○ New York City established as U.S. capital, 1788 ● { 9.7 / 10.3	*to*
14	Th.	**Holy Cross** ● President McKinley died from his wounds, 1901 ● { 10.3 / 10.0	*sizzlish.*
15	Fr.	ℂ on ℨ ● *Better break your word than do worse in keeping it.* { 10.4 / 10.2	*Badda-*
16	Sa.	Billy Durant founded General Motors, 1908 ● B. B. King born, 1925 ● Tides { 10.4 / 10.4	*bing,*
17	**A**	14th �>. af. ℣. ● Battle of Antietam, 1862	*badda-*
18	M.	♂ ♄ ℂ ● John Diefenbaker born, 1895 ● Tides { 10.0 / 10.6	*boom!*
19	Tu.	♂ ♃ ℂ ● Morning low of 15° F, Gunnison, Colo., 1987 ● { 9.8 / 10.5	*Followed*
20	W.	Ember Day ● Red Auerbach born, 1917 ● Guy Lafleur born, 1951 ● Tides { 9.5 / 10.4	*by*
21	Th.	**St. Matthew** ● Ted Erikson completed round-trip crossing of English Channel, 1965 ●	*a week*
22	Fr.	ℂ at ☍ ● ℂ runs high ● **Autumnal Equinox** ● Ember Day { 9.2 / 10.4	*of*
23	Sa.	Ember Day ● Planet Neptune discovered, 1846 ● Tides { 9.3 / 10.6	*gloom.*
24	**A**	15th �>. af. ℣. ● ℂ at perig. ● Tides { 9.7 / 10.9	*Blue*
25	M.	♂ ♂ ℂ ● Vasco Núñez de Balboa discovered Pacific Ocean, 1513 ●	*skies,*
26	Tu.	Johnny Appleseed born, 1774 ● T. S. Eliot born, 1888 ● Tides { 10.6 / 11.3	*golden*
27	W.	**New** ● Samuel Adams born, 1722 ● Thomas Nast born, 1840 ●	*haze;*
28	Th.	ℂ on ℨ ● 4 inches of snow, Hamilton, N.Y., 1836 ● Tides { 11.2	*McIntosh*
29	Fr.	**St. Michael** ● ♂ ♀ ℂ ● ♂ ♃ ℂ ● ♃ stat. { 11.2 / 11.2	*days.*
30	Sa.	**St. Jerome** ● **Rosh Hashanah** ● Truman Capote born, 1924 ●	

Remember, you can't steal second if you don't take your foot off first. – Mike Todd

2000 OCTOBER, The Tenth Month

All planets are now coming closer to Earth and brightening accordingly. Mars is still distant and dim but forms a nice predawn conjunction with the Moon on the 24th against a dark sky. In the evening, Venus, finally further up in the sky and more obvious, meets the Moon on the 29th. In much of the United States, October is one of the clearest months; it offers the year's best views of our galaxy's plane, the Milky Way, which bisects the sky at nightfall. Constellations set four minutes earlier each night, but autumn sunsets occur about two minutes earlier from night to night, causing the sky to look nearly identical each evening at dusk. Daylight Saving Time ends at 2:00 A.M. on the 29th.

☽	First Quarter	5th day	6th hour	59th minute
○	Full Moon	13th day	4th hour	53rd minute
☾	Last Quarter	20th day	3rd hour	59th minute
●	New Moon	27th day	3rd hour	58th minute

After 2:00 A.M. on October 29, Eastern Standard Time (EST) is given.

For an explanation of this page, see page 40; for values of Key Letters, see page 234.

Day of Year	Day of Month	Day of Week	☼ Rises h. m.	Key	☼ Sets h. m.	Key	Length of Day h. m.	Sun Fast m.	Declination of Sun ° '	High Tide Boston Light – A.M.	Bold – P.M.	☽ Rises h. m.	Key	☽ Sets h. m.	Key	☽ Place	☽ Age
275	1	**A**	6 42	C	6 25	B	11 43	26	3 s. 29	2¼	**2½**	10 A.M. 37	E	8 P.M. 55	B	LIB	4
276	2	M.	6 43	C	6 23	B	11 40	26	3 53	3	**3¼**	11 A.M. 39	E	9 32	B	SCO	5
277	3	Tu.	6 44	C	6 22	B	11 38	27	4 16	3¾	**4**	12 P.M. 38	E	10 12	B	OPH	6
278	4	W.	6 45	C	6 20	B	11 35	27	4 39	4¾	**4¾**	1 33	E	10 57	B	SAG	7
279	5	Th.	6 46	C	6 18	B	11 32	27	5 02	5½	**5¾**	2 22	E	11 P.M. 47	B	SAG	8
280	6	Fr.	6 47	C	6 16	B	11 29	27	5 25	6½	**6¾**	3 07	E	—	–	SAG	9
281	7	Sa.	6 48	C	6 15	B	11 27	28	5 48	7½	**7¾**	3 46	E	12 A.M. 42	B	CAP	10
282	8	**A**	6 49	C	6 13	B	11 24	28	6 11	8½	**8¾**	4 20	E	1 39	B	CAP	11
283	9	M.	6 51	C	6 11	B	11 20	28	6 33	9¼	**9½**	4 51	E	2 39	C	AQU	12
284	10	Tu.	6 52	C	6 10	B	11 18	29	6 56	10	**10¼**	5 20	D	3 41	C	AQU	13
285	11	W.	6 53	C	6 08	B	11 15	29	7 19	10¾	**11**	5 47	D	4 44	C	AQU	14
286	12	Th.	6 54	C	6 06	B	11 12	29	7 41	11¼	**11½**	6 15	C	5 49	D	CET	15
287	13	Fr.	6 55	D	6 05	B	11 10	29	8 04	**12**	—	6 43	C	6 55	D	PSC	16
288	14	Sa.	6 56	D	6 03	B	11 07	30	8 26	12¼	**12½**	7 13	B	8 03	E	CET	17
289	15	**A**	6 57	D	6 02	B	11 05	30	8 48	1	**1¼**	7 47	B	9 12	E	ARI	18
290	16	M.	6 59	D	6 00	B	11 01	30	9 10	1¾	**2**	8 27	B	10 23	E	TAU	19
291	17	Tu.	7 00	D	5 58	B	10 58	30	9 32	2½	**2¾**	9 13	B	11 A.M. 32	E	TAU	20
292	18	W.	7 01	D	5 57	B	10 56	30	9 53	3¼	**3½**	10 08	B	12 P.M. 38	E	GEM	21
293	19	Th.	7 02	D	5 55	B	10 53	31	10 15	4¼	**4½**	11 P.M. 10	B	1 37	E	GEM	22
294	20	Fr.	7 03	D	5 54	B	10 51	31	10 36	5¼	**5½**	—	–	2 29	E	CAN	23
295	21	Sa.	7 05	D	5 52	B	10 47	31	10 58	6½	**6¾**	12 A.M. 18	B	3 14	E	CAN	24
296	22	**A**	7 06	D	5 51	B	10 45	31	11 19	7½	**7¾**	1 28	C	3 51	E	LEO	25
297	23	M.	7 07	D	5 49	B	10 42	31	11 40	8½	**8¾**	2 40	C	4 25	D	LEO	26
298	24	Tu.	7 08	D	5 48	B	10 40	31	12 01	9½	**9¾**	3 50	D	4 55	D	VIR	27
299	25	W.	7 09	D	5 46	B	10 37	32	12 22	10¼	**10¾**	5 00	D	5 23	C	VIR	28
300	26	Th.	7 11	D	5 45	B	10 34	32	12 42	11	**11½**	6 08	D	5 51	C	VIR	29
301	27	Fr.	7 12	D	5 44	B	10 32	32	13 02	11¾	—	7 15	E	6 20	B	VIR	0
302	28	Sa.	7 13	D	5 42	B	10 29	32	13 23	12¼	**12½**	8 21	E	6 52	B	LIB	1
303	29	**A**	6 14	D	4 41	B	10 27	32	13 42	1	**12¼**	8 25	E	6 26	B	LIB	2
304	30	M.	6 16	D	4 40	B	10 24	32	14 02	12¾	**1**	9 26	E	7 05	B	OPH	3
305	31	Tu.	6 17	D	4 38	B	10 21	32	14 s. 21	1½	**1½**	10 A.M. 24	E	7 P.M. 49	A	SAG	4

OCTOBER hath 31 days. 2000

O suns and skies and flowers of June,
Count all your boasts together,
Love loveth best of all the year
October's bright blue weather. – Helen Hunt Jackson

D. M.	D. W.	Dates, Feasts, Fasts, Aspects, Tide Heights	*Weather* ↓
1	A	16th S. af. P. • Disney World opened, Orlando, Florida, 1971 •	*Wet,*
2	M.	St. Remigius • Mahatma Gandhi born, 1869 • Tides { 9.8 10.3	*we bet.*
3	Tu.	The *Mickey Mouse Club* show premiered on TV, 1955 • Tides { 9.3 9.8	*Autumn*
4	W.	St. Francis of Assisi • 9.6 inches of snow, Denver, Colo., 1969 •	*paints*
5	Th.	☾ at ☋ • ☾ runs low • Chester A. Arthur born, 1830 • { 8.4 9.1 •	*in*
6	Fr.	☾ at apo. • ☿ Gr. Elong (26° E.) • American Library Assoc. founded, 1876	*gold*
7	Sa.	☌ ♆ ☾ • *Don't give cherries to a pig; don't give advice to a fool.* • { 8.3 9.0	*and*
8	A	17th S. af. P. • ☌ ♅ ☾ • { 8.5 9.2 •	*umber—*
9	M.	Yom Kippur • Columbus Day • **Thanksgiving Day (Canada)** • { 8.9 9.5 •	
10	Tu.	Vice President Spiro T. Agnew resigned, 1973 • { 9.3 9.8	*masterpieces*
11	W.	Dorr Eugene Felt patented first dependable adding machine, 1887 • Tides { 9.7 10.1	*without*
12	Th.	☾ on Eq. • Columbus landed in the Bahamas, 1492 • Tides { 10.2 10.3	*number.*
13	Fr.	**Full Hunter's** ○ • White House cornerstone laid, 1792 •	*Treasures*
14	Sa.	Succoth • Chuck Yeager broke the sound barrier, 1947 • { 10.4 10.9 •	*worthy*
15	A	18th S. af. P. • ♆ stat. • Cole Porter died, 1964 • { 10.4 11.1	*of*
16	M.	☌ ♄ ☾ • ☌ ♃ ☾ • Noah Webster born, 1758 • Tides { 10.3 11.2	*a*
17	Tu.	St. Ignatius of Antioch • 2-inch hail, Colfax, Ill., 1988 •	*Florence*
18	W.	St. Luke • ☿ stat. • St. Luke's Little Summer • { 9.9 10.9 •	*washed*
19	Th.	☾ at ☊ • ☾ rides high • ☾ at perig. • Tides { 9.6 10.6	*away*
20	Fr.	*If we would have new knowledge, we must get a world of new questions.* • Tides { 9.4 10.4 •	*in*
21	Sa.	Tom Carvel, inventor of soft-serve ice-cream machine, died, 1990 • Tides { 9.3 10.3	*sudden*
22	A	19th S. af. P. • Timothy Leary born, 1920 •	*torrents.*
23	M.	First snow of the season reported, Chicago, Ill., 1988 • Tides { 9.9 10.5 •	*Watch*
24	Tu.	☌ ♂ ☾ • Toronto Blue Jays won the World Series, 1992 • Tides { 10.3 10.6 •	*for*
25	W.	St. Crispin • ☾ on Eq. • Minnie Pearl born, 1912 •	*monsoons!*
26	Th.	♅ stat. • *A bad woman can't make good applesauce.* • { 11.0 10.7 •	*Trick-*
27	Fr.	New ● • Privately operated subway began running in New York City, 1904 • { 11.1 —	*or-*
28	Sa.	Sts. Simon & Jude • Jonas Salk born, 1914 • Tides { 10.5 11.1	*treaters*
29	A	20th S. af. P. • **Daylight Saving Time ends, 2:00 A.M.** • ☿ in inf. ☌ •	
30	M.	☌ ♀ ☾ • Charles Atlas born, 1893 • Emily Post born, 1872 • { 9.9 10.6 •	*need*
31	Tu.	All Hallows Eve • Mount Rushmore completed, 1941 • { 9.5 10.2	*pontoons!*

Farmer's Calendar

■ Almost three years have passed — a long time, especially in the Federal City on the Potomac. They keep themselves busy down there; their lives are full, their memories short. It's different in the hustings, among the folk. Once we have earned the money to pay the taxes that keep things going in D.C., we haven't much to do. We sit around and tell each other stories. We recollect. We keep memory green.

It was our senior senator, fighting for the right, who turned the trick. The Senate was considering legislation authorizing $290 million for something called Sea Grant research, to be allocated to colleges in the region of the Great Lakes. Now in Vermont, $290 million is still thought to be pretty good money. *Hmmm,* mused our senator. Discreetly, he caused to be inserted into the text of the Sea Grant bill this sentence: *The term "Great Lakes" includes Lake Champlain.*

Champlain, of course, is the long, slender, deep lake that divides northwestern Vermont from New York. It is a nice lake, it is a good lake, but it is not a Great Lake — not even for 290 million bucks. Such at any rate was the position of the agitated legislators from states like Michigan when at last they got around to reading the law they were making. The press was also indignant, *The New York Times* accusing our crafty senator of "essentially rewriting the topography of North America." Up here we cheered our man on. All he was trying to do was bring home the bacon. Why did *The New York Times* think we'd sent him down there, anyway?

NOVEMBER, The Eleventh Month

Just seven days apart, Saturn and then Jupiter attain their closest and brightest positions to Earth this year, on the 19th and 26th, respectively. Both are exceptionally bright and high at midnight: Saturn's greatest brilliance since 1975 and Jupiter's highest ascent since 1989. Jupiter's brilliance, at magnitude -2.9, easily makes it the sky's brightest "star" after nightfall (brighter Venus having set during late twilight). Saturn, very bright but not dazzling at magnitude -0.4, conspicuously hovers nearby. Meanwhile, much less dramatically, Mercury makes its best morning appearances of the year from the 7th to the 24th in predawn twilight, hovering near the Moon on the 24th.

☽ First Quarter	4th day	2nd hour	27th minute
○ Full Moon	11th day	16th hour	15th minute
☾ Last Quarter	18th day	10th hour	24th minute
● New Moon	25th day	18th hour	11th minute

Times are given in Eastern Standard Time.

For an explanation of this page, see page 40; for values of Key Letters, see page 234.

Day of Year	Day of Month	Day of Week	☼ Rises h. m.	Key	☼ Sets h. m.	Key	Length of Day h. m.	Sun Fast m.	Declination of Sun ° '	High Tide Boston Light – A.M. **Bold – P.M.**		☽ Rises h. m.	Key	☽ Sets h. m.	Key	☽ Place	☽ Age
306	1	W.	6 18	D	4 37	B	10 19	32	14s. 40	2¼	**2½**	11ᴹ16	E	8ᴾᴍ37	B	SAG	5
307	2	Th.	6 19	D	4 36	B	10 17	32	14 59	3	**3¼**	12ᴾᴍ03	E	9 30	B	SAG	6
308	3	Fr.	6 21	D	4 35	B	10 14	32	15 18	4	**4**	12 44	E	10 26	B	CAP	7
309	4	Sa.	6 22	D	4 33	B	10 11	32	15 36	5	**5**	1 20	E	11ᴾᴍ25	B	CAP	8
310	5	**A**	6 23	D	4 32	B	10 09	32	15 54	5¾	**6**	1 52	D	—	—	CAP	9
311	6	M.	6 24	D	4 31	B	10 07	32	16 12	6¾	**7**	2 21	D	12ᴬᴍ25	C	AQU	10
312	7	Tu.	6 26	D	4 30	A	10 04	32	16 30	7½	**7¾**	2 48	D	1 27	C	AQU	11
313	8	W.	6 27	D	4 29	A	10 02	32	16 48	8¼	**8½**	3 15	D	2 31	D	PSC	12
314	9	Th.	6 28	D	4 28	A	10 00	32	17 05	9	**9¼**	3 42	C	3 36	D	CET	13
315	10	Fr.	6 29	D	4 27	A	9 58	32	17 22	9¾	**10**	4 11	C	4 44	D	PSC	14
316	11	Sa.	6 31	D	4 26	A	9 55	32	17 38	10¼	**10¾**	4 44	B	5 54	E	CET	15
317	12	**A**	6 32	D	4 25	A	9 53	31	17 54	11	**11½**	5 22	B	7 06	E	TAU	16
318	13	M.	6 33	D	4 24	A	9 51	31	18 10	11¾	**—**	6 07	B	8 18	E	TAU	17
319	14	Tu.	6 34	D	4 23	A	9 49	31	18 25	12¼	**12½**	7 00	B	9 28	E	TAU	18
320	15	W.	6 35	D	4 22	A	9 47	31	18 40	1¼	**1¼**	8 01	B	10 32	E	GEM	19
321	16	Th.	6 37	D	4 21	A	9 44	31	18 55	2	**2¼**	9 09	B	11ᴬᴍ28	E	GEM	20
322	17	Fr.	6 38	D	4 20	A	9 42	31	19 10	3	**3¼**	10 19	C	12ᴾᴍ15	E	CAN	21
323	18	Sa.	6 39	D	4 19	A	9 40	30	19 24	4	**4¼**	11ᴾᴍ30	C	12 55	E	LEO	22
324	19	**A**	6 40	D	4 19	A	9 39	30	19 38	5¼	**5½**	—	—	1 29	D	LEO	23
325	20	M.	6 42	D	4 18	A	9 36	30	19 51	6¼	**6½**	12ᴬᴍ40	D	1 59	D	LEO	24
326	21	Tu.	6 43	D	4 17	A	9 34	30	20 05	7¼	**7½**	1 49	D	2 27	D	VIR	25
327	22	W.	6 44	D	4 17	A	9 33	30	20 17	8¼	**8½**	2 56	D	2 54	C	VIR	26
328	23	Th.	6 45	D	4 16	A	9 31	29	20 30	9	**9½**	4 02	D	3 22	B	VIR	27
329	24	Fr.	6 46	D	4 15	A	9 29	29	20 42	9¾	**10¼**	5 07	E	3 51	B	LIB	28
330	25	Sa.	6 48	D	4 15	A	9 27	29	20 53	10½	**11**	6 12	E	4 24	B	LIB	0
331	26	**A**	6 49	E	4 14	A	9 25	28	21 04	11¼	**11¾**	7 14	E	5 01	B	SCO	1
332	27	M.	6 50	E	4 14	A	9 24	28	21 15	11¾	**—**	8 14	E	5 42	A	OPH	2
333	28	Tu.	6 51	E	4 14	A	9 23	28	21 26	12½	**12½**	9 09	E	6 29	A	SAG	3
334	29	W.	6 52	E	4 13	A	9 21	27	21 36	1	**1¼**	9 58	E	7 20	B	SAG	4
335	30	Th.	6 53	E	4 13	A	9 20	27	21s. 46	1¾	**2**	10ᴬᴍ41	E	8ᴾᴍ15	B	SAG	5

NOVEMBER hath 30 days. 2000

The year draws in the day
And soon will evening shut:
The laurels all are cut,
We'll to the woods no more. – A. E. Housman

D. M.	D. W.	Dates, Feasts, Fasts, Aspects, Tide Heights	Weather ↓
1	W.	All Saints • Montreal Canadiens goalie Jacques Plante invented face mask, 1959 •	*North*
2	Th.	All Souls • ☾ at ☋ • ☾ runs low • ☾ at apo. • { 8.7 9.4	*of*
3	F.	☌ ♆ ☾ • 31 automakers displayed cars at first National Auto Show, 1900 •	*the*
4	Sa.	☌ ♅ ☾ • Ben Crenshaw won his first pro tournament, 1973 • { 8.3 8.9	*notches*
5	**A**	21st S. af. P. • "Fawkes plot" never forgot. • Tides { 8.4 8.9 •	*are*
6	M.	John Philip Sousa born, 1854 • Adolph Sax born, 1814 • { 8.7 9.0 •	*splotches*
7	Tu.	☿ stat. • Election Day • Canada's transcontinental railway completed, 1885 • { 9.1 9.3	*of*
8	W.	☾ on Eq. • Wilhelm Roentgen "discovered" X-rays, 1895 • Tides { 9.6 9.6	*white,*
9	Th.	Kristallnacht, 1938 • Berlin Wall opened, 1989 • Bob Gibson born, 1935 •	*fore-*
10	Fr.	St. Leo the Great • *Sesame Street* premiered, 1969 • Tides { 10.6 10.1	*telling*
11	Sa.	St. Martin • Veterans Day • Full Beaver ○ • Sadie Hawkins Day	*a*
12	**A**	22nd S. af. P. • ☌ ♄ ☾ • ☌ ♃ ☾ • { 11.4 10.4	
13	M.	*You have to believe in happiness or happiness never comes.* • Tides { 11.7 — •	*future*
14	Tu.	☾ at perig. • Claude Monet born, 1840 • Aaron Copland born, 1900 • { 10.4 11.7	*that*
15	W.	☾ at ☊ • ☾ rides high • ☿ Gr. Elong. (19° W.) • { 10.2 11.5 •	*isn't*
16	Th.	Anne Murray became first Canadian to receive a gold record, 1970 • Tides { 10.0 11.2 •	*so*
17	Fr.	St. Hugh of Lincoln • 71° F, Minneapolis, Minn., 1953 •	*bright.*
18	Sa.	St. Hilda • First ticker tape parade, New York City, 1919 • Tides { 9.6 10.4	*Orion*
19	**A**	23rd S. af. P. • ♄ at ☍ • Tides { 9.6 10.1 •	*rears*
20	M.	Pelé scored his 1,000th career goal in Rio de Janeiro, 1969 • Tides { 9.8 10.0 •	*up*
21	Tu.	☾ on Eq. • ☌ ♂ ☾ • Dow Jones topped 5,000 mark, 1995 • { 10.1 9.9	*on a*
22	W.	*Make money your god and it will plague you like the devil.* • Tides { 10.4 9.9 •	*glistening*
23	Th.	St. Clement • Thanksgiving • Boris Karloff born, 1887 • { 10.7 9.9	*night,*
24	Fr.	☌ ☿ ☾ • Joseph F. Glidden patented barbed wire, 1874 • Tides { 10.8 9.9 •	*to*
25	Sa.	New ● • Carrie Nation born, 1846 • Joe DiMaggio born, 1914 • { 10.9 9.8	*hunt*
26	**A**	24th S. af. P. • J. B. Sutherland patented refrigerated railroad car, 1867 •	*in a*
27	M.	♃ at ☍ • 76° F, St. Louis, Missouri, 1989 • 18 inches of snow, Galena, S.D., 1989	*forest*
28	Tu.	Berry Gordy Jr., founder of Motown Record Corp., born, 1929 • Tides { 9.4 10.4 •	*of*
29	W.	☾ at ☋ • ☾ runs low • ☌ ♀ ☾ • { 9.2 10.2	*crystalline*
30	Th.	St. Andrew • ☌ ♆ ☾ • ☾ at apo. • { 8.9 9.8 •	*light.*

Our life is spent trying to find something to do with the time we have rushed through life trying to save. – Will Rogers

Farmer's Calendar

■ "Every man looks at his woodpile with a kind of affection," wrote Henry David Thoreau. He's right, too, isn't he? An ample woodpile has a familiar, reassuring presence. It's a satisfactory object in a way that's a little hard to account for, perhaps. We respond to the sight of a good woodpile with a level of contentment.

What is it that contents us? Not use, or not use alone. Today most of us know we do better to face the coming winter with a paid-up electric bill and a full oil barrel than with a big woodpile. Maybe we have an ancient, inherited memory of years when that woodpile was what stood between our forebears and the cold; but that kind of memory would lead us to look at our woodpile with anxiety rather than affection — the way we might, these days, look at our bank account.

It's not as fuel that a woodpile makes its particular appeal. It's as a symbol. We are cheered and comforted by our woodpile today because a woodpile is one of the stations of the year and expresses the essential ambiguity — of all seasonal work. It represents a job that we know we can do well enough but that we also know will never finally be done, woodpiles are built up that they may be torn down. Massive as they are, they're ephemeral. You'll have to build another next year, which you will then once more throw down. The woodpile reminds us of the fix we're in just by being alive on Earth. It connects us with the year, and so it connects us with one another. We may as well look at our woodpile with affection, then, for it makes us be philosophers.

Jupiter and Saturn dominate the heavens all night long throughout the month, retaining nearly their full brilliance. Both are fabulous through any telescope, whose users might also look toward Venus on the 11th, now more than 10 degrees above the horizon when darkness falls (the little bluish body to its right is Neptune). On the 24th and 25th, it's green Uranus that hovers to the right of dazzling Venus—an easy though rarely observed event for binocular users. In the early morning sky of the 20th, the Moon meets orange Mars and the blue star Spica. The winter solstice occurs on the 21st, at 8:37 A.M., EST. Although this date represents the year's longest night, the earliest sunset happened two weeks ago.

☽ First Quarter	3rd day	22nd hour	55th minute
○ Full Moon	11th day	4th hour	3rd minute
☾ Last Quarter	17th day	19th hour	41st minute
● New Moon	25th day	12th hour	22nd minute

Times are given in Eastern Standard Time.

For an explanation of this page, see page 40; for values of Key Letters, see page 234.

Day of Year	Day of Month	Day of Week	☼ Rises h. m.	Key	☼ Sets h. m.	Key	Length of Day h. m.	Sun Fast m.	Declination of Sun ° '	High Tide Boston Light — A.M. **Bold** — P.M.		☽ Rises h. m.	Key	☽ Sets h. m.	Key	☽ Place	☽ Age
336	1	Fr.	6 54	E	4 12	A	9 18	27	21s.55	2½	**2¾**	11ᴬ19	E	9ᴾ13	B	CAP	6
337	2	Sa.	6 55	E	4 12	A	9 17	26	22 04	3¼	**3½**	11ᴬ52	E	10 12	B	CAP	7
338	3	**A**	6 56	E	4 12	A	9 16	26	22 12	4¼	**4¼**	12ᴾ22	D	11ᴾ12	C	AQU	8
339	4	M.	6 57	E	4 12	A	9 15	25	22 20	5	**5¼**	12 49	D	—	—	AQU	9
340	5	Tu.	6 58	E	4 12	A	9 14	25	22 27	6	**6¼**	1 15	D	12ᴬ13	C	PSC	10
341	6	W.	6 59	E	4 12	A	9 13	25	22 34	6¾	**7**	1 41	C	1 16	D	CET	11
342	7	Th.	7 00	E	4 12	A	9 12	24	22 41	7½	**8**	2 09	C	2 21	D	PSC	12
343	8	Fr.	7 01	E	4 12	A	9 11	24	22 47	8¼	**8¾**	2 39	B	3 29	E	CET	13
344	9	Sa.	7 02	E	4 12	A	9 10	23	22 53	9	**9½**	3 14	B	4 40	E	ARI	14
345	10	**A**	7 03	E	4 12	A	9 09	23	22 58	9¾	**10½**	3 55	B	5 54	E	TAU	15
346	11	M.	7 04	E	4 12	A	9 08	22	23 03	10½	**11¼**	4 45	B	7 07	E	TAU	16
347	12	Tu.	7 04	E	4 12	A	9 08	22	23 07	11½	**—**	5 45	B	8 16	E	GEM	17
348	13	W.	7 05	E	4 12	A	9 07	21	23 11	12	**12¼**	6 53	B	9 19	E	GEM	18
349	14	Th.	7 06	E	4 12	A	9 06	21	23 15	1	**1**	8 05	B	10 11	E	CAN	19
350	15	Fr.	7 06	E	4 12	A	9 06	21	23 18	1¾	**2**	9 19	B	10 55	E	LEO	20
351	16	Sa.	7 07	E	4 13	A	9 06	20	23 20	2¾	**3**	10 31	C	11ᴬ32	D	LEO	21
352	17	**A**	7 08	E	4 13	A	9 05	20	23 22	3¾	**4**	11ᴬ41	C	12ᴾ03	D	LEO	22
353	18	M.	7 09	E	4 14	A	9 05	19	23 24	4¾	**5¼**	—	—	12 32	C	VIR	23
354	19	Tu.	7 09	E	4 14	A	9 05	19	23 25	5¾	**6¼**	12ᴬ48	D	12 59	C	VIR	24
355	20	W.	7 10	E	4 14	A	9 04	18	23 25	6¾	**7¼**	1 54	E	1 26	C	VIR	25
356	21	Th.	7 11	E	4 15	A	9 04	18	23 25	7¾	**8¼**	2 59	E	1 54	B	LIB	26
357	22	Fr.	7 11	E	4 15	A	9 04	17	23 25	8½	**9¼**	4 03	E	2 25	B	LIB	27
358	23	Sa.	7 11	E	4 16	A	9 05	17	23 25	9½	**10**	5 05	E	3 00	B	SCO	28
359	24	**A**	7 12	E	4 17	A	9 05	16	23 24	10	**10¾**	6 05	E	3 39	B	OPH	29
360	25	M.	7 12	E	4 17	A	9 05	16	23 22	10¾	**11½**	7 02	E	4 23	B	SAG	0
361	26	Tu.	7 12	E	4 18	A	9 06	15	23 19	11½	**—**	7 53	E	5 13	A	SAG	1
362	27	W.	7 13	E	4 19	A	9 06	15	23 17	12	**12**	8 39	E	6 07	B	SAG	2
363	28	Th.	7 13	E	4 19	A	9 06	14	23 14	12¾	**12¾**	9 19	E	7 04	B	CAP	3
364	29	Fr.	7 13	E	4 20	A	9 07	14	23 10	1½	**1½**	9 54	E	8 02	B	CAP	4
365	30	Sa.	7 13	E	4 21	A	9 08	13	23 06	2	**2¼**	10 24	E	9 02	C	AQU	5
366	31	**A**	7 13	E	4 22	A	9 09	13	23s.02	2¾	**3**	10ᴬ52	D	10ᴾ02	C	AQU	6

DECEMBER hath 31 days. 2000

He prayeth best, who loveth best
All things both great and small;
For the dear God who loveth us,
He made and loveth all. – Samuel Taylor Coleridge

D. M.	D. W.	Dates, Feasts, Fasts, Aspects, Tide Heights	*Weather* ↓
1	Fr.	☌ ♅ ☾ • 36.4 inches of snow, Marquette, Michigan, 1985 •	*Winter's*
2	Sa.	*Always leave something to wish for; otherwise you will be miserable from your very happiness.* •	*coming*
3	A	**1st S. in Advent** • Illinois became 21st state, 1818 • { 8.5 / 9.0 •	*fast*
4	M.	☌ ♇ ☉ • FDR ordered dissolution of the WPA, 1942 • Tides { 8.6 / 8.8	*and*
5	Tu.	Montgomery bus boycott began, 1955 • Martin Van Buren born, 1782 •	*furious,*
6	W.	St. Nicholas • ☾ on Eq. • Ira Gershwin born, 1896 • { 9.2 / 9.0 •	*Arctic*
7	Th.	St. Ambrose • Pearl Harbor attacked, 1941 • Tides { 9.7 / 9.2 •	*blast*
8	Fr.	Red Berenson born, 1941 • Sammy Davis Jr. born, 1925 • Tides { 10.3 / 9.6 •	*and*
9	Sa.	☌ ♄ ☾ • Clarence Birdseye born, 1886 • { 10.9 / 9.9	*snowflakes*
10	A	**2nd S. in Advent** • ☌ ♃ ☾ •	*flurrious.*
11	M.	Full Cold ○ • ☌ ♀ ♆ • Fiorello La Guardia born, 1882 •	*Your*
12	Tu.	☾ at ☊ • ☾ at perig. • Ed Koch born, 1924 • { 12.0 / — •	*parka*
13	W.	St. Lucy • ☾ rides high • Mary Todd Lincoln born, 1818 • { 10.4 / 12.1	*better*
14	Th.	Halcyon Days • *The secret of contentment is the realization that life is a gift, not a right.* •	*have*
15	Fr.	Alexandre Eiffel born, 1832 • Sitting Bull died, 1890 • Tides { 10.3 / 11.5 •	*tight*
16	Sa.	Boston Tea Party, 1773 • Margaret Mead born, 1901 • { 10.1 / 11.0 •	*strings.*
17	A	**3rd S. in Advent** • Arthur Fiedler born, 1894 •	*Hark! a*
18	M.	☾ on Eq. • Su-Lin, first giant panda sent from China to U.S., arrived, 1936 •	*herald*
19	Tu.	*People who make music together cannot be enemies, at least while the music lasts.* • { 10.0 / 9.5	*angel*
20	W.	☌ ♂ ☾ • Ember Day • Harvey S. Firestone born, 1868	*sings!*
21	Th.	St. Thomas • Winter Solstice • Beware the Pogonip. • { 10.2 / 9.2 •	*Glory*
22	Fr.	First day of Chanukah • Ember Day • E. A. Robinson born, 1869 • { 10.3 / 9.2	*to*
23	Sa.	☌ ♀ ♅ • Ember Day • -50° F at Williston, N.D., 1983 • { 10.4 / 9.2	*the*
24	A	**4th S. in Advent** • Tides { 10.4 / 9.2 •	*newborn*
25	M.	**Christmas Day** • New ● • Eclipse ☉ • ☿ in sup. ☌	
26	Tu.	St. Stephen • Boxing Day (Canada) • ☾ at ☋ • ☾ runs low •	*son!*
27	W.	St. John • Radio City Music Hall opened in New York City, 1932 • { 9.1 / 10.3	*Glory*
28	Th.	Holy Innocents • ☌ ♆ ☾ • ☾ at apo. • Tides { 9.0 / 10.1	*to*
29	Fr.	☌ ♅ ☾ • ☌ ♀ ☾ • U.S. branch of YMCA organized, 1851 •	*two*
30	Sa.	Sandy Koufax born, 1935 • Rudyard Kipling born, 1865 • { 8.9 / 9.7 •	*thousand*
31	A	*Each day that Fortune gives you, be it what it may, set down for gain.* – Horace • { 8.8 / 9.4	*one!*

Farmer's Calendar

■ It was a couple of years ago, around this time, that we in this section realized we might be into an endless autumn. Winter simply failed to arrive. Through December, the days held sunny and warm in the sixties and seventies, the skies held clear, and the Weather Bureau saw no winter in sight. Snow and ice were not merely put off; they seemed to have been dropped from the program.

The queer thing about this prolonged spell of fine weather was not the weather itself but how uneasy it made everybody. You would think that being able to work comfortably outdoors in your shirt in the middle of December would be a matter for glee and gratitude. Not at all. The mild days filled us with foreboding. We glanced nervously at the soft blue skies, we shook our heads. We told one another: "We'll pay for this."

We'll pay for this. What an odd idea! As though warm weeks in December were borrowed, or bought on the installment plan, to be paid for later, with interest and at an inconvenient time. People seemed to feel that to go ahead and enjoy the strange sunny season was not permitted; that to do so would increase the cost of the inevitable payment. And observe the important thing about this idea: It's not so. A warm, bright December is not a loan. It's a gift. No December will be required of us again, ever, not the cold ones, not the warm ones. An easy winter, when we've had it, is gone past retrieval. We know this to our sorrow, let us remember it to our joy. Let us learn to take the gift.

Best Sky Sights of the Next

The Magnificent Seven Total Solar Eclipses

(Four for Canada)

Totality causes humans and animals alike to moan and babble, as normally invisible deep-pink prominences leap from the Sun's edge like nuclear geysers. Alas, this ineffable experience of totality happens just once every 360 years, on average, from any given site on Earth.

August 21, 2017, will bring the first American totality: The 185-mile-wide shadow will slash the country from coast to coast — west to east — like a calligraphy brushstroke. Another mainland American totality will occur on **April 8, 2024,** followed by the longest eclipse in U.S. history (a six-minute totality) on **August 12, 2045,** that again will cross the country from the Pacific to the Atlantic — an inspiration, perhaps, for today's observers to stay healthy.

After a shorter totality over Georgia in **2052,** the continental United States will then receive a rare present: two total solar eclipses within a single year, on **May 11, 2078,** and **May 1, 2079.** Finally, the century will close with a totality for the north-central and mid-Atlantic states in September of **2099.** And that's it — seven opportunities in the next 100 years for stay-at-home Americans to stand fully in the Moon's shadow (we should note, however, that brief totalities occur in northern Alaska in **2033** and **2097**).

For Canadian eclipse addicts, the **April 8, 2024,** event will also be seen from the Maritime provinces. The next one, on **August 22, 2044,** will actually begin at sunrise on the border with Montana, then will hightail it northward through the western Prairies toward the North Pole. After that, it's a long wait until the eclipse of **May 1, 2079,** visible from the Maritimes, and the totality of **September 14, 2099,** seen in southwestern Canada.

Take your vitamins and stick around for the next century's super spectacles, including the longest total solar eclipse in U.S. history (in 2045) or the spectacular return of Halley's Comet in 2061.

by Bob Berman

Great Comets

In terms of sheer spectacle, the closest runner-up to solar totality is probably Earth's encounter with a Great Comet. While 1996's Hyakutake and 1997's Hale-Bopp did indeed break a 22-year Great Comet drought, neither was as spectacular — that

Century — Guaranteed!

is, bright, with a long tail — as some of the finest historical visitors. The most-demanding comet-lovers desire a comet with both qualities, like Halley's memorable 1910 visit, or the "Great January comet" of that same extraordinary year. Although most spectacular comets have initially uncharted orbits of thousands of years and therefore visit us with no advance notice, the one trusty short-period comet that *can* be predicted is also the most famous of all — Halley's comet.

Unfortunately, during Halley's most recent visit, in 1985 and '86, Earth was in nearly the worst possible position, the equivalent of the outfield bleacher seats. But the Earth/Halley geometry will be wonderful for its return in 2061. Then, it should span half the sky. Moreover, it will float in front of the stars of the Big Dipper, making it prominent for observers in the United States and Canada.

Meteor Showers

The finest reliable showers will continue to be summer's Perseids, from **August 11 to 13**, which will slowly creep to **August 12 to 14** as the century advances, and the rich Geminid display on the night of **December 13-14**, which will also migrate ahead one night toward century's end. Anyone can predict which years these will appear at their best by looking up the phases of the Moon for those dates. Meteors are greatly diminished from view by a Moon that falls between the first and last quarter phases.

Of course, for true spectacle, observers will be looking for a meteor "storm," the 50-to-100-shooting-stars-per-second display that happened in **1799**, **1833**, and **1966**. Right now, it appears that the on-again, off-again 33⅓-year periodicity of the Leonids should continue, giving us good opportunities in **2033**, **2066**, and **2099**.

Planetary Conjunctions

Truly awesome close encounters require a meeting of at least two of the three planets that can attain dazzling brilliance (Venus, Jupiter, and, rarely, Mars), or the Moon with one or more of these. We'll throw in bright but not brilliant Saturn and Mercury only when a meeting involving them is ultraclose. To qualify, the celestial targets must pass extremely close to each other in the night sky — perhaps even merge into a single, ultrabright, alien-looking sky object. (Although events involving Venus usually occur in twilight, the sky sightings below remain visible long enough to stand out against a satisfyingly dark backdrop.)

The following table presents a comprehensive list of the *best* planetary events of the 21st century that can be seen during the nightfall-to-10 P.M. period, when most people are willing to venture out.

(continued on next page)

Best Planetary Encounters

Date	Objects	Date	Objects
April 5, 2000	Ma, J	June 21, 2074	V, J
May 10, 2002	V, Ma	June 27, 2074	V, Mn, J
June 30, 2007	V, S	June 28, 2076	Ma, J
December 1, 2008	V, Mn, J	October 31, 2076	Mn, Ma, S
February 20, 2015	V, Mn, Ma	February 27, 2079	V, Ma
June 30-July 1, 2015	V, J	November 7, 2080	Ma, J, S
July 18, 2015	V, Mn, J	November 15, 2080	Ma, J, S
December 20, 2020	J, S	November 17, 2080	Mn, Ma, J, S
March 1, 2023	V, J	December 24, 2080	V, J
December 1-2, 2033	Ma, J	March 6, 2082	V, J
February 23, 2047	V, Ma	April 28, 2085	Mn, Ma, J
March 7, 2047	V, J	June 13, 2085	Me, V, J
May 13, 2066	V, Ma	May 15, 2098	V, Ma
July 1, 2066	V, S	June 29, 2098	V, J
March 14, 2071	V, J		

Attach this article to a refrigerator you plan to keep for ten decades. But there's no substitute for keeping your eyes wide open after nightfall — for many of the best celestial spectacles, such as awesome long-period comets, Northern Lights, and bolides (exploding meteors), arrive with little or no warning, brilliant bombshells in the heavens.   □ □

Spinning the Web: Go to **www.almanac.com** and click on **Article Links 2000** for Web sites related to this article. – *The Editors*

When Will the Moon Rise Today?

A lunar puzzle involves the timing of moonrise. Folks who enjoy the out-of-doors and the wonders of nature may wish to commit to memory the following gem:

**The new Moon always rises at sunrise
And the first quarter at noon.
The full Moon always rises at sunset
And the last quarter at midnight.**

Moonrise occurs about 50 minutes later each day than the day before. The new Moon is invisible because its illuminated side faces completely away from Earth, which occurs when the Moon lines up between Earth and the Sun. One or two days after the date of the new Moon, you can see it in the western sky as a thin crescent setting just after sunset. (See pages 60-86 for exact moonrise times.)

WHY ARE WE PRACTICALLY "GIVING AWAY"

"405 Woodworking Patterns For Only 2¢ Each?"

IF YOU LIKE TO CUT PATTERNS OUT OF WOOD, THIS IS THE SET FOR YOU! YOU'LL FIND A TREASURE HOUSE OF IDEAS INSIDE. 405 BEAUTIFUL WOODWORKING PATTERNS AND DESIGNS.

(By Frank K. Wood)

FC&A, a Peachtree City, Georgia, publisher, announced today that it is practically "giving away" an all-new set of *"405 Woodworking Patterns."*

- Welcome signs for every occasion.
- Glider swing, adirondak table and chair.
- Gardening grandparents and bunny.
- Swinging scarecrow and a scarecrow on a fence.
- Giant rocking horse, carousel and sea horse tables.
- Potato bin chest and collapsible basket.
- Birdhouses and birdfeeders in different styles.
- Ye olde English carolers, Christmas yard ornaments.

- Whizzing whirligigs like the rowing fisherman, flying eagle, flamingo, mallard duck and swimming fish.
- Christmas mouse for your house, Christmas train in case of rain!
- Santas galore.
- Shelf sitter's see-saw collection.
- Kitty door stop and four seasons perpetual calendar.
- Comical clowns, napkin rings and shelf brackets.
- Holstein cow — with udders that shudder and swinging tail too!
- Southwestern cactus collection.
- And much, much more!

Build all these wooden favorites. Illustrated plans include intricately detailed patterns and complete instructions. To order a set, just return this notice with your name and address and a check for $7.99 plus $3.00 shipping and handling, and we will send you *"405 Woodworking Patterns."* Or, for only $9.99 plus $3.00 shipping and handling, you can get both the basic set and an extra 100 patterns.

Plus, as a purchaser of our set of *"405 Woodworking Patterns,"* if pleased, about every two months you will also be eligible for a first look and free trial preview of all companion pattern sets printed in the years ahead.

Send your check along with your name and address to: **FC&A, Dept. AOF-00,** 103 Clover Green, Peachtree City, GA 30269.

You get a no-time-limit guarantee of satisfaction or your money back.

You must cut out and return this notice with your order. Copies will not be accepted!

IMPORTANT — FREE GIFT OFFER EXPIRES IN 30 DAYS

All orders mailed within 30 days will receive a free gift, *"50 Special, Seasonal, Woodworking Patterns,"* guaranteed. Order right away!   ©FC&A 1999

www.fca.com

Here's how to put time in a bottle — and keep it for posterity. by Howard Mansfield

With the world edging to war in the late 1930s, Dr. Thornwell Jacobs conceived the idea in 1936 to condense and entomb 6,000 years of human knowledge: the Bible and Donald Duck; the voices of Hitler and a champion hog caller; Franklin Roosevelt and Popeye the Sailor; Dante's *Inferno* and a script from *Gone with the Wind*; an electric Toastolator; drawings of inventions; historic newsreels; views of great cities; flower seeds; a quart of beer (Budweiser); 640,000 pages of microfilmed material; and a machine to teach the English language . . . the harvest of the preceding 72,000 months of human life.

Dr. Jacobs sealed his horde in 1940 in a room that had been an indoor swimming pool at Oglethorpe University in Atlanta, Georgia, where he was the college president. With great ceremony, a stainless-steel door was welded shut on the Crypt of Civilization, with this instruction: Do not open until May 28, 8113. (The year 1936 was the halfway point between the beginning

Right: Only 6,113 years to go before the Crypt of Civilization, a converted indoor swimming pool, is opened, with the intent of revealing 60 centuries of human knowledge.

of the Egyptian calendar, 6,177 years prior, and the year 8113, 6,177 years hence.) "The world is engaged in burying our civilization forever, and here in this crypt we leave it to you," said Dr. Jacobs. The modern time capsule, distinguished by a planned opening date, was born.

The phrase *time capsule* entered the language with the 1939 New York World's Fair. The

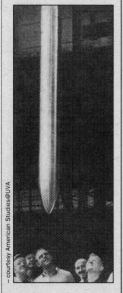

Left: The Westinghouse Time Capsule on display at the 1939 World's Fair in New York.

– courtesy American Studies@UVA

A TIME CAPSULE?

– courtesy Oglethorpe University

How to Make Your Own Time Capsule

■ If you make a time capsule, don't bury it — live with it, advises Paul Hudson of the International Time Capsule Society. "Make friends with it. Give it a birthday. Celebrate it. That way, you get an oral tradition and can preserve it longer." Place it in a secure indoor location — you may even want to keep it in the open, on your desk, on a bookshelf, in the lobby. In her West Halifax, Vermont, classroom, teacher Debbie Squires hung up a bright-yellow plastic bottle: her fifth- and sixth-graders' time capsule, to be opened at the end of the school year.

■ Choose a container that will keep the contents cool, dry, and dark. A safe is a good choice.

■ Make it personal, but leave out food or drink. "You're defining yourself when you do a time capsule," says Hudson.

■ Select a retrieval date: 50 years or less means the time capsule may be witnessed by your own generation.

■ Keep a list and photos of the contents. Mark the site with a plaque, and plan a memorable "sealing ceremony."

■ Register your project with the Time Capsule Society. To register, write to International Time Capsule Society at Oglethorpe University, 4484 Peachtree Rd. NE, Atlanta, GA 30319-2797.

– courtesy Oglethorpe University

Paul Hudson, cofounder of the International Time Capsule Society, holding one of the estimated 15,000 capsules now in existence.

Westinghouse Electric Corporation was looking for an attention-getter. G. Edward Pendray, an assistant to Westinghouse's president, taking his hint from Dr. Jacobs's crypt project, coined the term. The Westinghouse Time Capsule was a rocket-shaped messenger to the future — eight feet long and only eight

Japan's 1970 World Expo in Osaka buried two capsules, an upper one to be unearthed in the year 2000 . . . and a lower one to be opened in 5,000 years.

inches in diameter — made of Cupaloy, a trademarked copper-chromium-silver alloy, with a Pyrex glass lining, just like a Thermos bottle. Inside, sealed in nitrogen, are 100 objects of daily use; 10 million words (the Lord's Prayer in 300 languages, a biography of company president George Westinghouse); rules

for poker, bridge, golf, and football; a reproduction of Picasso's "Guernica"; and sheet music for "Flat Foot Floogie." It's all buried 50 feet under, to be opened in 5,000 years.

After Westinghouse, you couldn't have a World's Fair or big celebration without a time capsule. Japan's 1970 World Expo in Osaka buried two capsules, an upper one to be unearthed in the year 2000 and reburied every hundred years, and a lower one to be opened in 5,000 years. In 1994, Seoul, South Korea, marked its 600 years as a capital city with the Seoul Millennium Time Capsule, buried under Time Capsule Square and scheduled to be opened 400 years later.

But that's all changing — you don't need a fair to create a time capsule. "America is going time-capsule crazy right now. We all want to write ourselves into history, and this is the perfect moment," says Paul Hudson, a cofounder of the International Time Capsule Society. Hudson is registrar and lecturer in history at Oglethorpe University, home to the Crypt of Civilization.

The society estimates that there are 15,000 capsules worldwide, including about 5,000 that have been created in the last several years as the millennium approached. No part of Earth will be overlooked. Schools, museums, corporations, cities, and families are assembling an armada of memories. There are low-tech capsules, such as the locked pine hutch that students in an Austell, Georgia, school placed in the library to await the 25th class reunion; and old safes, strongboxes, and hiding places in statues. There are entire fleets of capsules: Tennessee buried 95 on the mall in Nashville (one for each county) for the state's bicentennial.

In 1996, Copenhagen created the largest such project in Europe: 900 time capsules, made by more than 16,000

Below: LegaSEA's time capsule is designed to sink to the ocean's floor, then bob to the surface using a timed float device.

– John Dunham, LegaSEA Time Capsule Project

people. The clear acrylic containers, stacked like building blocks, preserve a "cultural fingerprint" of Denmark.

For those who want to cast their message upon the waters, there is the LegaSEA oceanic time capsule, which is housed in a double-hulled, vacuum-sealed, "deep sea" glass sphere with a bronze "deployment stand." (Cost: $3,999, plus $499 for

---

All this activity would suggest that people in the future are going to be besotted with time capsules. Actually not: "More than 80 percent will be lost," says Hudson, buried and never to be found.

"final vacuseal.") The time capsule is dropped into international seas, descending 4,000 to 36,000 feet to await release at a chosen time 100 to 500 years in the future. The gold-plated "Automatic Release Mechanism" corrodes, freeing the capsule to float to the surface. ("Corrosion Release Error Factor: plus or minus 30 percent.")

Kinki University in Osaka, Japan, has plans for Antarctica with its BEST Capsule 2001 — Biological, Environmental, and Scientific Time Capsule. At midnight, January 1, 2001, it plans to bury a capsule 65 feet below the ice of Dome Fuji, containing DNA, mother's milk, seeds, air, seawater, rainwater, soil . . . all for scientists 1,000 years hence to study and perhaps use to clone extinct animals from the DNA. There will be 100,000 specimens in all. The university dreams of burying a BEST Capsule on the Moon.

All this activity would suggest that people in the future are going to be besotted with time capsules. Actually not: "More than 80 percent will be lost," says Hudson, buried and never to be found. "You really don't have to bury them, but people think you do. It's human nature: People forget them almost the next day. That's one reason we formed." The Time Capsule Society keeps a worldwide registry.

Such a registry would have helped Gas City, Indiana. For the city's centennial in 1992, the good citizens tore it apart looking for a time capsule buried 50 years earlier. Hundreds of people with shovels, backhoes, and even spoons attacked the city hall's lawn, toppling a 30-foot flagpole by destroying the concrete base. They never found the time capsule.

The Nine Most-Wanted Time Capsules

(according to the International Time Capsule Society)

1. The **"Bicentennial Wagon Train Time Capsule"** containing the signatures of 22 million Americans. President Gerald Ford arrived for the sealing ceremonies at Valley Forge on July 4, 1976, but someone had stolen the capsule.

2. The **M.I.T. Cyclotron Time Capsule.** In 1939, a group of M.I.T. engineers placed a brass capsule beneath an 18-ton magnet in a new cyclotron, to be opened in 50 years. In 1989, no one remembered it was there. The cyclotron has long since been deactivated. Will M.I.T. move the 36,000-pound lid and find the capsule?

(continued on page 100)

3. The most forgetful town — Corona, California — has lost track of 17 different capsules, dating back to the 1930s. "We just tore up a lot of concrete around the civic center," said the chairman of the town's centennial committee in 1986.

4. The M*A*S*H time capsule. In 1983, the cast of the TV show buried props and costumes somewhere in the Hollywood parking lot of 20th Century Fox.

5. The United States Capitol's cornerstone. In 1793, President George Washington officiated at a Masonic ritual in which a memorabilia-filled cornerstone was laid for the original U.S. Capitol. Over the years, the Capitol has undergone extensive expansion, but the original cornerstone has not been located.

6. The Gramophone Company's original sound recordings. In 1906, precious master-pressings of opera star Nellie Melba (of toast fame) and others were deposited behind the foundation stone of the new Gramophone factory (later HMV, then EMI). The container was removed in the 1960s, but someone ran off with it before it could be reburied.

7. The State of Washington celebrated its territorial centennial in 1953 by burying a two-ton time capsule near the state capitol in Olympia. The legislature did not approve funds to mark the spot, and the capsule was lost until 1959. A supplementary time capsule may have been interred beside the primary one or may be lurking in a closet at the capitol.

8. The Blackpool Tower cornerstone in Blackpool, Lancashire, England, was interred with great ceremony in the late 19th century. When a search was organized recently, fancy sensing equipment could not locate it, nor could clairvoyants called to the scene.

9. Citizens of Lyndon, Vermont, filled an iron box with proceedings of the town's centennial celebration in 1891, to be opened in 100 years. In 1991, citizens looked high and low but could not find the box. The burying ceremony may have been canceled because of rain.

Special Offer

to *Old Farmer's Almanac* Readers:

Is your town, school, or organization planning to prepare a time capsule as part of millennium festivities? What better item to include than a copy of this Almanac! We have reserved 1,000 copies of the 2000 edition for this use. A free copy of the newsstand edition will be sent upon request to any non-profit group that wants to tuck it into a time capsule. Please send us a note describing the project, and we will send you a free *2000 Old Farmer's Almanac*. We'll pay the postage, too. Write to Time Capsule Project, The Old Farmer's Almanac, Main St., Dublin, NH 03444.

☐☐

Spinning the Web: Go to www.almanac.com and click on **Article Links 2000** for Web sites related to this article. — *The Editors*

A Poultry Primer

Can you tell a boiler from a broiler? A rooster from a roaster? Having your own small flock of hens ensures a certain security in the 21st century. After all, in the grim uncertainty of the "Y2K," would you rather depend upon the computer chip or the chicken?

BY MARTHA WHITE

According to H. A. Highstone, a city-bred man who took up farming and lived to write about it in his *Practical Farming for Beginners,* published in 1940, "Anyone with brains enough to pound sand can successfully raise chickens." That may be so, but keeping poultry, like any year-round work, is not for the chickenhearted. Once your chicks arrive, feedings, waterings, coop cleanings, and egg gatherings follow in quick succession. Pounding sand may suddenly seem appealing.

Chickens are fascinating creatures, always aflutter with whims and worries, single-minded and determined when broody, and miraculous for their egg laying. Nothing heralds springtime like a newly hatched clutch of chicks, and nothing signals abundance so clearly as a steady supply of eggs for the kitchen and an occasional hen for the soup pot. Many families will consider a half dozen hens plenty to satisfy their daily egg requirements, but for the

A hen is only an egg's way of making another egg.

– Samuel Butler (1835-1902)

CONSIDER THE ROOSTER

If you plan to hatch some of your eggs into chicks, or if you prefer fertilized eggs for breakfast, you'll need a rooster or two. Otherwise, they're ornamental, sometimes feisty, and a lot of fun

for the Year 2000

sake of argument, we'll consider anything under two dozen birds a small flock. Once a hen starts laying, at about five months old, she'll average an egg on two out of three days — or about 20 a month. So, if hens are your idea of a nest egg for the future, here's how to get started.

BREEDS

■ With more than 100 recognized breeds to choose from, hen selection is your first high hurdle. Are you interested solely in eggs or meat, or do you prefer a dual-purpose bird? Brown eggs or white? Standard-size hens or smaller bantams? Just when you think you've been so clever to choose, say, a standard Wyandotte for its dual purpose and brown eggs, you'll still have to decide among the black, buff, Columbian, golden-laced, silver-laced, silver-penciled, and white Wyandottes. Clearly, this is no job for the featherbrained.

Color of Eggs

EGG LAYERS

Ancona	White
Australorp	Brown
California White	White
Hamburg	White or tinted
Lakenvelder	White or tinted
Leghorn	White

(continued on next page)

and trouble. Breeders suggest having a rooster for every 8 to 12 standard-size hens. A single cock can "accommodate," as they say, up to 18 hens. If you've ordered straight-run chicks (see Glossary, page 105) and ended up with several cocks, you may want to cull some or separate them from the hens to minimize pecking-order fights. Since roosters are prone to playing favorites, rotating two cocks among the flock may even things out.

Color of Eggs

EGG LAYERS
Minorca . . . . . . Chalk white
Production Red . . . . . Brown
Redcap . . . . White
Sex-Link . . . . Brown

MEAT BIRDS
Brahma . . . . Brown
Cochin . . . . Brown
Dark Cornish . . . . Brown
Jersey Giant . . . . Brown

DUAL-PURPOSE BIRDS
Araucana . . . . . . Blue green
Black Sex-Link . . . . . . Brown
Dominique . . . . Brown
Faverolle . . . Brown or tinted
Houdan (crested) . . . . White
New Hampshire . . . . . Brown
Orpington . . . . Brown
Red Sex-Link . . . . Brown
Rhode Island Red . . . Brown
Rock . . . . Brown
Sussex . . . . Brown
Wyandotte . . . . Brown

FEED *(and don't forget grit)*

■ For simplicity, most owners of small flocks buy commercial rations from their local feed stores. Young chicks will require "starter" feeds, and you may have a choice of medicated or nonmedicated versions. (If you can keep a healthy flock with the nonmedicated rations, do so.) Once the hens reach laying age, at approximately five months, you'll want to switch to layer rations with at least 16 percent protein.

Chicken feeds can be supplemented by homegrown or home-mixed rations of grains (oats, corn, barley, wheat, etc.), various brans, fish meal, alfalfa meal, bonemeal, etc. You can add food scraps from your table,

such as fruit and vegetable peels or leftover breads. Avoid offering raw potato peels (hard to digest), garlic or onions (which may alter the taste of eggs or meat), or anything spoiled.

Feeds bought from the store contain all the phosphorus and salt your hens will need, and they eliminate the need for grit. If you free-range your hens or supplement their diets, however, be sure to offer a hopper of grit to help the hens grind up any grains or plant matter they eat. Hens also need a hopper of ground oyster shells or other calcium source to prevent soft-shelled eggs. Fresh water should be in constant supply.

To dream of eggs signifies good luck or a wedding. A dream of broken eggs means a quarrel. To dream of many eggs indicates riches.

* * * * * * * *

WEATHER LORE

If a fowl stands

Can look upon an egg unmoved?

– Clarence Day (1874-1935)

FREE-RANGE OR CONFINED?

"Liberty and varied abundance are the two greatest essentials for poultry, old and young, to promote health, growth, beauty, and fertility," stated a poultryman in 1850. In confinement, contagious diseases such as coccidiosis can decimate a flock. Outdoors, predators such as raccoons, weasels, foxes, coyotes, hawks, and eagles can be problematic. Rats and snakes can threaten chicks or eggs. Some small farmers find a dog (or donkey) useful, others depend on the shotgun, while still others use fencing of various sorts.

HEN HOUSING

Even assuming free-range privileges, hens need a secure shelter for nesting, roosting at night, and escaping predators and bad weather. Most coop guides suggest about three square feet of space per adult bird. At a minimum, the coop should be easy to clean, be well ventilated but draft-free, include clean watering and feeding stations, and offer adequate roosts. Good, natural light is a plus, both for human and bird, and this together with standing headroom promotes more-frequent cleaning.

Dirt floors can work where the soil is sandy and the drainage reasonable, but a wooden floor is vastly easier to clean and protect. Cement floors work well, also. Good bedding, such as sawdust (untreated wood only), wood shavings, or chopped straw over a wooden or concrete floor is ideal.

(continued on next page)

CHICKEN TALK:
A GLOSSARY

BANTAM: A diminutive breed of domestic fowl

BOILER: A chicken 6 to 9 months old

BROILER: A cockerel of 2 or 3 pounds, at 8 to 12 weeks old

COCK: A male chicken; also called a rooster

COCKEREL: A young rooster, under 1 year old

FRYER: A chicken of 3 to 4 pounds, at 12 to 14 weeks old

HEN: A female chicken

NEST EGG: Literally, a china or wooden egg placed into the nest to encourage laying; figuratively, something set aside as security

POINT-OF-LAY PULLET: A young female just about to lay, near 5 months old

PULLET: A young female chicken, under 1 year old

ROASTER: A chicken of 4 to 6 pounds, over 12 to 14 weeks old

ROOSTER: A male chicken; also called a cock

SEXED CHICKS: Separated into only pullets or only cockerels

STRAIGHT RUN: Pullets and cockerels, mixed (unsexed or "as hatched")

on one leg, it is a sign of cold weather.

RULES OF THE ROOST

Hens perch on roosts about two feet off the ground and lay their eggs in nesting boxes. Simple 2x4s, placed on edge and rounded off, make fine roosts for the standard-size hen. Bantams will want a smaller pole, closer to an inch in width. As for the nest boxes, you'll know whether they're right by whether or not the hens use them. A 14x14-inch box, up to a foot deep and lined with clean hay, will accommodate even the larger breeds. Raised nests will require an outside perch to facilitate the hen's movement in and out. Since hens prefer a darkened nest, boxes can easily be stacked one above the other.

FUTURE GAINS

■ Assuming your neighbors don't mind your new feathered friends, the addition of poultry to your 21st-century assets will bring you much pleasure and not a few omelets and drumsticks. And, with luck, some of that "liberty and varied abundance" that are so good for hens may also prove beneficial to you.

WEATHER LORE

EXPECT RAIN IF

. . . hens spread and ruffle their tail feathers.

. . . cocks clap their wings in an unusual manner.

. . . hens take dustbaths and appear uneasy.

. . . fowls' wings droop.

. . . hens roost earlier than usual.

JOKES

Why did the chicken cross the road?
To get to the other side.

Why did the chicken cross the playground?
To get to the other slide.

Why did the dinosaur cross the road?
Because they didn't have chickens then.

■ Gather your eggs at noon, you gather them too soon.

■ Better an egg in peace than an ox in war.

■ As scarce as hens' teeth [i.e., nonexistent].

■ Don't put all your eggs in one basket. □□

Spinning the Web: Go to www.almanac.com and click on **Article Links 2000** for Web sites related to this article. – *The Editors*

BIO EAR - ELECTRONIC SOUND AMPLIFYING DEVICE

I'm Wearing Mine... And No One Can Tell!

**Why Pay $149.95?
Our Price
ONLY $49.95**

Provides You With A Little Extra Volume Enhancement That We All Need At Times

Frequency Range..........50-12,000Hz
Signal To Noise Ratio Less Than................25dB
Sensitivity Range.......-8dB
Weight (Battery Included) ..3.6 grams

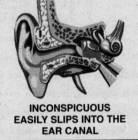

**INCONSPICUOUS
EASILY SLIPS INTO THE
EAR CANAL**

This compact, state-of-the-art electronic device can be easily concealed. No annoying, unsightly, behind-the-ear component. It's easy to use. Allows you to easily amplify the sounds around you. Imagine! Now you can hear clear, crisp sound. Great for the outdoors or today's shopping malls. All you do is slip our tiny, sound-amplifying component in the ear. Easily fits in right or left ear. That's it. The amplifying system is small enough to fit comfortably. Its lightweight design is ruggedly built to assure you that it will last a long, long time. You can take it anywhere. Ideal for watching TV, movies, sporting events, parties, or simply having a relaxing evening with a few good friends.

GREAT FOR PICKING UP DISTANT SOUND FROM ANYWHERE

Imagine how this small device will change your life. It can help you to hear those sounds which have eluded you before. Perhaps you simply got bored while watching TV, or it's been years since you appreciated the sound of birds chirping or rain gently pouring on your house. These are life's little special gifts. They were meant to be enjoyed. This compact, inconspicuous device can help put back the quality of life we all need and deserve. Comes with on/off switch and volume control. Three different sizes of ear tips to assure you of a proper fit everytime. Takes common, easy-to-find batteries. You get a 10-piece set including six replacement batteries and also a designer case to protect your sound amplifier when not in use. No wires. No tubes. We recommend you discuss this product with your physician. This is not a medical device.

It is in my best interest to have a medical evaluation, ideally from a physician that specializes in ear diseases. I am over 18 years old and voluntarily sign this waiver indicating that I do not wish at this time, to get a medical evaluation or test before purchasing the Bio-Ear.

THE
MOST
IMPORTANT
INVENTIONS
OF THE PAST
2,000
YEARS

... as nominated by scientists and experts around the world, collected by John Brockman, and published on the Web at www.edge.org. Here are excerpts from the nominations and explanations; go to the Web site for the whole nine yards.

"I think you'd have to go a long way to find a more important invention than the **basket.** Without something to gather into, you cannot have a gathering society of any complexity, no home and hearth, no division of labour, no humanity."

– Jeremy Cherfas, biologist and author of *The Seed Saver's Handbook*

"The **eraser.** As well as the delete key, Wite-Out, the Constitutional amendment, and all the other tools that let us go back and fix our mistakes."

– Douglas Rushkoff, author and lecturer on technology and culture

"The most important invention of the last two thousand years was **hay.** In earlier times, civilization could exist only in warm climates where horses could stay alive through the winter by grazing.... Sometime during the so-called dark ages, some unknown genius invented hay ... and civilization moved north over the Alps."

– Freeman Dyson, professor of physics, Institute for Advanced Study, Princeton, N.J.

"Western **classical music,** as epitomized in the compositions of Bach, Beethoven, Brahms, and above all Mozart. Classical music has probably given more pleasure to more individuals, with less negative fallout, than any other human artifact."

– Howard Gardner, professor of education, Harvard University

"Effectual health care. Not just antibiotics, not just birth control, not just anesthesia ... [but] also vitamin pills and — in some ways most wondrously cost-effective of all — **soap,** as in the soap doctors use to wash their hands."

– James J. O'Donnell, professor of classical studies, University of Pennsylvania

"The most important invention has been **reading glasses.** They have effectively doubled the active life of everyone who reads or does fine work — and prevented the world [from] being ruled by people under forty."

– Nicholas Humphrey, theoretical psychologist, New School for Social Research

"My personal favourite is the place-value notation system combined with the use of the symbol 0 for **zero** to denote a nonexistent number. [It] marks the birth of modern mathematics."

– V. S. Ramachandran, professor of neurosciences and psychology, University of California in San Diego

"The **Copernican Theory.** Generally, it was a counter-intuitive idea, and it ran opposite to the interpretation of [the] senses (not to mention the Church) — I mean, one could 'see'

the Sun going across the sky. . . . It took a lot of intellectual courage, and taught us more than just what it said."

– Michael Nesmith, artist and writer; former cast member of "The Monkees"

"My immediate response (without even thinking) was the **contraceptive pill.** My mother had six children in five and a half years and it was only the invention of the pill that saved our family from becoming a mini-nation-state in its own right."

– Margaret Wertheim, research associate, American Museum of Natural History

"The **concepts of democracy, of social justice,** and the belief in the possibility of creating a society free from the oppressions of class, race, and gender."

– Steven Rose, neurobiologist and author; director, Brain and Behaviour Research Group

"I am intrigued by the effects of such inventions as the **flag** — a symbol of belonging that millions will follow to ruin or victory independently of biological connectedness; or the **social security card** that signifies that we are not alone and our welfare is a joint problem for the community."

– Mihaly Csikszentmihalyi, professor of psychology and education, University of Chicago

"**Space travel.** Of course, it may be centuries before we know the full consequences."

– Reuben Hersh, mathematician and author

"**Religion.** Only two major religions have been invented in the last two millennia, Christianity and Islam. Try to imagine the last two millennia, or the present, without them."

– Stewart Brand, founder of the *Whole Earth Catalog*

"I propose the **clock** as the greatest invention. . . . It converted time from a per-

sonal experience into a reality independent of perception." – W. Daniel Hillis, physicist and computer scientist

"The greatest invention in the past two thousand years is the **printing press.** Next is the **Thermos bottle."**

– Leon Lederman, director emeritus of the Fermi National Accelerator Laboratory

"I have two suggestions. First, the **electric light**. . . . Having lived in Africa, where one is often forced to read from firelight, electricity is a godsend. My second suggestion for great inventions is the **aspirin.** . . . What a useful little pill."

– Marc D. Hauser, evolutionary psychologist, Harvard University

"I choose the **symphony orchestra.** . . . It establishes a dramatic link between two seemingly disparate worlds — the material world of science and the world of the psyche and the arts."

– Julian Barbour, theoretical physicist and author

"I'll choose two things — **chairs** and **stairs.** Apart from the fact that they rhyme, they also represent an imaginative leap by seeing the value to the human anatomy of an idealised platform in space at a certain height."

– Karl Sabbagh, writer and television producer for the BBC and PBS

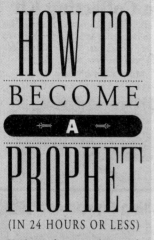

HOW TO
BECOME
‑‑ A ‑‑
PROPHET

(IN 24 HOURS OR LESS)

Here's a prediction: At the start of a new millennium, people will be nervous about the future. And that means big opportunities for prophets.

■ **In the old days, it took *years* to establish yourself as a big-time prophet. You had to journey to far-off lands, wear poorly cured animal skins, and run the risk of martyrdom in order to make a splash. Now we have the Internet. Set up a Web site with a snazzy URL, post your most-attention-grabbing prophecies, and bingo — in less than 24 hours, you're being denounced by Responsible Prophets for reckless disregard of truth.**

H. L. Mencken once said, "The prophesying business is like writing fugues; it is fatal to everyone save the man of absolute genius." Mencken was too pessimistic; you don't have to be a genius (or a man) to be a prophet. Just follow these six simple rules.

1 PREDICT THE PAST.

Sam Goldwyn, the legendary Hollywood producer and malapropist, once advised: "Never make predictions. Especially about the future."

There is more wisdom in that comment than you might think. Just about anything that might happen has happened before, and it's a safe bet it will happen again — someday. Wars and rumors of war? Guaranteed. Signs and portents in the heavens? A lead-pipe cinch. Earthquakes, volcanoes, floods, famines, plagues, riots, the fall of kingdoms, and the rise of false prophets? Check your daily newspaper.

The trick is not to let yourself be pinned down on when these things are going to happen. Which leads to our next rule . . .

2 AVOID SPECIFICS.

Geronimo Cardano, a 16th-century mathematician and astrologer, foretold that King Edward VI of England would fall desperately ill at the age of 55 years, 3 months, and 17 days. Unfortunately, the king ruined everything by dying at the age of 16. Cardano tried to recover his reputation by predicting his own death at the age of 75, and went so far as to kill himself in order to make it so.

Most successful prophets employ vague but colorful language to get around this problem. "In the fullness of time" is a convenient phrase, if a bit archaic. "Lo, it shall come to pass" has a nice ring to it. Remember, *anything* might happen in the long run. As the economist John Maynard Keynes pointed out, "In the long run, we are all dead."

3 PREDICT THE OBVIOUS.

You have to stay in touch with current events. For example, a smart would-be prophet will look at the newspapers in the fall of 1999 and issue a prophecy that sounds something like this:

"Lo, there will be signs and portents in the heavens (the Leonid meteor shower comes every November). And there will be great wailing and gnashing of teeth (something upsetting or startling will be happening in politics), and the false prophets (the media) will be confounded."

A corollary of this might be, "Predict what's *possible.*" For example, **saying that the Moon will turn the color of blood is not only poetic and exciting,** it's something that happens every now and then under certain atmospheric conditions. But you don't want to predict that the Moon will turn lime-green.

The Time of Doom Draws Near

4 LEAVE HOME.

As it says in the Bible, "A prophet is not without honor, save in his own country." A guy on a city street, raving about the end of the world, hardly merits a passing glance. Your Uncle Ike, who has been intercepting E-mail from the Trilateral Commission through his fillings for years, almost never sees his letters to the editor published. You, a prophet? Get a grip. We've known you all your life.

Ah, but **bill yourself as the Master Sukkimam, just in from the foothills of Bangladesh, and people sit up and take notice.** List a few advanced degrees from foreign educational institutions (Freedonia Technical-Mystical Institute, the Center for Intergalactic Pulchritude), and you'll be invited to the best parties.

5 LEAVE YOURSELF AN OUT.

When I was a freshman in college, a professor in introductory psychology told us about something called "cognitive dissonance." If I remember correctly, the term refers to situations in which the facts conflict with what we wish to believe. In such situations, we often find a way to ignore, deny, or distort the facts in order to defend the cherished belief or activity.

For example, take flying-saucer cults. Every now and then (especially approaching a new millennium), some prophet or other warns that Earth is about to be destroyed but that the faithful will be saved. Often the faithful are ordered to gather in high places, where they will be picked up in the nick of time by angels, or a flying saucer. **So the faithful pack their bags, quit their jobs, and show up on the mountaintop at the appointed time.**

(continued)

BY TIM CLARK

– illustrated by Eldon Doty

But — no flying saucer appears. No end of Earth. They all go home disillusioned and resolve never to be suckered again, right?

Wrong. *They believe in the prophet more strongly than ever.* Why? Cognitive dissonance. The clever prophet always leaves an out. Maybe it was the wrong mountaintop. Maybe the calculations were off. Or, more likely, the prophet appears to his people and says, "Your faith has saved the whole world!"

6 PREDICT INTERESTING STUFF.

I once represented *The Old Farmer's Almanac* on Geraldo Rivera's TV show (the old one, before he got respectable). It was taped for New Year's Day broadcast and the theme was "What to Expect in the Coming Year."

The guests included a Hollywood astrologer, a fashion maven, a political pundit, an economic forecaster, and me, the hick from New Hampshire.

Before the cameras rolled, the director told us he'd begin the show by focusing briefly on each of us for a quick prediction. "Make it short and exciting," he ad-vised us. I gave it my best shot.

"What's happening in the weather?" the announcer boomed.

"Hurricanes early and often," I said.

"Great!" the director cried.

"What's the latest in fashion?"

"Legs and cleavage!" shouted the fashion expert.

"Perfect!"

"What do the stars tell us about the stars?"

"Michael Jackson hears wedding bells!" the astrologer twinkled. The director was in ecstasy.

And then the economic forecaster.

"What's going on in the economy?"

"Big business will look more like small business, as executives try to respond more quickly to market trends, while medium-sized business . . ."

"Cut!" the director cried.

"I wasn't finished," the economist said.

"Shorter. More exciting," said the director. "Let's try it again, shall we?"

"What's going on in the economy?" the announcer intoned.

"Big business will look to small business for models of economic behavior, while . . ."

"Cut!"

You get the picture, even if the economic forecaster never did. Guess who got the most questions from the studio audience? **The folks wanted to know who Michael Jackson was going to marry. The astrologer was the star of the show. None of the rest of us got a single question.**

By the way, the astrologer predicted Michael would marry Whitney Houston. He actually married Lisa Marie Presley. And that poor economic forecaster was dead right. Big companies did start imitating smaller ones. But who cares? The successful prophet is often wrong — but never boring. □□

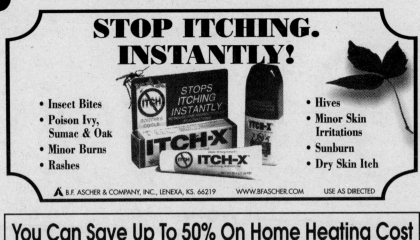

THE STATE OF

ROMANCE

IN THE YEAR 2000

It's a renaissance of romance. Romantic getaway bookings at bed and breakfasts are up 25 percent. Victoria's Secret, always ready to sell the sizzle, reported a 20 percent spike in sales just before Valentine's Day last year. And sales of cut roses — 1.2 billion stems a year in the United States — are blooming. Almanac writer **Christine Schultz** offers more evidence that matters of the heart still matter: In an era of spin control and global mergers, it's still love that makes the world go 'round.

♥ 1

FALLING IN LOVE WITH LOVE

Romance sells in books and movies. Do you know why?

ROMANCE IS WHAT AMERICA READS

♥ Roughly 14 percent of Americans spend some $750 million on 182 million romance novels every year, accounting for 49 percent of all paperback books sold in the United States, and outselling mystery, suspense, and science-fiction categories combined.

♥ The overwhelming majority of romance readers are women, approximately 45 million of them, of all ages and professions.

♥ About 59 percent of romance readers have attended college, according to *U.S. News & World Report*.

THE ROMANCE NOVEL'S GUIDE TO THE PERFECT LOVER (GUYS, TAKE NOTE)

If you were to study the heroes of most romance novels, this is what you'd conclude, according to *Men's Health*:

♥ Contrary to their reputation as bodice-rippers, romance novel heroes engage in scenes of long unlacings and unfastenings. In days of yore, all those layers of garments gave lovers time to consider the significance of the act, and modern-day women still cherish that idea.

♥ Romance novel heroes notice women's hair and eyes and clothes and napes of

— CORBIS/Hulton-Deutsch Collection

necks and say nice things about them in poetic detail. Readers would like their real-life men to do this on a daily basis. "Women are disappointed because the man initially does a lot of romantic things, but then he slacks off," says Michael Adamse, a clinical psychologist in Boca Raton, Florida.

❤ The seductive heroes of romance novels tend to be pirate kings, Viking lords, and ruthless barons, otherwise known as alpha males, who in real life lop off heads and don't stick around too long. So what does the heroine really want? A tough guy who will commit — in other words, fantasy.

❤ In the end, romance novels tend to support what most men suspected all along — that women want conversation, devotion, inner strength, and romance. "They understand, however, that all this may not be available in massive doses," notes *Men's Health*, "so they use romance novels like multivitamins, to supplement their actual diets."

ABOUT THE HANDSOME HUNK ON THE COVER . . .

❤ If one were to judge a romance novel by its cover, it would seem that women want a

muscle-pumped man, what *Men's Health* called the "cute Indian on Human Growth Hormone" look. But, says Julie Tetel Andresen, English professor at Duke University and author of a dozen romances, that's not the case. "The hunk on the cover is just a quick way to convey physical attraction," says Andresen. "The nonphysical virtues (such as honor, courage, loyalty, and respect) are the important ones, and those can be embodied in any man."

In days of yore, all those layers of garments gave lovers time to consider the significance of the act.

(continued)

❤ For a while, it looked like the century would end with the raw lyrics of today's R&B and gangsta rap instead of the romantic R&B love ballads of the years before. But a romance renaissance has turned the charts. "Gone are the baseball caps and saggy jeans; here instead are tuxes and boutonnieres," reports *Newsweek*.

THE CHASE
Searching for Mr. (or Ms.) Right

THE IDEAL GUY HAS A POSITIVE ATTITUDE ...

❤ When Harlequin Enterprises, Ltd., the world's leading publisher of romance novels, asked Canadian women to describe the one thing that would most attract them to their ideal man, 33 percent replied "a positive attitude"; 30 percent said "the way he makes me feel good about myself"; 21 percent said "a sense of humor"; 3 percent said they were looking for "smoldering, sexy looks"; and only 1 percent most desired "a sexy body."

... AND HE'S A FAB DAD

❤ After years of market research, a new line of Silhouette Romances has been introduced, devoted to the new pulp hero that women want: the Fabulous Father. "The relationship between hero and heroine has become equal, a partnership," writes David Borcherding in the *Romance Writer's Sourcebook*. But some critics are not impressed. "The 'Fab Dad' experiences no keen yearnings, save a placid wish to 'balance courtship with child rearing,'" *The New York Times* groused. "He is as docile and pliant as a winter-blooming shrub."

– photo: H. Armstrong Roberts

TRUE LOVE: IS IT DESTINY OR A LOT OF HARD WORK?

❤ There are those who say "we were meant to be," and those who say "we made it be." Psychologists now report that the way we view love greatly affects the route that our own romances take. Psychologist C. Raymond Knee reports in the *Journal of Personality and Social Psychology* that couples therapists and marriage manuals tend to support the growth-through-hard-work approach to a relationship, but destiny theorists believe that a couple should not stay stuck in a bad relationship in hopes that they can work it out: It's just not meant to be.

The "Fab Dad" tosses toddlers and understands teens (so much for the pirate king fantasy).

❤ *New York Times* columnist John Tierney has identified a new romantic custom called "spouse bounty," in which a single man or woman offers a reward (such as a new Mercedes or a paid vacation) to any friend who introduces him or her to the mate whom he or she ends up marrying. While the phenomenon does not yet appear to be widespread, Tierney reports, it's certainly been lucrative to the parties involved.

LIVING AN OCEAN APART

❤ With fast-track careers keeping more couples apart for longer periods of time, magazines are taking note of couples who make it work. During their marriage of nearly three decades, Texas strategist Joyce Scott and chemical engineer Lavanne Scott, parents of two sons, have lived apart twice for career opportunities. "The right person for you may be in Paris, France," says Mrs. Scott in *Jet* magazine, "and you are in Birmingham, Alabama. Why would you let that go just because you're separated by an ocean?"

DRIVE-BY DATING

❤ The "Cosmo woman" these days is encouraged to attract the man of her dreams

– H. Armstrong Roberts

In men's minds, a woman in a fast car is a racy woman hurtling toward her romantic destiny.

by driving a racy car, such as a red Porsche convertible, a powerful magnet that men can't resist. "In men's minds," reports *Cosmopolitan* magazine, "a woman in a fast car spells a racy woman who knows exactly what she wants and how to get it." Similarly, in an effort to distinguish a man's "drive-by dating potential," *Cosmopolitan* offers this road map:

"FERRARI: Owning such a high-performance car, his conversation is likely to consist of RPMs and engine size. He's probably more interested in his car's body than his girlfriend's.

"RANGE ROVER: An all-weather man who calls when he says he'll call. Chances are he'll stick around and handle relationship rough spots the way his car handles mountain roads.

"BMW: He probably wears a double-breasted suit, owns a portable phone, and goes to great lengths to behave like a gentleman and treat you like a lady.

"VOLVO: He doesn't like to take risks. If you hear your biological clock ticking loudly, he's the one for you. The Volvo man is a family man.

"CHEVY: Going from 0 to 60 in six seconds flat is less important to this regular guy than having a few beers with his pals. But he'll always reserve a special romantic time for the woman in his life."

(continued)

♥ A major survey in the United States found 1/3 of the women respondents — but only 1/6 of the men — saying they are uninterested in sex. Approximately 1/5 of the women — but only 1/10 of the men — said sex gave them no pleasure. Given those numbers, you might wonder why the latest sexual drug breakthrough, Viagra, has been for men. Now scientists are wondering if something similar could be invented to enhance sex for women.

LOVE IS WHERE YOU FIND IT

Texas, a cruise ship, the office

THE MOST ROMANTIC STATE

♥ In novels, the flashy urban romances of the '80s have now given way to the simpler, down-home love stories of the '90s, with the hottest homeplace these days being Texas. "It's a well-known fact in the industry right now that if you put 'Texas' in the title, your book will sell," says Debbie Macomber, author of Harlequin's best-selling *Heart of Texas* series. Of course, it doesn't hurt that several hundred romance writers call Texas home, but the attraction seems to go beyond that to the myth of the West and the rough-and-ready kind of hero the unforgiving landscape breeds. "Texas is larger than life and so are our men — they're stubborn, independent, proud," says Houston romance writer Rita Clay Estrada. "The challenge for our heroines here is trying to tame them."

Approximately ⅕ of the women — but only ⅒ of the men — said sex gave them no pleasure.

THE MOST ROMANTIC CITY

♥ The most romantic city at the turn of the new century, according to a *Ladies' Home Journal* survey of the country's 200 largest cities, is San Francisco. California's bay city topped the romance roster (followed by Denver, Colorado; Concord, California; and Salt Lake City, Utah) based on fabulous scenery, wining and dining, availability of fresh flowers, and romance-video rental rate. On the bottom end of the scale, despite its location in the most romantic state, was Brownsville, Texas.

– CORBIS/Hulton-Deutsch Collection

ROMANCE ON THE HIGH SEAS

❤ It appears that some 7 million passengers will take a cruise in the year 2000, as romance at sea experiences a wave of popularity following the movie *Titanic*. More than 20 new ships are being outfitted to set sail by 2001, many of which will

include chapels, because weddings at sea are standard fare. Carnival Lines reports 2,000 marriages a year.

ROMANCE IN THE OFFICE

❤ Sad to say, regulating office romance is the hottest issue at the turn of the century. "Today's fling is tomorrow's filing," says law professor Dennis Powers, author of *The Office Romance: Playing with Fire Without Getting Burned*. Some companies insist on "love contracts" for employees, ensuring that both parties agree to pursue an affair that is consensual and amorous, so that if the relationship sours, no legal action can be taken. Firms are adopting romance rules that range from straight no-dating-at-work policies to date-and-tell. The fact is, 15,000 complaints of sexual harassment are filed each year with the federal Equal Employment Opportunity Commission.

The good news is that love seems to be holding its ground. According to an American Management Association study, roughly one out of two office romances ends in long-term commitment or marriage — better odds than you'll find outside the workplace.

All sweethearts —

in the military, in the office, or elsewhere —

eventually must decide: Get hitched or ditched.

ROMANCE IN UNIFORM

❤ For the past two decades, romantic relationships were permitted under Army policy provided they weren't between superiors and subordinates in the same service or didn't cause favoritism. All that has changed. Following a year-long review by the Pentagon, toughened rules now prohibit fraternizing across any of the four services, even if the units don't interact. The Army will set a deadline by which existing sweethearts must get either hitched or ditched.

(continued)

❤ But what of those whose love is literally off the map? NASA advises its astronauts to prepare for separations by honestly discussing their hopes and fears with their spouses, and recommends that couples try not to be out of sight of each other for more than six weeks. To help bridge the galaxy gap, astronauts on the Mir space station phoned home weekly, interacted by video every other week, and got care packages sent in by rocket every two to three months. Astronaut Jerry Linenger, perhaps the most romantic of the bunch, had flowers sent to his wife every week.

....

If fashion is any indication of feeling, then romance is definitely back in style.

WHAT TO WEAR, WHAT TO SAY, HOW TO SMELL, IS E-MAIL OK?

Making sure you don't blow it.

ROMANCE IN MEN'S FASHION

❤ High-fashion designers have added romance to the latest look of men's clothing, including fanciful touches such as embroidered pants, Japanese draped coats, baby blue dragons, feathery fabrics, and black lace lining. But fear not, the overall masculine swagger has been kept intact.

ROMANTIC CLOTHES FOR WOMEN

❤ If fashion is any indication of feeling, then romance is definitely back in style. In a move away from the spare chic of white T-shirts, khakis, and black cardigans, designers are putting out lines of party dresses, camisoles, and pink frilly things. Jewelry, too, is back in vogue. "We're just all so tired of looking plain," notes Andrea Linett, a fashion writer at *Harper's Bazaar.* "Femininity now signifies the urban look." The trend, it seems, was a result not just of the booming economy, but of the nation's enchantment with the movie *Titanic,* which heralded an era of femininity and languid dress.

❤ *Mademoiselle* recently provided its long-distance romantics with a practical chart on phone rates — the numbers that make any heart beat faster. But better yet, the editors advised, *write* a love letter in your own true voice (and hand). Don't worry about sounding like an eloquent poet. Just let the

— CORBIS/Hulton-Deutsch Collection

lust and loneliness flow onto the page. Then reminisce about the past, add a keepsake from your time together, and dream about what you'll do when you're back in each other's arms.

WHAT THE NOSE KNOWS

❤ As the clock ticks toward the new millennium, overpowering perfumes of musk and patchouli have been replaced with more subtly sexy floral scents, reports *Cosmopolitan.* New fragrance technology has made perfumes capable of smelling like the real thing — fresh-cut flowers. The newest floral perfumes are named for the swing toward love: Ralph Lauren's "Romance," Calvin Klein's "Eternity," and Lancôme's "Ô Oui!"

Of course, the idea that our bodies send off invisible, odorless chemicals involved in sexual attraction has long been exploited by perfume-makers, who use pig pheromones (known as "boar taint") and compounds found in human sweat in their colognes, claiming that the smells will lure the opposite sexes together. Since human behavior is a complex blend of biology and experience, it remains to be seen how much aphrodisiac power pheromones really hold.

❤

LOVE ON-LINE

❤ The latest craze of love affairs is taking place in cyberspace, oftentimes with people falling in love with those they've never met, or haven't seen in years, or who are not always whom they say they are. "Experts say cyberspace is contributing to ruptured marriages at an alarming, albeit incalculable, rate," notes the *Alberta Report.*

The lure, of course, is that E-mailers, uninhibited by appearances, by real-life situations, or even by honesty, can make up identities for themselves. In their paper "Crossing the Line — On Line," psychologists David Greenfield and Alvin Cooper say that the Net is an ideal venue for seduction and adultery. "In cyberspace, there is no need to fear AIDS, pregnancy, or lipstick stains on the collar. Some people feel emboldened and experiment with their sexuality in ways they would likely avoid in the real-time, consequence-filled world."

Here are examples of people who followed through with cyberspace love affairs:

– H. Armstrong Roberts

❤ *Cosmopolitan* ran a story by a woman who had an on-line affair that led to a short and not-so-sweet marriage. The name of the story: "I Married a He Who Was Really a She!"

❤ New York City singer-songwriter Brian Gari met "Sarah" via an Internet romance ad. After many amorous E-mails, they arranged to meet at one of his performances. He

In cyberspace, some people experiment with their sexuality in ways they would likely avoid in the real-time world.

spotted her in the crowd right away. There was only one hitch — she was already married with children. She contemplated divorce. He wrote 70 songs inspired by his love for her. He released a CD called *Love Online,* then planned a stage musical. His imagined ending suggested undying love. Her real-life ending blocked his E-mail from her account.

❤ There is the occasional report of a successful relationship taking root in cyberspace, like *The New York Times* story of Susan Chang, who had almost given up on love till the man of her

(continued)

dreams, Randall Dean te Velde, answered her computerized personal ad. By the third E-mail, she was in love but hadn't met him in person. She snuck into his Tibetan Buddhism class one evening and, when class let out, introduced herself. Within a year, they were married in Brooklyn.

ADVICE FROM THE QUEEN OF STEAM

❤ Best-selling romance novelist Jackie Collins, called the "queen of steam" by *McCall's* magazine, uses strong and sexy heroines whom men meet once and can't get out of their minds. Her advice to women who want to have the same effect: "If you're in the mood for love, speak up. Men, like women, want to be wanted."

HOW TO KEEP THE LOVE LIGHT GLOWING

What to do (and what not . . .)

A ROOMFUL OF ROSES AND OTHER ROMANTIC MOMENTS

For those who need inspiration for romance, here are a few examples, courtesy of *Ebony* magazine:

❤ Will Smith, hating to be away from his love, Jada Pinkett, on her birthday, sent her enough roses to fill not a vase, but a room — literally, hundreds and hundreds of roses.

❤ For the 29th birthday of his wife, Tracey, Kenneth (Babyface) Edmonds rented the ballroom of the Beverly Hills Hotel to surprise her. She entered to find it overflowing with flowers, friends, and a full orchestra.

❤ Denzel Washington took his wife, Pauletta, and their four children on vacation to South Africa, where he renewed his marriage vows with Pauletta before Archbishop Desmond Tutu.

THE MARRIAGE PACT

❤ According to *Ladies' Home Journal,* the modern-day marriage pact goes like this: "A man

marries a woman hoping — praying — that this sweet young thing he's vowing to love and cherish won't change, ever. On the other hand, a woman marries a man hoping — insisting — he change, and soon. Of course, men don't change. Ever. Women — we start reinventing ourselves the minute we find out we're pregnant."

A woman marries a man hoping — insisting — he change, and soon. Of course, men don't change. Ever.

FINE WINE OR STALE BEER?

❤ If you ever wondered why the very thing that once made you crazy in love with your partner now makes you just plain crazy, Diane Felmlee, a sociology professor at the University of California-Davis, has the answer. In the early stages of love, she says, we wear the equivalent of rose-colored

glasses that give every quality a positive light and filter out any potential conflict areas. But what happens next, says Howard Rankin, author of *10 Steps to a Great Relationship*, is up to you: "What seemed like cute habits in the early stages of romance can mature like fine wine or ferment like stale beer."

LONGEST MARRIAGES ON RECORD

❤ The longest marriages on record lasted 86 years each. One was the marriage of cousins Sir Temulji Bhicaji Nariman and Lady Nariman, who wed in 1853 at the age of five. The other marriage of that length was between Lazarus Rowe and Molly Webber, of Greenland, New Hampshire. Married in 1743, when both were 18, they raised a large family and lived to see descendants of the fifth generation. Imagine.

– CORBIS/Hulton-Deutsch Collection

In the early stages of love, we wear the equivalent of rose-colored glasses that give every quality a positive light and filter out any potential conflict areas. But what happens next is up to you.

WARNING: YOU STILL CAN'T BOTTLE LOVE

❤ The miraculous results of that revolutionary pill, Viagra, have been gleefully guffawed at across the country. For the first time, we have a 50-milligram pill that in less than an hour will put the starch back in any man's romantic inklings. But the fact remains that Viagra is not

a desire drug. More than one middle-aged couple has discovered that you cannot simply take the pill and just lay quietly in bed or you are likely to fall asleep. As one *Texas Monthly* columnist put it, "Reawakening sexual desire requires a reacquaintance with romance . . . you can't kindle the fire of love with a pill."

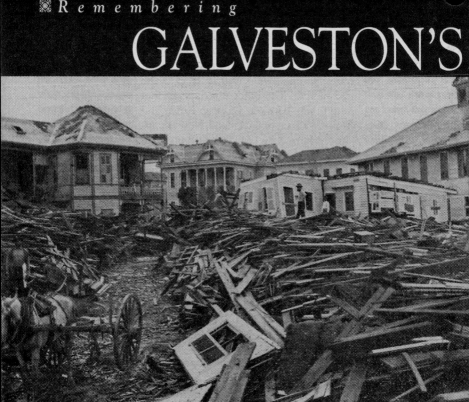

Top left and top right: Winds of 150 miles per hour and storm surges wreaked havoc on homes and large commercial buildings alike. **Above left:** Only the altar statue survived at St. Joseph's Church. **Above right:** The corner of 19th and N streets.

– photos: Texas State Library & Archives Commission

Over the years, Galveston had forgotten one thing: The sea that provided its wealth could also destroy its dreams in an instant. That terrifying moment came on Saturday, September 8, 1900, as a hurricane bore down on the "Queen City of the Gulf."

BY BOB
TREBILCOCK

"It is said that every wave of the sea has its tragedy, and it seems to be true here."

– from *The Great Galveston Disaster*, by Paul Lester

Near 9 P.M. on the evening of September 8, 1900, a group of men huddled together in the railroad depot in Galveston, Texas. On a typical night, the streets of Galveston would have been bustling. The locals called it the "Queen City of the Gulf." Located on an island about two miles off the Texas coast, and blessed with the only deepwater harbor in the state, Galveston was one of the wealthiest U.S. cities of its day: An estimated 70 percent of the South's cotton crop crossed its docks.

Tonight the streets of the busy port were empty. A hurricane-force wind beat on the sturdy depot. Waves from the Gulf of Mexico thundered ashore and flooded the streets to a depth of five feet or more. Buildings that had withstood storm after storm over the years were being torn from their foundations. The sounds of crumbling timbers, breaking glass, and screaming wind filled the night.

The depot was dark except for the dim light from a single lantern. The power plant and gas works had been destroyed hours earlier. One old man held a barometer up to the lantern. "27.90 and dropping," he said

– photos: Texas State Library & Archives Commission

mournfully. "We're gone. Nothing can exist in such a storm." The men waited to die.

Nearly 100 years after that terrible night, the storm that destroyed Galveston Island is still considered one of the deadliest natural disasters in U.S. history. A city of 37,789 was virtually wiped off the map. Every building on the island was damaged, and 3,600 homes — half the residences — were completely destroyed. At least 6,000 people are believed to have lost their lives that night, nearly one-sixth of the population; other estimates have put the loss at nearly double that figure.

The storm of 1900 moved slowly, providing ample warning. A Weather Bureau forecaster first noticed a disturbance in the Atlantic near the Windward Islands on August 30, 1900. By September 3, heavy rains were falling over Cuba. The following day, Dr. Isaac Cline, chief of the Galveston weather bureau, received his first bulletin and began to track the storm's progress.

On September 5, the storm reached hur-

At 3:40 P.M., the hurricane came ashore, and Galveston began to disappear under water. The train trestles and long wooden bridge that connected Galveston to the mainland were quickly submerged, eliminating any chance of escape from the island.

Galveston

ricane force as it passed over the Florida Keys. But the path was still unpredictable. Would it go north along the eastern seaboard to Boston, or west along the Gulf? Or maybe even turn on Central or South America? The following day, barometric conditions changed over the eastern United States, and the storm pushed to the northwest toward Louisiana and Texas.

On September 7, the storm was still hundreds of miles away when Dr. Cline raised the red-and-black flag that signaled an oncoming hurricane. The following morning, while his sons telegraphed storm readings to Washington, he went up and down the beaches of Galveston, warning people to find shelter on higher ground.

Few heeded Cline's warnings. Some even went to the shore to watch the waves roll in. When two women from Houston, vacationing in a beach cottage, donned their bathing suits to wade up to town, the neighbors next door laughed at their nervousness.

As the afternoon wore on, however, even longtime residents realized this storm meant business. At 3:40 P.M., the hurricane came ashore, and Galveston began to disappear under water. The train trestles and long wooden bridge that connected Galveston to the mainland were quickly submerged, eliminating any chance of escape from the island. Then the lights went out and the city sank into darkness. The winds shattered windows and tore off awnings and cornices. Slate roof tiles soared through the air like deadly shrapnel.

At 5:15 P.M., instruments at the weather service measured sustained winds of 84 miles per hour for five straight minutes. Then the instruments were blown off the roof. At the height of the storm, the winds reached an estimated 150 miles per hour. Frantic residents realized too late that they were trapped. "To leave a house was to drown," wrote Richard Spillane, the editor of the *Galveston Tribune*. "To remain was to court death in the wreckage. Such a night of agony has seldom been equaled."

Residents took shelter where they could find it. A woman who had just given birth was carried to a house a block away by a group of men who held her high above their heads in waist-deep water. The two women from Houston found a hiding spot in a stable. Nearly 1,000 crowded into the Tremont Hotel, even though part of the roof had been torn away.

"We were just as nearly like rats in a wire cage as anything could be," one survivor said later. The Reverend L. P. Davis, a local minister, lashed himself and his family to a tree trunk so they wouldn't blow away, and rode out the storm. Two women hugged one another for comfort in a wooden bathtub, which was carried out to sea. The next morning, the tide washed them back onto the beach, exhausted but alive.

Three miles from the city, the Sisters of Charity operated an orphanage on beachfront property. The dormitories housed 10 sisters and 93 children. That evening, the nuns and children crowded onto the second floor of one of the dormitories; the other had already collapsed. Tying their young charges to their cinctures with clotheslines, the nuns sang "Queen of the Waves," a favorite tune, to calm the children. One nun clutched two small orphans to her chest, promising that whatever happened, she would never let them go.

But the dormitory could not withstand the storm. All died except three boys, who floated for more than a day on an uprooted tree. The sister who promised never to let go was found across the bay, still clutching two children to her breast.

At 10 P.M., the railroad depot was one of the few buildings in Galveston still standing. The old man peered at his barometer again. "The pressure's rising," he announced, and whooped for joy. "The worst has passed. The storm will be over soon." Slowly, the wind and waves retreated to the sea. At midnight, the Moon peeked through the clouds. By 1:45 A.M. on September 9, the water level had dropped by two feet.

When the Sun came up in the morning, the water was gone and the bay was calm. Wreckage filled the landscape as far as the eye could see. Churches and schools lay in ruins. Once-proud homes were splinters. Enough debris washed up on shore across the bay at Texas City to build another town.

Corpses lined the streets and bobbed in the harbor like cordwood. "Nude forms of human beings were scattered everywhere," said F. B. Campbell, a cotton broker from Springfield, Massachusetts, who swam to safety that night. "No man could count them without going insane. It looked like a graveyard, where all the tenants of the tombs had been exhumed and the corpses thrown to the winds." In fact, the storm had scoured corpses from the local cemeteries, scattering the remains of the long-dead with the newly departed.

The living were barely better off. One distraught mother stood in the street and wailed, holding only the foot and leg of her child. The two Houston women who fled to a stable found a dead baby lying like a discarded toy in the backyard of their demolished cottage. The next-door neighbors who laughed when the two women evacuated all died in the storm.

There was no time for mourning. With thousands of bodies decaying in the hot sun, the stench of diseased flesh was overwhelming. Hundreds of bodies were loaded onto a barge and buried at sea, only to wash back up on shore days later. Eventually, the only way to deal with the corpses was to burn them along with the rubble. "The peculiar smell of burning flesh, so sickening at first, became horribly familiar within the next two months, when we lived in it and breathed it, day after day," wrote Clara Barton, the founder of what would become the American National Red Cross, who, at the age of 78, went to Galveston to direct the agency's relief effort.

And yet, out of this tragedy, hope survived and life went on. Four children were born during the hurricane. Five days after the town was virtually destroyed, Ernest A. Mayo, a lawyer running for prosecuting attorney, married Bessie Roberts in a ceremony at the Tremont Hotel. She had lost her parents and siblings; he had lost all his possessions. But they still had one another.

"You ask the *News* what is our estimate of Galveston's future and what the prospects are for building up the city," an editor from the *Galveston News* wrote soon after the storm. "Our wharves will be rebuilt, the sanitary conditions of the city will be perfected; new vigor and life will enter the community. . . . Galveston Island is still here, and here to stay."

That prediction came true. Galveston was rebuilt on higher ground, with a strong seawall. In the 100 years since the hurricane of 1900, storms have come and storms have gone, but Galveston remains. □ □

Spinning the Web: Go to **www.almanac.com** and click on **Article Links 2000** for Web sites related to this article. – *The Editors*

Galveston today, rebuilt on higher ground and protected by a seawall.

– Kevin Bartram

"We're looking for people

I F YOU WANT TO WRITE and see your work published, there's no better way to do it than writing books and stories for children and teenagers. Ideas flow naturally, right out of your own life. And while it's still a challenge, the odds of getting that first, unforgettable check from a children's publisher are better than they are from any other kind of publisher.

Your words will never sound as sweet as they do from the lips of a child reading your books and stories. And the joy of creating books and stories that truly reach young people is an experience you won't find anywhere else.

A surprisingly big market

But, that's not all. The financial rewards go far beyond most people's expectations, because there's a surprisingly big market out there for writers who are trained to tap it. More than $1.5 *billion* worth of children's books are purchased annually, and almost 500 publishers of books and 600 publishers of magazines related to children and teenagers buy freelance writing. That means that *there are thousands of manuscripts being purchased every month of the year!*

Yet two big questions bedevil nearly every would-be writer…"Am I really qualified?" and "How can I get started?"

"Am I really qualified?"

At the Institute of Children's Literature®, this is our definition of a "qualified person": someone with an aptitude for writing who can take constructive criticism, learn from it, and turn it into a professional performance.

To help us spot potential authors, we've developed a reliable test for writing aptitude based upon our 30 years of experience. It's free, and we don't charge for our evaluation. Those who pass are eligible to enroll and receive our promise:

You will complete at least one manuscript for submission to an editor or publisher by the time you finish the course.

You learn by corresponding with your own personal instructor—a nationally published writer or professional editor—in the privacy and comfort of your own home.

One-on-one training with your own instructor

Each relationship is tailored to the individual student's needs, yet every instructor works more or less the same way:

• When you're ready—at your own time and your own pace—you mail back each completed assignment.

• Your instructor reads it and rereads it to get everything out of it that you've put into it.

• Then he or she edits your assignment just the way a publishing house editor might—if he or she had the time.

Writing for Children and Teenagers is recommended for college credits by the Connecticut Board for State Academic Awards and approved by the Connecticut Commissioner of Higher Education.

The students' statements in this ad were provided voluntarily by them, without remuneration, from 1990 to 1998.

to write children's books"

• Your instructor mails it back to you with a detailed letter explaining his or her edits and tells you what your strong points and weaknesses are, and what you can do to improve.

It's a matter of push and pull. You push and your instructor pulls, and between you both, you learn how to write and how to market your writing.

"I hit pay dirt"

This method really works. The proof of the pudding is offered by our students.

"My first two attempts met with rejection, and on the third, I hit pay dirt with *Listen Magazine,*" says Marjorie Kashdin, East Northport, NY. "My instructor was invaluable...It's not everyone who has his own 'guardian editor!'"

"I was attracted by the fact that you require an aptitude test," says Nikki Arko, Raton, NM. "Other schools sign you up as long as you have the money to pay, regardless of talent or potential."

"...a little bird...has just been given...freedom"

"The course has helped me more than I can say," writes Jody Drueding, Boston, MA. "It's as if a little bird that was locked up inside of me has just been given the freedom of the garden."

Romy Squeri, Havertown, PA, says, "I met two of your students in my critique group and realized that they were the best writers there."

"I'd take the course again in a heartbeat!"

"I'd take the course again in a heartbeat!" says Tonya Tingey, Woodruff, UT. "It made my dream a reality."

"...it is comforting to know that there are still people out there who deliver what they promise," writes Meline Knago, Midland, TX. "The Institute is everything it says it is—and maybe even more."

Of course, not everyone gets published; we simply promise you the best training available.

FREE—Writing Aptitude Test and illustrated brochure

We offer a free Writing Aptitude Test to people who are interested in writing for children and teenagers, and we don't charge for our professional evaluation of it.

We also offer a free, illustrated brochure describing our course, *Writing for Children and Teenagers,* and introducing you to 64 of our instructors.

If your test reveals a true aptitude for writing, you'll be eligible to enroll. But that's up to you.

There is no obligation.

General Weather Forecast
1 9 9 9 - 2 0 0 0

(For detailed regional forecasts, see pages 136-155.)

Weather events will lead off the evening news more often than we'd like in the coming year, with record heat and cold, drought, floods, tornado outbreaks, and a couple of major hurricanes. Overall, the coming year will be warm, with below-normal precipitation in much of the country. Despite the abnormally large number of bouts with nature's worst, most of the time the weather will be favorable.

November through March will start relatively mild across much of the country. Temperatures will be well above normal in November and December in northern New England and in a broad east-to-west swath from the Ohio Valley to the West Coast. The Southeast and Florida will be significantly colder than normal in November and December. In January, cold air will dominate everywhere except the West Coast, the Desert Southwest, the northern Great Plains, and Texas. In February and March, well above normal temperatures will prevail in much of the eastern third of the country; the northern Great Plains, eastern Rockies, and West Coast will be colder than normal.

Precipitation will be above normal in the eastern Great Lakes and across the snowbelts of New York. Precipitation will be below normal along both coasts and in many interior locations in the South and West. **Snowfall** will be below normal in most of the country. Expect above-normal snowfall in northern New England, portions of the Great Lakes snowbelts, the southern Appalachians, a strip from Kansas City to central Illinois, the northern and central Rockies, and the Pacific Northwest.

For **millennium party-goers,** as the clock strikes midnight, the odds favor light snow across much of New England, with light rain from New York City to Washington, D.C., and westward to St. Louis. Elsewhere, expect dry weather, with relatively mild temperatures in the East and cold temperatures in much of the West.

April and May will bring warmer-than-normal temperatures to the eastern two thirds of the country, with relatively cool temperatures in the West. Rainfall will be above normal in portions of the South, central Great Plains, and West Coast. Watch for a major late-season snowstorm in the Rockies and foothills. Elsewhere, expect drier-than-normal weather.

June through August will be hotter than normal across most of the country. Expect an especially torrid summer from the eastern Rockies across the Great Plains, Great Lakes, and Ohio Valley all the way to the eastern seaboard from Virginia northward to New England. Elsewhere, temperatures will be near normal; the Pacific Northwest, Georgia, and Gulf Coast regions will be cooler than normal.

Rainfall will be well below normal through much of this period in the Northeast and Middle Atlantic states, with the potential for a drought. The drought will end with floods in August, as a couple of hurricanes threaten areas from North Carolina through New England. Dry weather will also bring drought to northern Florida, portions of the Ohio Valley, the Deep South, Texas, and Oklahoma.

September through October will be warmer than normal in northern New England, the Great Plains, the Deep South, the Tennessee and Ohio Valleys, the central Great Lakes, and the Desert Southwest. Elsewhere, temperatures should be normal or just below. Drought will continue in portions of the Deep South, Florida, Texas, and Oklahoma. The Pacific Northwest will experience excessive rain and flooding, and a mid-September hurricane will bring floods to the Northeast.

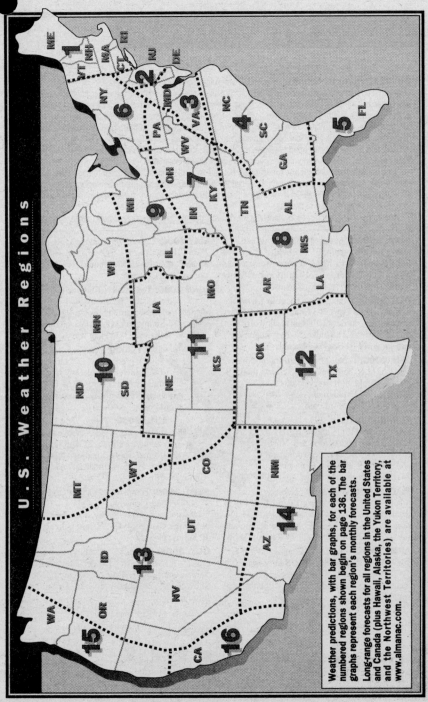

U.S. Weather Regions

Weather predictions, with bar graphs, for each of the numbered regions shown begin on page 136. The bar graphs represent each region's monthly forecasts.

Long-range forecasts for all regions in the United States and Canada (plus Hawaii, Alaska, the Yukon Territory, and the Northwest Territories) are available at www.almanac.com.

New England

SUMMARY: Overall, the coming winter will average close to normal in temperature and precipitation; snowfall will be above normal in the north but below normal elsewhere in the region. Although November and December will have some cold weather, most of the season will be relatively mild. Expect a big snowstorm in mid-December, but don't expect a January thaw — cold air will be persistent, capped by record low temperatures late in the month. Watch for a big snowstorm in early February, then relatively mild temperatures the rest of the month. March will be typical, with mild and cold air battling as spring takes hold.

April and May will start a trend toward warm and dry weather that could lead to a drought by midsummer. Both months will have above-normal temperatures and below-normal rainfall.

June through early August will be exceptionally hot and dry, with frequent heat waves. Temperatures will soar into the 90s everywhere in late July, with triple-digit temperatures setting records in some spots. A hurricane in mid-August will end the drought in eastern New England. Heavy rains throughout the region in late August will turn concerns from drought to flooding.

September will bring the season's last heat wave toward the middle of the month. October will be mild but wet.

NOV. 1999: Temp. 41° (2° below avg.; 1° above north); precip. 3" (1" below avg.). 1-8 Sunny, cool. 9-15 Mild, few showers. 16-18 Rain, then colder. 19-24 Chilly, rain; snow north. 25-30 Windy, cold, flurries.

DEC. 1999: Temp. 34° (3° above avg.); precip. 4.5" (1" above avg.). 1-3 Cold, snow. 4-8 Seasonable, few flurries. 9-15 Rain to snow. 16-18 Snowstorm. 19-23 Milder. 24-26 Colder, rain and snow. 27-31 Seasonable cold.

JAN. 2000: Temp. 23° (3° below avg.); precip. 1.5" (1.5" below avg.). 1-7 Snow, then clear and cold. 8-16 Very cold, flurries. 17-22 Moderating. 23-31 Snow, then record cold.

FEB. 2000: Temp. 29° (2° above avg.); precip. 4" (1" above avg.). 1-4 Rain, snow; then cold. 5-8 Northeaster. 9-18 Milder, occasional rain and snow. 19-23 Mild, some sun. 24-29 Colder, rain to snow.

MAR. 2000: Temp. 37° (1° below avg.); precip. 4" (0.5" above avg.). 1-5 Milder. 6-11 Rain, colder. 12-15 Cold, snow. 16-18 Heavy rain; snow north. 19-23 Colder, some rain and snow. 24-27 Sunny, mild. 28-31 Rain and snow.

APR. 2000: Temp. 51° (2° above avg.); precip. 2.5" (1" below avg.). 1-6 Sunny, warm. 7-10 Showers. 11-14 Cooler, some sun. 15-22 Rain, then cold. 23-30 Showers, then unseasonably warm.

MAY 2000: Temp. 59° (2° above avg.); precip. 2.5" (1" below avg.). 1-5 Clear, cool. 6-15 Seasonable, dry. 16-25 Hot, humid, few thunderstorms. 26-31 Cooler.

JUNE 2000: Temp. 68° (3° above avg.); precip. 2.5" (1" below avg.). 1-4 Coastal clouds, warm interior. 5-9 Rainy. 10-14 Sunny, hot. 15-22 Seasonable, few showers. 23-30 Heat wave.

JULY 2000: Temp. 75° (4° above avg.); precip. 2" (1.5" below avg.). 1-2 Showers, cool. 3-8 Hot, then thunderstorms, cool. 9-18 Hot, humid, hazy. 19-23 Cooler, showers. 24-31 Record heat.

AUG. 2000: Temp. 73° (3° above avg.); precip. 7" (3.5" above avg.). 1-5 Sunny, warm. 6-15 Hot, few thunderstorms. 16-18 Sizzling, then thunderstorms. 19-26 Warm; heavy rain. 27-31 Sunny, warm.

SEPT. 2000: Temp. 63° (2° above avg. north; 2° below south); precip. 3" (avg.). 1-4 Cooler. 5-10 Some rain. 11-14 Sunny, hot. 15-18 Thunderstorms, then cool. 19-25 Damp, dreary. 26-30 Sunny, pleasant.

OCT. 2000: Temp. 55° (2° above avg.); precip. 7" (3.5" above avg.). 1-3 Heavy rain. 4-9 Sunny, warm. 10-12 Rain, heavy south. 13-18 Showers. 19-24 Mainly dry. 25-31 Stormy; flooding rains.

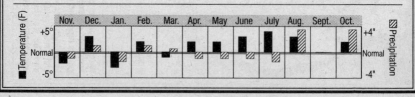

Greater New York–New Jersey

SUMMARY: November through March will be milder and drier than normal, with relatively little snow. Don't expect a January thaw, as the month will bring frequent cold spells. January will end with record cold following what will be the only big snowstorm of the season. Much of February and early March will be relatively mild. Winter will make a last gasp in mid-March, but overall we'll remember the winter as mild.

April and May will start a trend of above-normal temperatures and below-normal rainfall that will lead to a drought by midsummer.

June will start on the damp side, but the next widespread soaking rain will not come until August. Look for the first heat wave of the season in late June, with oppressive heat and humidity dominating July. Late June through July will be one of our hottest and driest periods in history. As July closes, many will wish for rain, but watch what you wish for. August will bring the possibility of two hurricanes, which would cause one of our rainiest months on record.

September will be more tranquil overall, despite the threat of another hurricane in midmonth. The first half of October will be stormy, with flooding rains; the second half, somewhat drier.

NOV. 1999: Temp. 44.5° (0.5° below avg.); precip. 3" (0.5" below avg.). 1-8 Sunny, cool. 9-12 Mild. 13-16 Heavy rain. 17-24 Seasonable, showers. 25-30 Sunny, chilly.

DEC. 1999: Temp. 37° (2° above avg.); precip. 4" (0.5" above avg.). 1-3 Cold, flurries. 4-13 Seasonable; rainy periods. 14-17 Flurries, cold. 18-22 Sunny, milder. 23-25 Rainy, windy, mild. 26-31 Few showers, mild.

JAN. 2000: Temp. 25° (4° below avg.); precip. 0.5" (2.5" below avg.). 1-7 Colder. 8-11 Cold; light snow. 12-16 Sunny, cold. 17-21 Seasonable, flurries. 22-26 Sunny, very cold. 27-31 Snowstorm, then record cold.

FEB. 2000: Temp. 35° (4° above avg.); precip. 4" (0.5" above avg.). 1-2 Rainy, milder. 3-5 Sunny, mild. 6-8 Rain to snow, colder. 9-15 Flurries, then sunny and milder. 16-19 Rain, then flurries and colder. 20-23 Cloudy, milder. 24-29 Heavy rain, colder.

MAR. 2000: Temp. 41.5° (1.5° above avg.); precip. 3" (0.5" below avg.). 1-6 Flurries, then mild. 7-11 Showers, mild. 12-14 Cold; light snow. 15-18 Heavy rain. 19-22 Colder; rain and snow. 23-28 Sunny, mild. 29-31 Seasonable.

APR. 2000: Temp. 53° (3° above avg.); precip. 2.5" (1" below avg.). 1-6 Sunny, warm. 7-10 Showers. 11-17 Sunny, then mild with showers. 18-23 Damp, chilly. 24-30 Sunny, hot.

MAY 2000: Temp. 61° (1° above avg.); precip.

2" (2" below avg.). 1-5 Seasonable; then cool, showers. 6-11 Warm. 12-16 Cool, then warming. 17-20 Hot, humid; thunderstorms. 21-31 Cool, then rain.

JUNE 2000: Temp. 70° (avg.); precip. 3.5" (1" below avg. north; 1" above south). 1-6 Windy, chilly; heavy rain. 7-13 Warm, dry. 14-22 Thunderstorms, hot; then cool. 23-30 Heat wave.

JULY 2000: Temp. 80° (5° above avg.); precip. 1" (3" below avg.). 1-5 Hot, humid; few thunderstorms. 6-11 Hot, hazy. 12-18 Hot, humid; searing sun. 19-26 Thunderstorms, cooler. 27-31 Oppressive heat and humidity.

AUG. 2000: Temp. 75.5° (2.5° above avg.); precip. 10" (6" above avg.). 1-5 Heavy thunderstorms, cooler. 6-9 Possible hurricane. 10-11 Sunny, warm. 12-15 Possible hurricane. 16-21 Thunderstorms, cooler. 22-26 Sunny, few showers. 27-31 Mostly dry.

SEPT. 2000: Temp. 65.5° (0.5° below avg.); precip. 2.5" (1" below avg.). 1-5 Sunny, cool. 6-9 Warm, dry. 10-12 Few thunderstorms. 13-16 Possible hurricane. 17-19 Rainy, cool. 20-26 Sunny, then rain. 27-30 Seasonable.

OCT. 2000: Temp. 57° (2° above avg.); precip. 6" (3" above avg.). 1-3 Rain. 4-8 Sunny, warm. 9-12 Flooding rains. 13-19 Cool, few showers. 20-24 Sunny, mild. 25-31 Rain, then cold.

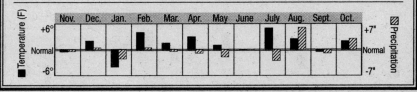

Middle Atlantic Coast

SUMMARY: November through March will be milder and drier than usual with below-normal snowfall. November and December will be close to normal in temperature but with little snowfall. January will bring winter's fury, with frequent cold spells and a snowstorm or two, particularly in the west and southeast. February and March will be relatively mild despite brief cold spells in early to mid-February and mid-March.

April and May will be warmer and drier than normal. Widely scattered thunderstorms will break out on many days in April. Expect the first heat wave of the season in late April, with a couple of hot spells in May.

June will start cool and damp, then turn sunny. A hot spell in late June will presage the month to come, one of the hottest and driest Julys in memory. High temperatures, high humidity, and sweltering sunshine will be the rule. The pattern is expected to change dramatically in August. Although the month will be hot, two hurricanes will threaten to make this one of the wettest Augusts on record.

September will bring a respite from heavy rain except for a possible hurricane in midmonth. October will be wet in the north, dry in the south.

NOV. 1999: Temp. 48° (1° below avg.); precip. 2" (1" below avg.). 1-6 Sunny, mild. 7-10 Sunny, mild. 11-15 Mild, damp. 16-24 Colder; showers then flurries. 25-28 Sunny. 29-30 Light rain and snow.

DEC. 1999: Temp. 40° (1° above avg.); precip. 3" (avg.). 1-3 Sunny, cold. 4-13 Seasonable; light rain. 14-17 Sunny, cold. 18-22 Sunny, mild. 23-25 Rainy, warm. 26-31 Mild, showers.

JAN. 2000: Temp. 30° (4° below avg.); precip. 1" (2" below avg.). 1-4 Sunny, cold. 5-8 Cold, some snow. 9-13 Sunny, cold. 14-17 Cold; light snow. 18-22 Cold. 23-26 Very cold. 27-31 Mild, then rain to snow.

FEB. 2000: Temp. 41° (4° above avg.); precip. 4.5" (1.5" above avg.). 1-2 Heavy rain. 3-5 Sunny, mild. 6-9 Rain to snow, then cold. 10-16 Mostly dry, cool. 17-29 Mild; frequent rain.

MAR. 2000: Temp. 47° (1° above avg.); precip. 3.5" (avg.). 1-3 Rain, then cold. 4-8 Warm, then showers. 9-14 Cold, rain to flurries. 15-19 Rain, then sun. 20-24 Showers, then sunny and cold. 25-31 Sun, turning warm.

APR. 2000: Temp. 60.5° (4.5° above avg.); precip. 3" (0.5" below avg.). 1-3 Thunderstorms, then cool. 4-9 Warm, thunderstorms. 10-18 Showers, warm east; chilly west. 19-24 Thunderstorms, then cool. 25-30 Dry, hot.

MAY 2000: Temp. 66° (1° above avg.); precip. 2.5" (1.5" below avg.). 1-4 Sunny, cool. 5-9 Hot; then rainy, cool. 10-14 Sunny. 15-20 Warm, thunderstorms. 21-23 Sunny, hot. 24-31 Thunderstorms, then delightful.

JUNE 2000: Temp. 72° (2° below avg.); precip. 3" (0.5" below avg.). 1-7 Cool; locally heavy thunderstorms. 8-13 Sunny. 14-20 Warm, few thunderstorms. 21-24 Sunny, pleasant. 25-30 Hot, humid.

JULY 2000: Temp. 83° (5° above avg.); precip. 2.5" (2" below avg.). 1-7 Warm, humid, few thunderstorms. 8-11 Hot, dry. 12-17 Heat wave, sizzling sun. 18-23 Hot, few thunderstorms. 24-26 Cool. 27-31 Hazy, hot, humid.

AUG. 2000: Temp. 78° (2° above avg.); precip. 9.5" (8" above avg. east; 2" above west). 1-5 Hot; then rain, cool. 6-9 Possible hurricane. 10-11 Sunny, warm. 12-14 Possible hurricane. 15-16 Sunny, hot. 17-20 Thunderstorms, then cool. 21-24 Sunny, hot. 25-31 Thunderstorms, then cool.

SEPT. 2000: Temp. 70.5° (0.5° above avg.); precip. 1.5" (2" below avg.). 1-5 Sunny, pleasant. 6-9 Thunderstorms, then cool. 10-12 Sunny, hot. 13-15 Possible hurricane. 16-20 Warm, showers. 21-30 Seasonable, showers.

OCT. 2000: Temp. 60° (1° above avg.); precip. 4" (2" above avg. north; 0.5" below south). 1-7 Showers. 8-10 Heavy rain. 11-18 Sunny, seasonable. 19-22 Gusty showers, then cool. 23-31 Warm, thunderstorms, then cold.

Baltimore

Washington

Richmond

Roanoke

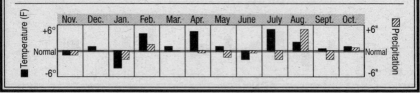

Honey, Garlic and Vinegar Better Than Prescription Drugs?

(SPECIAL) We know from scholars that ancient civilizations relied on their healing power for a wide variety of ailments. In fact, honey was so prized by the Romans for its medicinal properties that it was used instead of gold to pay taxes. Egyptian doctors believed garlic was the ultimate cure-all. And vinegar is said to have been used for everything from arthritis to obesity for thousands of years.

Today doctors and researchers hail the healing abilities of honey, garlic and vinegar as much more than folklore. Hundreds of scientific studies have been conducted on this dream team of healers. The results are conclusive on their amazing power to prevent and cure many common health problems.

These studies prove that this trio from nature's pharmacy can help **reduce blood pressure, lower cholesterol, improve circulation, lower blood sugar levels and help fight cancer.** Scientific evidence also indicates that they can be of medicinal value in the treatment of: **arthritis, athlete's foot, bronchitis, burns, colds and flu, cold sores, constipation, cramps, diarrhea, eczema, earaches, fatigue, fungus, heart problems, muscle aches, prostatitis, rheumatism, ringworm, sinus congestion, sore throat, urinary infections, virus and yeast infections and more.**

A new book called *Honey, Garlic & Vinegar Home Remedies*

is now available to the general public. It shows you exactly how to make hundreds of remedies using honey, garlic and vinegar separately and in unique combinations. Each preparation is carefully described along with the health condition for which it is formulated .

Learn how to prepare ointments, tonics, lotions, poultices, syrups and compresses in your own kitchen. Whip up a batch to treat:
- **ARTHRITIS:** Doctor reports that this remedy helps relieve the pain with no side effects
- **AGE SPOTS:** Watch them fade with this mixture
- **CORNS & CALLOUSES:** Get rid of them fast with this natural method
- **HEADACHE:** Enjoy fast relief without drugs
- **HEMORRHOIDS:** Don't suffer another day without this proven recipe
- **LEG CRAMPS:** Try this simple way to quick relief
- **MUSCLE ACHES:** Just mix up a batch of this and rub it on
- **STINGS & BITES:** Medical journals recommend this remedy to reduce pain and swelling fast
- **STOMACH PROBLEMS:** This remedy calms upset stomach and is noted in medical journals for ulcers
- **TOOTHACHE:** This remedy gives instant relief until you can get to the dentist
- **WEIGHT LOSS:** Secret reme-

dy speeds fat burn and flushes stubborn fat from hiding places

Discover all these health tips and more. You'll find: ***Dozens of easy-to-make beauty preparations for hair and skin, including a wrinkle smoother that really works. *Loads of delicious recipes using these health-giving super foods. *Tons of money-saving cleaning compounds to keep your home, car and clothing sparkling.**

Right now, as part of a special introductory offer, you can receive a special press run of the book *Honey, Garlic & Vinegar Home Remedies* for only $8.95 plus $1.00 postage and handling. Your satisfaction is 100% guaranteed. You must be completely satisfied, or simply return it in 90 days for a full refund — no questions asked.

HERE'S HOW TO ORDER: Simply print your name and address and the word "Remedies" on a piece of paper and mail it along with a check or money order for only $9.95 to: THE LEADER CO., INC., Publishing Division, Dept. HG880, P.O. Box 8347, Canton, Ohio 44711. (Make checks payable to The Leader Co., Inc.) VISA or MasterCard send card number and expiration date. Act now. Orders are filled on a first-come, first-served basis.

©2000 The Leader Co., Inc.

Piedmont and Southeast Coast

SUMMARY: November through March will be cooler and drier than normal. Above-average snowfall is expected, with major snowstorms in early December and mid-January. November through January will be colder than normal. February and March will be mild, but watch for a cold spell the second week of February and a late-season freeze in late March.

April and May will be warmer and drier than normal but with enough rain to avoid a significant drought.

June will be cool, with near-normal rainfall. The first heat wave of the season will start in late June, to remain with little relief through July. Rainfall in July will be above normal, with thunderstorms in the early part and second half of the month assuring adequate rainfall. The weather in August will be fairly typical across the south and west, with hot temperatures interrupted by cooling thunderstorms. In the northeast, a hurricane the second week of August will threaten the Outer Banks and even the Triangle.

September and October will be cooler and drier than normal, although another hurricane will threaten the Outer Banks in mid-September.

NOV. 1999: Temp. 53° (2° below avg.); precip. 4" (1" above avg.; avg. north). 1-4 Sunny; cold nights. 5-8 Sunny, pleasant. 9-15 Warm, rainy. 16-21 Cool, dry. 22-24 Heavy rain. 25-30 Sunny, cool.

DEC. 1999: Temp. 43° (3° below avg.; 0.5° below north); precip. 3" (1" below avg.). 1-3 Very cold, rain; snow north. 4-7 Cold, dry. 8-13 Chilly, rain. 14-17 Sunny, very cold. 18-23 Clouds and sun, warming. 24-28 Rain, cool. 29-31 Sunny, mild.

JAN. 2000: Temp. 37° (5° below avg.); precip. 3" (1" below avg.). 1-3 Sunny, cold. 4-9 Rain, then cold. 10-19 Cold, some rain and snow. 20-26 Sunny, cold. 27-31 Mild, showery; then cold.

FEB. 2000: Temp. 48° (4° above avg.); precip. 4" (0.5" above avg. north; 1" below south). 1-6 Mild, rain. 7-10 Sunny, cold. 11-16 Rain, then mild. 17-20 Showers, cool. 21-29 Warm; light rain north.

MAR. 2000: Temp. 55° (1° above avg.); precip. 2.5" (2" below avg.). 1-5 Thunderstorms, cool. 6-14 Warm south, rain north. 15-20 Seasonable, dry. 21-25 Some sun, late freeze. 26-31 Sunny, milder.

APR. 2000: Temp. 66° (4° above avg.); precip. 2.5" (1" below avg.). 1-4 Thunderstorms, then chilly. 5-10 Thunderstorms, mild. 11-15 Sunny, hot. 16-22 Thunderstorms, then cool. 23-30 Sunny, pleasant.

MAY 2000: Temp. 72° (2° above avg.); precip. 2" (1.5" below avg.). 1-5 Sunny, warm. 6-12 Seasonable, showers. 13-19 Warm, few thunderstorms. 20-24 Some sun, hot. 25-31 Sunny, warm.

JUNE 2000: Temp. 72° (4° below avg.); precip. 4" (avg.). 1-6 Showers, thunderstorms; cool. 7-12 Cool; light rain. 13-17 Seasonable, few thunderstorms. 18-22 Warm, few thunderstorms. 23-27 Sunny, warm. 28-30 Hot, thunderstorms.

JULY 2000: Temp. 80.5° (2° above avg. north; 1° below south); precip. 5.5" (1" above avg.). 1-6 Hot, humid, few thunderstorms. 7-11 Dry, very warm. 12-14 Hot, hazy. 15-21 Humid, thunderstorms. 22-31 Hot, few thunderstorms.

AUG. 2000: Temp. 79° (1° above avg.); precip. 2" (2" below avg.; 5" above northeast). 1-5 Hot. 6-9 Hot south, thunderstorms north. 10-13 Possible hurricane northeast. 14-17 Sunny, hot. 18-22 Thunderstorms, then cool. 23-31 Thunderstorms.

SEPT. 2000: Temp. 74° (avg.); precip. 1.5" (2" below avg.). 1-4 Sunny, warm. 5-12 Warm, few thunderstorms. 13-15 Hot south, possible hurricane northeast. 16-19 Sunny, hot. 20-22 Rain, cool. 23-30 Warm, dry.

OCT. 2000: Temp. 62.5° (1.5° below avg.); precip. 2" (1" below avg.). 1-7 Rain, cool. 8-15 Rain, then chilly. 16-22 Sunny, warmer. 23-31 Thunderstorms, then cold.

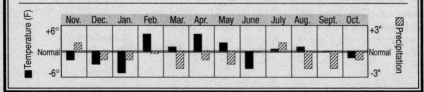

Florida

SUMMARY: Temperatures and rainfall will be below normal from November through March. November will be wetter than normal, with close to normal temperatures. December through February will average about 2 degrees colder than normal, with the greatest penetration of cold air in mid-January and early February. Early February will bring a freeze into central Florida, but the odds are against a severe freeze. Temperatures will warm up in late February, with warm and chilly weather alternating in March.

April and May will be warmer than normal, especially in the north, but below-normal rainfall will cause increasing concern. The best chance for a widespread soaking rain is in mid-May.

Although thunderstorms will occur in June, July, and August, overall activity will be slightly less than normal in most of the state. Temperatures will also be slightly below normal. Especially hot weather will occur in mid-August in the central and northern portions of the state and in mid-June and mid-July across the north. Although the hurricane season looks like it will be an active one, the main area threatened will be from the Carolinas into New England.

September and October will bring near-normal temperatures, with below-normal rainfall in the south but more rain than usual across the north.

NOV. 1999: Temp. 68° (avg.); precip. 3" (1" above avg.). 1-4 Sunny, cool. 5-10 Frequent rain. 11-14 Warm, few thunderstorms. 15-18 Cooler, few thunderstorms. 19-25 Sunny, seasonable. 26-30 Sunny, cool.

DEC. 1999: Temp. 59° (4° below avg.; avg. south); precip. 2" (0.5" below avg.). 1-7 Dry; frost north. 8-13 Chilly; occasional rain. 14-18 Sunny; cold nights. 19-31 Showers; then sunny, warm.

JAN. 2000: Temp. 57° (4° below avg.); precip. 2.5" (0.5" below avg.). 1-5 Sunny, seasonable. 6-10 Showers; then sunny, cold. 11-16 Showers; then sunny, seasonable. 17-21 Heavy thunderstorms, then cold. 22-25 Cold north, showers south. 26-31 Seasonable.

FEB. 2000: Temp. 63° (avg.; 3° above north); precip. 2" (1" below avg.). 1-5 Warm, then thunderstorms. 6-9 Very cold; possible freeze central. 10-14 Few showers. 15-21 Warmer; showers south. 22-29 Sunny, very warm.

MAR. 2000: Temp. 67° (avg.); precip. 2" (1.5" below avg.). 1-5 Sunny, cool. 6-16 Sunny, very warm. 17-25 Rainy, turning cold. 26-31 Dry, warmer.

APR. 2000: Temp. 73° (1° above avg.; 4° above north); precip. 1" (2" below avg.). 1-11 Warm north, seasonable south, few thunderstorms. 12-20 Sunny, hot north, seasonable south. 21-30 Sunny, warm days, comfortable nights.

MAY 2000: Temp. 78° (3° above avg. north; 0.5°

above south); precip. 3" (1" below avg.). 1-9 Sunny; heat wave north. 10-17 Warm, thunderstorms. 18-26 Hot, few thunderstorms. 27-31 Sunny, very warm.

JUNE 2000: Temp. 79° (1° below avg.); precip. 6" (3" below avg. north; 3" above south). 1-4 Sunny, very warm. 5-9 Thunderstorms south, showers north. 10-14 Heavy thunderstorms south. 15-21 Hot, few thunderstorms. 22-30 Hot, humid, few thunderstorms.

JULY 2000: Temp. 81° (1° below avg.); precip. 6" (1" below avg.). 1-10 Few thunderstorms, very warm. 11-20 More clouds than sun, daily thunderstorms. 21-31 More sun than clouds, daily thunderstorms.

AUG. 2000: Temp. 82.5° (0.5° above avg.); precip. 6" (1" below avg.). 1-3 Sunny, few thunderstorms. 4-8 Hot, few thunderstorms. 9-20 Very warm, daily thunderstorms. 21-26 Thunderstorms south and central, dry north. 27-31 Sunny, few thunderstorms.

SEPT. 2000: Temp. 81° (1° above avg.); precip. 6.5" (3" above avg. north; 2" below south). 1-13 Very warm; daily thunderstorms. 14-20 Hot north, few thunderstorms south and central. 21-25 Heavy rain north, dry south. 26-30 Heavy rain north, showers south.

OCT. 2000: Temp. 74° (1° below avg.); precip. 5" (1" below avg.). 1-8 Thunderstorms south, dry north. 9-15 Thunderstorms, then sunny and cool. 16-23 Pleasant. 24-31 Few showers.

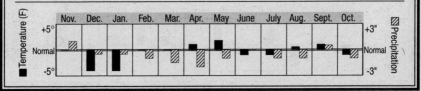

Upstate New York

SUMMARY: The coming winter will bring near-normal temperatures, with above-normal rainfall. Although snowfall in the snowbelts will be near or slightly above normal, elsewhere it is expected to be well below normal. November will be fairly typical, but December will be wetter and milder than normal, with heavy snow limited to the snowbelts. January will be very cold, especially at the middle and end of the month. February will be milder and rather wet. The best chance for a widespread snowstorm is in late March.

April and May will be warmer and drier than normal, with unseasonably hot weather in late April.

June through August will bring both drought and flooding. June and July will be hotter and drier than normal, with the hottest temperatures most likely in mid- and late June and in July. Record heat will occur in the second half of July, with the potential for drought. Widespread thunderstorms will help in early August, but a possible tropical storm in the second week, followed by more heavy rains, will bring flooding.

September will be fairly typical, but October will be as wet or wetter than August. Heavy rainstorms early and late in the month will bring flooding, with a cold spell late in the month.

NOV. 1999: Temp. 38° (1° below avg.); precip. 3" (0.5" below avg.). 1-8 Sunny, pleasant. 9-13 Mild, showers. 14-24 Colder, rain and snow. 25-30 Cold, snow.

DEC. 1999: Temp. 29° (2° above avg.); precip. 4.5" (1.5" above avg.). 1-8 Milder, flurries. 9-13 Rain, then cold, flurries. 14-18 Rain, cold; lake snows. 19-22 Sunny, milder. 23-31 Mild, rain.

JAN. 2000: Temp. 15° (6° below avg.); precip. 1.5" (1" below avg.). 1-5 Cold, flurries. 6-11 Cold, snow. 12-16 Very cold; lake snows. 17-21 Cold; occasional snow. 22-31 Bitter cold.

FEB. 2000: Temp. 27° (4° above avg.); precip. 4" (1.5" above avg.). 1-5 Snow to rain, mild. 6-9 Rain to snow, very cold. 10-13 Intermittent snow. 14-19 Mild, then rain to snow. 20-24 Mild, rainy. 25-29 Thunderstorms, colder.

MAR. 2000: Temp. 33° (avg.); precip. 4" (1" above avg.). 1-5 Cold, snow showers, then warmer. 6-10 Warmer, showers. 11-14 Cold, snow. 15-20 Seasonable, rain and snow. 21-24 Snowstorm. 25-28 Sunny, milder. 29-31 Rain, snow, then sunny.

APR. 2000: Temp. 51° (6° above avg.); precip. 2" (1" below avg.). 1-6 Rain and snow, then sunny, warm. 7-12 Showers, mild. 13-19 Showers, then pleasant. 20-23 Rainy, chilly. 24-30 Sunny, turning hot.

MAY 2000: Temp. 57° (1° above avg.); precip. 2.5" (1" below avg.). 1-5 Chilly, showers. 6-11 Seasonable. 12-18 Cool, then very warm. 19-21 Thunderstorms, then cooler. 22-25 Thunderstorms, warm. 26-31 Sunny and hot, then cooler with rain.

JUNE 2000: Temp. 67° (2° above avg.); precip. 1.5" (2" below avg.). 1-5 Warm west, showers east. 6-9 Cool, showers. 10-14 Sunny, hot. 15-20 Warm, thunderstorms. 21-24 Cool, then warmer. 25-30 Sunny, hot.

JULY 2000: Temp. 76° (5° above avg.); precip. 2.5" (2" below avg. east; avg. west). 1-5 Hot, dry. 6-8 Pleasant. 9-13 Hot, thunderstorms. 14-22 Cooler, then heat wave. 23-31 Very hot, thunderstorms.

AUG. 2000: Temp. 70.5° (2.5° above avg.); precip. 6" (2" above avg.; 6" above east). 1-5 Thunderstorms, then cooler. 6-9 Tropical rains possible. 10-12 Hot, humid. 13-15 Hot west, rain east. 16-21 Thunderstorms, then cooler. 22-26 Warm, thunderstorms. 27-31 Sunny, pleasant.

SEPT. 2000: Temp. 60° (1° below avg.); precip. 3.5" (avg.). 1-4 Sunny, cool. 5-10 Thunderstorms, warmer. 11-17 Sunny, hot, then cool. 18-22 Rainy, cool. 23-30 Rain, then pleasant.

OCT. 2000: Temp. 52° (2° above avg.); precip. 8" (5" above avg.). 1-3 Flooding rains. 4-7 Sunny, warm. 8-12 Flooding rains. 13-18 Dry, colder. 19-21 Rain, then flurries. 22-23 Warm. 24-31 Rain, colder.

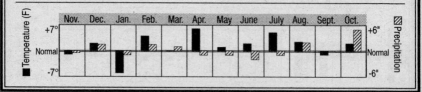

MACULAR DEGENERATION?

If you suffer symptoms of macular degeneration and are experiencing eye and vision problems, such as a gradual loss of clear focus, distorted vision, a gradual loss of color vision, or a dark or empty area in the center of your visual field, you should know about a new book called *The Macular Degeneration Handbook—Natural Ways to Prevent & Reverse It.*

The book contains a wealth of new information on this condition—what causes eye and vision problems, how to help halt and even reverse them, and how to protect yourself from macular degeneration and other eye problems.

The book gives you facts on the latest natural and alternative remedies and treatments that help improve your vision. You will learn all about these natural remedies and find out how and why they work.

You'll discover what to do to prevent and heal macular degeneration, what nutritional supplements may help, the best diet for healthy eyes, what chemicals to avoid to prevent further problems, and how specific over-the-counter and prescription drugs may contribute to the worsening of this condition.

The book also explains how your eyes work, basic eye care, ways to promote clear vision, how to cleanse your body of vision-destroying toxins, how to help heal and prevent glaucoma, cataracts, and retinal problems, and why over 12 million Americans suffer from macular degeneration.

Many people are putting up with vision loss due to macular degeneration and other eye problems because they are unaware of the new natural and alternative remedies, and the welcome help that is now available.

Get all the facts. *The Macular Degeneration Handbook* is available for only $12.95 *(plus $3 P&H)*. To order, send name and address with payment to United Research Publishers, Dept. FAV-2, 103 North Coast Highway 101, Encinitas, CA 92024. You may return the book within 90 days for a refund if you are not 100% satisfied.

IRRITABLE BOWEL SYNDROME?

If you want to get relief from irritable bowel syndrome, irritable colon and digestive problems—such as bloating, constipation, diarrhea, gas, stomach cramps, heartburn or pain and discomfort associated with foods—you should get a copy of the new book, *The Irritable Bowel Syndrome (IBS) & Gastrointestinal Solutions Handbook.*

The book reveals the latest natural, alternative and medical solutions to irritable bowel syndrome (IBS) and colon problems. The book reveals how virtually everyone can now control or end debilitating IBS, colon and digestive suffering, thanks to new scientific understandings of this problem.

Over 80 million people suffer from IBS or other digestive trouble. Many people are needlessly suffering because they are not aware of new ways to put an end to this misery. This book is of vital importance to anyone suffering IBS or digestive problems.

The book tells you what commonly causes IBS and digestive distress, how to alleviate symptoms, and how to prevent and protect yourself from future problems. The book reveals: ● what foods to avoid and what foods actually promote healing ● what you should know about gluten (found in grains) ● a simple natural way to stop painful spasms and relax the digestive tract ● how to clear up inflammation and promote healing and relief ● what you should know about peppermint oil ● why IBS is so often misdiagnosed by doctors.

The book explains in detail how the gastrointestinal tract works, how food is digested, why certain foods and activities cause difficulties, why some foods take up to 4 days to pass through your digestive tract, and why gastrointestinal problems are increasing at a startling rate.

Get all the latest facts. Put an end to this condition once and for all. The book is available for only $12.95 *(plus $3 P&H)*. To order, send name and address with payment to United Research Publishers, Dept. FAS-6, 103 North Coast Highway 101, Encinitas, CA 92024. You may return the book within 90 days for a refund if not completely satisfied. ◼

Greater Ohio Valley

SUMMARY: November through March will be milder and slightly drier than normal, with below-normal snowfall. November and December will be milder than normal, with mostly light snow in late November and mid-December. Although Thanksgiving will be white, Christmas will be mild and damp. January will be much colder, with widespread snow in the first ten days and with the coldest temperatures of the season late in the month. February and March will be milder than normal, despite a couple of cold spells. Expect unusually warm weather with heavy rain during February. March will be drier, with alternating warm and cold spells.

April and May will be warmer and drier than usual, with some very warm temperatures in late April.

June will be cooler than normal before a hot July and August. The season's first heat wave is expected in late June, with very hot temperatures in mid-July and record heat to close the month. August will have several hot spells. Expect below-normal rainfall from June through August, especially in the east, where a drought is possible. Although some thunderstorms will bring local downpours, for the most part, they will be scattered.

September and October will be typical, as temperatures gradually cool down. Look for the first widespread freeze in mid- to late October.

NOV. 1999: Temp. 47° (2° above avg.); precip. 1.5" (2" below avg.). 1-10 Sunny, pleasant. 11-15 Showers, warm. 16-21 Colder, showers, flurries. 22-24 Rain east, snow west. 25-30 Cold, flurries.

DEC. 1999: Temp. 39° (4° above avg.); precip. 4" (1" above avg.). 1-2 Sunny, cold. 3-12 Seasonable, showers, flurries. 13-17 Much colder, snow showers. 18-21 Some sun, milder. 22-24 Rainy, warm. 25-31 Mild, rain.

JAN. 2000: Temp. 24° (5° below avg.); precip. 1.5" (1" below avg.). 1-4 Colder. 5-10 Cold; occasional snow. 11-14 Cold, flurries. 15-21 Cold, snow showers. 22-26 Very cold, flurries. 27-31 Rain south, snow north, very cold.

FEB. 2000: Temp. 35° (3° above avg.); precip. 5" (2" above avg.). 1-5 Rain, then mild. 6-9 Snow, then colder. 10-15 Rain, becoming warm. 16-20 Rain, colder. 21-29 Warm, thunderstorms.

MAR. 2000: Temp. 44° (1° above avg.); precip. 3" (1" below avg.). 1-3 Cold, snow showers. 4-9 Dry, warm. 10-14 Thunderstorms, then colder with rain, snow. 15-17 Rain, then flurries. 18-24 Cold, snow. 25-31 Sunny, warmer.

APR. 2000: Temp. 59° (6° above avg.); precip. 3" (1" below avg.). 1-5 Sunny, cold then milder. 6-9 Warm, thunderstorms. 10-13 Sunny, warm. 14-19 Warm, thunderstorms. 20-25 Seasonable. 26-30 Sunny, warm.

MAY 2000: Temp. 63° (avg.); precip. 3.5" (0.5" below avg.). 1-9 Cooler, showers. 10-15 Sunny, warm. 16-19 Warm, thunderstorms. 20-22 Pleasant. 23-26 Thunderstorms, then sunny. 27-31 Sunny, warmer.

JUNE 2000: Temp. 69° (3° below avg.); precip. 2.5" (1" below avg.). 1-8 Chilly, showers. 9-15 Sunny, warmer. 16-20 Cooler, thunderstorms. 21-25 Sunny, warm. 26-30 Hot, some sun, afternoon thunderstorms.

JULY 2000: Temp. 81° (5° above avg.); precip. 4" (1" below avg. east; 1" above west). 1-4 Warm, humid, thunderstorms. 5-9 Sunny, dry. 10-15 Hot, humid; scattered thunderstorms. 16-25 Very warm, some sun, thunderstorms. 26-31 Hot.

AUG. 2000: Temp. 76° (2° above avg.); precip. 1.5" (2" below avg.). 1-5 Hot, thunderstorms. 6-9 Cooler, showers. 10-15 Hot, dry. 16-21 Thunderstorms, then cooler. 22-25 Turning hot, thunderstorms. 26-31 Sunny.

SEPT. 2000: Temp. 70° (2° above avg.); precip. 3.5" (1" below avg. east; 2" above west). 1-3 Sunny. 4-8 Hot, thunderstorms, then cooler. 9-15 Sunny, hot. 16-19 Rain. 20-25 Warm, showers. 26-30 Sunny.

OCT. 2000: Temp. 56° (avg.; 1° below west); precip. 3.5" (1" above avg.). 1-3 Heavy thunderstorms. 4-7 Sunny, cool. 8-14 Chilly, rainy. 15-18 Sunny, seasonable. 19-22 Rain, then freeze. 23-27 Warm, then rainy and cool. 28-31 Sunny.

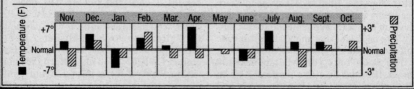

Deep South

SUMMARY: November through March will bring less rain and snow than normal, with dry weather in the south. Temperatures will be near normal in the east, milder in the west. The coldest temperatures will occur in mid-December, mid-January, early February, and late March. The best chance for snow or ice is in mid-December, January, and early February. November and December will be milder and drier than normal, followed by a cold January, then mild and dry weather in February and March.

Drought will be a problem in some areas in April and May, though locally heavy thunderstorms will prevent a widespread drought. Watch for hot weather in mid-April and early May.

Look for fairly normal weather from June through August, with hot days and scattered thunderstorms. Although thunderstorms in the south will cause local flooding, the north will remain quite dry. Heaviest rains in the south will occur in early and late July and early August. Temperatures from June through August will be near or slightly below normal in the north and a bit cooler than normal in the south. The hottest temperatures will be in late June, mid-July, and mid-August.

Expect above-normal rainfall in September to bring relief in the north while the south dries out. October will be drier than normal throughout the region.

NOV. 1999: Temp. 55° (1° above avg.); precip. 1.5" (2.5" below avg.). 1-9 Sunny, turning warmer. 10-14 Warm, showers. 15-20 Sunny, cool. 21-23 Warm, showers. 24-27 Sunny, seasonable. 28-30 Thunderstorms.

DEC. 1999: Temp. 45.5° (2° above avg. west; 1° below east); precip. 6" (1" above avg.). 1-5 Cool, showers. 6-11 Thunderstorms, then sunny, cold. 12-15 Cold, flurries northeast. 16-20 Sunny, warmer. 21-24 Warm, thunderstorms. 25-31 Rain, then sunny, warm.

JAN. 2000: Temp. 35° (4° below avg.); precip. 3.5" (1" below avg.; 2" above south). 1-5 Mild, rain south, flurries north. 6-9 Sunny, cold south; rain, snow north. 10-14 Rain south, snow north. 15-20 Sunny, cold. 21-25 Cold, rain south, flurry north. 26-31 Milder, then rain.

FEB. 2000: Temp. 45° (2° above avg.); precip. 2.5" (2" below avg.). 1-4 Rain, then sunny. 5-8 Rain, snow north, then cold. 9-13 Dry. 14-17 Colder, rain; snow northwest. 18-23 Warm, rainy. 24-29 Sunny, warm south, rain north.

MAR. 2000: Temp. 55° (2° above avg.); precip. 1" (3" below avg.; 1" above north). 1-4 Showers, cooler. 5-8 Sunny, hot. 9-13 Sunny, hot south, thunderstorms north. 14-17 Thunderstorms, colder. 18-24 Showers, then cold. 25-31 Milder, thunderstorms.

APR. 2000: Temp. 65° (2° above avg.); precip. 4" (1" above avg. east; 2" below west). 1-4 Pleasant north, thunderstorms south. 5-15 Warm, thunderstorms, then hot. 16-30 Warm, thunderstorms.

MAY 2000: Temp. 73° (2° above avg.); precip. 4.5" (avg.; 5" above central). 1-5 Hot, mainly dry. 6-15 Warm; local thunderstorms. 16-22 Warm, thunderstorms north. 23-31 Thunderstorms, then sunny.

JUNE 2000: Temp. 74° (4° below avg.); precip. 3.5" (avg.). 1-10 Cool, thunderstorms. 11-17 Sunny, warm. 18-30 Hot, humid, thunderstorms.

JULY 2000: Temp. 82° (2° above avg.; 1° below south); precip. 1.5" (2" below avg.; 3" above south). 1-6 Sunny, hot north, thunderstorms south. 7-18 Warm, thunderstorms. 19-26 Hot north, rain south. 27-31 Warm, showers.

AUG. 2000: Temp. 81° (1° above avg.); precip. 0.5" (2.5" below avg.; 3" above south). 1-6 Humid, showers. 7-11 Thunderstorms south, sunny north. 12-16 Sunny, hot. 17-24 Thunderstorms, then sunny. 25-31 Thunderstorms.

SEPT. 2000: Temp. 78° (4° above avg.); precip. 2" (2" above avg. north; 5" below south). 1-11 Sunny, warm. 12-17 Sunny, hot. 18-25 Thunderstorms north, hot south. 26-30 Sunny, warm.

OCT. 2000: Temp. 62° (2° below avg.); precip. 1" (2" below avg.). 1-6 Thunderstorms, then cooler. 7-14 Showers, then sunny. 15-18 Sunny, warmer. 19-24 Cooler, showers. 25-31 Sunny.

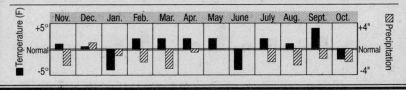

Chicago and Southern Great Lakes

SUMMARY: Another relatively mild winter is on the way, with temperatures from November through March averaging a little above normal, precipitation near normal, and snowfall below normal. November and December will be rather mild, with light snowfall. Snow will arrive for Christmas before the year ends mild and damp. January will be the only month that is colder than normal. Although lake snows will be more active, much of the region is expected to get below-normal amounts. February and March will bring milder weather again, especially mid- to late February, with some warm spells in March. Winter's heaviest general snowfall will come in late March.

April is expected to be exceptionally warm. May will also be warmer than normal, with heavy thunderstorms in midmonth.

June will start and end hot, but a couple of cool spells will leave temperatures near normal overall. July will be one of our hottest months on record, followed by a very hot August. Look for several new record high temperatures in the second half of July and the first half of August. Rainfall will be near or a bit below normal, with drought averted by a few heavy thunderstorms.

Temperatures will continue above normal in September and October, with record-setting heat in mid-September. October will start and end with rain, but much of midmonth will be dry.

NOV. 1999: Temp. 42° (2° above avg.); precip. 1.5" (1" below avg.). 1-5 Sunny, cool. 6-12 Rain, then sunny, mild. 13-17 Seasonable, showers. 18-24 Cool, rain; snow west. 25-30 Colder, some snow.

DEC. 1999: Temp. 32° (4° above avg.); precip. 3" (0.5" above avg.). 1-6 Seasonable, snow showers. 7-13 Rain and snow. 14-17 Colder, flurries. 18-21 Sunny, mild. 22-25 Rain, then colder, snow. 26-31 Very mild, rainy.

JAN. 2000: Temp. 19° (3° below avg.); precip. 1" (0.5" below avg.). 1-7 Mild, flurries, sprinkles. 8-15 Colder, flurries. 16-20 Cold, snow. 21-25 Flurries, very cold. 26-31 Cold, snow showers.

FEB. 2000: Temp. 28° (3° above avg.); precip. 2.5" (1" above avg.). 1-4 Cloudy, milder. 5-9 Colder; occasional snow. 10-13 Seasonable. 14-16 Mild, rainy. 17-19 Cooler, dry. 20-23 Mild, rain. 24-29 Warm, thunderstorms, then colder.

MAR. 2000: Temp. 38° (1° above avg.); precip. 1.5" (1" below avg.; 1" above east). 1-3 Cold, snow. 4-9 Sunny, warm. 10-14 Thunderstorms, then colder. 15-18 Mild, thunderstorms, then colder with snow. 19-23 Very cold, with snow. 24-31 Becoming sunny, mild.

APR. 2000: Temp. 57° (8° above avg.); precip. 2" (1" below avg.). 1-3 Sunny, cool. 4-7 Sunny, warm. 8-20 Warm, showers, thunderstorms. 21-25 Sunny, pleasant. 26-30 Record heat, then showers.

MAY 2000: Temp. 60.5° (1.5° above avg.); precip. 3.5" (avg.). 1-5 Showers, cool. 6-16 Sunny, pleasant. 17-19 Thunderstorms, warm. 20-24 Cooler, showers. 25-29 Sunny, pleasant. 30-31 Hot.

JUNE 2000: Temp. 70° (avg.); precip. 3" (1" below avg.). 1-5 Hot, then thunderstorms. 6-9 Chilly, showers. 10-14 Sunny, hot. 15-22 Thunderstorms, then sunny, cool. 23-30 Hot, humid, thunderstorms.

JULY 2000: Temp. 80° (6° above avg.); precip. 4" (1" above avg. west; 1" below east). 1-4 Hot, thunderstorms. 5-8 Sunny, warm. 9-13 Hot, humid, thunderstorms. 14-17 Sunny, hot, humid. 18-22 Thunderstorms, then record heat. 23-31 Very hot, thunderstorms.

AUG. 2000: Temp. 75° (3° above avg.); precip. 4.5" (1" above avg.; 1" below south). 1-2 Thunderstorms, cooler. 3-7 Some sun, warm. 8-10 Rain east, sunny west. 11-16 Record heat. 17-20 Thunderstorms, then sunny. 21-25 Hot, thunderstorms. 26-31 Sunny.

SEPT. 2000: Temp. 66° (2° above avg.); precip. 3.5" (avg.). 1-4 Sunny, hot. 5-9 Thunderstorms, cooler. 10-14 Record heat. 15-19 Thunderstorms, cooler. 20-24 Seasonable. 25-30 Very warm, then rain.

OCT. 2000: Temp. 53° (1° above avg.); precip. 4" (1" above avg.). 1-6 Rain, then sunny. 7-14 Cool, showery. 15-18 Sunny, milder. 19-25 Showers, chilly, then sunny. 26-31 Rain, colder.

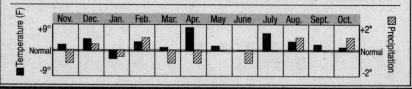

Northern Great Plains–Great Lakes

SUMMARY: November through March will be milder and drier than normal with below-normal snowfall. The season will start exceptionally mild, with temperatures well above normal in November and December. There will be periods of snow in mid-December, but just barely. January is expected to be colder than normal in the east, but a bit milder than normal in the west. February will be much colder than usual, with possible record low temperatures. March will bring rapid changes, veering from very cold to unseasonably mild spells and back again. No heavy snowstorms are expected during the season, with the best chance for widespread snow in late November, late December, late January, early and mid-February, and late March.

April and May will be very warm, with below-normal rainfall. Look for hot days from late April to mid-May.

June through August will be hotter and somewhat drier than normal, especially in late July and mid-August. Although rainfall will be a bit below normal, thunderstorms in mid-June, early and late July, and early August will avert a drought.

September and October will be fairly normal, with possible record hot temperatures toward mid-September. Look for very warm temperatures in mid-October. However, winter will gain the upper hand with cold temperatures and snow in late October.

NOV. 1999: Temp. 39° (7° above avg.); precip. 1" (0.5" below avg.). 1-9 Sunny, mild. 10-19 Very mild, sunny, then a shower. 20-26 Colder, snowy periods. 27-30 Seasonable, some sun.

DEC. 1999: Temp. 27° (8° above avg.); precip. 0.5" (0.5" below avg.). 1-7 Seasonable, flurries. 8-12 Mild, sun and clouds. 13-20 Sunny, very mild. 21-26 Seasonably cold, snow showers. 27-31 Sunny, cold.

JAN. 2000: Temp. 12.5° (2° below avg. east; 3° above west); precip. 1.5" (0.5" above avg.). 1-5 Some sun, cold. 6-10 Cold, snow showers east. 11-14 Sunny, very cold. 15-18 Occasional snow. 19-25 Very cold east, mild west. 26-31 Snowy periods.

FEB. 2000: Temp. 11° (5° below avg.); precip. 1" (avg.). 1-4 Cold, some snow. 5-9 Sunny, very cold. 10-12 Sunny, milder. 13-17 Snow and ice, very cold. 18-22 Very cold, snow showers. 23-29 Milder, then cold, flurries.

MAR. 2000: Temp. 26° (2° below avg.); precip. 1.5" (avg.). 1-5 Very cold, then very mild. 6-8 Mild, showers. 9-16 Much colder, flurries. 17-22 Some sun, record cold. 23-27 Sunny, warm. 28-31 Colder, rain to snow.

APR. 2000: Temp. 51° (7° above avg.); precip. 1" (1" below avg.). 1-7 Sunny, warm. 8-12 Warm, dry. 13-19 Cooler, thunderstorms east and central. 20-25 Sunny, very warm. 26-30 Hot, then showers, cooler.

MAY 2000: Temp. 59° (3° above avg.); precip. 2.5" (0.5" below avg.). 1-4 Chilly, showers. 5-10 Sunny, hot west. 11-17 Thunderstorms west, then sunny, hot. 18-23 Cooler, rainy. 24-31 Sunny, then thunderstorms.

JUNE 2000: Temp. 65° (avg.); precip. 3" (1" below avg.). 1-6 Chilly, rainy. 7-10 Sunny, warmer. 11-14 Warm, thunderstorms. 15-22 Warm, dry. 23-30 Hot, thunderstorms.

JULY 2000: Temp. 76° (3° above avg.); precip. 4.5" (1" above avg.). 1-6 Hot, thunderstorms. 7-15 Sunny, hot. 16-20 Thunderstorms, then cooler. 21-31 Hot, humid, thunderstorms.

AUG. 2000: Temp. 75° (4° above avg.); precip. 3" (0.5" below avg.). 1-5 Warm, thunderstorms. 6-10 Sunny, warm. 11-15 Hot, thunderstorms. 16-24 Hot west, thunderstorms east. 25-31 Sunny, hot.

SEPT. 2000: Temp. 59° (avg.); precip. 3.5" (0.5" above avg.). 1-4 Seasonable. 5-8 Showers, then cool. 9-12 Sunny, hot. 13-21 Showers, colder. 22-26 Sunny, becoming warmer. 27-30 Sunny west, showers east.

OCT. 2000: Temp. 48° (2° above avg.); precip. 1.5" (0.5" below avg.). 1-5 Sunny, warm. 6-16 Seasonable. 17-21 Showers, then very warm. 22-26 Colder, rain to snow. 27-31 Cold, flurries.

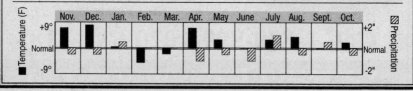

Central Great Plains

SUMMARY: Temperatures and precipitation will be fairly normal in the west from November through March, with a mild first half and cold second half, and slightly below-normal snowfall. In the east, temperatures will be slightly milder than normal, with near-normal precipitation and below-normal snowfall. Only in the central part of the region is above-normal snowfall expected. The coldest periods will be in mid- and late January and early February, with record cold in late March. The best chance for heavy snow is in late December, mid- and late January, mid-February, and mid-March.

April and May will be warmer than normal, especially in the east. A snowstorm will hit the west in early April. Rainfall will be above normal in central areas but below normal elsewhere.

June through August will be hotter than normal, with below-normal rainfall in most spots. The hottest temperatures will occur in late June, early and late July, and mid-August. June will be drier than normal, which will fuel concern of a summer drought, but widespread thunderstorms in late June, mid- and late July, and August will bring sufficient rainfall.

September will feature alternating hot and cooler periods, with heavy thunderstorms in midmonth. Mid-October will bring the first snow of the season in the west, with snow showers in many spots toward month's end.

NOV. 1999: Temp. 46° (5° above avg.); precip. 1.5" (1.5" below avg. east; avg. west). 1-12 Warm. 13-20 Warm west; showers east. 21-25 Snow west, sunny east. 26-30 Showers east, mild west.

DEC. 1999: Temp. 33° (4° above avg.); precip. 2.5" (0.5" above avg.). 1-8 Sunny west, flurries central, rain east. 9-13 Snow; sunny west. 14-20 Sunny, warmer. 21-24 Colder, rain east, snow west. 25-27 Milder. 28-31 Snow west; rain east.

JAN. 2000: Temp. 21° (3° below avg.); precip. 1" (avg.). 1-4 Cold west, mild east. 5-9 Cold, flurries. 10-16 Mild, then colder with snow. 17-20 Cold, flurries. 21-25 Milder west; cold, snow east. 26-31 Cold, snow.

FEB. 2000: Temp. 28° (2° above avg. east; 4° below west); precip. 2" (0.5" above avg.). 1-4 Sunny, milder. 5-8 Snow, cold. 9-12 Sunny, mild. 13-15 Snow west, rain east. 16-19 Sunny, cold, flurries. 20-23 Cold west, rain east. 24-29 Warmer, then rain.

MAR. 2000: Temp. 40° (avg.; 2° below west); precip. 1" (1" below avg.). 1-7 Turning warm. 8-12 Colder, rain and snow. 13-20 Much colder, snow. 21-31 Record cold, then warmer.

APR. 2000: Temp. 59° (7° above avg.; 3° above west); precip. 2" (1" below avg.). 1-4 Sunny, seasonable. 5-8 Warm, rain east, snow west. 9-13 Sunny, very warm east. 14-18 Pleasant west, thunderstorms east. 19-30 Warm, thunderstorms.

MAY 2000: Temp. 64° (2° above avg.); precip. 3.5" (0.5" below avg.; 2" above central). 1-4 Thunderstorms. 5-7 Sunny west, rain central and east. 8-15 Sunny, warm, rain west. 16-21 Showers. 22-24 Thunderstorms. 25-31 Warm, rain.

JUNE 2000: Temp. 70° (2° below avg.); precip. 3" (1" below avg.). 1-7 Cool, showers. 8-12 Sunny east, thunderstorms west. 13-16 Sunny, very warm. 17-30 Warm, then hot, thunderstorms.

JULY 2000: Temp. 81.5° (3.5° above avg.); precip. 3.5" (avg.). 1-14 Hot, thunderstorms. 15-19 Warm; heavy rain. 20-26 Record heat. 27-31 Thunderstorms.

AUG. 2000: Temp. 76.5° (1.5° above avg.); precip. 2.5" (1" below avg.; 1" above west). 1-7 Very warm, thunderstorms. 8-15 Hot, thunderstorms west. 16-19 Sunny, hot. 20-24 Thunderstorms west, sunny and hot east. 25-31 Warm, thunderstorms central.

SEPT. 2000: Temp. 68° (2° above avg.); precip. 4.5" (1.5" above avg.). 1-4 Sunny, hot. 5-8 Thunderstorms, cooler. 9-13 Sunny, hot. 14-18 Thunderstorms. 19-22 Cool, rainy. 23-25 Sunny, warm. 26-30 Sunny west, rain east.

OCT. 2000: Temp. 55° (2° below avg. east; 2° above west); precip. 2" (1" below avg.). 1-5 Showers east, then sunny and warm. 6-13 Cool, rainy east. 14-19 Colder with snow west, seasonable east. 20-24 Warmer, then showers. 25-31 Colder, rain and snow.

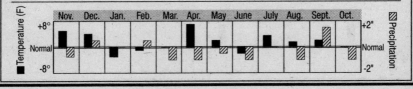

Texas–Oklahoma

SUMMARY: November through March will be milder and drier than normal, with below-normal snowfall in the north. Temperatures will average about 2 degrees above normal overall, and 4 degrees above normal in November and December. Coldest periods will occur in early and late December, the first half of January, mid-February, and mid- to late March. The best chance for snow in the north is in late December, early January, and mid-March. Rainiest periods are most likely in mid- to late December, mid- and late January, and mid-March.

April and May will be warmer than normal, with near-normal rainfall in the north and drier, sunnier than normal weather in the south.

The summer season will bring slightly cooler and drier weather than normal, with no major heat waves. Hottest periods will be in early, mid-, and late July, and early August. The usual thunderstorms will develop, but they will miss often enough to cause drought in some spots. The best chance for widespread thunderstorms is in early August. A hurricane in late August will pass south of the Valley but close enough to bring heavy rain.

September and October will bring near-normal temperatures but below-normal rainfall. The best chance for a soaking rain is in late September. Rainfall in mid-October will be especially sparse.

NOV. 1999: Temp. 60° (4° above avg.); precip. 1" (1" below avg.). 1-3 Sunny. 4-8 Sunny, showers south. 9-16 Showers east, then sunny. 17-22 Sunny, warm. 23-30 Sunny, warm; clouds south.

DEC. 1999: Temp. 53° (4° above avg.); precip. 0.5" (1" below avg.; 0.5" above north). 1-4 Seasonable. 5-7 Rain south, colder with snow north. 8-12 Sunny, cool. 13-19 Sunny, warmer. 20-25 Turning colder, rain south, snow north. 26-31 Warm, cloudy, showers.

JAN. 2000: Temp. 44° (1° below avg.; 1° above south); precip. 2.5" (1" above avg.). 1-6 Cloudy, cool, rain with snow north. 7-14 Cool, rainy, flurries north. 15-19 Rain south. 20-26 Sunny, mild. 27-31 Rain.

FEB. 2000: Temp. 51° (1° above avg.); precip. 0.5" (1" below avg.). 1-4 Sunny, cool. 5-8 Chilly, flurries north. 9-12 Sunny, milder. 13-18 Rain, then colder, flurries north. 19-22 Cloudy, warm. 23-29 Sunny, warm.

MAR. 2000: Temp. 57° (1° below avg. north; 1° above south); precip. 1.5" (1" below avg.). 1-4 Sunny and warm; rain south. 5-10 Sunny, warm. 11-17 Rain, snow north, then colder. 18-24 Showers, then record cold. 25-31 Sprinkles, turning cold.

APR. 2000: Temp. 70° (4° above avg.); precip. 2" (1" below avg.). 1-7 Clouds, thunderstorms. 8-16 Sunny, turning warm. 17-30 Scattered thunderstorms, then sunny and warm.

MAY 2000: Temp. 73° (1° above avg.); precip. 4.5" (2" above avg. north; 2" below south). 1-2 Sunny, warm. 3-7 Scattered thunderstorms. 8-16 Thunderstorms, sunny south. 17-20 Warm. 21-25 Showers, thunderstorms. 26-29 Sunny, warm. 30-31 Thunderstorms north.

JUNE 2000: Temp. 79° (1° below avg.); precip. 2.5" (1" below avg.). 1-5 Thunderstorms, sunny south. 6-9 Dry, cool. 10-15 Thunderstorms north, dry south. 16-22 Thunderstorms, then sunny and warm. 23-30 Sunny, thunderstorms east.

JULY 2000: Temp. 84° (avg.); precip. 2" (0.5" below avg.). 1-5 Sunny, hot. 6-12 Warm, thunderstorms. 13-31 Hot; scattered thunderstorms.

AUG. 2000: Temp. 82.5° (0.5° below avg.); precip. 2" (1" below avg.; 3" above south). 1-8 Hot, humid; widespread thunderstorms. 9-12 Sunny, hot. 13-16 Sunny, thunderstorms east. 17-28 Warm, thunderstorms. 29-31 Sunny, possible hurricane south.

SEPT. 2000: Temp. 78° (2° above avg.); precip. 3" (1" below avg.). 1-4 Sunny, very warm. 5-9 Humid, thunderstorms. 10-22 Thunderstorms, hot; cooler northwest. 23-30 Warm, thunderstorms south; cool, rain north.

OCT. 2000: Temp. 66° (1° below avg.); precip. 1" (2" below avg.). 1-7 Sunny, warm, then thunderstorms. 8-13 Sunny, cool. 14-21 Sunny, warm. 22-26 Showers, then sunny, cool. 27-31 Warmer, showers.

Map labels: Amarillo, Oklahoma City, Dallas, Houston, San Antonio

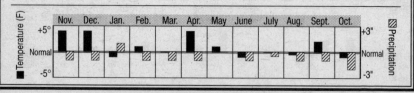

Blacklisted Cancer Treatment Could Save Your Life

Baltimore, MD—As unbelievable as it seems the key to stopping many cancers has been around for over 30 years. Yet it has been banned. Blocked. And kept out of your medicine cabinet by the very agency designed to protect your health—the FDA.

In 1966, the senior oncologist at St. Vincent's Hospital in New York rocked the medical world when he developed a serum that **"shrank cancer tumors in 45 minutes!"** 90 minutes later they were gone... Headlines hit every major paper around the world. Scientists and researchers applauded. Time and again this life saving treatment worked miracles, but the FDA ignored the research and hope he brought and shut him down.

You read that right. He was not only shut down—but also forced out of the country where others benefited from his discovery. That was 32 years ago. How many other treatments have they been allowed to hide?

Decades ago, European research scientist Dr. Johanna Budwig, a six-time Nobel Award nominee, discovered a totally natural formula that not only protects against the development of cancer, but has actually healed people all over the world diagnosed with incurable cancer. This is not conjecture or guesswork—but the results of scientific research.

After 30 years of study, Dr. Budwig discovered that the blood of seriously ill cancer patients was deficient in certain substances and nutrients. Yet, healthy blood always contained these ingredients. It was the lack of these nutrients that allowed cancer cells to grow wild and out of control.

By simply eating a combination of two natural and delicious foods (found on page 127) not only can cancer be prevented—but in case after case it was actually healed! "Symptoms of cancer, liver dysfunction, and diabetes were completely alleviated." Remarkably, what Dr. Budwig discovered was a totally natural way for eradicating cancer.

However, when she went to publish these results so that everyone could benefit—**she was blocked by manufacturers with heavy financial stakes!** For over 10 years now her methods have proved effective—yet she is denied publication—blocked by the giants who don't want you to read her words.

What's more, the world is full of expert minds like Dr. Budwig who have pursued cancer remedies and come up with remarkable natural formulas and diets that work for hundreds and thousands of patients. *How to Fight Cancer and Win* author William Fischer has studied these methods and revealed their secrets for you—so that you or someone you love may be spared the horrors of conventional cancer treatments.

As early as 1947, Virginia Livingston, M.D., isolated a cancer-causing microbe. She noted that every cancer sample analyzed (whether human or other animal) contained it.

This microbe—a bacteria that is actually in each of us from birth to death—multiplies and promotes cancer when the immune system is weakened by disease, stress, or poor nutrition. Worst of all, the microbes secrete a special hormone protector that short-circuits our body's immune system—allowing the microbes to grow undetected for years. No wonder so many patients are riddled with cancer by the time it is detected. But there is hope even for them...

Dr. Livingston has a delicious diet on page 76 of *How to Fight Cancer and Win* to help stop the formation of cancer cells and shrink tumors.

They walked away from traditional cancer treatments... and were healed! Throughout the pages of *How to Fight Cancer and Win* you'll meet real people who were diagnosed with cancer—suffered through harsh conventional treatments—only to be miraculously healed by natural means! Read their stories.

Skeptical but desperate... Magda W. "I was told by the most expert of doctors that I would have to be operated on to cut out the cancerous tumor that was causing a swelling under my eye. When I heard about Dr. Budwig's natural formula (as outlined in *How to Fight Cancer and Win*), I was skeptical but desperate for help. The doctors at the University hospital gave me many exhausting tests. One told me, "If I didn't have your previous x-rays and medical history in front of me, I wouldn't believe that you ever had cancer."

The Diet Saved my Life... When Scotty A. experienced blurred vision, loss of balance and coordination, plus a complete shutdown of his bladder, he went to a nearby medical research center for a series of tests. The examination showed arachnoidal bleeding due to a brain tumor. Scotty was discharged and sent home to die in peace. A friend told him of Dr. Budwig's formula. "After 8-weeks on the diet, I was able to walk unaided for the first time in months. My health improved so rapidly that I was soon able to return to my work part time. The Budwig diet saved my life!"

Prostate Cancer Reversed! Diagnosed with prostate cancer, Mr. I.M. began conventional treatments that included drugs, surgery, chemotherapy and radiation. He was in continual pain and vomited violently. After 5 years of enduring these harsh treatments, Mr. I.M. said enough! Then he began this special diet—and within 6 months he was no longer in pain.

Cervical Cancer Stopped! Miss G. was diagnosed as having cervical cancer at the young age of 27. As a nurse, she opted for traditional treatment of surgery—but the cancerous cells came back. Before giving up hope she turned to the diet in chapter 9—and 6 months later her doctor said her cancer was gone. He called it a "spontaneous remission!"

Less than 1 year to live...J.J. couldn't believe his ears when doctors told him he had less than a year to live. He tried chemotherapy. Experimental drugs. Intravenous injections—nothing was working and the treatments were worse than the disease. After so much suffering he began the diet in Chapter 9—after a year, blood tests showed no signs of cancer and the tumor in his neck had virtually disappeared.

Claim your book today and you will be one of the lucky few who no longer have to wait for cures that get pushed "underground" by big business and money-hungry giants.

To get your copy of *How to Fight Cancer and Win* call **1-888-821-3609** (ask for Dept. 1107) to order by credit card. Or write "Fight Cancer—Dept. 1107" on a plain piece of paper with your name, address, phone number (in case we have a question about your order) and a check for $19.95 plus $4.00 S&H (MD residents, add 5% sales tax) and mail to: **Agora Health Books, Dept. 1107, P.O. Box 977, Frederick, MD 21705-9938.**

If you are not completely satisfied, return the book within one year for a complete and total refund—no questions asked. This will probably be the most important information you and your loved ones receive—so order today!

© 1999 Agora Health Books

Rocky Mountains

SUMMARY: Winter will be colder and drier than normal, with near- to above-normal snowfall. After a mild November, temperatures from December through March will average about 4 degrees colder than normal. The coldest temperatures are expected in late December, January, and mid-February. Most spots will get two or three heavy snowstorms in late November, mid-January, late February, and late March.

The first half of April will be cold, with a chance of snow. Late April and early May will be milder, though perhaps cold enough in mid-May for a widespread snowstorm. Overall, both months will be about 3 degrees cooler than normal, with near-normal precipitation and above-normal snowfall.

June through August will be a bit hotter and drier than normal. Still, despite below-normal rainfall, thunderstorms will be frequent enough to avoid a drought in most spots. The best chance for substantial rains is in early to mid-June, mid-July, and mid-August. Expect hot days in early and mid-June, most of July, and August.

September and October will bring near-normal temperatures and precipitation as the countdown to winter begins. Expect a hot start to September, a pleasant end to the month, and showers and cool temperatures in between. The first real wintry chill is expected in late October.

NOV. 1999: Temp. 46° (4° above avg.); precip. 1.5" (0.5" above avg.). 1-5 Sunny, mild. 6-12 Mild, showers. 13-22 Sunny, rather mild. 23-30 Turning colder, heavy snow and rain.

DEC. 1999: Temp. 27° (1° below avg.); precip. 0.5" (0.5" below avg.). 1-3 Sunny. 4-6 Snow showers. 7-11 Turning colder. 12-20 Sunny, seasonably cold. 21-23 Very cold. 24-31 Cold, snow showers.

JAN. 2000: Temp. 21° (5° below avg.); precip. 0.5" (0.5" below avg.). 1-3 Sunny, cold. 4-9 Cold, flurries. 10-15 Snow, some heavy. 16-24 Sunny, cold. 25-31 Cold, periods of snow.

FEB. 2000: Temp. 25° (7° below avg.); precip. 0.5" (0.5" below avg.). 1-9 Sunny, cold, then milder. 10-14 Snow, then very cold. 15-19 Snow, cold east, some sun west. 20-24 Periods of snow. 25-29 Sunny, cold.

MAR. 2000: Temp. 36° (3° below avg.); precip. 1.5" (0.5" below avg.). 1-8 Sunny, turning milder. 9-16 Cold; occasional snow. 17-22 Mild west, cold east. 23-25 Sunny, milder. 26-31 Cold; locally heavy snow.

APR. 2000: Temp. 45° (3° below avg.); precip. 2" (avg.). 1-6 Cold, rain and snow. 7-11 Milder east, snow showers west. 12-17 Colder, rain, mountain snow. 18-21 Mild east, snow central and west. 22-30 Mild, rain.

MAY 2000: Temp. 54° (3° below avg.); precip. 2" (avg.). 1-7 Rain, then sunny, warm. 8-12 Colder, rain and snow. 13-16 Sunny, warm. 17-23 Warm, then cooler. 24-31 Warm, then cooler with showers and mountain snow.

JUNE 2000: Temp. 66° (avg.); precip. 1" (0.5" below avg.). 1-6 Sunny, hot. 7-12 Cooler, showers. 13-18 Sunny, turning hot. 19-30 Showers west, sunny and warm east.

JULY 2000: Temp. 72° (2° below avg.; 2° above east); precip. 1" (avg.). 1-5 Sunny, hot east, cool west. 6-11 Hot west, cool east, thunderstorms. 12-20 Sunny, hot; scattered thunderstorms. 21-31 Sunny, hot.

AUG. 2000: Temp. 74° (2° above avg.); precip. 0.5" (0.5" below avg.). 1-6 Sunny, hot days, mountain thunderstorms. 7-11 Hot, some sun, scattered thunderstorms. 12-16 Sunny, hot. 17-22 Warm; scattered thunderstorms. 23-31 Sunny, hot.

SEPT. 2000: Temp. 62° (1° below avg.); precip. 1" (avg.). 1-8 Sunny, hot. 9-15 Showers, then cool. 16-22 Rather cool, showers. 23-30 Sunny, pleasant.

OCT. 2000: Temp. 54° (1° above avg.); precip. 0.5" (0.5" below avg.). 1-4 Sunny, warm days; cold nights. 5-13 Sunny, warm. 14-23 Turning cooler, showers. 24-31 Mild, then colder with mountain snows.

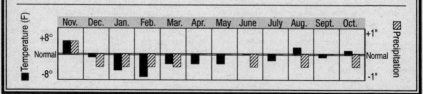

Desert Southwest

SUMMARY: November through March will be warmer and drier than normal. Most places that get snow will get less than usual. November will be warmer than normal, with showers only early and late in the month. Look for some cold periods in December, with showers limited to early and late in the month. January will be wetter, with showers possible during the first half of the month. Although cold temperatures are expected in the second half of January, the coldest weather of the season will hold off until mid-February. Late February and March will be quite a bit milder, with a cold spell in mid-March.

April and May will bring near-normal temperatures, with continued below-normal rainfall. The season's first hot weather is expected in late April, with several hot spells in May. The best chance for widespread rain is in mid- or late April, and in May in the east.

June through August will be a bit cooler than normal, with above-normal rainfall. Most spots will have to wait until early July for thunderstorms, when they will be scattered about the region until late August. Expect the hottest temperatures in early and mid-June, early July, and early September.

September and October will be warmer and a bit drier than normal, with the best chance for rain in mid- and late September. Anticipate chilly nights in the second half of October.

NOV. 1999: Temp. 62° (5° above avg.); precip. 0.1" (0.5" below avg.). 1-3 Sunny, seasonable. 4-8 Warm, showers. 9-17 Sunny, warm days. 18-22 Sunny, warm. 23-30 Very warm, showers.

DEC. 1999: Temp. 48° (avg.; 2° above east); precip. 0.5" (0.5" below avg.). 1-6 Cooler, showers, mountain snow. 7-13 Sun and clouds, cool. 14-18 Sunny, warm. 22-27 Sunny, cold. 28-31 Mild, showers.

JAN. 2000: Temp. 46° (1° below avg.); precip. 1.1" (0.5" above avg.). 1-5 Cool, showers. 6-9 Milder, showers. 10-15 Cold, rain, mountain snow. 16-20 Sunny, cold. 21-27 Mild. 28-31 Sunny, cold.

FEB. 2000: Temp. 50° (2° below avg.); precip. 0.2" (0.4" below avg.). 1-6 Sunny, cold. 7-10 Milder. 11-13 Showers, mild. 14-19 Record cold. 20-22 Cloudy, milder. 23-29 Mild, some sun.

MAR. 2000: Temp. 58° (avg.); precip. 0.2" (0.4" below avg.). 1-10 Sunny, mild. 11-17 Showers, then colder. 18-20 Sunny, warmer. 21-24 Colder, snow showers east. 25-31 Sunny; chilly nights.

APR. 2000: Temp. 66° (avg.); precip. 0" (0.4" below avg.). 1-11 Sunny, turning warmer. 12-18 Clouds, spot showers, then cooler. 19-24 Sunny, turning warmer. 25-30 Scattered showers, cool then hotter.

MAY 2000: Temp. 73° (1° below avg.); precip. 0" (0.3" below avg.). 1-5 Hot, then cooler, showers east. 6-11 Sunny, hot. 12-18 Warm, thunderstorms east. 19-23 Sunny, pleasant. 24-31 Hot, thunderstorms east, then cooler.

JUNE 2000: Temp. 84° (avg.); precip. 0.3" (avg.). 1-6 Sunny, hot. 7-9 Cooler. 10-15 Sunny, becoming hot. 16-19 Very hot, a shower east. 20-30 Sunny, warm.

JULY 2000: Temp. 86° (2° below avg.); precip. 2" (1" above avg.). 1-4 Sunny, hot. 5-12 Hot; scattered thunderstorms. 13-21 Warm, a few thunderstorms. 22-31 Hot; scattered thunderstorms.

AUG. 2000: Temp. 87° (avg.); precip. 1.5" (avg.). 1-7 Hot; scattered thunderstorms. 8-12 Rather hot, mostly dry. 13-17 Hot west, showers east. 18-24 Hot; scattered thunderstorms east, hot west.

SEPT. 2000: Temp. 83° (2° above avg.); precip. 1" (avg.). 1-5 Sunny, hot. 6-9 Hot, thunderstorms east. 10-14 Cooler; scattered thunderstorms. 15-21 Showers east. 22-25 Sunny, warm. 26-30 Scattered thunderstorms, turning cooler.

OCT. 2000: Temp. 73° (2° above avg.); precip. 0.4" (0.4" below avg.). 1-12 Sunny, warm. 13-18 Cloudy, turning cooler. 19-31 Sunny, warm days; crisp nights.

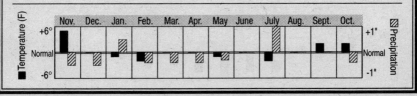

Pacific Northwest

SUMMARY: November through March will be cooler and a bit drier than normal, with some rain on most days and snowfall near or above normal. The stormiest periods are most likely in early November, the second and fourth weeks of December, mid-January, and early and mid-February. Accumulating snow will reach all the way to the coast in mid- to late February and early March. Temperatures from November through January will be above normal, then relatively cool in February and March.

April and May will be exceptionally cool, with temperatures 4 to 5 degrees below normal. April will be much rainier than normal, with a major storm to start the month. Rain in May will not be as heavy or as frequent.

Relatively cool weather will continue from June through August, with near-normal rainfall. The hottest temperatures will occur in early June, late July, and early and late August. The best chance for significant rainfall is in late June, early and late July, and mid-August.

September and October will be cooler and rainier than normal, with widespread rainfall in the second half of September and heavy rainstorms in early, mid-, and late October. Look for the last warm spell in mid-September, with colder temperatures prevailing by late October.

NOV. 1999: Temp. 50° (4° above avg.); precip. 6" (1" above avg. north; 1" below south). 1-7 Mild, rain. 8-12 Rain, some heavy. 13-19 Mild, showers north. 20-22 Mild, rain. 23-30 Colder, showers, mountain snow.

DEC. 1999: Temp. 42° (avg.); precip. 5" (1" below avg.; 1" above north). 1-6 Rainy, some sun. 7-10 Heavy rain, mild. 11-15 Sunny, colder. 16-23 Cold, rainy; snow inland. 24-27 Rainy, milder. 28-31 Colder, showers and flurries.

JAN. 2000: Temp. 43° (2° above avg.); precip. 4" (2" below avg.). 1-7 Chilly, showers, snow inland. 8-12 Rain, mountain snow. 13-19 Some sun, mild; rainy periods. 20-23 Occasional sun. 24-31 Rain, then showers.

FEB. 2000: Temp. 40° (4° below avg.); precip. 4" (0.5" below avg.). 1-3 Rain. 4-6 Cold, some sun. 7-12 Rain and snow. 13-16 Sunny, cold. 17-26 Rain turning to snow. 27-29 Sunny, cold.

MAR. 2000: Temp. 43° (4° below avg.); precip. 2.5" (1" below avg.). 1-3 Some sun, chilly. 4-9 Cold, rain and snow. 10-15 Sunny, cold. 16-20 Chilly, rainy, snow inland. 21-27 Rain, milder. 28-31 Sunny, pleasant.

APR. 2000: Temp. 45° (5° below avg.); precip. 4.5" (2" above avg.). 1-7 Stormy. 8-14 Chilly, rainy periods. 15-21 Cold, rain, snow inland. 22-27 Cool, showers. 28-30 Sunny, pleasant.

MAY 2000: Temp. 52° (4° below avg.); precip. 2" (avg.). 1-5 Sunny, pleasant, showers north. 6-11 Chilly, rainy. 12-19 Cool, sprinkles. 20-31 Chilly then milder, some rain.

JUNE 2000: Temp. 60.5° (2.5° below avg.); precip. 1.5" (avg.). 1-4 Sunny, hot. 5-11 Sunny, cool. 12-16 Dry, warmer. 17-26 Chilly, some showers. 27-30 Sun then clouds, cool.

JULY 2000: Temp. 65° (3° below avg.); precip. 1.5" (0.5" above avg.). 1-5 Cool, showers. 6-9 Sunny, warmer. 10-15 Showers, then sunny and cooler. 16-18 Sunny, warmer. 19-25 Cool, showers. 26-31 Sunny, becoming hot.

AUG. 2000: Temp. 68° (1° below avg.); precip. 0.5" (0.5" below avg.). 1-3 Hot, then a shower. 4-11 Sunny, pleasant. 12-16 Sunny and warm, showers north. 17-22 Sunny, pleasant. 23-26 Cool. 27-31 Sunny, turning hot.

SEPT. 2000: Temp. 61° (3° below avg.); precip. 2.5" (0.5" above avg.). 1-7 Sunny, pleasant. 8-12 Cool, showers. 13-17 Dry. 18-23 Warm, rainy periods. 24-30 Sunny, then rain.

OCT. 2000: Temp. 55° (1° below avg.); precip. 6.5" (3" above avg.). 1-5 Heavy rain. 6-18 Sunny periods, some showers. 19-21 Heavy rain. 22-24 Mild, showers. 25-31 Heavy rain, colder.

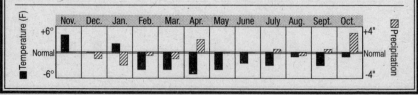

California

SUMMARY: November through March will be cooler and a bit drier than normal. Heavy rain is likely in early and late November. Watch for dense fog in the Valley in mid-November and through much of December. Elsewhere, December will be generally sunny despite rainy episodes to start and end the month. Watch for thunderstorms toward mid-January, with other rainy periods early and late in the month. February will be very sunny but with heavy rain in midmonth. March will be drier than usual, with showers early and late in the month.

April will bring nearly as much rain as February and March combined. May will start with rain, but the rest of the month will be dry, with some hot spells.

June through August will be almost normal, with the usual coastal clouds and fog, and nearly 100 percent of the possible sunshine in the Valley. The best chance for a shower is in late July. Hottest temperatures in the Valley will occur in late August, with other particularly hot spells in early June, mid- and late July, and early and mid-August. Look for record heat in coastal sections in late August, when temperatures in Los Angeles will soar well beyond the century mark.

September and October will be drier than normal, with near-normal temperatures.

NOV. 1999: Temp. 56° (avg. north; 2° above south); precip. 4" (1.5" above avg.). 1-3 Sunny, warm. 4-7 Heavy rain. 8-11 Sunny, then rain. 12-14 Sunny. 15-19 Cool north, warm south, dense fog in the Valley. 20-25 Sunny inland, coastal fog. 26-30 Rainy periods.

DEC. 1999: Temp. 48° (2° below avg.); precip. 2.5" (avg.). 1-4 Rainy. 5-20 Cool north, warm south, dense fog in the Valley. 21-24 Sunny, cool. 25-31 Rainy.

JAN. 2000: Temp. 47° (2° below avg.); precip. 3" (0.5" below avg. north; 1" above south). 1-3 Sunny, chilly. 4-6 Showers, thunderstorms. 7-9 Some sun. 10-14 Thunderstorms. 15-22 Sunny, cool. 23-27 Clouds, rain. 28-31 Sunny, chilly.

FEB. 2000: Temp. 50° (2° below avg.); precip. 1.5" (1.5" below avg.). 1-4 Sunny, cool. 5-10 Sun and clouds, warmer. 11-12 Rain. 13-19 Sunny, chilly. 20-22 Rain. 23-29 Sunny, cool.

MAR. 2000: Temp. 54° (1° below avg.); precip. 1" (1.5" below avg.). 1-6 Sunny, warm, then showers. 7-18 Sunny, cool. 19-22 Sunny, warmer. 23-31 Showers, then sunny and cooler.

APR. 2000: Temp. 56° (2° below avg.); precip. 2" (0.5" above avg.). 1-4 Sunny, pleasant. 5-8 Showers north, warm south. 9-10 Sunny. 11-17 Cool, rainy. 18-21 Sunny, then showers. 22-30 Chilly, showers, then milder.

MAY 2000: Temp. 62° (1° below avg.); precip. 0.6" (avg. north; 0.5" above south). 1-7 Rain, then sunny and warm. 8-11 Sunny, cool. 12-15 Sunny, hot. 16-22 Coastal clouds, sunny inland. 23-28 Hot, then cloudy and cool. 29-31 Sunny, hot.

JUNE 2000: Temp. 66° (1° below avg.); precip. 0" (0.1" below avg.). 1-4 Hot inland, coastal clouds. 5-11 Sunny and cooler inland, clouds and sun coast. 12-20 Sunny. 21-30 Cool, sun inland, coastal clouds.

JULY 2000: Temp. 69° (1° below avg.); precip. 0" (avg.). 1-5 Sunny, warm. 6-15 Sunny, rather hot. 16-25 Morning coastal fog, otherwise sunny and pleasant. 26-28 Sunny, hot. 29-31 Some sun, possible shower.

AUG. 2000: Temp. 72° (2° above avg.); precip. 0" (avg.). 1-14 Sunny and hot, cool north coast. 15-19 Hot in the Valley, cooler elsewhere. 20-24 Sunny, warm. 25-31 Heat wave.

SEPT. 2000: Temp. 66° (1° below avg.); precip. 0.1" (0.2" below avg.). 1-8 Cool sea breeze, hot elsewhere. 9-13 Cooler, sun and clouds. 14-30 Sunny and warm in the Valley, clouds and sun elsewhere.

OCT. 2000: Temp. 62° (1° above avg. north; 1° below south); precip. 0.3" (0.5" below avg.). 1-4 Sunny, hot inland. 5-10 Cooler, showers. 11-16 Cloudy, seasonable. 17-21 Coastal clouds, shower north, sunny elsewhere. 22-25 Sunny, very warm. 26-31 Cooler, perhaps a shower.

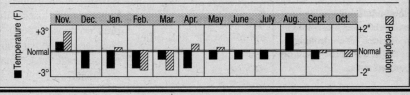

Bonemeal is a great bulb fertilizer, right? (Not really.) Poinsettias are toxic, aren't they? (Nope.) For real green-thumb wisdom, please read on.

by Doc and Katy Abraham

MYTH

A colder-than-normal winter will kill bugs in my garden so there will be fewer insect pests the following growing season.

FACT

■ If you think that cold weather kills bugs, you're mistaken. Insects are tough and will take all the cold that Mother Nature can give them. Some species' bloodstreams contain as much as 50 percent glycerol, a natural antifreeze!

MYTH

Homemade sprays are not as effective as store-bought pesticides for controlling insects in the garden and on houseplants.

FACT

■ In many cases, remedies you make yourself work just as well as the high-powered pesticides. Here is a USDA formula that is safe around pets and children, and good for the environment:

Add 1 teaspoon of liquid dishwashing detergent to 1 cup of cooking oil and shake vigorously. Add 1 cup of rubbing alcohol. Add 2 teaspoons of this mixture to 1 cup of plain water and shake well to emulsify. Pour into a spray or pump bottle and use at 10-day intervals, or more often, if needed.

Murphy's Oil Soap, used at a rate of ¼ cup per gallon of warm water, will kill whiteflies, mites, aphids, scale, and other pests.

MYTH

Certain plants can be grown in pots on decks and patios to repel mosquitoes.

FACT

■ We know of no plants that produce oils strong enough to repel mosquitoes any farther away than the surface of their leaves. If you rub the leaves of certain plants (rosemary, scented geraniums, and basil, among others) onto your skin, the oils and aromas can help discourage mosquitoes from biting you there, but it is a fallacy to think that any plant can "squirt" a mosquito repellent into the air.

Actually, your best defense against mosquitoes is the bat: Using its own radar, a bat can find and eat 500 mosquitoes an hour! (A bug zapper, by contrast, is worse than useless: It kills the very insects that prey on mosquitoes.) So build yourself a bat house to encourage these amazing creatures.

Why They're WRONG

MYTH

It is a good idea to buy lady beetles by the gallon to release into the greenhouse and garden.

FACT

■ Most beetles take flight a short time after being released, so it probably is not gardening money wisely spent. However, if you see lady beetles *(Hippodamia convergens)* in the home or garden, don't destroy them. They will eat all the aphids they can find.

MYTH

Oak leaves should be used as mulch on acid-loving plants.

FACT

■ Oak leaves are often singled out as beneficial for the acid-lovers, but they are not as acidic as many others. Even loads

of leaves rarely change the acidity to below 6.5, which is fine for most vegetables and ornamentals.

MYTH

Bonemeal makes a great bulb fertilizer.

FACT

■ Back in the old days, bonemeal *was* used for bulbs and all kinds of flowers and vegetables, and it did a good job. Today, bonemeal isn't what it used to be. Old-style bonemeal was made from bones, cartilage, and other tissue scraps and was a good source of nitrogen, phosphorus, and many micronutrients. Nowadays, bonemeal is made from bones that have been steamed to remove the nitrogen-rich marrow. What remains is mostly phosphorus. Steamed bonemeal is not a balanced fertilizer, but it will contribute phosphorus if worked into the root zone when planting bulbs.

MYTH

It's not a good idea to use wood ashes in your garden because they contain radiation.

FACT

■ Wood ashes are safe to use, and gardeners should have no fear of using them on vegetable gardens. Ashes *do* contain the naturally occurring radioactive isotope Potassium 40 (K40); this is a fact of nature that cannot be avoided. All living things on Earth contain K40, a compound that's been around since "day one" and is needed for growth.

Wood ashes are beneficial in that they act as a key to unlock soil nutrients so that plants can take them up. Very large quantities may make the soil too alkaline, but you can check for this with a soil test.

(c o n t i n u e d)

Poinsettias are toxic.

F A C T

■ Poinsettias are not toxic. Most poison control centers have taken poinsettias off their toxic-plant list, and the Humane Society no longer warns that they are toxic to pets. This doesn't mean you should make a poinsettia salad or encourage your pets to chew on your holiday plants (but why would you?).

MYTH

Green moss on the surface of the soil will kill houseplants.

F A C T

■ It's unsightly, but green moss is not harmful in itself. It is, however, a signal of poor drainage. Repot, adding perlite or sand to the soil mixture, and occasionally use the tines of a fork to loosen the soil surface.

MYTH

Allow houseplants to go dry before you water.

F A C T

■ Every time a plant wilts, it loses between one and four days of flowering life, according to Yoder Brothers, North America's largest grower of chrysanthemums. A safe rule is to keep the soil uniformly moistened, which will vary from plant to plant according to size of pot, exposure to heat and sun, humidity in your home, and the individuality of the plant. Do not water if the soil feels moist or soggy; *do* water as soon as it starts to dry out.

MYTH

Clay pots are better for houseplants than plastic or glazed pots.

F A C T

■ Any kind of pot is good as long as you don't overwater. Clay pots evaporate half the water you give them directly through their walls, so you are less likely to overwater and suffocate the plant's roots. Plants in plastic or glazed pots lose no water through the walls of the pot, so plants dry out more slowly.

If houseplants are in a variety of containers, don't automatically water them all at the same time, and never let a houseplant sit in water.

MYTH

It doesn't pay to use leftover seeds of flowers and vegetables.

F A C T

■ Most unused seeds remain viable for two or three years if stored in a cool, dry place in tightly sealed jars with a drying agent, or dessicant, of some kind. Our favorite drying agent? Powdered milk. Use one part seeds to one part powdered milk, and store in a tightly sealed glass jar. Lightweight plastic bags are not moistureproof.   □□

Doc and Katy Abraham's latest book is Green Thumb Wisdom *(published in 1996 by Storey Communications, Inc., Pownal, VT 05261).*

BE HONEST: Do You Know What pH Is?

Most gardeners (including us!) have barely a clue. Here's the scoop on this important fact about your soil. by Jon Vara

Ask a home gardener to name some key attributes of a successful garden and you'll probably hear about soil fertility, moisture, weed control, and choosing varieties well adapted to local conditions. But another equally important factor — the pH of the soil — may go unmentioned.

Many gardeners never have more than a vague, general idea of what soil pH is or how it can best be managed. And that's

The capital *H* represents the element hydrogen. The lowercase *p* stands for "power of," and the letters together are shorthand for "the negative logarithm of the hydrogen-ion concentration, or pH = -log[H+]." But you knew that.

too bad, because this is one area where a little knowledge can make a big difference. In short, if the pH is unsuitable, plants will do poorly no matter how well-tended they are in other respects.

So what *is* meant by the pH of a soil? Broadly speaking, it's a sort of chemical snapshot that reflects how acidic — or, less commonly, how alkaline — a given soil is at a given point in time. The letters *pH* aren't an abbreviation but a form of scientific notation in which the capital *H* represents the element hydrogen. The lowercase *p* stands for "power of," and the letters together are shorthand for "the negative logarithm of the hydrogen-ion concentration, or pH = -log[H+]." But you knew that.

Actually, you can live a perfectly normal life without understanding that the pH of a substance depends on the relative concentrations of two types of hydrogen ions: If the positive *cations* (pronounced kat-eye-ens) outnumber the negative *anions* (pronounced an-eye-ens), the substance is said to be acidic. If the anions predominate, it's said to be alkaline. If the two types of ions are perfectly balanced, the pH is said to be neutral.

Even if you never learn the difference between an anion and an onion, you should know that pH is measured on a

RANGE OF ALKALINITY

14.0
13.0
12.0
11.0
10.0
9.0
8.0
NEUTRAL — 7.0
6.0
5.0
4.0
3.0
2.0
1.0

RANGE OF ACIDITY

TREES AND SHRUBS

Apple	5.0 - 6.5
Ash	6.0 - 7.5
Azalea	4.5 - 6.0
Basswood	6.0 - 7.5
Beautybush	6.0 - 7.5
Beech	5.0 - 6.7
Birch	5.0 - 6.5
Blackberry	5.0 - 6.0
Blueberry	4.0 - 6.0
Boxwood	6.0 - 7.5
Cherry, sour	6.0 - 7.0
Chestnut	5.0 - 6.5
Crab apple	6.0 - 7.5
Currant, black	6.0 - 7.5
Currant, red	5.5 - 7.0
Dogwood	5.0 - 7.0
Elder, box	6.0 - 8.0
Fir, balsam	5.0 - 6.0
Fir, Douglas	6.0 - 7.0
Gooseberry	5.0 - 6.5
Hazelnut	6.0 - 7.0
Hemlock	5.0 - 6.0
Hickory	6.0 - 7.0
Hydrangea, blue-flowered	4.0 - 5.0
Hydrangea, pink-flowered	6.0 - 7.0
Juniper	5.0 - 6.0
Laurel, mountain	4.5 - 6.0
Lemon	6.0 - 7.5
Lilac	6.0 - 7.5
Maple, sugar	6.0 - 7.5
Oak, white	5.0 - 6.5
Orange	6.0 - 7.5
Peach	6.0 - 7.0
Pear	6.0 - 7.5
Pecan	6.4 - 8.0
Pine, red	5.0 - 6.0
Pine, white	4.5 - 6.0
Plum	6.0 - 8.0
Raspberry, red	5.5 - 7.0
Rhododendron	4.5 - 6.0
Spruce	5.0 - 6.0
Walnut, black	6.0 - 8.0
Willow	6.0 - 8.0

VEGETABLES

Asparagus	6.0 - 8.0
Bean, pole	6.0 - 7.5
Beet	6.0 - 7.5
Broccoli	6.0 - 7.0

pH Preferences of Selected Garden Crops, Trees, Shrubs, and Flowers

Brussels sprouts	6.0 - 7.5
Carrot	5.5 - 7.0
Cauliflower	5.5 - 7.5
Celery	5.8 - 7.0
Chives	6.0 - 7.0
Cucumber	5.5 - 7.0
Garlic	5.5 - 8.0
Kale	6.0 - 7.5
Lettuce	6.0 - 7.0
Pea, sweet	6.0 - 7.5
Pepper, sweet	5.5 - 7.0
Potato	4.8 - 6.5
Pumpkin	5.5 - 7.5
Radish	6.0 - 7.0
Spinach	6.0 - 7.5
Squash, crookneck	6.0 - 7.5
Squash, Hubbard	5.5 - 7.0
Tomato	5.5 - 7.5

FLOWERS

Alyssum	6.0 - 7.5
Aster, New England	6.0 - 8.0
Baby's-breath	6.0 - 7.0
Bachelor's button	6.0 - 7.5
Balloon flower	5.0 - 6.0
Bee balm	6.0 - 7.5
Begonia	5.5 - 7.0
Black-eyed Susan	5.5 - 7.0
Bleeding heart	6.0 - 7.5
Canna	6.0 - 8.0
Carnation	6.0 - 7.0
Chrysanthemum	6.0 - 7.5
Clematis	5.5 - 7.0
Coleus	6.0 - 7.0
Coneflower, purple	5.0 - 7.5
Cosmos	5.0 - 8.0
Crocus	6.0 - 8.0
Daffodil	6.0 - 6.5
Dahlia	6.0 - 7.5
Daisy, Shasta	6.0 - 8.0
Daylily	6.0 - 8.0
Delphinium	6.0 - 7.5
Foxglove	6.0 - 7.5
Geranium	6.0 - 8.0
Gladiolus	5.0 - 7.0
Hibiscus	6.0 - 8.0
Hollyhock	6.0 - 8.0
Hyacinth	6.5 - 7.5
Iris, blue flag	5.0 - 7.5
Lily-of-the-valley	4.5 - 6.0
Lupine	5.0 - 6.5
Marigold	5.5 - 7.5
Morning glory	6.0 - 7.5
Narcissus, trumpet	5.5 - 6.5
Nasturtium	5.5 - 7.5
Pansy	5.5 - 6.5
Peony	6.0 - 7.5
Petunia	6.0 - 7.5
Phlox, summer	6.0 - 8.0
Poppy, oriental	6.0 - 7.5
Rose, hybrid tea	5.5 - 7.0
Rose, rugosa	6.0 - 7.0
Snapdragon	5.5 - 7.0
Sunflower	6.0 - 7.5
Tulip	6.0 - 7.0
Zinnia	5.5 - 7.0

scale from 0 to 14, on which the neutral point occurs at exactly 7, with lower numbers representing increasing acidity and higher ones increasing alkalinity. The outer edges of the pH scale are the realm of substances such as battery acid and drain cleaner. Soils occupy a band near the center of the scale, ranging from a low of 4.5 or so to a high of about 9.5.

What to Do About pH

A pH of 6.5 is just about right for most home gardens, since most plants thrive in the 6.0 to 7.0 (slightly acidic to neutral) range. Some plants (blueberries, azaleas) prefer more strongly acidic soil, while a few do best in soil that is neutral to slightly alkaline (ferns, asparagus).

An accurate soil test will tell you where your pH currently stands and will specify the amount of lime or sulfur that is needed to bring it up or down to the appropriate level.

Soils in moist, temperate areas (most of the eastern half of the United States and Canada) tend to be moderately to strongly acidic, while those in very dry regions, such as the intermountain West, are often strongly alkaline and sometimes saline. Excess acidity is usually counteracted by applying finely ground limestone, and alkaline soils are frequently treated with gypsum (calcium sulfate) or ground sulfur.

Which of these should you add, and how much should you use? The most common approach is to collect a soil sample every other year or so and have it tested by a qualified soil-testing laboratory. (To find a laboratory in your area, call your county agricultural agent or the agriculture department of your state university.)

An accurate soil test will tell you where your pH currently stands and will specify the amount of lime or sulfur — or perhaps some other locally available soil amendment — that is needed to bring it up or down to the appropriate level. This information is essential, because the pH reading alone merely tells you where you are, not how to get where you want to be.

Why? Soils often have different needs even if their pH levels are identical. A highly acidic, sandy soil with a pH of 4.5, for example, might require 5 pounds of lime per 100 square feet to bring it into the 6.5 to 7.0 range, whereas a clay or muck soil with the same initial pH of 4.5 might require the addition of 15 pounds or more to accomplish the same result. This is because coarse-grained (sandy) soils that contain little organic matter respond to the action of lime or sulfur much more readily than fine-grained (clay or muck) soils that are rich in organic matter.

But no matter what kind of soil you have to work with, make a habit of keeping an eye on its pH level and tweaking it back into line as necessary. You'll be repaid with a garden that's healthier, more vigorous, and just plain more rewarding. And chemistry aside, that's what gardening is all about. ☐☐

Spinning the Web: Go to **www.almanac.com** and click on **Article Links 2000** for Web sites related to this article. – *The Editors*

Pollution
Disease
Corruption
Poverty
Civil Unrest
Terrorism
Drugs
Natural Disaster
Social Decay
War

Read about God's solution to atrocities that plague our world and his wonderful plan for mankind in this free booklet:

"Why God Permits Evil"

Call toll-free **1-800-234-DAWN**

or send your request to:

The Bible Answers
Dept. F-Box 60, General Post Office
New York, NY 10116

Your Fresh Fruits and Vegetables Need Water!

FREE INFO!

Now, find all the water you need with a water well you drilled yourself!

Since 1962, thousands of happy gardeners and homeowners around the world have discovered the **Hydra-Drill™** secret. They drilled their own wells and their gardens prove it! You can, too. Call or write us today and we'll send you a big, free package of information about drilling your own well with the **Hydra-Drill™**. We carry everything you need for your home water requirements, including pumps, tanks, and water purification products. We can even have your water tested for you.

Ask about our "How To..." video!

Call Today for FREE Water Well Drilling Information Package

1-800-333-7762
(Ask for Operator 8292)

DeepRock 8292 Anderson Road
Opelika, AL 36802

☐ **YES!** Send the **FREE INFORMATION PACKAGE** and the illustrated guide **HOW TO DRILL YOUR OWN WATER WELL.**

Print Name

Address

City/State/Zip

Phone (must have)   © 1995 DeepRock

Outdoor Planting Table

2 0 0 0

■ The best time to plant flowers and vegetables that bear crops above ground is during the *light* of the Moon; that is, from the day the Moon is new to the day it is full. Flowering bulbs and vegetables that bear crops below ground should be planted during the *dark* of the Moon; that is, from the day after it is full to the day before it is new again. The Moon Favorable columns at right give these Moon days, which are based on the Moon's phases for 2000 and the safe periods for planting in areas that receive frost. Consult **page 166** for dates of frosts and lengths of growing seasons. See the **Left-Hand Calendar Pages 60-86** for the exact days of the new and full Moons.

Aboveground Crops Marked (*)

(E) means Early   (L) means Late

* Barley	
* Beans	(E)
	(L)
Beets	(E)
	(L)
* Broccoli Plants	(E)
	(L)
* Brussels Sprouts	
* Cabbage Plants	
Carrots	(E)
	(L)
* Cauliflower Plants	(E)
	(L)
* Celery Plants	(E)
	(L)
* Collards	(E)
	(L)
* Corn, Sweet	(E)
	(L)
* Cucumber	
* Eggplant Plants	
* Endive	(E)
	(L)
* Flowers	(All)
* Kale	(E)
	(L)
Leek Plants	
* Lettuce	
* Muskmelon	
Onion Sets	
* Parsley	
Parsnips	
* Peas	(E)
	(L)
* Pepper Plants	
Potato	
* Pumpkin	
Radish	(E)
	(L)
* Spinach	(E)
	(L)
* Squash	
Sweet Potatoes	
* Swiss Chard	
* Tomato Plants	
Turnips	(E)
	(L)
* Watermelon	
* Wheat, Spring	
* Wheat, Winter	

Planting Dates	Moon Favorable	Planting Dates	Moon Favorable	Planting Dates	Moon Favorable	Planting Dates	Moon Favorable
2/15-3/7	2/15-19, 3/6-7	3/15-4/7	3/15-19, 4/4-7	5/15-6/21	5/15-18, 6/2-16	6/1-30	6/2-16
3/15-4/7	3/15-19, 4/4-7	4/15-30	4/15-18	5/7-6/21	5/7-18, 6/2-16	5/30-6/15	6/2-15
8/7-31	8/7-15, 8/29-31	7/1-21	7/1-16	6/15-7/15	6/15-16, 7/1-15	—	—
2/7-29	2/20-29	3/15-4/3	3/20-4/3	5/1-15	5/1-3	5/25-6/10	5/25-6/1
9/1-30	9/14-26	8/15-31	8/16-28	7/15-8/15	7/17-29	6/15-7/8	6/17-30
2/15-3/15	2/15-19, 3/6-15	3/7-31	3/7-19	5/15-31	5/15-18	6/1-25	6/2-16
9/7-30	9/7-13, 9/27-30	8/1-20	8/1-15	6/15-7/7	6/15-16, 7/1-7	—	—
2/11-3/20	2/11-19, 3/6-19	3/7-4/15	3/7-19, 4/4-15	5/15-31	5/15-18	6/1-25	6/2-16
2/11-3/20	2/11-19, 3/6-19	3/7-4/15	3/7-19, 4/4-15	5/15-31	5/15-18	6/1-25	6/2-16
2/15-3/7	2/20-3/5	3/7-31	3/20-31	5/15-31	5/19-31	5/25-6/10	5/25-6/1
8/1-9/7	8/16-28	7/7-31	7/17-29	6/15-7/21	6/17-30, 7/17-21	6/15-7/8	6/17-30
2/15-3/7	2/15-19, 3/6-7	3/15-4/7	3/15-19, 4/4-7	5/15-31	5/15-18	6/1-25	6/2-16
8/7-31	8/7-15, 8/29-31	7/1-8/7	7/1-16, 7/30-8/7	6/15-7/21	6/15-16, 7/1-16	—	—
2/15-29	2/15-19	3/7-31	3/7-19	5/15-6/30	5/15-18, 6/2-16	6/1-30	6/2-16
9/15-30	9/27-30	8/15-9/7	8/15, 8/29-9/7	7/15-8/15	7/15-16, 7/30-8/15	—	—
2/11-3/20	2/11-19, 3/6-19	3/7-4/7	3/7-19, 4/4-7	5/15-31	5/15-18	6/1-25	6/2-16
9/7-30	9/7-13, 9/27-30	8/15-31	8/15, 8/29-31	7/1-8/7	7/1-16, 7/30-8/7	—	—
3/15-31	3/15-19	4/1-17	4/4-17	5/10-6/15	5/10-18, 6/2-15	5/30-6/20	6/2-16
8/7-31	8/7-15, 8/29-31	7/7-21	7/7-16	6/15-30	6/15-16	—	—
3/7-4/15	3/7-19, 4/4-15	4/7-5/15	4/7-18, 5/4-15	5/7-6/20	5/7-18, 6/2-16	5/30-6/15	6/2-15
3/7-4/15	3/7-19, 4/4-15	4/7-5/15	4/7-18, 5/4-15	6/1-30	6/2-16	6/15-30	6/15-16
2/15-3/20	2/15-19, 3/6-19	4/7-5/15	4/7-18, 5/4-15	5/15-31	5/15-18	6/1-25	6/2-16
8/15-9/7	8/15, 8/29-9/7	7/15-8/15	7/15-16, 7/30-8/15	6/7-30	6/7-16	—	—
3/15-4/7	3/15-19, 4/4-7	4/15-30	4/15-18	5/7-6/21	5/7-18, 6/2-16	6/1-30	6/2-16
2/11-3/20	2/11-19, 3/6-19	3/7-4/7	3/7-19, 4/4-7	5/15-31	5/15-18	6/1-15	6/2-15
9/7-30	9/7-13, 9/27-30	8/15-31	8/15, 8/29-31	7/1-8/7	7/1-16, 7/30-8/7	6/25-7/15	7/1-15
2/15-4/15	2/20-3/5, 3/20-4/3	3/7-4/7	3/20-4/3	5/15-31	5/19-31	6/1-25	6/1, 6/17-25
2/15-3/7	2/15-19, 3/6-7	3/1-31	3/6-19	5/15-6/30	5/15-18, 6/2-16	6/1-30	6/2-16
3/15-4/7	3/15-19, 4/4-7	4/15-5/7	4/15-18, 5/4-7	5/15-6/30	5/15-18, 6/2-16	6/1-30	6/2-16
2/1-29	2/1-4, 2/20-29	3/1-31	3/1-5, 3/20-31	5/15-6/7	5/19-6/1	6/1-25	6/1, 6/17-25
2/20-3/15	3/6-15	3/1-31	3/6-19	5/15-31	5/15-18	6/1-15	6/2-15
1/15-2/4	1/21-2/4	3/7-31	3/20-31	4/1-30	4/1-3, 4/19-30	5/10-31	5/19-31
1/15-2/7	1/15-20, 2/5-7	3/7-31	3/7-19	4/15-5/7	4/15-18, 5/4-7	5/15-31	5/15-18
9/15-30	9/27-30	8/7-31	8/7-15, 8/29-31	7/15-31	7/15-16, 7/30-31	7/10-25	7/10-16
3/1-20	3/6-19	4/1-30	4/4-18	5/15-6/30	5/15-18, 6/2-16	6/1-30	6/2-16
2/10-29	2/20-29	4/1-30	4/1-3, 4/19-30	5/1-31	5/1-3, 5/19-30	6/1-25	6/1, 6/17-25
3/7-20	3/7-19	4/23-5/15	5/4-15	5/15-31	5/15-18	6/1-30	6/2-16
1/21-3/1	1/21-2/4, 2/20-3/1	3/7-31	3/20-31	4/15-30	4/19-30	5/15-6/5	5/19-6/1
10/1-21	10/14-21	9/7-30	9/14-26	8/15-31	8/16-28	7/10-31	7/17-29
2/7-3/15	2/7-19, 3/6-15	3/15-4/20	3/15-19, 4/4-18	5/15-31	5/15-18	6/1-25	6/2-16
10/1-21	10/1-13	8/1-9/15	8/1-15, 8/29-9/13	7/17-9/7	7/30-8/15, 8/29-9/7	7/20-8/5	7/30-8/5
3/15-4/15	3/15-19, 4/4-15	4/15-30	4/15-18	5/15-6/15	5/15-18, 6/2-15	6/1-30	6/2-16
3/23-4/6	3/23-4/3	4/21-5/2	4/21-5/2	5/15-6/15	5/19-6/1	6/1-30	6/1, 6/17-30
2/7-3/15	2/7-19, 3/6-15	3/15-4/15	3/15-19, 4/4-15	5/1-31	5/4-18	5/15-31	5/15-18
3/7-20	3/7-19	4/7-30	4/7-18	5/15-31	5/15-18	6/1-15	6/2-15
1/20-2/15	1/21-2/4	3/15-31	3/20-31	4/7-30	4/19-30	5/10-31	5/19-31
9/1-10/15	9/14-26, 10/14-15	8/1-20	8/16-20	7/1-8/15	7/17-29	—	—
3/15-4/7	3/15-19, 4/4-7	4/15-5/7	4/15-18, 5/4-7	5/15-6/30	5/15-18, 6/2-16	6/1-30	6/2-16
2/15-29	2/15-19	3/1-20	3/6-19	4/7-30	4/7-18	5/15-6/10	5/15-18, 6/2-10
10/15-12/7	10/27-11/11, 11/25-12/7	9/15-10/20	9/27-10/13	8/11-9/15	8/11-15, 8/29-9/13	8/5-30	8/5-15, 8/29-30

Frosts and Growing Seasons

Courtesy of National Climatic Center

■ Dates given are normal averages for a light freeze (32° F); local weather and topography may cause considerable variations. The possibility of frost occurring after the spring dates and before the fall dates is 50 percent. The classification of freeze temperatures is usually based on their effect on plants, with the following commonly accepted categories: **Light freeze:** 29° to 32° F — tender plants killed; little destructive effect on other vegetation. **Moderate freeze:** 25° to 28° F — widely destructive effect on most vegetation; heavy damage to fruit blossoms and tender and semihardy plants. **Severe freeze:** 24° F and colder — heavy damage to most plants.

CITY	Growing Season (days)	Last Frost Spring	First Frost Fall	CITY	Growing Season (days)	Last Frost Spring	First Frost Fall
Mobile, AL	272	Feb. 27	Nov. 26	North Platte, NE	136	May 11	Sept. 24
Juneau, AK	133	May 16	Sept. 26	Las Vegas, NV	259	Mar. 7	Nov. 21
Phoenix, AZ	308	Feb. 5	Dec. 15	Concord, NH	121	May 23	Sept. 22
Tucson, AZ	273	Feb. 28	Nov. 29	Newark, NJ	219	Apr. 4	Nov. 10
Pine Bluff, AR	234	Mar. 19	Nov. 8	Carlsbad, NM	223	Mar. 29	Nov. 7
Eureka, CA	324	Jan. 30	Dec. 15	Los Alamos, NM	157	May 8	Oct. 13
Sacramento, CA	289	Feb. 14	Dec. 1	Albany, NY	144	May 7	Sept. 29
San Francisco, CA	*	*	*	Syracuse, NY	170	Apr. 28	Oct. 16
Denver, CO	157	May 3	Oct. 8	Fayetteville, NC	212	Apr. 2	Oct. 31
Hartford, CT	167	Apr. 25	Oct. 10	Bismarck, ND	129	May 14	Sept. 20
Wilmington, DE	198	Apr. 13	Oct. 29	Akron, OH	168	May 3	Oct. 18
Miami, FL	*	*	*	Cincinnati, OH	195	Apr. 14	Oct. 27
Tampa, FL	338	Jan. 28	Jan. 3	Lawton, OK	217	Apr. 1	Nov. 5
Athens, GA	224	Mar. 28	Nov. 8	Tulsa, OK	218	Mar. 30	Nov. 4
Savannah, GA	250	Mar. 10	Nov. 15	Pendleton, OR	188	Apr. 15	Oct. 21
Boise, ID	153	May 8	Oct. 9	Portland, OR	217	Apr. 3	Nov. 7
Chicago, IL	187	Apr. 22	Oct. 26	Carlisle, PA	182	Apr. 20	Oct. 20
Springfield, IL	185	Apr. 17	Oct. 19	Williamsport, PA	168	Apr. 29	Oct. 15
Indianapolis, IN	180	Apr. 22	Oct. 20	Kingston, RI	144	May 8	Sept. 30
South Bend, IN	169	May 1	Oct. 18	Charleston, SC	253	Mar. 11	Nov. 20
Atlantic, IA	141	May 9	Sept. 28	Columbia, SC	211	Apr. 4	Nov. 2
Cedar Rapids, IA	161	Apr. 29	Oct. 7	Rapid City, SD	145	May 7	Sept. 29
Topeka, KS	175	Apr. 21	Oct. 14	Memphis, TN	228	Mar. 23	Nov. 7
Lexington, KY	190	Apr. 17	Oct. 25	Nashville, TN	207	Apr. 5	Oct. 29
Monroe, LA	242	Mar. 9	Nov. 7	Amarillo, TX	197	Apr. 14	Oct. 29
New Orleans, LA	288	Feb. 20	Dec. 5	Denton, TX	231	Mar. 25	Nov. 12
Portland, ME	143	May 10	Sept. 30	San Antonio, TX	265	Mar. 3	Nov. 24
Baltimore, MD	231	Mar. 26	Nov. 13	Cedar City, UT	134	May 20	Oct. 2
Worcester, MA	172	Apr. 27	Oct. 17	Spanish Fork, UT	156	May 8	Oct. 12
Lansing, MI	140	May 13	Sept. 30	Burlington, VT	142	May 11	Oct. 1
Marquette, MI	159	May 12	Oct. 19	Norfolk, VA	239	Mar. 23	Nov. 17
Duluth, MN	122	May 21	Sept. 21	Richmond, VA	198	Apr. 10	Oct. 26
Willmar, MN	152	May 4	Oct. 4	Seattle, WA	232	Mar. 24	Nov. 11
Columbus, MS	215	Mar. 27	Oct. 29	Spokane, WA	153	May 4	Oct. 5
Vicksburg, MS	250	Mar. 13	Nov. 18	Parkersburg, WV	175	Apr. 25	Oct. 18
Jefferson City, MO	173	Apr. 26	Oct. 16	Green Bay, WI	143	May 12	Oct. 2
Fort Peck, MT	146	May 5	Sept. 28	Janesville, WI	164	Apr. 28	Oct. 10
Helena, MT	122	May 18	Sept. 18	Casper, WY	123	May 22	Sept. 22
Blair, NE	165	Apr. 27	Oct. 10	*Frosts do not occur every year.			

Gardening by the Moon's Sign

■ It is important to note that *the placement of the planets through the signs of the zodiac is not the same in astronomy and astrology.* The *astrological* placement of the Moon, by sign, is given in the table below. (The *astronomical,* or actual, placement is given in the **Left-Hand Calendar Pages, 60-86.**)

For planting, the most fertile signs are the three water signs: Cancer, Scorpio, and Pisces. Good second choices are Taurus, Virgo, and Capricorn.

Weeding and plowing are best done when the Moon occupies the sign of Aries, Gemini, Leo, Sagittarius, or Aquarius. Insect pests can also be handled at these times. Transplanting and grafting are best done under a Cancer, Scorpio, or Pisces Moon. Pruning is best done under an Aries, Leo, or Sagittarius Moon, with growth encouraged during waxing (from the day of new to the day of full Moon) and discouraged during waning (from the day after full to the day before new Moon). (The dates of the Moon's phases can be found on **pages 60-86.**) Clean out the garden shed when the Moon occupies Virgo so that the work will flow smoothly. Fences and permanent beds can be built or mended when Capricorn predominates. Avoid indecision when under the Libra Moon.

Moon's Place in the Astrological Zodiac

	NOV. 1999	DEC. 1999	JAN. 2000	FEB. 2000	MAR. 2000	APR. 2000	MAY 2000	JUNE 2000	JULY 2000	AUG. 2000	SEPT. 2000	OCT. 2000	NOV. 2000	DEC. 2000
1	LEO	VIR	SCO	SAG	CAP	PSC	ARI	TAU	CAN	VIR	LIB	SCO	CAP	AQU
2	VIR	LIB	SCO	CAP	AQU	PSC	ARI	GEM	CAN	VIR	SCO	SAG	CAP	AQU
3	VIR	LIB	SAG	CAP	AQU	ARI	TAU	GEM	LEO	VIR	SCO	SAG	AQU	PSC
4	LIB	SCO	SAG	AQU	AQU	ARI	TAU	CAN	LEO	LIB	SAG	CAP	AQU	PSC
5	LIB	SCO	CAP	AQU	PSC	ARI	GEM	CAN	VIR	LIB	SAG	CAP	AQU	ARI
6	LIB	SAG	CAP	AQU	PSC	TAU	GEM	LEO	VIR	SCO	SAG	CAP	PSC	ARI
7	SCO	SAG	CAP	PSC	ARI	TAU	CAN	LEO	LIB	SCO	CAP	AQU	PSC	ARI
8	SCO	SAG	AQU	PSC	ARI	GEM	CAN	VIR	LIB	SAG	CAP	AQU	ARI	TAU
9	SAG	CAP	AQU	ARI	TAU	GEM	LEO	VIR	SCO	SAG	AQU	PSC	ARI	TAU
10	SAG	CAP	PSC	ARI	TAU	CAN	LEO	LIB	SCO	SAG	AQU	PSC	TAU	GEM
11	SAG	CAP	PSC	TAU	TAU	CAN	VIR	LIB	SCO	CAP	AQU	PSC	TAU	GEM
12	CAP	AQU	PSC	TAU	GEM	LEO	VIR	SCO	SAG	CAP	PSC	ARI	GEM	CAN
13	CAP	AQU	ARI	GEM	GEM	LEO	VIR	SCO	SAG	AQU	PSC	ARI	GEM	CAN
14	AQU	PSC	ARI	GEM	CAN	VIR	LIB	SCO	CAP	AQU	ARI	TAU	GEM	LEO
15	AQU	PSC	TAU	CAN	CAN	VIR	LIB	SAG	CAP	AQU	ARI	TAU	CAN	LEO
16	AQU	ARI	TAU	CAN	LEO	LIB	SCO	SAG	CAP	PSC	ARI	GEM	CAN	VIR
17	PSC	ARI	GEM	LEO	LEO	LIB	SCO	CAP	AQU	PSC	TAU	GEM	LEO	VIR
18	PSC	ARI	GEM	LEO	VIR	LIB	SAG	CAP	AQU	ARI	TAU	CAN	LEO	LIB
19	ARI	TAU	CAN	LEO	VIR	SCO	SAG	CAP	PSC	ARI	GEM	CAN	VIR	LIB
20	ARI	TAU	CAN	VIR	LIB	SCO	SAG	AQU	PSC	TAU	GEM	LEO	VIR	SCO
21	TAU	GEM	LEO	VIR	LIB	SAG	CAP	AQU	PSC	TAU	CAN	LEO	LIB	SCO
22	TAU	GEM	LEO	LIB	SCO	SAG	CAP	PSC	ARI	TAU	CAN	LEO	LIB	SCO
23	GEM	CAN	VIR	LIB	SCO	SAG	AQU	PSC	ARI	GEM	LEO	VIR	SCO	SAG
24	GEM	CAN	VIR	SCO	SCO	CAP	AQU	PSC	TAU	GEM	LEO	VIR	SCO	SAG
25	CAN	LEO	LIB	SCO	SAG	CAP	AQU	ARI	TAU	CAN	LEO	LIB	SAG	CAP
26	CAN	LEO	LIB	SAG	SAG	AQU	PSC	ARI	GEM	CAN	VIR	LIB	SAG	CAP
27	LEO	VIR	LIB	SAG	CAP	AQU	PSC	TAU	GEM	LEO	VIR	SCO	SAG	CAP
28	LEO	VIR	SCO	SAG	CAP	AQU	ARI	TAU	CAN	LEO	LIB	SCO	CAP	AQU
29	VIR	LIB	SCO	CAP	CAP	PSC	ARI	GEM	CAN	VIR	LIB	SAG	CAP	AQU
30	VIR	LIB	SAG	—	AQU	PSC	TAU	GEM	LEO	VIR	SCO	SAG	AQU	PSC
31	—	SCO	SAG	—	AQU	—	TAU	—	LEO	LIB	—	SAG	—	PSC

A Month-by-Month Astrological Timetable for 2000

■ The following yearlong chart is based on the Moon's sign and shows the most favorable times each month for certain activities. *by Celeste Longacre*

	JAN.	FEB.	MAR.	APR.	MAY	JUNE	JULY	AUG.	SEPT.	OCT.	NOV.	DEC.
Give up smoking	21, 22, 25, 26	4, 22	3, 30	3, 26	1, 24, 28	20, 25	17, 22	18, 27	15, 24	21, 25	17, 21	14, 18
Begin diet to lose weight	21, 22, 25, 26	4, 22	3, 30	3, 26	1, 24, 28	20, 25	17, 22	18, 27	15, 24	21, 25	17, 21	14, 18
Begin diet to gain weight	8, 9, 13, 14	9, 18	7, 16	12, 17	9, 14	6, 10	3, 7	4, 13	10, 27	7, 12	3, 8	1, 6, 28
Cut hair to encourage growth	15, 16	11, 12	10, 11	6, 7, 17	14, 15	10, 11	7, 8	4, 5, 31	1, 2, 28	9, 10	6, 7	8, 9
Cut hair to discourage growth	25, 26	22, 23	21	29, 30	3, 31	27, 28	24, 25	21, 22	17, 18	14, 15	21, 22	18, 19
Have dental care	23, 24	20, 21	18, 19	14, 15	12, 13	12, 13	5, 6	1, 2	25, 26	23, 24	19, 20	16, 17
End old projects	4, 5	3, 4	4, 5	2, 3	2, 3	1, 2	29, 30	27, 28	25, 26	25, 26	23, 24	9, 10
Start new projects	7, 8	6, 7	7, 8	5, 6	5, 6	3, 4	2, 3	30, 31	28, 29	28, 29	26, 27	12, 13
Entertain	21, 22	18, 19	16, 17	12, 13	9, 10	6, 7	3, 4, 31	1, 2, 27, 28	24, 25	20, 21	17, 18	14, 15
Go camping	3, 4, 30	27, 28	25, 26	21, 22	19, 20	15, 16	12, 13	8, 9, 10	5, 6	2, 3, 4, 30	26, 27	23, 24
Plant above-ground crops	10, 11, 19	7, 8, 16	14, 15	10, 11	7, 8, 16, 17	4, 5, 12, 13	10, 11	6, 7	2, 3, 12, 30	9, 10, 28	6, 7	3, 4, 30, 31
Plant below-ground crops	1, 28, 29	24, 25	5, 22, 23	19, 20, 29, 30	26, 27	22, 23	20, 21, 28, 29	16, 17, 25, 26	21, 22	18, 19	15, 16, 23, 24	12, 13, 21, 22
Destroy pests and weeds	13, 14	9, 10	7, 8	4, 5	1, 2, 28, 29	25, 26	22, 23	18, 19	15, 16	12, 13	8, 9	6, 7
Graft or pollinate	19, 20	15, 16	14, 15	10, 11	7, 8	4, 5	1, 2, 29	25, 26	21, 22	18, 19	15, 16	12, 13
Prune to encourage growth	13, 14	9, 10	16, 17	5, 12	9, 10	6, 7	3, 12, 13	8, 9	5, 6	2, 3	8, 9	6, 7
Prune to discourage growth	30, 31	27, 28	25, 26	21, 22	19, 28, 29	25, 26	22, 23	18, 19, 27	24, 25	20, 21	17, 18	14, 15
Harvest above-ground crops	15, 16	11, 12	10, 11	14, 15	12, 13	8, 9	5, 6	2, 3	8, 9	4, 5	10, 28, 29	8, 9, 26
Harvest below-ground crops	23, 24	20, 21	23, 24	24, 25	3, 31	27, 28	24, 25	21, 22	25, 26	14, 15	19, 20	17, 18
Cut hay	13, 14	9, 10	7, 8	4, 5	1, 2, 28, 29	25, 26	22, 23	18, 19	15, 16	12, 13	8, 9	6, 7
Begin logging	5, 6, 7	2, 3	1, 28, 29	24, 25	21, 22	17, 18	15, 16	11, 12	7, 8	4, 5, 6	28, 29	25, 26
Set posts or pour concrete	5, 6, 7	2, 3	1, 28, 29	24, 25	21, 22	17, 18	15, 16	11, 12	7, 8	4, 5, 6	28, 29	25, 26
Breed	28, 29	24, 25	22, 23, 24	19, 20	16, 17	12, 13	10, 11	6, 7	2, 3, 30	1, 28, 29	24, 25	21, 22
Wean	21, 22, 25, 26	4, 22	3, 30	3, 26	1, 24, 28	20, 25	17, 22	18, 27	15, 24	21, 25	17, 21	14, 18
Castrate animals	8, 9	4, 5	30, 31	26, 27	24, 25	20, 21	17, 18	13, 14	10, 11	7, 8	3, 4	1, 2, 28, 29
Slaughter	1, 2, 28, 29	24, 25	23, 24	19, 20	16, 17	12, 13	10, 11	6, 7	2, 3, 30	1, 27, 28	23, 24	21, 22

Secrets of the Zodiac

Ancient astrologers associated each of the signs with a part of the body over which they felt the sign held some influence. The first sign of the zodiac — Aries — was attributed to the head, with the rest of the signs moving down the body, ending with Pisces at the feet.

The Man of Signs

♈	Aries, head.	**ARI**	*Mar. 21-Apr. 20*
♉	Taurus, neck	**TAU**	*Apr. 21-May 20*
♊	Gemini, arms	**GEM**	*May 21-June 20*
♋	Cancer, breast.	**CAN**	*June 21-July 22*
♌	Leo, heart	**LEO**	*July 23-Aug. 22*
♍	Virgo, belly	**VIR**	*Aug. 23-Sept. 22*
♎	Libra, reins.	**LIB**	*Sept. 23-Oct. 22*
♏	Scorpio, secrets	**SCO**	*Oct. 23-Nov. 22*
♐	Sagittarius, thighs . .	**SAG**	*Nov. 23-Dec. 21*
♑	Capricorn, knees . . .	**CAP**	*Dec. 22-Jan. 19*
♒	Aquarius, legs	**AQU**	*Jan. 20-Feb. 19*
♓	Pisces, feet	**PSC**	*Feb. 20-Mar. 20*

Astrology and Astronomy

■ Astrology is a tool we use to time events according to the *astrological* placement of the two luminaries (the Sun and the Moon) and eight planets in the 12 signs of the zodiac. Astronomy, on the other hand, is the charting of the *actual* placement of the known planets and constellations, taking into account precession of the equinoxes. As a result, *the placement of the planets in the signs of the zodiac are not the same astrologically and astronomically.* (The Moon's *astronomical* place is given in the **Left-Hand Calendar Pages, 60-86,** and its *astrological* place is given in **Gardening by the Moon's Sign, page 167.**)

Modern astrology is a study of synchronicities. The planetary movements do not cause events. Rather, they explain the "flow," or trajectory, that events tend to follow. Because of free will, you can choose to plan a schedule in harmony with the flow, or you can choose to swim against the current.

The dates given in **A Month-by-Month Astrological Timetable (page 169)** have been chosen with particular care to the astrological passage of the Moon. However, because other planets also influence us, it's best to take a look at all indicators before seeking advice on major life decisions. A qualified astrologer can study the current relationship of the planets and your own personal birth chart to assist you in the best possible timing for carrying out your plans.

Planet Mercury Does What?

■ Sometimes when we look out from our perspective here on Earth, the other planets appear to be traveling backward through the zodiac. (They're not actually moving backward; it just looks that way to us.) We call this *retrograde motion.*

Mercury's retrograde periods, which occur three or four times a year, can cause travel delays and misconstrued communications. Plans have a way of unraveling, too. However, this is an excellent time to research or look into the past. Intuition is high during these periods, and coincidences can be extraordinary.

When Mercury is retrograde, astrologers advise us to keep plans flexible, allow extra time for travel, and avoid signing contracts. It's OK and even useful to look over projects and plans, because we may see them with different eyes at these times. However, our normal system of checks and balances might not be active, so it's best to wait until Mercury is direct again to make any final decisions. In 2000, Mercury will be retrograde from February 21 to March 14, June 23 to July 17, and October 18 to November 8.

– Celeste Longacre

PALMS
A·N·D
Portents

Try to read this without glancing even once at your own palm.

by Gita M. Smith

Across the South, on byways and in towns, the signs of palm readers rise out of the ground in salute, fingers spread skyward. Some fight a losing battle with kudzu and southern sunshine. Others are well-lit, freshly painted beacons signaling a practitioner of the ancient art of reading the maps we were born with.

The art of palmistry is old, though no one can say exactly when the first palmist picked up a hand to discern human fate. Spanish cave drawings of hands with distinct palm lines are thought to date back perhaps 12,000 years. Egyptian, Greek, and Biblical accounts dating back thousands of years tell of man's attempts to plot the future in the lines of the hand.

Aristotle presented a treatise on palmistry to Alexander the Great, and the ancient Romans included palm reading in parliamentary procedure. Napoleon kept a palmist, Marie Anne Le Norman, at his court to perform readings for him and the empress Josephine. In more recent times, psychiatrist Carl Jung believed that palmistry could unearth thoughts held deep within the subconscious. He used the ancient practice to evaluate patients as well as to forecast their future dilemmas.

The theory behind palmistry is that the grooves, creases, and lines of the hand are the result of the brain's constant nervous impulses. This repeated channeling of wants, needs, deeds, and subconscious thoughts to the hands produces a map to the inner self.

"Reading the palm, I can tell you the past, present, and future, all your troubles, whether your husband or wife is telling the truth, whether there will be court dates in the future and how they will go, what to do about money, health, everything," claims psychic reader Chief Little Eagle. He shares a home and attached buildings on the southbound side of the Troy Highway (U.S. 231), below Montgomery, Alabama, with Valencia Valentina, "Palm, card, spiritual reader and advisor." They are open seven days a week to counsel the hopeful and the worried who travel that stretch of road. Little Eagle, a full-blooded Cherokee whose voice is as gruff as gravel, says that he has been looking for life's answers in people's palms for 45 years.

Across the Georgia border, and also of Native American heritage, is Mrs. Roberts, with a business location in the airport district of College Park, where international travelers can find her. Mrs. Roberts has been decoding the mysteries of the hand for 35 years. Her manner is as soothing as chamomile and rich with the promise of better days ahead. She calls her customers "sweetheart" and says she has the powers "to heal and take away bad elements as well."

Today, as in the days of Aristotle and Napoleon, practitioners look at the three or four deepest and longest lines in the hand: the two horizontal ones, heart above and head below, and the diagonal or vertical lines of life and fate. "The hand has four elements, like the four legs of a table," says Mrs. Roberts. "If a table has a missing leg, it cannot stand. The palm shows us if something is wrong."

The **fate line** is the most vertical of the hand's deep lines. If it reaches its most common goal, the middle finger, it is a portent of material and financial prosperity. If it branches toward the index finger, the individual will likely achieve his or her worldly ambitions. A bend toward the pinkie indicates success in communication and knowledge, science, medicine,

Heart line

Head line

Life line

Fate line

Most practitioners look at both hands during a reading — their interpretation of the nature versus nurture debate.

or public relations. People who are free spirits, however, may not possess a fate line at all.

It is a misconception that the **life line,** which usually starts midway between the thumb and the index finger and curves down toward the wrist lines, needs to be long. "I have seen people with no life line who were very healthy," Mrs. Roberts reassures. A positive outlook can override a poor constitution, making it impossible for palmists to predict an early death from an abbreviated mark. However, palmists maintain that a long, strong life line correlates with longevity, while a shorter or fainter formation implies physical frailty.

The horizontal **heart line** gauges a person's emotions. A strong, long mark indicates a tenderhearted soul, while the owner of a faint or abbreviated line is ruled more by the mind than the heart.

Finally, the horizontal **head line** measures intelligence. A general explanation, according to palmist Ray Douglas, is that the length of the line indicates the standard of intelligence, the depth signifies the ability to focus, and the direction reveals the type of intelligence. For example, if the head line slopes up toward the pinkie, the owner is strong on common sense, with a good head for making money. If the head line slopes downward, it indicates a creative, artistic temperament.

The hand's fleshiness; the length, shape, and angle of the fingers; the circular, raised areas at the base of the fingers, or the mounts; and the color and vitality of the hand all contribute to a reading. The length of the thumb is said to reveal willpower (the longer the thumb, the more strong-willed), while the shape of the fingertips may indicate artistic sensitivity (ovoid fingertips show a drive toward artistic creativity).

Most practitioners look at both hands during a reading — their interpretation of the nature versus nurture debate. According to the *Journal of Palmistry,* published by the Palmistry Center in Westmount, Quebec, a person's dominant hand generally represents life since birth and where you are likely to be headed, and the other reflects inherited traits and past lives.

Prices for palm readings generally range between $20 and $35 but may be privately quoted if a customer has a difficult question that requires lengthy study. For example, removing a bad spell or a hex is a more complicated and expensive procedure, Mrs. Roberts explains. "In these modern times, as unlikely as it sounds, that still goes on," she says.

Palmistry has arrived in cyberspace, too. Web sites abound, and the curious can buy "The Art of Palmistry," a CD-ROM for home computers, published by Arc Media, Inc.

But missing from the do-it-yourself method is the adventure. To drive down a road one afternoon and pull up to a bejeweled, giant palm — and sit down with a stranger who claims to possess "true sight" and knowledge of your palm's deepest secrets — is far more compelling than reading a book or staring at a computer screen.

Such a detour is all that's left of the state fair midway and the beaded, secret booth at the county fair, where our mothers forbade us to go. It beckons to us, with the promise of supernatural knowledge, or something close to it. And sometimes we just have to follow.

□ □

Home Remedies

Ever wish your pet could talk? We're often left guessing about what ails them. When our animal companions aren't feeling up to par, a visit to the veterinarian can bring relief. But what about those times when you can't get to the vet quickly, or the problem isn't serious? Here are some ways to help your pet at home.

— CORBIS/Paul Kaye; Cordaiy Photo Library Ltd.

by Jana Rygas, D.V.M.

Injuries and Accidents

Cuts, Scrapes, and Abrasions: Mix together 1 pint water, ½ teaspoon salt, and ½ teaspoon calendula tincture; soak an injured paw in this. If the wound is on the body, put the solution into a squirt bottle or large syringe and gently apply it to the injured area. Repeat the soaking or application every 4 to 6 hours for the first 24 hours.

Bites and Scratches: Make up a solution of 1 pint water, ½ teaspoon salt, and ½ teaspoon echinacea/goldenseal tincture. (You can also use a strong brew of echinacea/goldenseal tea if no tincture is available.) Rinse out fresh wounds and punctures with large amounts of this solution, using a squirt bottle or syringe. Hydrogen peroxide may also be used to clean wounds, but it can damage delicate tissues.

Cat-fight wounds are notorious for forming abscesses. If the abscess is draining, clean it with the echinacea/goldenseal solution. Caution: Wear latex gloves when handling an abscess.

Tissue Trauma: If your pet falls, gets stepped on, is in a fight, or is otherwise bruised, the homeopathic remedy arnica can speed recovery. Give 2 pellets of arnica 30c once per hour for 3 hours following the injury. Many vets use arnica before and after surgery to hasten healing.

Choking: You can perform the Heimlich maneuver on animals. This technique uses a quick, firm thrust at the level of the diaphragm to create air pressure that will expel a foreign object from the windpipe. Lift a small pet, or reach over the back of a large one and raise the back legs, so that the rear end is elevated over the head. Place your hands around the lowest part of the chest and give a

Your Pets

quick, gentle thrust inward and upward. Remember to scale the force of your thrust to the size of your pet. For smaller pets, imagine you are performing this on an infant or toddler.

Chronic Health Problems

Cowpie Stool: When your dog scavenges something from the compost pile, it irritates the bowel; this creates nerve impulses that signal the gut to speed up. When food moves too quickly through the gut, the result is loose stools. In dogs and cats with

---

DID YOU KNOW?

■ Animal injuries and deaths from automobiles are so common that HBC — hit by car — is one of the first acronyms that veterinary students learn.

■ If your pet is sprayed by a skunk, the most effective antidote is to bathe the pet in a mixture of 1 quart hydrogen peroxide, 1/4 cup baking soda, and 1 teaspoon liquid soap. Work the solution into the fur (avoid the eyes), then rinse.

---

chronic inflammatory bowel disease, the gut responds as if irritated at the slightest stress or change of diet.

The herb slippery elm can help restore a pet's comfort and the pet owner's sanity. Available as powder or capsules, slippery elm coats the lining of the gastrointestinal tract, counteracting the irritation and allowing stools to firm up. Put 1 tablespoon of the powder (break open capsules) into 1 pint of water and bring to a boil to thicken. Let it cool, and administer by mouth, a teaspoon or less for small pets, several tablespoons for large dogs, every 2 to 4 hours, until the gut settles

POISONS

Dogs and cats are curious, hungry, and low to the ground. Keep them away from these:

■ **ACETAMINOPHEN OR ASPIRIN.** Extremely poisonous to cats.

■ **ANTIFREEZE.** It tastes sweet but can cause fatal kidney damage.

■ **CHOCOLATE.** The darker the chocolate, the more dangerous to a dog.

■ **DECAYING COMPOST OR GARBAGE.** Dogs will scavenge the unthinkable.

■ **PRESCRIPTION MEDICINES.** A human dose can be an enormous overdose for a dog or cat.

■ **RAT POISON.** Evidence of internal bleeding may not show up for two weeks.

■ **SLUG BAIT (METALDEHYDE).** Can cause drooling, shaking, and seizures.

First Aid for Poisoning

■ If you know the source and can find the container, keep it with you as you call your vet or your local poison control center for advice.

■ If advised by a veterinarian to induce vomiting, and if your pet seems normal and alert, take your pet to the kitchen or bathroom or put it into its kennel. Add 1/4 cup hydrogen peroxide to 1/4 cup water and gently administer 1 to 2 teaspoonfuls of this by mouth, using a syringe or child's medicine spoon. The pet should vomit within 5 minutes; if not, administer one more dose. Do not induce vomiting if the poison is unknown. Caustic poisons can do more damage coming back up.

■ Follow any additional advice from your vet, such as taking the animal in to be checked, or feeding your pet something to dilute the poison.

When Is It Safe to Use Home Remedies?

Before you try home treatments, ask yourself these questions:

- **Is there only one thing wrong?** More than one abnormal sign (e.g., diarrhea plus vomiting) may be too serious for home care.

- **Are the vital functions (breathing, temperature, urination, drinking, eating, healthy gum color) in order?** If any are off, check with your vet.

- **Is your pet behaving normally?** Unusual behavior or lethargy can indicate a serious problem.

- **Is the cause known?** A severe injury (hit by a car) should be checked out even if the pet seems OK.

- **Is an external or internal part of the body affected?** A problem with the skin or a foot is less likely to be dangerous than an internal problem.

- **Are the eyes involved?** Eye problems can become serious quickly.

- **Is this a young, healthy animal, or an older pet with a history of health problems?**

> **"Outside of a dog, a book is man's best friend. Inside of a dog, it's too dark to see."** – Groucho Marx

down (usually 8 to 24 hours).

A temporary fast and a change to a bland diet also help. Remove food for 8 hours (keep fresh water available); then feed a small amount of gruel made from water, cooked white rice, and shredded cooked chicken. Phase in regular food after 48 hours.

Itchiness: Pruritis (the medical term for chronic itchiness) affects more than half of pet dogs and many cats. Flea allergy dermatitis is especially common. For ongoing problems, get your vet's recommendations, and try one of these low-tech remedies:

- **OATMEAL BATH.** Put uncooked oatmeal, or rolled oats, into a sock or nylon stocking and run a tubful of warm to lukewarm water over it. Soak your dog (it's a rare cat that will stand for this) in the water, ideally for 5 to 10 minutes. If your pet dislikes bathing, apply the soaked stocking as a poultice to the sore areas. No rinsing needed.

- **ALOE VERA.** Break off a piece of the plant and apply the thick juice directly to areas that look raw. (If you use commercial aloe, be sure to find some without preservatives or additives, since pets are bound to lick it off.)

- **JOJOBA, ALMOND, OR OLIVE OIL.** Mix 1 part oil to 10 parts warm water in a spray bottle and spritz your pet. Massage in with a towel. This helps to break up scabs or scales.

- **HOT SPOTS.** This type of moist dermatitis develops when bacteria multiplies rapidly in an area that has already been scratched raw or is under a mat of tangled fur, and intense itching and pain result. If you see a hot spot developing, clip the hair around it, then clean the area thoroughly. Keep it open and apply calendula soaks (see Cuts, Scrapes, and Abrasions, page 176). Do not use cream. See your vet if the hot spot persists.

Itchy ears: Aloe vera or the contents of a vitamin E capsule can soothe red or inflamed areas of the ear. A gentle cleaning with a cotton swab or gauze dipped into vegetable oil can help to remove a buildup of wax and dirt. Remember that dog and cat ear canals take a right-angle turn at the base of the ear, and be careful not to jam anything deep into the ear canal.

D I D   Y O U   K N O W ?

■ Far more cats die because emergency hospitals or shelters can't trace an owner than from catching a collar on a fence, the common reason owners give for not keeping a collar and ID tag on a cat.

Sore or runny eyes: A simple rinse of sterile saline solution can help a mild eye irritation. Continue as drops every 4 hours, until clear. If symptoms increase, have the vet check the pet's eyes.

Arthritis: Ease chronic pain from hip dysplasia, disk disease, and other types of arthritis in dogs with these home remedies:

■ Massage helps to relieve muscle tensions that contribute to pain. Be gentle. Start from the center of the body and work your way outward. If feet are too sensitive, leave them alone.

■ Nutritional research suggests that supplements containing chondroitin sulfate and glucosaminoglycans can help inflamed or damaged joints. Check with your vet or health-food store.

■ Egg-crate foam and other creature comforts can bring relief to older and arthritic pets. Buy enough foam for two or three beds, cover the foam with washable covers (easy to make from old towels), and put them into the places your pet likes to sleep.

Pest Control

Flea control: The most successful antiflea tools I've seen are a good diet fed to your pet and nontoxic borate salts applied around the home to control flea eggs and larvae. The best place for a flea collar is in the bag of your vacuum cleaner, so the fleas you sweep up stay put. Adding garlic and brewer's

HOME FIRST-AID KIT FOR PETS

Household or pharmacy items:

■ activated charcoal (absorbs recently ingested poison)

■ milk of magnesia (neutralizes acid poisons)

■ vinegar (neutralizes alkali poisons)

■ hydrogen peroxide, 3% (induces vomiting after a poisoning; make sure supply is fresh)

■ digital thermometer (well worth the extra cost)

■ roll of gauze (for bandages or to muzzle an injured pet)

■ Telfa pads for wounds

■ dropper bottle

■ empty squirt bottle or large (35-mL to 50-mL) plastic syringe

■ sterile saline solution or bottled water

Health-food store items:

■ calendula tincture

■ echinacea/goldenseal tincture

■ aloe vera plant or juice

■ vitamin E capsules

■ calendula or combination herbal cream

■ slippery-elm bark powder, about 1/2 cup

■ arnica 30c

■ jojoba or other natural oil

yeast to the diet hasn't been proved to work, but many people swear by it. Give your dog a flea bath with a limonene shampoo, and flea-comb him thoroughly while he's in the water so the fleas drown.

How to pull a tick: Worries about leaving the head in are overstated. If you are concerned, apply vaseline or some flea spray to the tick, wait a few seconds, then pull it out. (Please, no matches!)

Worms: Dogs and cats get roundworms, hookworms, tapeworms, and whipworms. Tapeworm segments appear as wiggling, rice-like particles in the stool. Worms are easily treated with conventional medication. Feeding ground pumpkin seeds can make your pet's intestines less hospitable to worms. Grind the seeds in a blender and feed ½ teaspoon to 1 tablespoon per meal (depending on the size of your pet) for 1 week out of every month.

If your pet scoots around on his bottom, this rarely indicates worms; most likely, anal sac problems are the cause. Anal sacs are filled by small glands below the tail. They are the reason dogs sniff each other's rears. The sacs empty regularly on their own; if they don't, itching and burning cause the animal to drag his or her bottom. You can empty the sacs by gently squeezing the areas on both sides of the anus at the 4 o'clock and 8 o'clock positions. Be sure to wear gloves and step to one side as you do this! If the sacs don't empty easily or seem impacted, see your vet. □ □

How Old Is Your Dog?

Multiplying your dog's age by seven is easy, but it doesn't always hold true. The more carefully graded system at right has the human equivalency years piled onto a dog's life more quickly during the dog's rapid growth to maturity, after which each year for a dog becomes the equivalent of four human years, and after age 13 it slows down to 2½ years.

Dog Age (years)	Equivalent Human Age (years)	Dog Age (years)	Equivalent Human Age (years)
½	10	15	73
1	15	16	75½
2	24	17	78
3	28	18	80½
4	32	19	83
5	36	20	85½
6	40	21	88
7	44	22	90½
8	48	23	93
9	52	24	95½
10	56	25	98
11	60	26	100½
12	64	27	103
13	68	28	105½
14	70½	29	108

WHO WAS LEIF ERIKSSON?

(AND WHY SHOULD WE CARE?)

It's true — the Viking voyage to North America 1,000 years ago didn't really change history. Leif's explorations never led to permanent settlement. Only a few pieces of physical evidence have been found to corroborate the Viking presence. What we are celebrating this year, therefore, is the millennium of a historic encounter between Europeans and North Americans. One could say it was the original Family Reunion.

by John Fleischman

SCANDINAVIA

UNITED KINGDOM

ICELAND

GREENLAND

ATLANTIC OCEAN

LABRADOR

NEWFOUNDLAND

Newfoundland, they say, is shaped like a fist, waving its index finger northward in an eternal "We're Number One!" salute. The cause for celebration lies at the very tip of the wagging finger, where the Long Range Mountains end at Cape Bauld. Just west of the cape, facing the distant coast of Labrador across the Strait of Belle Isle, is a shallow bay with a gravel beach backed by a grassy terrace. This is L'Anse aux Meadows. At first glance, it looks unremarkable: an archaic sod hut surrounded by wooden palings, a few grassy mounds, a Parks Canada Visitor Centre, a parking lot. Yet this is an important place, one the United Nations agency UNESCO declared to be a "World Heritage Site." America was discovered here.

At least, it was discovered from the European point of view, in or about the year

– Culver Pictures, Inc.

1000, by Leif Eriksson and his Vikings. From the native point of view, the Vikings from Greenland were the strange and unwelcome discovery. From the broader view of the entire human species, L'Anse aux Meadows was the site of our first Family Reunion.

Like many family reunions, it was a strained affair. The rough-mannered Vikings often didn't make a good impression on strangers. They called the natives "Skraelings," lumping together all the different Eskimo and Indian peoples they encountered while leapfrogging the North Atlantic. What the Skraelings called the Vikings is unknown but probably not something polite. But then the two branches of the human family tree hadn't seen each other in 900,000 years. It was bound to be rocky.

That's how Kevin McAleese sees it. He is the curator of archaeology for the Newfoundland Museum. "This is the history of how the people from one side of the world met up with the people from the other side of the world," McAleese says. "That journey began about 900,000 years ago in Africa. Our species split up. There were the people who turned 'left,' in a sense, and went to Europe. They met up in Newfoundland and Labrador with the people

Top and above right: *The Viking encampment replica at L'Anse aux Meadows.* Above left: *Genuine Viking artifacts found here include needle hone, spindle whorl, and knitting needle (modern coin shown for scale).*

who'd turned 'right' out of Africa and eventually traveled across Asia into Alaska and the Americas."

It took roughly 899,000 years for the two great waves of human migration to roll all the way around the planet and finally bump into each other on the coast of

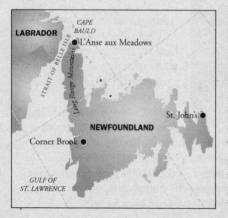

Atlantic Canada. "Full Circle," McAleese calls it. He is organizing a Viking-Skraeling first-contact exhibit by that name to celebrate the 1,000th anniversary of the brief family reunion (see "Viking Exhibits This Year," page 185).

Leif Eriksson would be just another pretty legend, if not for L'Anse aux Meadows. In this place, Leif left his unmistakable calling card, a Viking village where iron was smelted and planked ships repaired, 500 years before Columbus found his New World. Yet until these excavations, the Viking claims to having reached America first hung by the silver thread of the Icelandic sagas. The sagas were authentic, but they had not been written down until 200 years after Leif's voyages to "Vinland," a paradise of mild climate, wild grapes, and broad meadows. But where was Vinland? Was it Newfoundland or Cape Cod or even Miami Beach? Was it real?

The Vinland epics start with a luckless Icelander, Bjarni Herjolfsson, bound for Greenland in A.D. 986, who missed his landfall and was blown far to the west to an unknown shore of rocks and dense woods. Herjolfsson, in no mood for discovery, turned back for Greenland, where he told his tales to Leif, the second son of the two-fisted Erik the Red (who had been thrown out of Iceland for murdering too many of his enemies). Leif bought Herjolfsson's boat and in about the year 1000 set off for the west. Jumping from island to island, Leif finally reached Vinland. After wintering over, he returned to Greenland to recruit larger expeditions.

According to the sagas, there were at least three more Vinland settlements. All failed to take root: The Skraelings were hostile; the Vikings fell out with each other. The survivors returned to Greenland, carrying tales of a rich, temperate country that was impossible to settle because of fierce Skraelings. Great stories, said scholars who later studied the Icelandic sagas, but at bottom just folk tales.

Then in 1960, the Norwegian explorer Helge Ingstad and his archaeologist wife,

VIKING EXHIBITS THIS YEAR

The Smithsonian's **NATIONAL MUSEUM OF NATURAL HISTORY** unveiled an exhibit entitled "Vikings: The North Atlantic Saga" in Washington, D.C., last April. The Smithsonian exhibit includes historic Viking, Indian, and Eskimo artifacts as well as maps, interactive displays on the challenges of navigating the North Atlantic, and more. Over the next two years, the Smithsonian exhibit will tour museums in the United States and Canada.

In St. John's, the **NEWFOUNDLAND MUSEUM** will open "Full Circle: Viking-Skraeling First Contact" in June 2000. The draw here is a choice array of Viking materials from L'Anse aux Meadows and from Ellesmere Island. "Full Circle" will move to Corner Brook, Newfoundland, in September 2000, and then on to museums in mainland Canada.

Parks Canada has updated its Visitor Centre at **L'ANSE AUX MEADOWS** for the 1,000th anniversary. Visitors can enter a sod Viking hall replica and see how Leif and his captains whiled away the long winter nights in the New World. Also on display, and possibly under sail in warm weather, will be *Snorri*, the Viking *knarr* replica that retraced Leif's voyage two years ago.

Historical interpreters reenact Viking ways at L'Anse aux Meadows.

– courtesy Parks Canada/Shane-Kelly/1998

The excavators found discarded ships' planks made from European woods, hand tools, a bronze pin, a glass bead, and a soapstone spindle-whorl that hinted at the presence of women.

ONBOARD THE SNORRI

Rediscovering America is not for the fainthearted or those who like to stay dry. Or so writer Hodding Carter discovered when he set out to retrace Leif's voyage to Vinland. Carter built a 55-foot replica of a _knarr_, the beamy open boat the Vikings preferred for trade and exploration over their more famous dragon ships, and sailed it from Greenland to Newfoundland. The first attempt ended when _Snorri's_ stern began to break up, and it was towed back to Greenland.

Carter's second attempt, in 1998, was a success. Wet and cold, the sailors reached L'Anse aux Meadows in 87 days. Carter, who is writing a book about his experiences as a do-it-yourself Viking, says he has new admiration for Viking navigational skills and restlessness.

Carter named his replica ship _Snorri_ after the first European baby born in the New World, the son of Thorfinn Karlsefni, an Icelander who married Gudrid, the widow of one of Leif's brothers. As for his boat, Carter adds, "_Snorri_ turned out to be an apt name, because everyone on board snored really loudly. Except the captain."

On her first voyage, in 1997, Snorri *sailed near Erik the Red's farm in southern Greenland. Soon after,* Snorri *had to be towed to port for repairs.*

– Russell Kaye

*I*n the nearly 40 years since L'Anse aux Meadows, no further Viking settlements have been found in eastern Canada or New England.

Anne Stine Ingstad, uncovered L'Anse aux Meadows. Excavations by the Ingstads and later by Parks Canada revealed three Viking halls with clusters of smaller buildings, all patterned in the Icelandic manner with many layers of sod covering a timber frame. There were a smithy and an iron-smelting furnace, a carpentry shop, and a boat repair yard. The excavators found discarded ships' planks made from European woods, hand tools, a bronze pin, a glass bead, and a soapstone spindle-whorl that hinted at the presence of women. Equally intriguing, the excavators found butternuts, which do not grow in Newfoundland.

But it wasn't Vinland, says Birgitta Wallace, who recently retired as the Parks Canada archaeologist for L'Anse aux Meadows. Or at least it was not one of the lush Vinland settlements blessed with wild grapes and butternuts. L'Anse aux Meadows is too far north. The site is tundra, a bare grassy plain with access to the sea but little protection from storms. Most critically, there were no barns or livestock enclosures, both needed for permanent settlement. L'Anse aux Meadows was a repair base, Wallace believes, a staging area for Viking explorations further south into the warmer Gulf of St. Lawrence, where butternuts grow. *(continued)*

The "Norse Penny" is one of a handful of Viking artifacts that experts acknowledge as credible evidence of their presence in North America.

In the nearly 40 years since L'Anse aux Meadows, no further Viking settlements have been found in eastern Canada or New England. Experts acknowledge only two other pieces of Viking evidence: 1) a wealth of 12th-century Viking items — a piece of chain mail, a scrap of woolen cloth, a carpenter's plane, and a merchant's balance for weighing coins — scattered over Paleo-Eskimo sites on remote Ellesmere Island in the Canadian Arctic; and 2) the "Norse Penny," a small silver coin struck for the Norwegian king Olav Kyrre between 1065 and 1080. It was uncovered in Brooklin, Maine, in 1974 by an amateur archaeologist. Bruce Bourque, the curator of archaeology at the Maine State Museum in Augusta, believes the coin reached Maine through Indian trading routes. Historians regard other "evidence" of Norse America — runestones from Minnesota and Maine; a stone tower in Newport, Rhode Island; various maps — as "not credible" Viking artifacts.

Birgitta Wallace thinks the whole Vinland period might have lasted 20 to 30 years, with no more than 60 to 100 Vikings moving about in the region at any time. There is no evidence, for example, that the Vikings introduced new diseases or new technologies to the Skraelings. The first contact between the two halves of the world was a glancing blow, Wallace says.

Could things have gone differently? William Fitzhugh, director of the Arctic Study Center at the Smithsonian's National Museum of Natural History, says the medieval Norse were, at heart, farmers and shepherds. They couldn't stay in the New World because they couldn't find safe pastures. To pasture their livestock (and to gather butternuts), the Vikings had to move south into the warmer Gulf of St. Lawrence. Here they hit an ethnic brick wall — the Skraelings. In the sagas, the Vikings win every battle. In real life, the Algonkian peoples of the St. Lawrence won the war, driving the Vikings out and putting off a European invasion for 500 years.

When Europeans returned to North America in the wake of Columbus, they came in great numbers with new viruses and new weapons. This second contact shattered Native America. There was a different opportunity in A.D. 1000, when the Vikings could have been the bridge. The ring of history closed for a moment at L'Anse aux Meadows. For that brief moment and for what might have been, all human beings — all Vikings, all Skraelings, and all in between — can celebrate. □ □

Spinning the Web: Go to www.almanac.com and click on **Article Links 2000** for Web sites related to this article. – *The Editors*

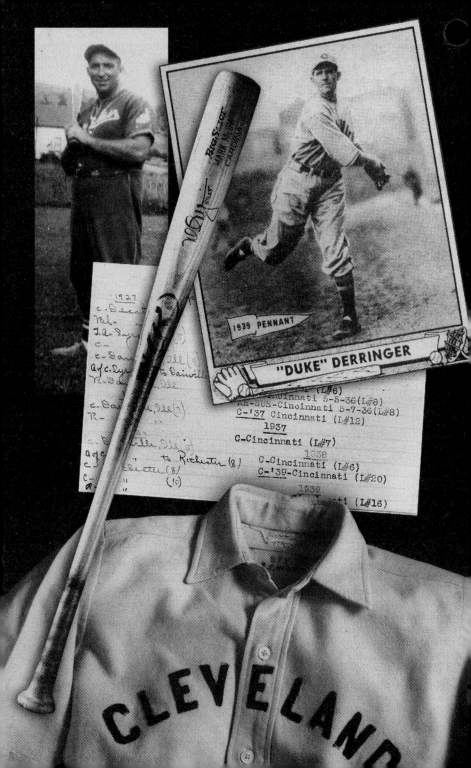

"DUKE" DERRINGER

1939 PENNANT

Big Stick
MARK NOGN
CARDINAL

1937

C-Cincinnati 5-5-36(L#8)
AL-SUS-Cincinnati 5-7-36(L#8)
C-'37 Cincinnati (L#12)

1937
C-Cincinnati (L#7)

1938
C-Cincinnati (L#6)
C-'39-Cincinnati (L#20)

1939
C-Cincinnati (L#16)

CLEVELAND

Five Stories

Even if you've been to the Baseball Hall of Fame in Cooperstown,

from the

New York, it's unlikely you know these stories. They're the ones the

Hall of Fame

staff members tell to each other.

I f you are one of the millions who have walked the corridors of the National Baseball Hall of Fame and Museum in Cooperstown, New York, you will understand why the museum staff does not laugh when security guards say they hear the voices of baseball's immortals when they patrol the darkened halls at night. Over 7,000 objects are on display, and each one tells a story to baseball fans. Here are Ty Cobb's spikes, Babe Ruth's bat, Shoeless Joe Jackson's shoes, a cornerstone from Brooklyn's Ebbets Field saved by the demolition crew, the resin bag Ralph Branca fingered just before pitching to Bobby Thomson.

And for every memory put behind a glass display case, there are hundreds more in rooms never seen by visitors. Too many stories, too much emotion spilled in countless games for the Hall ever to be silent. So the museum staff understands the night voices.

I went to Cooperstown looking for the stories that the Hall of Fame staff members tell among themselves. Not surprisingly, some memories come with no object attached except the human heart. **(continued)**

by Mel Allen

The National Baseball Hall of Fame keeps over a half million photos in its archives. Yet one photo is of a man who played not a single inning of professional baseball, a photo that today lies hidden from view. In 1994, workers renovating the Hall moved a display case that highlighted baseball during World War II. Beneath the case, they found a photograph of a smiling, burly man holding a baseball bat. His baseball jersey said "Sinclair." Attached was this handwritten note:

"You were never to [sic] tired to play catch. On your days off you helped build the Little League field. You always came to watch me play. You were a Hall of Fame Dad. I wish I could share this moment with you. Your son, Pat."

The workers gave the photo to Ted Spencer, curator of exhibits. Though Spencer and his staff tried to identify the player in the photo, their search came up empty. Soon after, *Sports Illustrated* ran a story about the mysterious photo. A writer for the *Wellsville* (N.Y.) *Daily Reporter* remembered there had been a Sinclair Oil team in town. He showed the story to old-timers in the town of about 9,000 people in southwestern New York. Someone said it looked like "Big Joe" O'Donnell. His son, Pat, ran the Blarney Stone tavern.

People in Wellsville knew Pat's father as a man who loved baseball. It was his ballplaying that helped Joe, a Pennsylvania farm boy, land a job at the Sinclair Refinery in Wellsville. The factory team took its games seriously, and Big Joe was a standout catcher for the team in the 1940s and '50s. Big Joe died in 1966.

One day in the summer of 1988, Pat toured the Hall of Fame, bringing along a photo of his father. "I just wanted to have him with me when I visited the Hall of Fame," Pat says. "He'd always wanted to go, but we never did." Pat sat down on a bench and hastily scrawled a message to his father. When no one was looking, he quickly wedged it underneath a display case. When he got home, he told only his wife, his son, his mother, and his sister that Big Joe was now in the Hall of Fame.

Six years after he placed his dad's photo under the case, Pat O'Donnell told his story to the newspaper, and now a movie is in the works. Today, Big Joe remains in the Hall of Fame. When the renovations were finished, Ted Spencer quietly slipped the photo beneath another display, along with a note for some future curator who might find it, urging him to leave the picture in the Hall forever as a "gift to every parent who has taken the time to play baseball with his or her children."

Big Joe O'Donnell *(above)* finally made it to the Baseball Hall of Fame, thanks to his son, Pat.

– photo: National Baseball Hall of Fame Library, Cooperstown, N.Y.

Each year, about 10,000 people come to the Hall of Fame library. They slip thin white gloves over their hands because the clippings and photos are old and fragile. Some of the visitors are baseball scholars researching a book. Some are searching for something else.

In November 1997, a woman named Helen Derringer came to Cooperstown from Cincinnati. Her father, Paul Derringer, had risen from the poverty of a Kentucky tobacco farm to become a star pitcher for the Cincinnati Reds through the 1930s and into the '40s. A six-time all-star, he won 223 games. One season he won 25 games.

But his baseball heroics were finished by the time Helen was born. Her father never spoke about his baseball career. Except for a few mementos — a bronzed glove, a World Series ring, an all-star award — it was as though he had never played. The father Helen knew declared bankruptcy, and, deeply embarrassed, moved his family to Florida. Her Paul Derringer was an unsuccessful businessman who died in 1987.

Ten years later, Helen came to Cooperstown hoping to find some Paul Derringer baseball cards in the many memorabilia stores on Main Street. She bought two, at $40 a card. A storekeeper told her that the Hall of Fame kept a library and that she probably could find a lot more about her father there.

"I made a mad dash for the library," she says. "I told them I had never seen my father play. Well, they brought me his original contract card, and on the back there was the record of where he had played each year. I didn't know he played in Decatur, Illinois. I didn't know he came to Cincinnati in a trade, and I didn't know he'd been traded for Leo Durocher.

Paul Derringer's contract card. His 1940 baseball card (page 190) gives his nickname, "Duke."

– National Baseball Hall of Fame Library, Cooperstown, N.Y.

Dad didn't talk about his games. Never, never, never. In a film clip, I saw him walk out onto the field. He was so young, so tall and gangly. He smiled, and I thought, 'This was my father.' Well, I just started crying, and I couldn't stop."

Jim Gates, the librarian of the National Baseball Library, brought Helen a film of her father teaching children to play baseball. She heard his voice as he showed them how to grip a ball, how to hold the bat. "I was just astounded. Who is this person? He loved kids. He would have been a tremendous coach. That was the best of my father," she says. It was as if she was learning her own history for the first time. "For the first time, I appreciated and understood what the game meant to him. Now I'm going to get the whole family to come back with me. We're all going to find Paul Derringer." **(continued)**

His name was R. Emmett Heidrick and he played only 19 games for the Cleveland Spiders in 1898. His family gave the uniform to the Hall of Fame. When it was not on display as an example of the 19th-century uniform, it sat downstairs in its box.

In 1994, the Hall brought several hundred artifacts to Japan, including the Heidrick shirt. Curator Ted Spencer was putting it onto a mount. "I was just chit-chatting, when all of a sudden my eye jumped. We'd had that jersey for 15 years. I'd handled it so many times. Suddenly I saw 'D. T. Y.' in red letters inside the collar above the black 'R. E. Heidrick.' I said, 'Oh, my God, that's Cy Young's initials' — Denton True Young. Cy Young had played for Cleveland. He left there in 1898 and the team handed the shirt to the next young player. Here was this irre-placeable part of baseball history and I'd never known it."

As Spencer told me this story in the Hall, he casually picked up the pants from the box. Pants rarely leave the boxes, since the jersey is almost always the only part that is displayed. He suddenly saw, for the first time, "D. T. Young" clearly printed inside the waistband.

R. E. Heidrick inherited the great Cy Young's baseball jersey, whose initials in the shirt went unnoticed for nearly a hundred years.

– National Baseball Hall of Fame Library, Cooperstown, N.Y.

The Amazing Acerra Brothers

A few years ago, a young man named Jim Acerra phoned the Hall of Fame. He was calling, he said, on behalf of his father and his uncles. They had once been part of the Acerra Brothers baseball team. Now they were old men, and he wanted to bring them to Cooperstown.

The more the museum officials learned about the brothers, the more intrigued they became. Jim's grandparents, Louis and Elizabeth Acerra, had 17 children in Long Branch, New Jersey. A dozen of their boys became baseball players. The age difference between the oldest, Anthony, and the youngest, Louis Jr., was 25 years. For 22 consecutive years, an Acerra brother had played baseball for Long Branch High. Their father, "Pop," was the coach.

The Acerra Brothers started playing semipro ball throughout the Northeast in 1938, one of 17 all-brother baseball teams. The Acerras stayed together longer than any of the teams. One brother turned down a scholarship to Holy Cross, two others turned down professional contract offers. Six brothers enlisted in World War II, all at different times. Keeping the team together came first. They played their final game in 1952.

Cooperstown welcomed them — not as tourists but as part of the Hall of Fame. On

I Know Impotence

Imagine being able to feel like a young man again.

After heart surgery and medications left me impotent, I worked with a urologist to design safe and effective products that any man can successfully use to regain sexual potency. Since 1989, Vet-Co has become a leading world-class manufacturer of quality medical impotence products.

Forget the cheap toy and novelty products, all Vet-Co products are FDA registered and covered by Medicare. Our products are recommended by impotence specialists around the world. All products are discreetly shipped to your door. Why wait another day to live your life to the fullest; call one of my trained counselors today to learn more.

Sincerely,

Sol Shapiro

Sol Shapiro
President Vet-Co, Inc.

Ask about our Medicare-NO Out-of-Pocket Expense Program*

You deserve the best! Great for...

- Men who want immediate results.
- Men who want a safe and reliable form of treatment.
- Anyone unsuccessful with prescription medications for impotence.
- Men wanting a natural, non-invasive option.
- Effective treatment without discussing the problem with local pharmacy.

CALL 1-800-827-8382
for Confidential FREE Information Package!

VET-CO, INC.
VACUUM ERECTION
TECHNOLOGIES

- FDA Registered • 30-Day Money-Back Guarantee • Urologist Recommended
- Easy To Use • Discreetly Shipped • Member Better Business Bureau

*Must have medicare as your primary health insurance and secondary insurance coverage. No HMOs. Must have met annual medicare deductible. Sold by prescription only.

Covered by Your Medicare

- National Baseball Hall of Fame Library, Cooperstown, N.Y.

Between 1938 and 1952, twelve brothers from the Acerra family formed a traveling baseball team.

Saturday, June 14, 1997, Paul, Alfred, Robert, William, Fred, Edward, and Richard Acerra, now in their 70s and 80s, stood before an audience in the Grandstand Theater, while their nephew, Jim, presented his father's uniform to the Hall of Fame.

Jim had tears in his eyes because his father, James, the team's star pitcher, had died only three weeks before. He told the audience, "This is a family that never allowed sibling rivalry, infighting, or even success to tear them apart. Their team was a reflection of something greater, something that 15 years, many hardships, the lure of professional contracts, and even a World War could not destroy."

A Prayer for a Bat: Enshrining the Home-Run Chase of 1998

■ During the 1998 season, while the world watched as Mark McGwire of the Cardinals and Sammy Sosa of the Cubs closed in on Roger Maris's home-run record of 61, the Hall of Fame had a chase of its own.

Jeff Idelson of the Hall of Fame staff brought Roger Maris's historic bat to St. Louis for the Cubs-Cardinals series early in September. "We wanted both McGwire and Sosa to see their link with history. First we met with Sosa and showed him the Maris bat. He swung it. It was the same weight and length as his bat. He immediately gave us the black Rawlings bat he used to break Hack Wilson's Cubs record of 57 home runs.

"Then we went to the Cardinals clubhouse. Mark took the barrel of the bat and rubbed it over his heart, saying, 'Roger, you're with me now.' He told us, 'Don't worry. When I hit 62, I'll take care of you guys.'" He hit number 62 on September 8 and gave the bat to Idelson.

Meanwhile, John Ralph of the Hall of Fame flew to Chicago as the Cubs went on to play the Brewers. Sammy Sosa slammed four homers in the series, also reaching 62. Within hours, Sosa's bat had joined McGwire's and Maris's in the Hall of Fame.

Then Sosa went to San Diego and struck out five or six times with a new bat. "He said he missed his old bat," Idelson says. "I agreed to wipe a handkerchief over the bat and say a prayer. I had security turn off the alarm system. I opened the case, wiped the handkerchief on the bat, and said a prayer for Sammy. I overnighted the handkerchief to him. That night he hit a grand slam, for 63."

Today, inside a tall glass case at the Hall, visitors can see Mark McGwire's flame-treated, 35-inch, 32-ounce bat that hit his record-breaking home run number 62 on the night of September 8, 1998. Beside the bat is the ball, which was caught by a groundskeeper. The Roger Maris bat and ball, and Sammy Sosa's prayed-over bat and ball are there, too.

□ □

📶 **Spinning the Web:** Go to www.almanac.com and click on **Article Links 2000** for Web sites related to this article. – *The Editors*

Mark McGwire used this bat — now on display in Cooperstown — to hit his record-breaking 62nd home run.

- National Baseball Hall of Fame Library, Cooperstown, N.Y.

The Old Farmer's Almanac

2000 Engagement Calendar

Try your hand at these puzzles, compiled for
The Old Farmer's Almanac by Raynor R. Smith Sr., mathematics teacher at Keene
Middle School in Keene, New Hampshire.

Answers appear on page 228.

1 In the year 2000, my father will be 10 years older than my mother, but neither will have reached the half-century mark. The sum of their ages will be exactly seven times the sum of my sister's and mine. If I will be 6 years old and am younger than my sister, how old will my sister, my mother, and my father be? (No fractional parts of a year are used in our ages).

2 Jordan is trying to climb up the pole at Times Square to put up the New Year's

Eve 2000 ball, but he is having a serious problem. He climbs ¼ of the way up, gets tired, pauses at that spot for a moment, and slides back ½ the distance he's climbed. If he continues to climb that same distance (¼ the length of the pole), sliding back ½ the distance each time, how many upward climbs will it take Jordan to reach the top?

3 The seventh-grade class at Fungwald Middle School needs to raise $300 for its "Year 2000" class trip. The students have decided to sell computer discs. They can buy the discs in a box of 5 for $4, then repackage them and sell them in packs of 3 for $4. How many discs will they have to buy and sell in order to make their $300?

4 Zunker's Jewelry Store is having a huge "Year 2000" sale, with everything in the store being offered at 30% off the regular price. If you pay cash, you will receive an additional 10% off the sale price. What will you pay, in cash, for a $100 bracelet?

5 The fourth-grade students at Fungwald Elementary School find 7 huge boxes on the playground that seem to be identical. Miss Holly, their teacher, tells them that each box is identical except one. Inside that one is a package of passes to the July 4, 2000, fireworks extravaganza. The students can have the passes if they can find out in only two attempts (and without opening any boxes) which one contains the passes! How do they do it?

6 The cuckoo clock in Grandma's kitchen has just cuckooed three o'clock and formed a right angle. At 3:45 P.M., when Grandma's "Celebration 2000" cake is done, what is the measure of the angle formed by the hands of Grandma's cuckoo clock? Cassidy thinks she knows, do you?

7 At the T-Bird Gas Station in Keene, New Hampshire, there is a sign that advertises the "Early Morning Special." The sign says: "12-Ounce Coffee, Dunkin' Donut, and Newspaper, all for .99¢." If you pay for the "Early Morning Special" with a $1 bill, how much change should you get?

8 Symbols:

Take the # of " in every ',
x by the # of ' in every yard,
+ the # of rods in every furlong.
This really isn't hard.

+ the # of ' in every mile,
and the # of ounces in every #,
÷ by the # of pecks in every bushel.
? # have you found?

9 A man jogs away from home, takes three left turns and arrives home confronted by two masked men. Why isn't the man worried?

10 A ball is dropped and bounces upward ½ the distance it traveled to the ground when it was dropped. If Jordan climbs a ladder and drops a ball from 38 feet off the ground, how far will the ball have traveled when it hits the ground for the fifth time?

11 Clair asks her mathematics teacher, Mr. Smith, if he can change three tens into nine fifty with a little bit of geometry? She has him stumped! How does she do it?

12 At the Cheshire Fair, Marty entered a giant plum that she had grown. The plum weighed 10 pounds, 95% of which was water. After sitting on display at the fair for four days, it is now 80% water. How much does the plum now weigh?

□ □

Favorite Foods for

For example, the Snow family of North Carolina insist on their Hypocrite Pie. And a Maine family always buries their reunion dinner down in a hole in the ground . . .

Several years ago, in honor of my extended family's first reunion, a cousin printed up T-shirts touting the weekend's agenda. "Hike. Eat. Swim. Eat. Talk. Eat. Play Ball. Eat," the shirts read. And that's exactly what we did.

Food has always been central to every gathering in my family, just as it plays a vital role in the family life of virtually everyone else that I know. At the estimated 200,000 family reunions across the United States each year, food often is the tie that binds, uniting generations over coffee cake and homemade chicken and dumplings.

The Smith/Smart family, with roots north of Bangor, Maine, has been holding family reunions for 75 years. The culinary centerpiece is pulled from a hole in the ground — baked beans made

Family Reunions

by Robin Bloksberg

in an outdoor bean hole. According to family member John Madden, whose father and grandfather were lumberjacks, family history has it that when the loggers were sent downriver to drive the logs to the mill, camp cooks would precede them each day by land. The cooks would put a pot of beans on top of coals in a hole beside the river, so that the beans would be ready when the river drivers arrived late in the day. Today, those bean-hole baked beans are a staple at Smith/Smart family reunions.

The Greenia family of Michigan also showcased an old family recipe at a recent reunion. "When we went to the farm to visit Grandma, we could almost always expect coffee cake," recalls family member Diane Timmons. So when 100 relatives gathered for their first reunion in many years, Maggie O'Donnell Hasenjager pulled out her copy of the original recipe for

– background painting: "Family Gathering" by Barbara Appleyard

her great-grandmother's coffee cake, and baked up a bunch of them to share.

Potluck and covered-dish meals are common at rural reunions, says *Reunions* magazine editor Edith Wagner, especially if most guests live nearby. When the Deskins family of Virginia gets together each year, family members bring along enough homegrown and homemade foods — among them tomatoes, beans, pickles, pickled eggs, hand-gathered honey, and a bevy of cakes — to fill six long folding tables. The Snow family of North Carolina also favors covered-dish meals at their reunions, with baked country ham, sweet-potato cobbler, and other regional specialties — plus Grandma Snow's famous Hypocrite Pie — filling the groaning board.

For 50 years, the W. R. Powell family of San Saba County, Texas, has gathered each year on the third weekend in June. Saturday afternoon is always reserved for ice-cream making. Everyone brings freezers and ingredients like chocolate chips, peaches, strawberries, and peanut butter to flavor their concoctions. The tradition began decades ago when the family matriarch decided to teach the younger generation how things were done in the olden days. Today those children are adults themselves, carrying on the ice-cream-making custom.

Some families decide to preserve their culinary history by assembling their own personalized cookbooks. These can be inexpensive productions, created with a home computer and a photocopy machine, such as the one Norma Corbett Bruce made for the Corbett family of Illinois. With nearly 50 pages of recipes, the booklet tells the story of a family through its favorite foods. (Several publishers have programs to help families produce personalized cookbooks; one of the biggest is Cookbook Publishers, Inc., Lenexa, Kansas; 800-227-7282.)

If you're among the thousands of Americans planning your own family reunion to celebrate the millennium, remember this: Whether you opt for a sit-down dinner, a picnic lunch, or a potluck gathering, if your heart's in it, everyone will have a great time. In fact, if anyone ever doubted that food is the tie that binds, they need only attend a family reunion to find out otherwise.

Mother's Old-Fashioned Homemade Chicken and Dumplings

From Shirley Wollard Woodlock, Waco, Texas

Shirley Wollard Woodlock learned to make chicken and dumplings while watching her mother, Jennie Wollard Nunn. "Hers were made to perfection," recalls Shirley. "She would always say, 'Don't forget the bay leaves and the pepper.'" Now Shirley always makes her mother's chicken and dumplings to bring to Wollard family reunions. The recipe was passed down from Shirley's grandmother, who grew up in the hills of Tennessee.

1 whole fryer chicken or hen
4 to 5 bay leaves
salt and pepper, to taste
4 to 6 tablespoons butter
pepper, to taste

Dumplings:
1 teaspoon salt
1/2 cup oil
3/4 cup water
2 small eggs
3 cups flour

Wash the chicken and place into a large Dutch oven. Cover well with plenty of water and add bay leaves. Add salt and pepper, and the butter (the more butter, the richer the dish).

(continued)

"They gasped when I sprayed beer on my lawn. But you should see my golf-course green grass now!"

MILWAUKEE (Special) That's right — I spray beer on my lawn, and use baby shampoo, ammonia, and instant tea to grow mouth watering vegetables and flowers prettier than a florist!

My name is Jerry Baker, and I'm known as America's Master Gardener. I've got hundreds of amazing lawn and garden secrets and "make-it-yourself" home remedies I'd like to share with you. The best part is *you'll save money since everything you need to make them is found in your home!*

Your Plants Will Love 'Em, Too

Since 1964, I've taught over 19.8 million people how to beautify their yards and gardens using common household products on my national radio show – *On the Garden Line*, on *Good Morning America*, *The Tonight Show*...in *Sports Illustrated*, *Mature Outlook*...and in my 40 best-selling lawn and gardening books.

Now, you can get an *extraordinary collection* of my all-time favorite tonics for super lawns, trees, shrubs, flowers, vegetables, roses and houseplants in my new *Year 'Round Garden Magic Program.* This jam-packed program reveals over 200 of my amazing secrets like how a little corn syrup and baby shampoo will invigorate your trees. Plus, you'll learn how...

- Instant tea energizes flowers
- Ashes make bulbs bloom bigger
- Roses love banana peels
- Laundry soap controls crabgrass
- Whiskey – the key to houseplant success
- Tabasco Sauce® stimulates perennials
- Pantyhose produces heftier tomatoes

Cures For Your Toughest Gardening Problems

You'll also learn that...
- Beer bombs lawn thatch
- Coke® really gets your compost a cookin'
- Epsom salts power packs soil
- Mouthwash fights off lawn disease
- Chewin' tobacco sends pests a packin'

Have Fun, Save Money and Enjoy a *Showcase* Yard!

Do my 200+ secrets really work? You bet! Enthusiastic gardeners write: "Our flowers never stood so tall"..."My lawn is magnificent... great program... and very, **very** inexpensive to boot"... "Giant produce in giant quantities." I love hearing how much fun people are having mixing up my homemade formulas, and *how much money they are saving* by using common household products.

Save 67% and Receive 4 FREE Gifts

My *Year 'Round Garden Magic Program* is just $9.95 (a $12.95-value). Plus, I'll send you my step-by-step "Growing Power" cassette tape (a $9.95-value), FREE. *And, if you order within 7 days,* I'll send you 3 extra FREE gifts – a "Garden Secrets" Summary Chart, handy Calendar Reminder Stickers and a handsome carrying case (a $6.95-value). That's a total value of $29.85 for just $9.95, a 67% savings!

TO ORDER: Simply print your name, address and the words "Garden Secrets" on a piece of paper, and mail it with only $9.95 plus $2.95 S&H (total – **$12.90**) to Year Round Garden Magic, P.O. Box 1001, Dept. 1393, Wixom, MI 48393. VISA/ MasterCard send card number, signature, and expiration date.

Want to save even more? Order an extra copy for family and friends for only $20.00 postage paid.

There's no risk - you're protected by my 100% money-back guarantee for 90 days. **So order today!**

Bring to a boil over medium-high heat, and cook, uncovered, until the chicken is well done, about 1 hour.

Remove the chicken from the broth. Discard the bay leaves. When the chicken has cooled, remove the meat from the bone and return the deboned chicken to the broth. About ½ to ¾ pot of broth should remain.

For dumplings: In a large bowl, mix together the salt, oil, water, and eggs. Slowly add the flour to the mixture, blending it constantly with a fork. Stir only long enough to mix the dough.

Turn the dough out onto a floured board. Pinch the dough in half, and roll out until thin, about ¼ inch. Slice the dough into ½-inch-wide strips, and cross-slice into pieces 4 to 8 inches long, for ease in handling.

Bring the broth and chicken back to a boil, and pepper well to taste. Drop the dumpling strips into the boiling stock. Boil approximately 20 minutes, uncovered, stirring occasionally to prevent sticking, until the dumplings are done (they'll be puffy). Most of the broth will be absorbed. Serve with red pinto beans and corn bread.

Makes 8 to 10 servings.

Health Salad
From Olive Weybright Corbett, Mount Morris, Illinois, via daughter Norma Bruce

When Olive Weybright Corbett was a teenager in the 1920s, she often stayed overnight with her friend Arlene, whose mother made this salad. "Arlene and I took turns chopping the cabbage in a wooden bowl," Corbett wrote in a recently assembled family cookbook. "We would bring the cabbage, carrot, and apples up from the cellar under the kitchen." Today, this salad is a favorite at Corbett family get-togethers.

1/2 head cabbage
1 carrot
1 large apple (any good eating apple)
1/2 cup raisins
1/2 cup mayonnaise-style salad dressing (like Miracle Whip)

2 tablespoons sugar
1 teaspoon cider vinegar
6 tablespoons evaporated milk

Shred the cabbage and carrot. Dice the apple, leaving the skin on to add color to the salad. Mix these ingredients together with the raisins. In a separate bowl, sweeten the salad dressing with the sugar. Add cider vinegar to the dressing, and thin with evaporated milk. Pour the dressing over the dry ingredients, mix well, and refrigerate for at least an hour before serving.

Makes about 6 servings.

Bean-Hole Baked Beans
From John Madden, Keene, New Hampshire

For 75 years, the Smith/Smart family has gathered annually in Maine to enjoy each other's company and feast on a potluck meal. There's always one staple: real bean-hole baked beans. John Madden, whose mother was a Smart, says that the family sometimes has three pots of beans going at once. ("They eat a lot of beans up there, morning, noon, and night sometimes," says John's wife, Evelyn.) John suggests using a three-legged, cast-iron kettle with a flared sheet metal cover to bake the beans in. For a 1½- or 2-gallon pot, increase the following basic recipe by three times.

1 pound dried beans (yellow eye or pea beans work well)
1/4 pound salt pork, cut up
1 teaspoon dry mustard
3/4 teaspoon salt
1/4 teaspoon pepper
1/4 cup molasses

Pick over the beans, remove any bad ones and take out any pebbles, then wash beans. Soak beans overnight in plenty of water to cover. Meanwhile, dig a two-foot-wide bean hole to have it ready for the next day (be sure the hole is at least two feet deep). Collect eight to ten fist-size rocks, along with an ample supply of softwood, like pine or hemlock.

The next morning, add water to the

beans to cover, and parboil the beans until the skins pop when you blow on them (about 20 minutes). In the meantime, fill the bean hole about ¾ full of wood and light a fire. Place the rocks on top, and add more wood.

Drain the beans. In a large iron pot that has a flared cover, put in a layer of salt pork, half the beans, the rest of the salt pork, and the rest of the beans. Mix the mustard, salt, and pepper into the molasses, and pour into the pot. Fill the pot with hot water, just to cover the beans. Place a brown paper shopping bag between the pot and its top to make a seal.

When the fire has burned down to red-hot coals and the rocks are red hot (after 1 to 1½ hours), use a long-handled spade to push the rocks to one side of the hole. Carefully set the pot into the hole so it's level. Nestle the rocks around the pot, and use one large hot rock to weight the top.

Cover the pot and hole with four to six inches of soil (checking first to make sure the lid is on tight so no dirt gets into the beans), and let it cook for 8 hours. Shovel off the dirt and remove the pot. If the beans seem dry, make a ½-inch indentation in the beans, add a little boiling water, and let it set in before eating.

Serves 6 to 8.

Sauerkraut-and-Sausage Casserole

From Allen Snow, Thurmond, North Carolina

The Snow family of North Carolina documents their family history as far back as the 18th century, when patriarch John Snow — who had "quite the sense of humor," according to family historian, Allen Snow — named one son Frost And Snow and another Ice And Snow. Today, family history lives on not only in the annual Snow family reunions, but also in a bound collection of recipes that Allen assembled and published. This recipe, one of Allen's own, is a simple-to-make covered dish.

1 pound fully cooked Polish sausage, cut into 1/2-inch slices
1 tablespoon dried, minced onions
2 apples, cored and quartered
1 can (27 ounces) sauerkraut (undrained)
1 cup water
1/2 cup brown sugar
2 teaspoons caraway seed
snipped parsley (optional)

Mix all ingredients (except parsley) and bake, covered, in a 2½-quart baking dish at 350° F for 1 hour. Garnish with fresh snipped parsley.   **Serves 6.**

Grandma Snow's Hypocrite Pie

From Ida Victoria Holder Snow, Dobson, North Carolina

Another Snow family favorite is this pie, made from an old family recipe. Family historian Allen Snow says the pie got its name because, deceptively, it looks like a simple egg-custard pie — while in actuality it's a dried-apple pie.

2 cups dried apples
about 3/4 teaspoon sugar
about 1/2 teaspoon cinnamon
1 unbaked, 9-inch deep-dish pie shell
3 eggs
1/2 cup sugar
1/4 teaspoon salt
2 cups milk
1 teaspoon vanilla extract
nutmeg or allspice

In a medium saucepan, cover apples with water. Cook over medium heat for 15 to 20 minutes, or until the apples are tender and the water is absorbed (stir often so the fruit won't burn). Season with ¾ teaspoon sugar and ½ teaspoon cinnamon, or to taste. When mixture is cool, spoon into a deep-dish unbaked pie shell to make a half-inch layer of fruit.

Beat eggs. Add sugar, salt, milk, and vanilla. Pour the mixture over the fruit and bake at 350° F until custard is done, about

The biggest surprise on this innovative compact sound machine...is the price

Zenith Audio, a leading electronics manufacturer, designs a "Small Footprint," "Big Sound" stereo system and drives the price below $100.

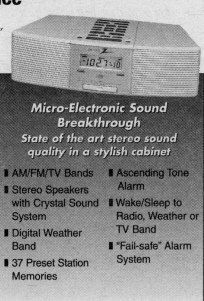

Zenith Audio has developed a Digital Stereo Clock Radio that boasts the acoustic quality and practical features of stereo radios four times as expensive. You'll be amazed at the sound quality and powerful bass you get from a radio this small and this affordable. This stereo radio features an 11-key handheld remote control and an input jack for CD players or other audio sources.

Loaded with features. The AM/FM radio features digital tuning for pinpoint reception and crystal-clear sound. It picks up TV and WEATHER signals with 13 TV channels and 7 Weather channels, so your Zenith Audio Clock Radio is a great source of news, entertainment and information. You can program the unit's memory for 37 preset stations, and the tuning buttons can operate either manually or in an automatic search mode.

Practical functions. The clock has several alarm functions, waking you to either radio, TV, weather or a buzzer. The sleep timer allows you to fall asleep to up to 90 minutes of music, TV or weather and then shuts off automatically. In the morning, if you need a few extra minutes

Micro-Electronic Sound Breakthrough
State of the art stereo sound quality in a stylish cabinet

- AM/FM/TV Bands
- Stereo Speakers with Crystal Sound System
- Digital Weather Band
- 37 Preset Station Memories
- Ascending Tone Alarm
- Wake/Sleep to Radio, Weather or TV Band
- "Fail-safe" Alarm System

of sleep, press the SNOOZE bar. The radio or alarm tone stops for 10 minutes and then sounds again.

Factory direct risk-free offer. This product comes with a one-year manufacturer's limited warranty and Comtrad's exclusive risk-free home trial. If you are not satisfied for any reason, simply return it within 90 days for a full "No Questions Asked" refund.

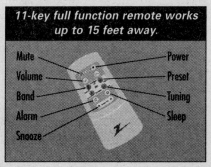

11-key full function remote works up to 15 feet away.

Mute — Power
Volume — Preset
Band — Tuning
Alarm — Sleep
Snooze

Zenith Crystal Clear Stereo
.... **$99.95** $12 S&H
Please specify white or black.
Please mention promotional code **4245-16212.**

For fastest service, call toll-free 24 hours a day
800-992-2966

Virginia residents only—please include 4.5% sales tax.

comtradindustries
2820 Waterford Lake Drive, Suite 102 Midlothian, VA 23112

40 minutes. Sprinkle top with nutmeg or allspice. **Serves 8 to 10.**

Grandma DuRussel's Coffee Cake

From Maggie O'Donnell Hasenjager, Troy, Michigan

Along with a pig roast with all the fixin's, Grandma DuRussel's coffee cake was a big hit at a Greenia family reunion in Capac, Michigan.

2 cups water
1-1/2 cups sugar
1/2 cup (1 stick) butter, cut into chunks
1/4 teaspoon salt
2 eggs, beaten
8 cups flour, divided into 2 equal portions
1-1/2 cups raisins
2 packages yeast
1 teaspoon sugar
1/3 cup warm water
a few tablespoons milk or cream

Topping:
1-1/2 tablespoons flour
3/4 cup brown sugar
1 tablespoon cinnamon
1/2 cup chopped pecans
2 tablespoons melted butter

Heat water to a simmer, and add the sugar, butter, and salt. When the butter has melted, remove from heat and cool to lukewarm. Add eggs.

Put 4 cups of flour into a mixing bowl. Add the raisins, and then the cooled liquid. Soften (proof) two packages of yeast in a little warm water, along with 1 teaspoon of sugar. Add proofed yeast and 4 more cups of flour to the dough. Mix well, and knead slightly. Place into a greased mixing bowl, cover with a towel, and place into a cool oven with a bowl of very hot water. Allow the dough to rise about 1 hour, until it has doubled in bulk.

Divide the dough into 4 pieces. Place into 4 greased, round 8-inch or 9-inch cake pans. Let rise again until double in bulk, about 40 minutes.

Meanwhile, make the topping by combining the 1½ tablespoons of flour with the brown sugar, cinnamon, and pecans. Melt 2 tablespoons of butter, and blend it with the other topping ingredients.

When the dough has risen for the second time, brush the tops with milk or cream, then sprinkle with topping. Bake at 350° F for 30 minutes. **4 cakes serve about 32.**

Pecan Pie Bars

From Kay McKee, Richland Springs, Texas

The Powells of Texas are "a cookin' bunch of people," says family member Kay McKee. So McKee asked everyone for favorite recipes and family stories, and published a cookbook. Not surprisingly, given the family's roots in the heart of Texas pecan country, more than a few of the recipes feature pecans. This is just one of them.

Crust:
2 cups flour
1/2 cup powdered sugar
1 cup (2 sticks) butter or margarine

Filling:
1 can sweetened condensed milk
1 egg
1 teaspoon vanilla extract
1 package (10 ounces, or about 2 cups) almond brickle chips, such as Heath Bits O' Brickle
1 cup chopped pecans

Mix together the flour and powdered sugar. Chop in the butter, until the mixture resembles coarse cornmeal. Press into a 13x9-inch pan. Bake for 15 minutes at 350° F. Cool. Mix together the filling ingredients, and pour on top of the cooled crust. Bake for an additional 25 minutes at 350° F. Cool before cutting into bars.
Makes about 30 bars.

□□

OLD FARMER'S ALMANAC CALENDARS FOR 2000!

WALL CALENDARS

- ❖ Large, full-color grid with plenty of room to write
- ❖ Heavy stock that is easy to write on with pen or pencil
- ❖ Opens to 10-5/8" x 16"
- ❖ Each calendar only $6.99 plus shipping and handling

EVERY DAY CALENDARS

- ❖ Handy page-per-day format
- ❖ Daily wit and wisdom based on each calendar's topic
- ❖ Gift boxed, plastic easel-backed, 5-1/4" x 5-3/8"
- ❖ Each calendar only $9.95 plus shipping and handling

ITEM #OF00CGC — $6.99 each

ITEM #OF00CHH — $6.99 each

ITEM #OF00CEV
$9.95 each

ITEM #OF00CEH
$9.95 each

ITEM #OF00CEW
$9.95 each

ITEM #OF00CHR
$9.95 each

ITEM #OF00CAD — $6.99 each

ITEM #OF00CCK — $6.99 each

TO ORDER:

BY MAIL: Send order with payment, including postage and handling*, to The Old Farmer's Almanac, P.O. Box 37370, Boone, IA 50037-0370. (U.S. funds drawn on a U.S. bank only, please.)

BY CREDIT CARD: Call TOLL-FREE 800-223-3166 (Visa or MasterCard).

Please mention key **#CAAOFCFP** when ordering.

*Postage & Handling Schedule

Total Cost	Shipping Charge
Up to $8.99	$2.95
$9.00 - $15.99	$3.95
$16.00 - $24.99	$4.95
$25.00 - $49.99	$5.95

Sharing My Best

APPLE RECIPES

They should see you nicely into the new millennium and beyond.

BY KEN HAEDRICH

A century ago, in New York State alone, more than 700 varieties of apples were grown. Among them were 'Summer Rambo', 'Old Nonpareil', 'Sops of Wine', and 'Roxbury Russet'. Today, only about 20 varieties are grown commercially in the entire country — and even those 20 have had a tough go of it. The fanciful old varieties have been weeded out by a marketplace that values uniformity over flavor.

Yet the apple is the very picture of endurance: firm, all muscular curves, holds up well in storage. More so than any other native-grown fruit, apples are always there. I love apple-apricot tarts in summer, apple cakes in March, and apple dumplings all winter.

Do I regret the fact that I may never have a slice of apple pie made with 'Yellow Bellflower' or 'Westfield Seek-No-Further' apples? To a point. Beyond that, I've always thought that regret is the least appetizing form of revenge: I'd rather bake than stew. Here are five of my apple favorites, to see you nicely into the new millennium and beyond.

Apple Crumble Bars

These will get high marks with the brown-baggers and after-school snack crowd, among others. The crumble mixture also makes an excellent topping for pies and fruit crisps.

Crumble mixture:
1 cup all-purpose flour
1 cup old-fashioned rolled oats
3/4 cup packed light-brown sugar
1 teaspoon ground cinnamon
pinch of salt
1/2 cup (1 stick) plus 2 tablespoons cold unsalted butter, cut into pieces

Apple filling:
3 large cooking apples
1 tablespoon butter
2 tablespoons packed light-brown sugar
1/2 cup raisins
1 teaspoon lemon juice

Preheat oven to 350° F and lightly butter an 8x8-inch baking pan; set aside. For crumble mixture: Put flour, oats, brown sugar, cinnamon, and salt into the bowl of a food processor; pulse to mix. Add the butter and pulse repeatedly, until the mixture just starts to get clumpy. Press half the mixture into the bottom and slightly up the sides of the pan. Refrigerate.

For apple filling: Peel and core the apples. Slice two of them and cut the other into bite-size chunks. Heat the butter in a medium nonreactive skillet. Stir in the apples and sauté over medium heat for 2 minutes to soften. Stir in the brown sugar, raisins, and lemon juice and sauté 1 minute longer. Remove from heat; cool.

Spread cooled filling over bottom crust. Sprinkle remaining crumble mixture over apples and press gently to pack. Bake for 35 minutes. Transfer to a rack to cool thoroughly. Slice and serve. You'll get a cleaner cut if you refrigerate bars for 30 minutes before slicing. **Makes 9 bars.**

Cider-Cooked Apple Dumplings with Vanilla Custard Sauce

These dumplings can be poached in cider or half-and-half cream. You can serve the dumplings with their broth or use the custard sauce.

1-1/2 cups unbleached all-purpose flour
1/3 cup yellow cornmeal
3 tablespoons sugar
1-1/2 teaspoons baking powder
1/2 teaspoon salt
1/2 teaspoon ground nutmeg

(continued)

3 tablespoons cold unsalted
   butter, cut into pieces
1/2 cup milk
1 large egg
1/2 teaspoon vanilla extract
1 large apple, peeled, cored,
   and finely chopped
1/2 cup dried currants or raisins
1 quart cider or half-and-half
Vanilla Custard Sauce (recipe below)

*M*ix the first six (dry) ingredients in a medium bowl. Add the butter and use your fingers to rub it in to make a coarse meal. Whisk milk, egg, and vanilla in a small bowl. Make a well in the center of the dry ingredients; add liquid all at once and stir to combine, mixing in apple and currants.

Bring the cider (or half-and-half) to a simmer in a wide, nonreactive, covered deep skillet. Spoon 8 equal portions of dough into the simmering liquid. Cover, reduce heat, and simmer gently — without removing the lid — for 10 minutes. Remove from heat and let dumplings sit, covered, for 5 minutes longer.

Transfer dumplings to dessert bowls. Serve with the poaching liquid or Vanilla Custard Sauce. **Makes 8 dumplings.**

VANILLA CUSTARD SAUCE

6 large egg yolks
1/2 cup sugar
2 cups whole milk
1/2 teaspoon vanilla extract

♥ Whisk yolks and sugar in a medium bowl to blend. Bring milk to a simmer in a medium saucepan. Gradually whisk hot milk into yolk mixture. Return mixture to saucepan. Stir over medium-low heat for about 5 minutes, until custard thickens enough to leave a path on the back of a wooden spoon when you draw a finger across it. Do not boil the sauce or it will curdle. Strain into a small bowl and stir in the vanilla. If desired, chill until cold, about 3 hours. **Makes about 2-1/2 cups.**

Apple Crumb Kuchen

This is the sort of buttery, crumb-topped apple cake everyone loves. Take it on hikes or to a potluck; there's plenty here.

Topping:
1 cup coarsely chopped pecans
1/2 cup packed light-brown sugar
2 tablespoons unbleached all-purpose flour
1 teaspoon cinnamon
2 tablespoons cold unsalted butter, cut
   into pieces

Cake:
1/2 cup milk
1/2 cup sour cream or plain yogurt
2-3/4 cups all-purpose flour
2 teaspoons baking powder
1/2 teaspoon baking soda
3/4 teaspoon salt
1 cup (2 sticks) unsalted butter, softened
1 cup sugar
3/4 cup packed light-brown sugar
3 large eggs, at room temperature
finely grated zest of 1 lemon
1 teaspoon vanilla extract
2 cups chopped, peeled apples

*F*or topping: Blend pecans, brown sugar, flour, and cinnamon in the bowl of a food processor until nuts are finely chopped. Add butter and pulse machine repeatedly until clumps begin to form. Transfer to a bowl and refrigerate.

For cake: Preheat oven to 350° F. Butter and flour a 13x9-inch baking pan, preferably glass. Whisk milk and sour cream in a small bowl and set aside. Sift flour, baking powder, baking soda, and salt into a bowl. Using an electric mixer, cream the butter in a large bowl, gradually beating in both sugars until thick and creamy. Add the eggs, one at a time, beating well after each addition. Mix in the zest and vanilla. Alternately add flour mixture and liquid ingredients to creamed mixture in three stages, each time blending until smooth.

Spread half the batter into the prepared pan. Cover evenly with apples. Spoon remaining batter over apples, and smooth it. Sprinkle with topping. Bake the cake on the center rack for about 45 minutes, until a tester inserted into the center comes out clean; cover cake with foil if top is getting too dark. Cool in the pan, on a rack, for at least 2 hours before slicing.

Makes 12 large servings.

Maple Baked Apples

I love these for breakfast, cold, swimming in light cream, but they also make a nice warm winter dessert. Use 'Golden Delicious' apples, as indicated here, because they hold their shape better than most.

6 large 'Golden Delicious' apples
1 cup walnut pieces
1/3 cup raisins
1/4 cup sweetened flaked coconut
2 tablespoons real maple syrup
1 teaspoon grated lemon zest
1/4 teaspoon cinnamon
1/4 teaspoon ground nutmeg
6 tablespoons apricot preserves
1 cup apple cider
2 tablespoons unsalted butter

Preheat oven to 375° F. Core the apples, and peel only the upper third

of each one. Using a sharp paring knife, score the apples all around where the flesh and peel meet; this will help to keep them from bursting. Cut a small crater into the top of each apple to hold extra filling, and cut a tiny bit off the bottoms, so they sit up without falling. Place the apples into a large, shallow glass baking dish.

Put walnuts, raisins, and coconut into the bowl of a food processor; chop finely. Transfer to a bowl and mix in maple syrup, zest, and spices. Divide filling equally among the apples, pressing it into the cores. Spread 1 tablespoon preserves over the top of each.

Heat cider and butter in a small saucepan until butter melts. Pour into baking dish. Cover loosely with foil and bake for 40 minutes. Uncover and bake until tender, basting every 10 minutes. (To test for doneness, insert a small paring knife into an apple — it should feel tender throughout.) Total cooking time will be about 1 hour. Serve warm, with the pan juice, or refrigerate and serve cold the next day.

Makes 6 servings.

Apple, Cranberry, and Pear Pie

I always throw extra bags of cranberries into the freezer when they're on sale in the fall, so I can make this pie throughout the year.

Pastry:
1-1/2 cups all-purpose flour
1 tablespoon sugar
1/4 teaspoon salt
1/2 cup (1 stick) cold unsalted butter, cut up
1 egg yolk
3 tablespoons cold water

(continued)

Apple Buying Guide

'Braeburn' ❤ Tart, sweet, and aromatic. Excellent fresh; good for baking.

'Cortland' ❤ Crisp, tart, good pie apple. Flesh does not turn brown quickly.

'Fuji' ❤ Crisp, juicy, and sweet. Excellent snacking apple; good for baking.

'Gala' ❤ Has a yellow-orange skin with red striping. Juicy and sweet, with a good crisp texture. Good baking apple.

'Golden Delicious' ❤ Sweet; tender skin. Not the most flavorful apple, but one of the best all-round for baking because it holds its shape in the oven.

'Granny Smith' ❤ Bright-green skin; crisp, with tart and tangy flavor. Good in pies, but mix with other, juicier apples for best results.

'Jonagold' ❤ A cross between 'Golden Delicious' and 'Jonathan'. Has a tangy-sweet flavor. Good for cooking or snacking.

'McIntosh' ❤ Juicy; bruises easily. Excellent for applesauce; fair for baking.

'Red Delicious' ❤ Crisp, sweet, somewhat bland, with a distinctive heart shape. Best eaten fresh; not a good choice for pies or baked apples.

'Rome Beauty' ❤ Primarily a baking apple; the flavor intensifies with cooking.

'Winesap' ❤ Juicy-tart snacking apple favored by cider-makers. Spicy flavor, good for baking.

Filling:
**2 cups fresh
    cranberries
2 large baking apples,
    peeled, cored,
    and thinly sliced
2 large ripe pears, peeled, cored, and chunked
3/4 cup packed light-brown sugar
1-1/2 tablespoons quick-cooking tapioca
finely grated zest of 1 lemon
juice of 1/2 lemon
1/4 teaspoon ground cloves
crumble mixture (from Apple Crumble Bars, page 211)**

*F*or pastry: Combine flour, sugar, and salt in a food processor; pulse to mix. Add the butter and pulse 5 or 6 times to make small crumbs. In a small bowl, whisk yolk and water. Add to processor, pulsing just until the pastry starts to get clumpy. Dump crumbs onto a counter and pack them like a snowball. Knead pastry 2 or 3 times. Place onto a piece of plastic wrap and flatten into a ¼-inch-thick disk. Wrap and refrigerate for 1 hour. When chilled, roll into a 12-inch circle on a sheet of waxed paper. Invert over a 9-inch deep-dish pie pan; peel off paper and tuck pastry into pan. Sculpt edge into an upstanding rim. Freeze.

Preheat oven to 400° F. For filling: Combine all the filling ingredients — except crumble mixture — in a large bowl; mix well. Let fruit sit for 5 minutes, then turn it into the pie shell. Bake on the center rack for 25 minutes (make crumble mixture while the pie is baking). Remove pie from oven and spread a thick layer of crumble mixture over the top; you may not need all of it (leftovers can be used on muffins). Reduce heat to 350° F and bake another 35 to 40 minutes, until the juices bubble thickly. Cool on a rack before slicing. **Makes 8 to 10 servings.**

☐☐

TECHNOLOGY UPDATE

"For years I had trouble sleeping restfully — now I know the problem was in my mattress!"

NatureSleep™ Platinum features comfort zones that match your body's shape and promote restful, therapeutic sleep.

The distinct comfort zones in NatureSleep Platinum have revolutionized the sleep-product industry. They reduce sleep stress— especially strain on the spine—and cradle those areas of the body prone to increased pressure.

by Christine Wolf

Traditional mattresses leave your lower back and legs unsupported and hinder proper circulation. Even expensive waterbeds, which are supposed to distribute weight evenly, fail to support the body properly. Your spine arches downward, in a position specialists refer to as "hammocking," causing excessive strain on the back. Scientists and doctors agree that the ideal position is a neutral body posture in which the different parts of the human body are supported individually and evenly. This is the secret behind NatureSleep Platinum, the revolutionary product that turns any bed into the ideal sleep surface.

Scientific solution. Anatomic Concepts, a medical products research and manufacturing company, has designed the ultimate mattress pad. Using research originally conducted for hospitals, this innovative company developed an effective, affordable way to transform any mattress into a specially-designed sleep surface that closely matches the shape of the human body. It features a patented five-zone sleep surface that holds the body in a neutral posture and redistributes pressure during sleep.

Comfort zones. The distinct comfort zones in NatureSleep Platinum have revolutionized the sleep-product industry. They reduce sleep stress— especially strain on the spine—and cradle those areas of the body prone to increased pressure. Until now, only the most expensive and most

advanced mattress products featured this degree of technology, but now you can get it without even buying a new mattress.

Installs in seconds. NatureSleep Platinum fits right over your existing mattress, uses normal sheets and turns any bed into an anatomically-correct and incredibly comfortable sleep surface. The five comfort zones have been created using a computer-designed grid pattern and are engineered to accommodate people of all heights and sizes.

Risk-free. Try it for yourself, it comes with a one-year manufacturer's limited warranty and Comtrad's exclusive risk-free home trial. If for any reason you are not completely satisfied, return your purchase within 90 days for a full refund, "No Questions Asked."

NatureSleep™ Platinum mattress pad: Sizes Twin through King starting at
. . . .**$59.95** $9.95 S&H
Virginia and California residents only, please include applicable sales tax.

Please mention promotional code **6057-16213.**

For fastest service, call toll-free 24 hours a day

800-992-2966

comtradindustries
2820 Waterford Lake Drive, Suite 102 Midlothian, VA 23112

Winning Recipes

in the 1999 Recipe Contest

First Prize

Crescent City Banana Bundles

Bundles:

2 cans (8 ounces each) refrigerated crescent dinner rolls

4 medium firm-ripe bananas

8 teaspoons brown sugar

1/2 cup coarsely chopped pecans

1/2 cup white chocolate chips

Sauce:

1/2 cup (1 stick) butter

1/2 cup brown sugar

2 tablespoons orange juice or rum

6 tablespoons coarsely chopped pecans

For Serving:

8 scoops vanilla ice cream or frozen yogurt

Preheat oven to 375° F. Divide crescent rolls into 8 rectangles and press perforations to seal. On a lightly floured surface, roll each rectangle to a 6x6-inch square. Peel and cut bananas in half crosswise. Cut each half into ½-inch slices and put into center of squares. Sprinkle each pile with 1 teaspoon brown sugar, 1 tablespoon pecans, and 1 tablespoon white chocolate chips. Bring corners and sides up and pinch together in center to form a bundle. Place onto an ungreased baking sheet. Bake 17 to 20 minutes, until golden brown and crisp.

Meanwhile, in a small saucepan, bring butter, brown sugar, and orange juice or rum to a boil. Add pecans and boil for 1 to 2 minutes, until slightly thickened; keep warm. To serve, place 1 bundle onto each plate. Place 1 scoop of ice cream or frozen yogurt alongside, and spoon sauce over both. **Serves 8.**

Julie DeMatteo, Clementon, New Jersey

Second Prize

Lemon Cream and Raspberry Tart

Caramel Crunch Crust:

1/3 cup packed dark-brown sugar

1/2 cup toasted and finely ground pecans

1/2 cup flour

1/2 teaspoon cinnamon

1/2 teaspoon ginger

1/4 teaspoon salt

6 tablespoons cold unsalted butter, cut into small pieces

Preheat oven to 375° F. In a food processor, pulse all crust ingredients until combined, about 40 seconds. Press dough evenly into bottom and up sides of a 9-inch round tart pan with a fluted rim. Bake crust in middle of oven 20 minutes, and cool in pan on rack.

Lemon Cream Filling:

6 ounces cream cheese, at room temperature

1/2 cup lemon curd, at room temperature

Topping:

12 ounces raspberries (fresh or frozen)

In a food processor or mixer, whip cream cheese until light and fluffy, and gradually add the lemon curd, continuing to whip until mixture is combined.

Fill cooled crust with lemon cream and top with raspberries. **Serves 8.**

Veronica Betancourt, Antioch, California

Third Prize

Summer Peach Crisp

Topping:

2/3 cup packed brown sugar
1/2 cup rolled oats
1/2 cup toasted sliced almonds
1/2 cup flour
3 tablespoons sugar
1/2 cup (1 stick) butter

Filling:

1/4 cup flour
1/3 cup sugar
1/2 teaspoon cinnamon
1/4 teaspoon nutmeg
1/8 teaspoon ginger
8 cups peeled and sliced ripe peaches (or nectarines)
1/4 cup peach nectar or orange juice

Preheat oven to 400° F. In a bowl, stir together the brown sugar, oats, almonds, ½ cup flour, and 3 tablespoons sugar. Using a pastry blender, cut in the butter until mixture resembles coarse crumbs.

In a large bowl, stir together the ¼ cup flour, ⅓ cup sugar, cinnamon, nutmeg, and ginger. Add the peach slices and nectar or orange juice. Toss to coat. Transfer filling to an ungreased 3-quart rectangular baking dish. Sprinkle topping over the filling. Bake for 30 to 35 minutes, or until fruit is tender and topping is golden. Serve warm or cold. If desired, top with ice cream. **Serves 10.**

Mike Potoroka, Goodeve, Saskatchewan

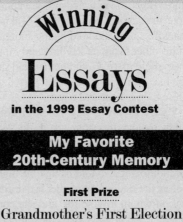

Winning Essays

in the 1999 Essay Contest

My Favorite 20th-Century Memory

First Prize

Grandmother's First Election

My grandmother was born in 1893 in Rochester, New York, on the family farm. I grew up in her house on Canton Street. Every election day, she told us this story, the tale of her first election.

Women had just gotten the vote. My great-grandfather had a wife and two daughters who were of age and American citizens. On election day, they woke up early and harnessed the horses to the wagon for the ride down Lyell Avenue to the polling place. It was a lovely day, sunny and clear, and knowing it was the day of their first vote made the sisters sit straight and smile wide at people they passed.

As they drove up to the voting poll, my grandmother and her sister, Mary, could see a few dozen men standing in front of the building, holding bats and rakes. It seemed that the men didn't want young ladies to vote.

Great-grandfather parked the wagon across the street. He helped his wife and daughters out. Grandmother heard him reaching under the wagon seat. He pulled out his double-barreled shotgun and loaded it in full view of the men, then said, "Boys, my wife and girls are gonna vote, thank you. Come on, girls." Taking his wife's arm and holding the shotgun in his other hand, he led the family into the polling place. Grandmother said she felt like Moses when the water parted — those men just cleared a path.

Every election day when Grandmother told us this story, she'd add, "Always vote. It was not an easy right to obtain and one you should never give up." Grandmother also told us that the night before the election, her father had drilled her on whom to vote for, and she confided, "I would have had chicken-coop duty for a year if he knew how I voted!"

Mary C. Taylor, Bergen, New York

The Day I Sold Three Pencils to Albert Einstein

As a teen in 1950, I worked after school at a Woolworth store in Princeton, New Jersey. My counter held neatly arranged stationery supplies. One afternoon, a short, disheveled man with long, unruly gray hair came to my counter. I had seen him before, walking on Nassau Street, his hands clasped behind his back. He always muttered to himself and walked as though studying the sidewalk.

Now he was fiddling with the Ticonderoga pencils. He examined the stack, chose three, then dug deep into his pocket for loose change. I said, "That will be 15 cents, please." He stretched out his hand to me. His palm held an assortment of coins, pocket lint, and scraps of paper. He mumbled something, and I realized that he wanted me to choose the correct amount of money from his hand. I took three nickels, thanked him, and watched him walk away.

I still wonder if Albert Einstein, the genius whose theory of relativity set him apart in the world of physics, hadn't mastered the simple skill of making change!

Ethel P. Ughetta,
Neshanic Station, New Jersey

How I Became a Jets Fan

It was early January of 1968, and my dad surprised me with tickets to Super Bowl II at the Orange Bowl in Miami for my 15th birthday. It was a dream come true for a sports-minded young man. The game was between the Green

Bay Packers (Vince Lombardi, Bart Starr, Ray Nitschke, and others) and the Oakland Raiders (George Blanda, Fred Biletnikoff, and John Madden as a linebacker coach). What a matchup!

At halftime, my dad pointed out the young upstart quarterback of the New York Jets, Joe Namath, sitting five rows in front of us. I got up my courage and, with my program in hand, went up to him and asked for his autograph. He graciously accepted and told me to keep an eye on the Jets.

I immediately became a Jets fan. And next season, there they were, playing in Super Bowl III. My dad got us tickets again, and as I cheered my heart out, the Jets beat the Colts, just as Joe had predicted.

I still have my signed program and cherish it as a reminder of my youth and the wonderful times I shared with my dad. By the way — tickets cost $12 back then!

Tom McLeod, Leslie, Arkansas

Honorable Mention

A Visit to the Eternal Flame

A gray wind rolled down the Potomac River and whipped through Arlington National Cemetery on November 22, 1964. Washington, D.C.'s monuments were hidden in a shroud of mist.

We sloshed through soaked grass and dodged muddy ruts to reach John F. Kennedy's grave site, just one year old. I shivered behind the white picket fence surrounding the still-mounded grave. We gazed into the eternal flame a few feet away, each of us absorbed in private grief.

Nobody noticed the limousine that slipped out of the fog until it stopped be-

side us and two men got out. They parted our small crowd and opened the gate to the grave. The chauffeur opened the limousine's back door. Two passengers emerged, heads bowed. Each carried a wreath to the grave. They placed the wreaths, then knelt for a short, silent prayer.

When the men stood up and acknowledged us, we realized they were Robert and Edward Kennedy. They got back into their limousine and it disappeared into the mist.

Carol P. Bartold, Glendale, California

Announcing the 2000 Essay Contest

What This Country Needs Is . . .

■ What do you think would make our society better? Whether it's as nostalgic as a horse and buggy, as practical as a better mousetrap, or as visionary as the Bill of Rights, let us know what it is, and why, in 200 words or less. Cash prizes (first prize, $100; second prize, $75; third prize, $50) will be awarded for the best original essays. All entries become the property of Yankee Publishing Incorporated, which reserves all rights to the materials submitted. Winners will be announced in the 2001 edition of *The Old Farmer's Almanac* and posted on our Web site at www.almanac.com. Deadline is February 1, 2000. Please type all essays. Address: Essay Contest, The Old Farmer's Almanac, P.O. Box 520, Dublin, NH 03444; or send E-mail (subject: Essay Contest) to almanac@yankeepub.com.

THAT SCANDALOUS DANCE CALLED

The  altz

Two hundred years ago, a new dance whirled into society, shocking the sensibilities of respectable folk on both continents. It wasn't the sexy tango or the racy cancan, but an indecent new dance called the waltz.

Picture a gilded ballroom, with the strains of Johann Strauss's "The Blue Danube" filling the perfumed air. Whirling in circles around the floor are couples performing the waltz, one of the best-loved dances of all time. Well — maybe not *all* time. When the waltz made its debut with the dawn of the 19th century, it was feared as "the devil's greatest invention."

For those who have blocked out junior-high dancing class or who don't share today's interest in ballroom dancing, the waltz is a graceful couple's dance done in three-quarter time, performed to music of the same name. The first beat of a waltz rhythm (both in music and in dance) is accented, followed by two lighter beats. It's the dance where you whisper "ONE two three, ONE two three" while whirling around the room.

Eighteenth-century ballrooms were dominated by stilted minuets, sprawling gavottes, and stiff chaconnes, all rigid dances executed at arm's length and without body contact. Like the ballroom itself, the dancers were governed by strict rules of social intercourse.

In 1800, the spirit of freedom that had prompted the French and American revolutions ignited the world of dance, as well. The waltz (from the German *walzen,* meaning "to turn or roll") twirled onto the scene, adapted from two popular central-European folk dances, the *Weller* and the *Ländler,* and from the French *contredanse,* in which couples faced each other and executed a turning motif called a valse. As tourists flocked to Vienna, the waltz capital of the world, just to see and hear the sensational new dance, ballroom dancing as we know it was born.

As with any revolution, there were critics. "Waltzing is the main source of weakness of the body and mind of our generation," wrote one gentleman. Religious officials tried banning all gliding and waltzing. Reporters in Italy, France, and Hungary commented on the "erotic nature" of the waltz, and a London newspaper fretted about "how uneasy an English mother would be to see her daughter so familiarly treated . . ."

BY VICTORIA DOUDERA

Just what was so shocking? Never before had a gentleman held a lady to him in a closed position (now called a ballroom hold). Never before had couples in polite society appeared to dance as if for their own pleasure. And the speed! "Vertigo is one of the great inconveniences of the waltz," a dancer noted in 1836. "The character of this dance, its rapid turnings, the clasping of the dancers, their exciting contact . . ."

Even more shocking, the new dance used the classical ballet position of turned-out toes, compounding the "familiar" posture. The positions are "so dirty and vulgar as to be disgusting," said one detractor.

Dancing masters of the day were also vocal opponents, mainly because the waltz threatened their livelihood. Complicated court dances like the quadrille and the minuet required many lessons to learn. But the basic steps of the waltz could be mastered quickly. Why, some dancers could pick up the steps just by watching it!

All the commotion only increased its popularity, and slowly but surely, the waltz was accepted in the polite circles of Paris, London, and New York. It was not danced in Boston until 1834, when a dancing master named Lorenzo Papanti gave an exhibition of the new dance at the Beacon Hill home of one Mrs. Otis. By the middle of the 19th century, the waltz was here to stay.

Dances need music, and the waltz was no exception.

(c o n t i n u e d)

TEN FAVORITE WALTZES
(how many can you hum?)

- "The Anniversary Waltz" (Dave Franklin and Al Dubin, 1941)

- "The Skaters' Waltz" (Emile Waldteufel, 1882)

- "The Tennessee Waltz" (Redd Stewart and Pee Wee King, 1948)

- "The Blue Danube" (Johann Strauss the Younger, 1867)

- "The Minute Waltz" (Frédéric Chopin, 1846-47)

- "Goodnight, Irene" (Huddie Ledbetter, aka Leadbelly, and John Lomax, 1936)

- "La Valse" (Maurice Ravel, 1919-20)

- "The Mephisto Waltz" (Franz Liszt, 1860)

- "The Waltz of the Flowers," from The Nutcracker (Pyotr Ilich Tchaikovsky, 1892)

- "The Jitterbug Waltz" (Fats Waller, 1942)

Two Austrian composers, Johann Strauss the Younger and Franz Lanner, greatly boosted the new dance by writing beautiful music. A young Frédéric Chopin visited Vienna in the 1830s and became enamored of the new sound. Soon he was writing waltzes himself. Johannes Brahms shocked the musical world when he, too, was inspired to write this new type of music.

The original waltz of two centuries ago is known today as the Viennese. It's faster (50 to 60 measures per minute) than today's typical waltz and characterized by a constant, lively turning of the couples. A slower version, at first called the Boston, developed around the close of the 19th century. It was distinguishable by a slower tempo (30 to 40 measures per minute), long gliding steps, and more forward and backward movement. The Boston evolved into what is known today as the American Waltz — the dance of Fred Astaire and Ginger Rogers. Another modification, the Hesitation, was introduced at about the same time. It involves taking one step to the three beats of a measure.

The era of the Charleston, the 1920s, saw the development of a new waltz, the English, now known as the International Waltz. Played at a set tempo of 31 measures per minute, it's a complicated dance in which the couples remain in a ballroom hold (no spontaneous twirling) and execute diagonal patterns across the ballroom. The fancy International Waltz has become enormously popular.

In fact, ballroom dancing in general is again in vogue. Mary Schaufert, of the United States Amateur Ballroom Dancers Association, says that its membership has more than doubled over the past five years: "From swing and Latin to the good old waltz, ballroom dancing is fun, it's healthy, and anyone from age 6 on up can do it."

Doris Pease, senior editor at the magazine *Dancing USA*, has confidence that efforts to add DanceSport — the new name for competitive ballroom dancing — to the Olympics will succeed during the next decade. And when that happens, the grandparent of ballroom dancing, the waltz, will be there.

Once the dance of peasants, the waltz has become the dance of athletes. But it's also the dance of royalty at coronations, and heads of state at inaugurals. The dance of happily married couples celebrating golden wedding anniversaries. And the dance of cowboys at local watering holes. Despite new steps, new styles, scandal, and criticism, the waltz has endured.

LEARN TO
WALTZ
(and More)

🔳 Interested in learning the scandalous waltz or another ballroom dance? The USABDA and the National Dance Council of America estimate that 17.7 million Americans go ballroom dancing several times a year. Of these, 150,000 are serious dancers who take lessons two or more times a week, and 16,000 are competitors. Contact the United States Amateur Ballroom Dancers Association, Inc., for more information. The number is 800-447-9047; its Web site is www.usabda.org. □ □

🖥 **Spinning the Web:** Go to **www.almanac.com** and click on **Article Links 2000** for Web sites related to this article. – *The Editors*

The (Sickening) SECRETS of WINNING an EATING CONTEST

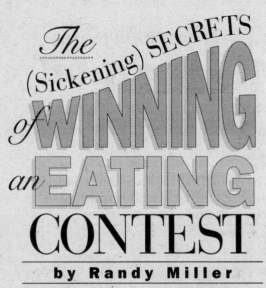

by Randy Miller

It was Ben Franklin who wrote, "Eat to live, and not live to eat," but the present-day popularity of eating contests suggests we could add "eat to compete" to his old adage. We visited food fairs and festivals around the country and spoke with some champion chompers to get their advice on a winning strategy.

EGGS

■ We're talking about hard-boiled, pickled quail eggs, and a contest in Texas to see how many of them you can eat in 60 seconds. The World Championship of Pickled-Quail-Egg Eating is a highlight of the annual Prairie Dog Chili Cook-Off, held at Traders Village in Grand Prairie, and there is one contestant who flies high above the flock. Lester Tucker, age 45, has won seven championships, setting a world record in 1998 by downing 42 quail eggs (each one about the size of a giant olive) in a minute. The rules are strict. At the end of the 60 seconds, says Tucker, "your mouth has got to be clean or you're dis-quail-ified."

CEREAL

Stephanie Solomon and an impressed Tony the Tiger.

■ Stephanie Solomon's teammates on the Cornell University novice women's crew team were amazed at how much cereal she always ate for breakfast. When their dining hall announced a cereal-eating contest (cosponsored by Kellogg Company), Stephanie ate her way to a championship, spooning down nine bowls of Frosted Flakes cereal (with milk) in three minutes. Stephanie lined up seven bowls to begin. "You don't breathe and you don't chew. You just swallow," she recalls. Asked to describe her inner thoughts during the serial cereal eat-off, Solomon compared it with rowing: "I hit the wall, but I just kept going. I went out hard at the beginning, found my rhythm, kept steady throughout, and pushed through the pain." Of such grit, Champions of Breakfast are made.

Tucker's technique is simple: "I swallow them whole. If one gets hung in my throat, I swallow another and they both go down." Lester's wife, Mary, serves as coach, counting the fast-disappearing eggs and keeping track of the time. On the day of the contest, does Lester forgo breakfast to leave room? "Nope, I eat all the time," he says. When asked if the 50-egg barrier will ever be broken, Tucker offers this hard-boiled answer: "I doubt it. But I'll be back next year."

Lester Tucker — pickled-quail-egg-eating champion.

– photo courtesy
Alicia Smith Buescher

LOBSTER

■ If you are a lobster-lover between the ages of 8 and 12, head for the Maine Lobster Festival, held in Rockland each August. According to the rules of the festival's lobster-eating contest, you must crack open a 1-1/4-pound lobster using only your hands or other body part (like a foot) and be the first to eat all the meat in the lobster's claws, knuckles, and tail. Past winners have usually accomplished this in about a minute and a half, according to festival spokesperson Alice Knight. "If you're good, you rip out a claw and break it into three sections, using your fist to whap it. And you chew while you're doing the next piece." The festival's all-time winning mark for eating a lobster is 53 seconds, "held by a boy who knew exactly where the meat was," recalls Knight. "He must have grown up eating lobster!"

■ When the days are long, the sun is hot, and the corn is ripe, downtown Urbana, Illinois, shucks its usual routine in favor of the Urbana Sweet Corn Festival. How many ten-inch ears of cooked 'Colorado' sweet corn can a person eat in one minute? Serious contestants know it's more efficient to move the corn cob instead of their mouth. Andy Baylor's unique approach earned him the 1998 championship, when he ate 13 ears of corn in just one minute. Baylor, a long-haired disc jockey

at WZNF radio in Urbana, held the corn vertically, raked it upward against his upper teeth, then rotated the cob for the next pass, creating a new art form that required him to get his chin out of the way while catching the flying kernels in his mouth. "I approached it like I was some kind of ancient machine, a hybrid of a human and the old manual typewriter — *rrrrrr-ding! rrrrr-ding!*" explains Baylor. "I ended up a mess of hair, corn, and emotion. I felt like I was a performer!" Baylor intends to compete again.

(c o n t i n u e d)

CHEESE CURDS

■ Father Jim Vanden Hogen knows cheese. He and his 13 siblings grew up on a small farm in Wisconsin. "My parents were from Holland, and cheese was always popular in our family — we made blocks of it." Cheese curds, formed during the initial stage of cheese-making, when the milk solids separate from the liquid whey, are rubbery and mild. Father Jim, the parish priest in Little Chute, Wisconsin, won the cheese-curd-eating contest at the Great Wisconsin Cheese Festival in 1997. He was the fastest to eat a half pound of the peanut-size clumps and offers this advice on quick curd consumption: "Take in six to eight at a time; chew them quickly but not too much, just to break them down; then wash them down with a sip of water. I like cheese curds," he adds, "but you can't take time to enjoy them. I make sure I am hungry before competing, and hungry to win!" Father Jim's post-contest regimen includes drinking a glass of prune juice, "so as not to get all bound up with the cheese."

OKRA

■ What's green and slimy and slides right down? *Abelmoschus esculentus,* of course, but only when it's boiled. Folks in Irmo, South Carolina, put on an annual festival in its honor called the Okra Strut. Sergeant Jesse Belue of the local sheriff's department is known for more than keeping the peace: He is a four-time eating-contest winner. Sergeant Belue uses his fingers to shovel in the allotted two pounds of cooked okra pods. It takes him 20 to 30 seconds to finish. "Don't think about what you're eating," he advises. Fortunately, there's no rule that the okra has to stay down. "I go to the nearest porta-johnny and get rid of it. You'll have a rude awakening the next day if you don't!"

Winner: Sergeant Jesse Belue, second from the left, at the Irmo Okra Strut. He has won four years in a row.

PIE

■ Pies are everywhere, as are the contests to eat them. At the Kentucky State Fair in Louisville, where the competition is open only to senior citizens, contestants have two minutes to eat as many nine-inch chocolate, banana, or lemon custard pies as they can. To date, the record is 2½ pies. Carla Miller, director of public

relations for the fair, says, "We use crust-less pies for safety, and the best eaters suck it in, like a vacuum cleaner — they almost inhale it. I saw one fellow get pie stuck up his nose!"

At the Machias (Maine) Wild Blueberry Festival, contestants have one minute to down as much of a nine-inch, two-crust wild blueberry pie as they can. Helen Vose, who bakes some of the 200 pies used throughout the festival, notes that "once they get most of the top crust eaten, they're on their way."

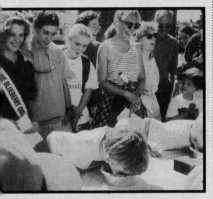

Machias (Maine) Wild Blueberry Festival pie-eating contest. The rules bar use of hands. – photo courtesy Helen Vose

Fred Grossblatt, of Los Angeles, a veteran of the pie wars, has a strategy for the single-crust cream pies offered at the Benton County (Oregon) Fair: "Bend down part of the aluminum pie plate, and in every bite, take a bit of crust. You don't want to leave all that crust until the end!" Grossblatt's best time for eating a whole pie is one minute and 47 seconds.

Most pie-eating contests have one thing in common: You can't use your hands. And most contestants probably share the belief, at least at the outset, that beauty is in the pie of the beholder.

WHERE TO COMPETE

OKRA
Irmo Okra Strut
P.O. Box 212334
Columbia, SC
29221-2334
September 29-30,
2000 (27th annual)
803-781-9878

LOBSTER
Maine Lobster Festival
P.O. Box 552
Rockland, ME 04841
August 2-6, 2000
(53rd annual)
207-596-0376

PIE
Kentucky State Fair
Heritage Hall
Kentucky Fair &
Exposition Center
P.O. Box 37130
Louisville, KY
40233-7130
Held in August, 2000
(97th annual)
502-367-5184
(call for dates)

Machias Wild Blueberry Festival
c/o Centre Street
Congregational
Church
P.O. Box 265
Machias, ME 04654
August 18-19, 2000
(25th annual)
207-255-6665

CORN
Urbana Sweet Corn Festival
111 West Main St.
Urbana, IL 61801
August 26, 2000
(25th annual)
217-344-3872

PICKLED QUAIL EGGS
Prairie Dog Chili Cook-Off
Traders Village
2602 Mayfield Rd.
Grand Prairie, TX
75052
April 8-9, 2000
(25th annual)
972-647-2331

CHEESE CURDS
Great Wisconsin Cheese Festival
1940 Buchanan St.
Little Chute, WI
54140-1414
June 2-4, 2000
(12th annual)
920-788-7390

☐☐

Answers to

Mr. Smith's MADDENING Mind-Manglers

From page 198.

1. The sister is 6 years old and is the older of twins (or the sister was born early in the year and her sibling late in the same year). The mother is 37, the father is 47, and the sum of their ages is 84.

■ My age = 6   Sister's age = x
Mother's age = n
Father's age = n +10
Because we know that neither parent has reached the half-century mark, the oldest that Mom can be is 39, and dad 49. We guess and check solutions by substituting in ages for the unknown child. 88 is the largest total possible for the parents, so:

$$7(6 + x) < 89$$
$$42 + 7x < 89$$
$$7x < 47$$
$$x < 6.714$$

Therefore, we know that the sister is less than 7 years old, which makes her 6, and she must either be the older of twins or have been born earlier in the same year!

2. 7 climbs

■ Jordan has climbed ⅛ of the flagpole after each slide backward (½ of ¼ equals ⅛). Therefore, he will reach the top on the 7th climb and not slide back. (6 x ⅛ = ¾ and ¾ + ¼ = 1 whole)

3. 565 discs

■ By buying 5 discs for $4 and selling 3 discs for $4, the students will essentially get 2 free discs from every 5-pack they buy for making their profit. They need to sell 75 packs of 3 free discs at $4 each to make $300.
75 x 3 = 225 free discs
They need to buy 113 packs (at 2 free discs per pack) to get 225 (or 226) free discs for selling.
113 x 5 = 565 discs

4. $63

■ Most people think they will pay $60 because 30% + 10% = 40%. However, the 10% discount is taken off the sale price ($70), not the regular price, which means you save another $7. Thus, the final price is $63.

5. The students take the boxes to the seesaw and, for their first attempt, put three boxes on each end. If the seesaw balances, then the seventh box is the one that weighs the most and has the tickets. If the seesaw doesn't balance, they take the three boxes that weigh the most and, for their second attempt, put one of those boxes on each end. Again, if the seesaw balances, then the third box is the one that has the tickets. If it doesn't balance, the heavy one is it. Thus, after two attempts, they will know the correct box.

6. 157.5°

■ Each 5-minute section is equivalent

to 30°, and the hour hand has moved ¾ of the way within the 3 to 4 section (or 22.5°), leaving 7.5°. The minute hand is 5 full sections away, from 4 to 9, or 150°. Add the remaining 7.5° to the hour hand, for a total of 157.5°.

7. 99¢ change
■ The sign reads .99¢, which is really 99/100 of 1 cent, which is less than 1 penny. Therefore, the sign should be corrected either to $0.99, which is 99/100 of a dollar, or to 99¢, which is the correct way of writing 99 cents.

8. 1,343 (or 1,379 if " is used as seconds and ' is used as minutes)
■ Take 12 inches in every foot
Times 3 feet in every yard = 36
Plus 40 rods in every furlong = 76
Plus 5,280 feet in every mile = 5,356
Plus 16 ounces in every pound = 5,372
Divided by 4 pecks in every bushel = 1,343

9. Because he is a batter who has just hit a home run. The masked men are the catcher and umpire!

10. 109¼ feet

■ 1st time hits ground = 38 feet
1st bounce up = 19 feet
2nd time hits ground = 19 feet
2nd bounce up = 9½ feet
3rd time hits ground = 9½ feet
3rd bounce up = 4¾ feet
4th time hits ground = 4¾ feet
4th bounce up = 2⅜ feet
5th time hits ground = 2⅜ feet
Total: 109¼ feet

11. If you write down 10 10 10 and simply put a small segment over the 1 in the middle 10, you make 10 T0 10, or 9:50!

12. 2.5 pounds
■ Originally, the plum was 95% water (or 9.5 pounds) and 5% pit and pulp (or 0.5 pound). Now it is 80% water and therefore 20% pit and pulp. Since now 20% of the weight is 0.5 pound, here is the ratio:

$$\frac{.20 \text{(the new weight)}}{.20} = \frac{0.5 \text{ pounds}}{.20}$$

The new weight = 2.5 pounds
(Or if 20% [pit and pulp] is 0.5 pounds, then 80% [water] is 4 times 0.5, or 2 pounds. Added together, the total weight is 2.5 pounds.) □□

Makeshift Measurers

■ When you don't have a measuring stick or tape, use what is at hand. To this list, add any other items that you always (or nearly always) have handy.

Credit card: 3-3/8" x 2-1/8"
Business card (standard): 3-1/2" x 2"
Floor tile: 12" square
Dollar bill: 6-1/8" x 2-5/8"
Quarter (diameter): 1"
Penny (diameter): 3/4"
Sheet of paper: 8-1/2" x 11"
    (legal size: 8-1/2" x 14")

Your foot/shoe: _____

Your outstretched arms, fingertip to
    fingertip: _____

Your shoelace: _____

Your necktie: _____

Your belt: _____

THE GREATEST BARGAINS
• OF THE LAST 100 YEARS •

For instance, if, in 1909, you'd kept your Honus Wagner baseball card that came free in a pack of cigarettes, you could sell it today for $640,000. But *you* can decide which of the following was the greatest bargain of them all.

BY KENNETH M. SHELDON

Taking Stock of the Century

■ One hundred years ago, the "high-tech" stock of the day was General Electric. With the introduction of washing machines, vacuum cleaners, and other electric devices, wise investors predicted that GE stock would be a safe bet — and they were right. Over the course of the century, GE stock has split eight times (twice offering 4-for-1 and once 3-for-1 splits). If you had purchased a single share of GE stock in 1901 (at a cost of between $183.50 and $289.75), you would now have 1,536 shares, with a total worth of over $150,000.

∽ The Original ∽ REAL THING

■ For a somewhat smaller investment, say a nickel, you could have turned to a patent-medicine-turned-soft-drink-manufacturer, purchased a bottle of Coca Cola, and tucked it away for safekeeping. Coke's original stoppered bottles (before the 1917 advent of the "hobble-skirt" design) are known as Hutchinson bottles. According to antique Coke-bottle dealer Reggie Lynch, an unopened Hutchinson Coke bottle with label and stopper is worth about $5,000 today. (Of course, the Coke might be a little flat.)

– courtesy Reggie Lynch

A Penny Saved

■ You might have better luck finding a 1909 penny. That was the year the U.S. Mint changed the design from the Indian Head to the Lincoln Head. Some of the first Lincoln pennies had the initials of the designer, Victor D. Brenner, inscribed on the reverse of the coin, near the rim. The pennies

A BARGAIN IN THE CARDS

- Card Collectors' Company

■ **The turn of the** century saw the birth of the baseball card. The very first cards came not with bubble gum but in cigarette packages. Tobacco companies used them to stiffen the soft cigarette packages. The cards proved popular, but not every ballplayer wanted to be identified with smoking. Honus Wagner, star shortstop for the Pittsburgh Pirates, asked the American Tobacco Company in 1909 to stop distributing cards with his image, which the company did — but not before a few cards were released.

Today, the Honus Wagner card is the most valuable of all baseball cards. If you were to find one, it could be worth as much as $640,000 — the price actually paid for a card in 1996. Not bad considering it came free in a pack of Sweet Caporal cigarettes.

... minted at the San Francisco mint and carrying the "S" mint mark along with Brenner's initials are especially valuable: A "gem quality" 1909-S VDB (as it is known to coin collectors) is worth $2,000 today.

- photo: Museum of the American Numismatic Association

- Smithsonian Institution Libraries, Smithsonian Institution

A High-Flying Rarity

■ **In 1918, the U.S. Post Office** marked the inauguration of air mail service with a new 24-cent stamp depicting the plane that would carry the mail, a biplane known as the Jenny. On the day of issuance, a stamp collector named William T. Robey went to a Washington, D.C., post office and asked the clerk for a sheet of the stamps. "He brought forth a full sheet, and my heart stood still," Robey later told an interviewer. Due to a printing mistake, the image of the plane appeared upside-down, making the stamps an instant rarity.

The postal service tried to buy back the stamps, but Robey refused. As far as is known, the 100 stamps in the sheet, later broken up, are the only ones to have escaped the eyes of postal inspectors. Today, they are among the most valuable stamps known, each fetching as much as $100,000.

(continued)

The Best Dime Ever Spent

■ If you had walked past a newsstand in 1938, you could have plunked down a dime to buy a copy of *Action Comics #1*. That's the comic book that introduced a blue-suited "visitor from another planet," who chose the name Superman. While not the first comic book to be published, *Action Comics #1* heralded the Golden Age of comics by introducing the superhero.

Today's comic books dazzle with special graphics and holographic covers. But none of the current crop is likely to top the value of that first *Action Comics*, a copy of which was sold for **$137,500 in 1995.**

– Photofest / © DC Comics

A Burger, Fries, and a Slice of History

■ If you had lived in Lubbock, Texas, in the 1950s, you could have heard Charles Hardin ("Buddy") Holley for nothing — surely one of the entertainment bargains of the century. Buddy and his band, The Crickets, often performed for free at local teen hangouts like the Hi-D-Ho drive-in. Lis-

– courtesy Lubbock Convention and Visitors Bureau

tening to this likable young man who broke new ground in rock 'n' roll was a real bargain that will "Not Fade Away" with time. You may want to think twice before you tell the kid next door to turn down his amplifier.

A Sweet Deal

– Richard Geary, *Pez Collectibles*

■ Remember those candy dispensers you had when you were a kid, the ones with the heads of cartoon characters on top? Pez candies, introduced in Austria in the 1920s, were breath mints for smokers. When the company brought Pez to the United States in 1952, they added plastic heads to the dispensers and fruit flavoring to the mints.

Until a few years ago, only a few people collected Pez dispensers. Now, however, there are thousands of "Pezheads," as they call themselves. If you check your attic, you might find a "Make-A-Face" Pez dispenser (a kind of "Mr. Potatohead" Pez with exchangeable parts), which sold for 79 cents in 1972. The most valuable of all Pez dispensers, it sells for as much as $5,500.

Making Book ON First Editions

■ A first edition doesn't have to be ancient to be valuable. If you had purchased the first printing of a novel by an unknown Southern lawyer named John Grisham — A

A MONSTER

OF A BARGAIN

■ In the fall of 1998, three friends were flea-marketing near Oakland, California, and bought a set of luggage from the 1930s for $100. Included with the set was a briefcase that was locked and rusted shut. At home, they opened the briefcase to find a folded poster for the original 1931 movie *Frankenstein*. The poster was a "6-sheet," the largest of display posters made, the most valuable, and the hardest to find in good condition.

It was an incredible find, says Stephen Fishler, of Metropolis Collectibles, a dealer in movie memorabilia. Fishler purchased the poster for his own collection for a sum that he will only say is "in the six figures."

– courtesy Stephen Fishler

Time to Kill — your initial $10 investment in 1989 would have grown to $2,500 by now (later editions don't count). A search of flea markets and library sales (especially in Mississippi and thereabouts) might still turn up a copy. Or you could pick up the first novel from the next Grisham . . . if you can figure out who that will be.

A Mickey Mouse Land Deal

■ Prior to 1965, central Florida was known largely for orange groves, swamps, and alligators. Then, as the *Kissimmee Gazette* reported, "Miami interests have put together about 30,000 acres of land in Osceola and Orange counties. . . . No one will say publicly what the land is for."

It turned out that the "Miami interests" were acting on behalf of Walt Disney, who didn't want his plans to leak out. Disney paid about $200 an acre for a chunk of waterlogged wilderness twice the size of Manhattan (a real-estate bargain from an earlier era).

Today, the "Reedy Creek Improvement District," as Disney World is officially known, includes the Magic Kingdom, Epcot Center, Disney-MGM Studios, the new Animal Kingdom Park, 19 resorts, and three water parks. The most recent addition is Celebration, a 4,900-acre planned community of storybook homes on tree-lined streets. Quarter-acre lots in Celebration sell for up to $80,000 — or 1,600 times more than the original price Disney paid. □□

■ **Spinning the Web:** Go to **www.almanac.com** and click on **Article Links 2000** for Web sites related to this article. *– The Editors*

– Photofest/©Walt Disney Pictures

Time Corrections

■ Times of sunrise/sunset and moonrise/moonset, selected times for observing the visible planets, and transit times of the bright stars are given for Boston on **pages 60-87, 50-51, and 54.** Use the Key Letter shown to the right of each time on those pages with this table to find the number of minutes, already adjusted for different time zones, that you must add to or subtract from Boston time to get the correct time for your city. (Because of complex calculations for different locales, times may not be precise to the minute.) If your city is not listed, find the city closest to you in latitude and longitude and use those figures. Boston's latitude is 42° 22' and its longitude is 71° 03'. Canadian cities appear at the end of the table. For further information on the use of Key Letters and this table, see **How to Use This Almanac, page 39.**

Time Zone Code: Codes represent *standard time.* Atlantic is –1, Eastern is 0, Central is 1, Mountain is 2, Pacific is 3, Alaska is 4, and Hawaii-Aleutian is 5.

City	North Latitude ° '	West Longitude ° '	Time Zone Code	A (min.)	B (min.)	C (min.)	D (min.)	E (min.)
Aberdeen, SD	45 28	98 29	1	+37	+44	+49	+54	+59
Akron, OH	41 5	81 31	0	+46	+43	+41	+39	+37
Albany, NY	42 39	73 45	0	+ 9	+10	+10	+11	+11
Albert Lea, MN	43 39	93 22	1	+24	+26	+28	+31	+33
Albuquerque, NM	35 5	106 39	2	+45	+32	+22	+11	+ 2
Alexandria, LA	31 18	92 27	1	+58	+40	+26	+ 9	– 3
Allentown–Bethlehem, PA	40 36	75 28	0	+23	+20	+17	+14	+12
Amarillo, TX	35 12	101 50	1	+85	+73	+63	+52	+43
Anchorage, AK	61 10	149 59	4	–46	+27	+71	+122	+171
Asheville, NC	35 36	82 33	0	+67	+55	+46	+35	+27
Atlanta, GA	33 45	84. 24	0	+79	+65	+53	+40	+30
Atlantic City, NJ	39 22	74 26	0	+23	+17	+13	+ 8	+ 4
Augusta, GA	33 28	81 58	0	+70	+55	+44	+30	+19
Augusta, ME	44 19	69 46	0	–12	– 8	– 5	– 1	0
Austin, TX	30 16	97 45	1	+82	+62	+47	+29	+15
Bakersfield, CA	35 23	119 1	3	+33	+21	+12	+ 1	– 7
Baltimore, MD	39 17	76 37	0	+32	+26	+22	+17	+13
Bangor, ME	44 48	68 46	0	–18	–13	– 9	– 5	– 1
Barstow, CA	34 54	117 1	3	+27	+14	+ 4	– 7	–16
Baton Rouge, LA	30 27	91 11	1	+55	+36	+21	+ 3	–10
Beaumont, TX	30 5	94 6	1	+67	+48	+32	+14	0
Bellingham, WA	48 45	122 29	3	0	+13	+24	+37	+47
Bemidji, MN	47 28	94 53	1	+14	+26	+34	+44	+52
Berlin, NH	44 28	71. 11	0	– 7	– 3	0	+ 3	+ 7
Billings, MT	45 47	108 30	2	+16	+23	+29	+35	+40
Biloxi, MS	30 24	88 53	1	+46	+27	+11	– 5	–19
Binghamton, NY	42 6	75 55	0	+20	+19	+19	+18	+18
Birmingham, AL	33 31	86 49	1	+30	+15	+ 3	–10	–20
Bismarck, ND	46 48	100 47	1	+41	+50	+58	+66	+73
Boise, ID	43 37	116 12	2	+55	+58	+60	+62	+64
Brattleboro, VT	42 51	72 34	0	+ 4	+ 5	+ 5	+ 6	+ 7
Bridgeport, CT	41 11	73 11	0	+12	+10	+ 8	+ 6	+ 4
Brockton, MA	42 5	71 1	0	0	0	0	0	– 1
Brownsville, TX	25 54	97 30	1	+91	+66	+46	+23	+ 5
Buffalo, NY	42 53	78 52	0	+29	+30	+30	+31	+32
Burlington, VT	44 29	73 13	0	0	+ 4	+ 8	+12	+15
Butte, MT	46 1	112 32	2	+31	+39	+45	+52	+57
Cairo, IL	37 0	89 11	1	+29	+20	+12	+ 4	– 2
Camden, NJ	39 57	75 7	0	+24	+19	+16	+12	+ 9
Canton, OH	40 48	81 23	0	+46	+43	+41	+38	+36
Cape May, NJ	38 56	74 56	0	+26	+20	+15	+ 9	+ 5
Carson City–Reno, NV	39 10	119 46	3	+25	+19	+14	+ 9	+ 5

City	North Latitude ° '		West Longitude ° '		Time Zone Code	Key Letters				
						A (min.)	B (min.)	C (min.)	D (min.)	E (min.)
Casper, WY	42	51	106	19	2	+19	+19	+20	+21	+22
Charleston, SC...........	32	47	79	56	0	+64	+48	+36	+21	+10
Charleston, WV..........	38	21	81	38	0	+55	+48	+42	+35	+30
Charlotte, NC	35	14	80	51	0	+61	+49	+39	+28	+19
Charlottesville, VA.......	38	2	78	30	0	+43	+35	+29	+22	+17
Chattanooga, TN	35	3	85	19	0	+79	+67	+57	+45	+36
Cheboygan, MI	45	39	84	29	0	+40	+47	+53	+59	+64
Cheyenne, WY	41	8	104	49	2	+19	+16	+14	+12	+11
Chicago–Oak Park, IL	41	52	87	38	1	+ 7	+ 6	+ 6	+ 5	+ 4
Cincinnati–Hamilton, OH .	39	6	84	31	0	+64	+58	+53	+48	+44
Cleveland–Lakewood, OH..	41	30	81	42	0	+45	+43	+42	+40	+39
Columbia, SC	34	0	81	2	0	+65	+51	+40	+27	+17
Columbus, OH	39	57	83	1	0	+55	+51	+47	+43	+40
Cordova, AK.............	60	33	145	45	4	–55	+13	+55	+103	+149
Corpus Christi, TX	27	48	97	24	1	+86	+64	+46	+25	+ 9
Craig, CO................	40	31	107	33	2	+32	+28	+25	+22	+20
Dallas–Fort Worth, TX.....	32	47	96	48	1	+71	+55	+43	+28	+17
Danville, IL..............	40	8	87	37	1	+13	+ 9	+ 6	+ 2	0
Danville, VA.............	36	36	79	23	0	+51	+41	+33	+24	+17
Davenport, IA	41	32	90	35	1	+20	+19	+17	+16	+15
Dayton, OH	39	45	84	10	0	+61	+56	+52	+48	+44
Decatur, AL..............	34	36	86	59	1	+27	+14	+ 4	– 7	–17
Decatur, IL..............	39	51	88	57	1	+19	+15	+11	+ 7	+ 4
Denver–Boulder, CO	39	44	104	59	2	+24	+19	+15	+11	+ 7
Des Moines, IA	41	35	93	37	1	+32	+31	+30	+28	+27
Detroit–Dearborn, MI......	42	20	83	3	0	+47	+47	+47	+47	+47
Dubuque, IA	42	30	90	41	1	+17	+18	+18	+18	+18
Duluth, MN	46	47	92	6	1	+ 6	+16	+23	+31	+38
Durham, NC	36	0	78	55	0	+51	+40	+31	+21	+13
Eastport, ME	44	54	67	0	0	–26	–20	–16	–11	– 8
Eau Claire, WI...........	44	49	91	30	1	+12	+17	+21	+25	+29
Elko, NV	40	50	115	46	3	+ 3	0	– 1	– 3	– 5
Ellsworth, ME............	44	33	68	25	0	–18	–14	–10	– 6	– 3
El Paso, TX	31	45	106	29	2	+53	+35	+22	+ 6	– 6
Erie, PA	42	7	80	5	0	+36	+36	+35	+35	+35
Eugene, OR	44	3	123	6	3	+21	+24	+27	+30	+33
Fairbanks, AK............	64	48	147	51	4	–127	+ 2	+61	+131	+205
Fall River– New Bedford, MA	41	42	71	9	0	+ 2	+ 1	0	0	– 1
Fargo, ND	46	53	96	47	1	+24	+34	+42	+50	+57
Flagstaff, AZ.............	35	12	111	39	2	+64	+52	+42	+31	+22
Flint, MI.................	43	1	83	41	0	+47	+49	+50	+51	+52
Fort Myers, FL	26	38	81	52	0	+87	+63	+44	+21	+ 4
Fort Scott, KS	37	50	94	42	1	+49	+41	+34	+27	+21
Fort Smith, AR	35	23	94	25	1	+55	+43	+33	+22	+14
Fort Wayne, IN	41	4	85	9	0	+60	+58	+56	+54	+52
Fresno, CA...............	36	44	119	47	3	+32	+22	+15	+ 6	0
Gallup, NM	35	32	108	45	2	+52	+40	+31	+20	+11
Galveston, TX............	29	18	94	48	1	+72	+52	+35	+16	+ 1
Gary, IN.................	41	36	87	20	1	+ 7	+ 6	+ 4	+ 3	+ 2
Glasgow, MT.............	48	12	106	38	2	– 1	+11	+21	+32	+42
Grand Forks, ND.........	47	55	97	3	1	+21	+33	+43	+53	+62
Grand Island, NE.........	40	55	98	21	1	+53	+51	+49	+46	+44
Grand Junction, CO	39	4	108	33	2	+40	+34	+29	+24	+20
Great Falls, MT...........	47	30	111	17	2	+20	+31	+39	+49	+58
Green Bay, WI...........	44	31	88	0	1	0	+ 3	+ 7	+11	+14
Greensboro, NC	36	4	79	47	0	+54	+43	+35	+25	+17

City	North Latitude ° '	West Longitude ° '	Time Zone Code	Key Letters				
				A (min.)	B (min.)	C (min.)	D (min.)	E (min.)
Hagerstown, MD.........39 39		77 43	0	+35	+30	+26	+22	+18
Harrisburg, PA 40 16		76 53	0	+30	+26	+23	+19	+16
Hartford–New Britain, CT . . 41 46		72 41	0	+ 8	+ 7	+ 6	+ 5	+ 4
Helena, MT 46 36		112 2	2	+27	+36	+43	+51	+57
Hilo, HI 19 44		155 5	5	+94	+62	+37	+ 7	−15
Honolulu, HI 21 18		157 52	5	+102	+72	+48	+19	− 1
Houston, TX 29 45		95 22	1	+73	+53	+37	+19	+ 5
Indianapolis, IN........39 46		86 10	0	+69	+64	+60	+56	+52
Ironwood, MI 46 27		90 9	1	0	+ 9	+15	+23	+29
Jackson, MI.............42 15		84 24	0	+53	+53	+53	+52	+52
Jackson, MS 32 18		90 11	1	+46	+30	+17	+ 1	−10
Jacksonville, FL 30 20		81 40	0	+77	+58	+43	+25	+11
Jefferson City, MO 38 34		92 10	1	+36	+29	+24	+18	+13
Joplin, MO..............37 6		94 30	1	+50	+41	+33	+25	+18
Juneau, AK 58 18		134 25	4	−76	−23	+10	+49	+86
Kalamazoo, MI 42 17		85 35	0	+58	+57	+57	+57	+57
Kanab, UT 37 3		112 32	2	+62	+53	+46	+37	+30
Kansas City, MO........39 1		94 20	1	+44	+37	+33	+27	+23
Keene, NH..............42 56		72 17	0	+ 2	+ 3	+ 4	+ 5	+ 6
Ketchikan, AK...........55 21		131 39	4	−62	−25	0	+29	+56
Knoxville, TN 35 58		83 55	0	+71	+60	+51	+41	+33
Kodiak, AK..............57 47		152 24	4	0	+49	+82	+120	+154
LaCrosse, WI............43 48		91 15	1	+15	+18	+20	+22	+25
Lake Charles, LA 30 14		93 13	1	+64	+44	+29	+11	− 2
Lanai City, HI 20 50		156 55	5	+99	+69	+44	+15	− 6
Lancaster, PA 40 2		76 18	0	+28	+24	+20	+17	+13
Lansing, MI.............42 44		84 33	0	+52	+53	+53	+54	+54
Las Cruces, NM 32 19		106 47	2	+53	+36	+23	+ 8	− 3
Las Vegas, NV 36 10		115 9	3	+16	+ 4	− 3	−13	−20
Lawrence–Lowell, MA. . . 42 42		71 10	0	0	0	0	0	+ 1
Lewiston, ID 46 25		117 1	3	−12	− 3	+ 2	+10	+17
Lexington–Frankfort, KY. . . 38 3		84 30	0	+67	+59	+53	+46	+41
Liberal, KS 37 3		100 55	1	+76	+66	+59	+51	+44
Lihue, HI...............21 59		159 23	5	+107	+77	+54	+26	+ 5
Lincoln, NE.............40 49		96 41	1	+47	+44	+42	+39	+37
Little Rock, AR..........34 45		92 17	1	+48	+35	+25	+13	+ 4
Los Angeles–Pasadena– Santa Monica, CA 34 3		118 14	3	+34	+20	+ 9	− 3	−13
Louisville, KY...........38 15		85 46	0	+72	+64	+58	+52	+46
Macon, GA 32 50		83 38	0	+79	+63	+50	+36	+24
Madison, WI 43 4		89 23	1	+10	+11	+12	+14	+15
Manchester–Concord, NH . . 42 59		71 28	0	0	0	+ 1	+ 2	+ 3
McAllen, TX 26 12		98 14	1	+93	+69	+49	+26	+9
Memphis, TN 35 9		90 3	1	+38	+26	+16	+ 5	− 3
Meridian, MS 32 22		88 42	1	+40	+24	+11	− 4	−15
Miami, FL 25 47		80 12	0	+88	+57	+37	+14	− 3
Miles City, MT 46 25		105 51	2	+ 3	+11	+18	+26	+32
Milwaukee, WI 43 2		87 54	1	+ 4	+ 6	+ 7	+ 8	+ 9
Minneapolis–St. Paul, MN . . 44 59		93 16	1	+18	+24	+28	+33	+37
Minot, ND 48 14		101 18	1	+36	+50	+59	+71	+81
Moab, UT 38 35		109 33	2	+46	+39	+33	+27	+22
Mobile, AL 30 42		88 3	1	+42	+23	+ 8	− 8	−22
Monroe, LA.............32 30		92 7	1	+53	+37	+24	+ 9	− 1
Montgomery, AL.........32 23		86 19	1	+31	+14	+ 1	−13	−25
Muncie, IN..............40 12		85 23	0	+64	+60	+57	+53	+50
Nashville, TN 36 10		86 47	1	+22	+11	+ 3	− 6	−14
Newark–East Orange, NJ . . . 40 44		74 10	0	+17	+14	+12	+ 9	+ 7

City	North Latitude °	'	West Longitude °	'	Time Zone Code	A (min.)	B (min.)	C (min.)	D (min.)	E (min.)
New Haven, CT	41	18	72	56	0	+11	+ 8	+ 7	+ 5	+ 4
New London, CT	41	22	72	6	0	+ 7	+ 5	+ 4	+ 2	+ 1
New Orleans, LA	29	57	90	4	1	+52	+32	+16	− 1	−15
New York, NY	40	45	74	0	0	+17	+14	+11	+ 9	+ 6
Norfolk, VA	36	51	76	17	0	+38	+28	+21	+12	+ 5
North Platte, NE	41	8	100	46	1	+62	+60	+58	+56	+54
Norwalk–Stamford, CT	41	7	73	22	0	+13	+10	+ 9	+ 7	+ 5
Oakley, KS	39	8	100	51	1	+69	+63	+59	+53	+49
Ogden, UT	41	13	111	58	2	+47	+45	+43	+41	+40
Ogdensburg, NY	44	42	75	30	0	+ 8	+13	+17	+21	+25
Oklahoma City, OK	35	28	97	31	1	+67	+55	+46	+35	+26
Omaha, NE	41	16	95	56	1	+43	+40	+39	+37	+36
Orlando, FL	28	32	81	22	0	+80	+59	+42	+22	+ 6
Ortonville, MN	45	19	96	27	1	+30	+36	+40	+46	+51
Oshkosh, WI	44	1	88	33	1	+ 3	+ 6	+ 9	+12	+15
Palm Springs, CA	33	49	116	32	3	+28	+13	+ 1	−12	−22
Parkersburg, WV	39	16	81	34	0	+52	+46	+42	+36	+32
Paterson, NJ	40	55	74	10	0	+17	+14	+12	+ 9	+ 7
Pendleton, OR	45	40	118	47	3	− 1	+ 4	+10	+16	+21
Pensacola, FL	30	25	87	13	1	+39	+20	+ 5	−12	−26
Peoria, IL	40	42	89	36	1	+19	+16	+14	+11	+ 9
Philadelphia–Chester, PA	39	57	75	9	0	+24	+19	+16	+12	+ 9
Phoenix, AZ	33	27	112	4	2	+71	+56	+44	+30	+20
Pierre, SD	44	22	100	21	1	+49	+53	+56	+60	+63
Pittsburgh–McKeesport, PA	40	26	80	0	0	+42	+38	+35	+32	+29
Pittsfield, MA	42	27	73	15	0	+ 8	+ 8	+ 8	+ 8	+ 8
Pocatello, ID	42	52	112	27	2	+43	+44	+45	+46	+46
Poplar Bluff, MO	36	46	90	24	1	+35	+25	+17	+ 8	+ 1
Portland, ME	43	40	70	15	0	− 8	− 5	− 3	− 1	0
Portland, OR	45	31	122	41	3	+14	+20	+25	+31	+36
Portsmouth, NH	43	5	70	45	0	− 4	− 2	− 1	0	0
Presque Isle, ME	46	41	68	1	0	−29	−19	−12	− 4	+ 2
Providence, RI	41	50	71	25	0	+ 3	+ 2	+ 1	0	0
Pueblo, CO	38	16	104	37	2	+27	+20	+14	+ 7	+ 2
Raleigh, NC	35	47	78	38	0	+51	+39	+30	+20	+12
Rapid City, SD	44	5	103	14	2	+ 2	+ 5	+ 8	+11	+13
Reading, PA	40	20	75	56	0	+26	+22	+19	+16	+13
Redding, CA	40	35	122	24	3	+31	+27	+25	+22	+19
Richmond, VA	37	32	77	26	0	+41	+32	+25	+17	+11
Roanoke, VA	37	16	79	57	0	+51	+42	+35	+27	+21
Roswell, NM	33	24	104	32	2	+41	+26	+14	0	−10
Rutland, VT	43	37	72	58	0	+ 2	+ 5	+ 7	+ 9	+11
Sacramento, CA	38	35	121	30	3	+34	+27	+21	+15	+10
St. Johnsbury, VT	44	25	72	1	0	− 4	0	+ 3	+ 7	+10
St. Joseph, MI	42	5	86	26	0	+61	+61	+60	+60	+59
St. Joseph, MO	39	46	94	50	1	+43	+38	+35	+30	+27
St. Louis, MO	38	37	90	12	1	+28	+21	+16	+10	+ 5
St. Petersburg, FL	27	46	82	39	0	+87	+65	+47	+26	+10
Salem, OR	44	57	123	1	3	+17	+23	+27	+31	+35
Salina, KS	38	50	97	37	1	+57	+51	+46	+40	+35
Salisbury, MD	38	22	75	36	0	+31	+23	+18	+11	+ 6
Salt Lake City, UT	40	45	111	53	2	+48	+45	+43	+40	+38
San Antonio, TX	29	25	98	30	1	+87	+66	+50	+31	+16
San Diego, CA	32	43	117	9	3	+33	+17	+ 4	− 9	−21
San Francisco–Oakland–San Jose, CA	37	47	122	25	3	+40	+31	+25	+18	+12
Santa Fe, NM	35	41	105	56	2	+40	+28	+19	+ 9	0

City	North Latitude ° '	West Longitude ° '	Time Zone Code	A (min.)	B (min.)	C (min.)	D (min.)	E (min.)
Savannah, GA	32 5	81 6	0	+70	+54	+40	+25	+13
Scranton–Wilkes-Barre, PA.	41 25	75 40	0	+21	+19	+18	+16	+15
Seattle–Tacoma–Olympia, WA	47 37	122 20	3	+ 3	+15	+24	+34	+42
Sheridan, WY	44 48	106 58	2	+14	+19	+23	+27	+31
Shreveport, LA	32 31	93 45	1	+60	+44	+31	+16	+ 4
Sioux Falls, SD	43 33	96 44	1	+38	+40	+42	+44	+46
South Bend, IN	41 41	86 15	0	+62	+61	+60	+59	+58
Spartanburg, SC	34 56	81 57	0	+66	+53	+43	+32	+23
Spokane, WA	47 40	117 24	3	−16	− 4	+ 4	+14	+23
Springfield, IL	39 48	89 39	1	+22	+18	+14	+10	+ 6
Springfield–Holyoke, MA	42 6	72 36	0	+ 6	+ 6	+ 6	+ 5	+ 5
Springfield, MO	37 13	93 18	1	+45	+36	+29	+20	+14
Syracuse, NY	43 3	76 9	0	+17	+19	+20	+21	+22
Tallahassee, FL	30 27	84 17	0	+87	+68	+53	+35	+22
Tampa, FL	27 57	82 27	0	+86	+64	+46	+25	+ 9
Terre Haute, IN	39 28	87 24	0	+74	+69	+65	+60	+56
Texarkana, AR	33 26	94 3	1	+59	+44	+32	+18	+ 8
Toledo, OH	41 39	83 33	0	+52	+50	+49	+48	+47
Topeka, KS	39 3	95 40	1	+49	+43	+38	+32	+28
Traverse City, MI	44 46	85 38	0	+49	+54	+57	+62	+65
Trenton, NJ	40 13	74 46	0	+21	+17	+14	+11	+ 8
Trinidad, CO	37 10	104 31	2	+30	+21	+13	+ 5	0
Tucson, AZ	32 13	110 58	2	+70	+53	+40	+24	+12
Tulsa, OK	36 9	95 60	1	+59	+48	+40	+30	+22
Tupelo, MS	34 16	88 34	1	+35	+21	+10	− 2	−11
Vernal, UT	40 27	109 32	2	+40	+36	+33	+30	+28
Walla Walla, WA	46 4	118 20	3	− 5	+ 2	+ 8	+15	+21
Washington, DC	38 54	77 1	0	+35	+28	+23	+18	+13
Waterbury–Meriden, CT	41 33	73 3	0	+10	+ 9	+ 7	+ 6	+ 5
Waterloo, IA	42 30	92 20	1	+24	+24	+24	+25	+25
Wausau, WI	44 58	89 38	1	+ 4	+ 9	+13	+18	+22
West Palm Beach, FL	26 43	80 3	0	+79	+55	+36	+14	− 2
Wichita, KS	37 42	97 20	1	+60	+51	+45	+37	+31
Williston, ND	48 9	103 37	1	+46	+59	+69	+80	+90
Wilmington, DE	39 45	75 33	0	+26	+21	+18	+13	+10
Wilmington, NC	34 14	77 55	0	+52	+38	+27	+15	+ 5
Winchester, VA	39 11	78 10	0	+38	+33	+28	+23	+19
Worcester, MA	42 16	71 48	0	+ 3	+ 2	+ 2	+ 2	+ 2
York, PA	39 58	76 43	0	+30	+26	+22	+18	+15
Youngstown, OH	41 6	80 39	0	+42	40	+38	+36	+34
Yuma, AZ	32 43	114 37	2	+83	+67	+54	+40	+28

CANADA

City	North Latitude ° '	West Longitude ° '	Time Zone Code	A (min.)	B (min.)	C (min.)	D (min.)	E (min.)
Calgary, AB	51 5	114 5	2	+13	+35	+50	+68	+84
Edmonton, AB	53 34	113 25	2	− 3	+26	+47	+72	+93
Halifax, NS	44 38	63 35	−1	+21	+26	+29	+33	+37
Montreal, QC	45 28	73 39	0	− 1	+ 4	+ 9	+15	+20
Ottawa, ON	45 25	75 43	0	+ 6	+13	+18	+23	+28
Peterborough, ON	44 18	78 19	0	+21	+25	+28	+32	+35
Saint John, NB	45 16	66 3	−1	+28	+34	+39	+44	+49
Saskatoon, SK	52 10	106 40	1	+37	+63	+80	+101	+119
Sydney, NS	46 10	60 10	−1	+ 1	+ 9	+15	+23	+28
Thunder Bay, ON	48 27	89 12	0	+47	+61	+71	+83	+93
Toronto, ON	43 39	79 23	0	+28	+30	+32	+35	+37
Vancouver, BC	49 13	123 6	3	0	+15	+26	+40	+52
Winnipeg, MB	49 53	97 10	1	+12	+30	+43	+58	+71

The Twilight Zone

How to determine the length of twilight and the times of dawn and dark

■ Twilight is the period of time between dawn and sunrise, and again between sunset and dark. Both dawn and dark are defined as moments when the Sun is 18 degrees below the horizon. The latitude of a place and the time of year determine the length of twilight. To find the latitude of your city or the city nearest you, consult the **Time Corrections table, page 234.** Use that figure in the chart at the right with the appropriate date, and you will have the length of twilight in your area.

To determine when dawn will break and when dark will descend, apply the length of twilight to the times of sunrise and sunset. Follow the instructions given in **How to Use This Almanac, page 39,** to determine sunrise/sunset times for a given locality. Subtract the length of twilight from the time of sunrise for dawn. Add the length of twilight to the time of sunset for dark.

Latitude	25° N to 30° N	31° N to 36° N	37° N to 42° N	43° N to 47° N	48° N to 49° N
	H M	H M	H M	H M	H M
Jan. 1 to Apr. 10	1 20	1 26	1 33	1 42	1 50
Apr. 11 to May 2	1 23	1 28	1 39	1 51	2 04
May 3 to May 14	1 26	1 34	1 47	2 02	2 22
May 15 to May 25	1 29	1 38	1 52	2 13	2 42
May 26 to July 22	1 32	1 43	1 59	2 27	—
July 23 to Aug. 3	1 29	1 38	1 52	2 13	2 42
Aug. 4 to Aug. 14	1 26	1 34	1 47	2 02	2 22
Aug. 15 to Sept. 5	1 23	1 28	1 39	1 51	2 04
Sept. 6 to Dec. 31	1 20	1 26	1 33	1 42	1 50

	Boston, Mass. (latitude 42° 22')	Eugene, Ore. (latitude 44° 3')
Sunrise, August 1	5:37 A.M.	5:58 A.M.
Length of twilight	−1:52	−2:13
Dawn breaks	3:45 A.M., EDT	3:45 A.M., PDT
Sunset, August 1	8:03 P.M.	8:33 P.M.
Length of twilight	+1:52	+2:13
Dark descends	9:55 P.M., EDT	10:46 P.M., PDT

Tidal Glossary

Apogean Tide: A monthly tide of decreased range that occurs when the Moon is farthest from Earth (at apogee).

Diurnal: Experiencing one high water and one low water during a tidal day of approximately 24 hours.

Mean Lower Low Water: The arithmetic mean of the lesser of a daily pair of low waters, observed over a specific 19-year cycle called the National Tidal Datum Epoch.

Neap Tide: A tide of decreased range that occurs twice a month, when the Moon is in quadrature (during the first and last quarter Moons, when the Sun and the Moon are at right angles to each other relative to Earth).

Perigean Tide: A monthly tide of increased range that occurs when the Moon is closest to Earth (at perigee).

Semidiurnal: Having a period of half a tidal day. East Coast tides, for example, are semi-diurnal, with two highs and two lows during a tidal day of approximately 24 hours.

Spring Tide: A tide of increased range that occurs at times of syzygy each month. Named not for the season of spring, but from the German *springen* ("to leap up"), a spring tide also brings a lower low water.

Syzygy: The nearly straight-line configuration that occurs twice a month, when the Sun and the Moon are in conjunction (on the same side of Earth at the new Moon) and when they are in opposition (on opposite sides of Earth at the full Moon). In both cases, the gravitational effects of the Sun and the Moon reinforce each other, and tidal range is increased.

Vanishing Tide: A mixed tide of considerable inequality in the two highs or two lows, so that the "high low" may become indistinguishable from the "low high." The result is a vanishing tide, where no significant difference is apparent.

Tide Corrections

■ Many factors affect the times and heights of the tides: the coastal configuration, the time of the Moon's southing (crossing the meridian), and the Moon's phase. Use this table to calculate the *approximate* times and heights of high water at the places shown. The figures for High Tide on the **Left-Hand Calendar Pages 60-86** are the times of high tide at Commonwealth Pier in Boston Harbor. The heights of some of these tides, reckoned from Mean Lower Low Water, are given on the **Right-Hand Calendar Pages 61-87.** For the times and heights of high water at any of the following places, apply the time difference to the times of high water at Boston **(pages 60-86)** and the height difference to the heights at Boston **(pages 61-87).**

Estimations derived from this table are not meant to be used for navigation. *The Old Farmer's Almanac* accepts no responsibility for errors or any consequences ensuing from the use of this table.

National Ocean Service (NOS) tide predictions for the East Coast, West Coast, and Caribbean regions are printed in *Reed's Nautical Almanacs,* Thomas Reed Publications, Inc., 13A Lewis St., Boston, MA 02113; 800-995-4995. Tide predictions for many other reference stations around the country are also listed at NOS's Web site, www.opsd.nos.noaa.gov/tp4days.html.

Coastal Site	Difference: Time (h. m.)	Height (ft.)
Canada		
Alberton, PE	−5 45**	−7.5
Charlottetown, PE	−0 45**	−3.5
Halifax, NS	−3 23	−4.5
North Sydney, NS	−3 15	−6.5
Saint John, NB	+0 30	+15.0
St. John's, NF	−4 00	−6.5
Yarmouth, NS	−0 40	+3.0
Maine		
Bar Harbor	−0 34	+0.9
Belfast	−0 20	+0.4
Boothbay Harbor	−0 18	−0.8
Chebeague Island	−0 16	−0.6
Eastport	−0 28	+8.4
Kennebunkport	+0 04	−1.0
Machias	−0 28	+2.8
Monhegan Island	−0 25	−0.8
Old Orchard	0 00	−0.8
Portland	−0 12	−0.6

Coastal Site	Difference: Time (h. m.)	Height (ft.)
Rockland	−0 28	+0.1
Stonington	−0 30	+0.1
York	−0 09	−1.0
New Hampshire		
Hampton	+0 02	−1.3
Portsmouth	+0 11	−1.5
Rye Beach	−0 09	−0.9
Massachusetts		
Annisquam	−0 02	−1.1
Beverly Farms	0 00	−0.5
Boston	0 00	0.0
Cape Cod Canal		
East Entrance	−0 01	−0.8
West Entrance	−2 16	−5.9
Chatham Outer Coast	+0 30	−2.8
Inside	+1 54	*0.4
Cohasset	+0 02	−0.07
Cotuit Highlands	+1 15	*0.3
Dennis Port	+1 01	*0.4
Duxbury–Gurnet Pt.	+0 02	−0.3
Fall River	−3 03	−5.0
Gloucester	−0 03	−0.8
Hingham	+0 07	0.0
Hull	+0 03	−0.2
Hyannis Port	+1 01	*0.3
Magnolia–Manchester	−0 02	−0.7
Marblehead	−0 02	−0.4
Marion	−3 22	−5.4
Monument Beach	−3 08	−5.4
Nahant	−0 01	−0.5
Nantasket	+0 04	−0.1
Nantucket	+0 56	*0.3
Nauset Beach	+0 30	*0.6
New Bedford	−3 24	−5.7
Newburyport	+0 19	−1.8
Oak Bluffs	+0 30	*0.2
Onset–R.R. Bridge	−2 16	−5.9
Plymouth	+0 05	0.0
Provincetown	+0 14	−0.4
Revere Beach	−0 01	−0.3
Rockport	−0 08	−1.0
Salem	0 00	−0.5
Scituate	−0 05	−0.7
Wareham	−3 09	−5.3
Wellfleet	+0 12	+0.5
West Falmouth	−3 10	−5.4
Westport Harbor	−3 22	−6.4
Woods Hole		
Little Harbor	−2 50	*0.2
Oceanographic Inst.	−3 07	*0.2
Rhode Island		
Bristol	−3 24	−5.3
Narragansett Pier	−3 42	−6.2

Coastal Site	Difference:	Time (h. m.)	Height (ft.)	Coastal Site	Difference:	Time (h. m.)	Height (ft.)
Newport		−3 34	−5.9	Norfolk		−2 06	−6.6
Pt. Judith		−3 41	−6.3	Virginia Beach		−4 00	−6.0
Providence		−3 20	−4.8	Yorktown		−2 13	−7.0
Sakonnet		−3 44	−5.6	**North Carolina**			
Watch Hill		−2 50	−6.8	Cape Fear		−3 55	−5.0
Connecticut				Cape Lookout		−4 28	−5.7
Bridgeport		+0 01	−2.6	Currituck		−4 10	−5.8
Madison		−0 22	−2.3	Hatteras			
New Haven		−0 11	−3.2	Inlet		−4 03	−7.4
New London		−1 54	−6.7	Kitty Hawk		−4 14	−6.2
Norwalk		+0 01	−2.2	Ocean		−4 26	−6.0
Old Lyme				**South Carolina**			
Highway Bridge		−0 30	−6.2	Charleston		−3 22	−4.3
Stamford		+0 01	−2.2	Georgetown		−1 48	*0.36
Stonington		−2 27	−6.6	Hilton Head		−3 22	−2.9
New York				Myrtle Beach		−3 49	−4.4
Coney Island		−3 33	−4.9	St. Helena			
Fire Island Light		−2 43	*0.1	Harbor Entrance		−3 15	−3.4
Long Beach		−3 11	−5.7	**Georgia**			
Montauk Harbor		−2 19	−7.4	Jekyll Island		−3 46	−2.9
New York City–Battery		−2 43	−5.0	St. Simon's Island		−2 50	−2.9
Oyster Bay		+0 04	−1.8	Savannah Beach			
Port Chester		−0 09	−2.2	River Entrance		−3 14	−5.5
Port Washington		−0 01	−2.1	Tybee Light		−3 22	−2.7
Sag Harbor		−0 55	−6.8	**Florida**			
Southampton				Cape Canaveral		−3 59	−6.0
Shinnecock Inlet		−4 20	*0.2	Daytona Beach		−3 28	−5.3
Willets Point		0 00	−2.3	Fort Lauderdale		−2 50	−7.2
New Jersey				Fort Pierce Inlet		−3 32	−6.9
Asbury Park		−4 04	−5.3	Jacksonville			
Atlantic City		−3 56	−5.5	Railroad Bridge		−6 55	*0.1
Bay Head–Sea Girt		−4 04	−5.3	Miami Harbor Entrance		−3 18	−7.0
Beach Haven		−1 43	*0.24	St. Augustine		−2 55	−4.9
Cape May		−3 28	−5.3				
Ocean City		−3 06	−5.9				
Sandy Hook		−3 30	−5.0				
Seaside Park		−4 03	−5.4				
Pennsylvania							
Philadelphia		+2 40	−3.5				
Delaware							
Cape Henlopen		−2 48	−5.3				
Rehoboth Beach		−3 37	−5.7				
Wilmington		+1 56	−3.8				
Maryland							
Annapolis		+6 23	−8.5				
Baltimore		+7 59	−8.3				
Cambridge		+5 05	−7.8				
Havre de Grace		+11 21	−7.7				
Point No Point		+2 28	−8.1				
Prince Frederick							
Plum Point		+4 25	−8.5				
Virginia							
Cape Charles		−2 20	−7.0				
Hampton Roads		−2 02	−6.9				

* Where the difference in the Height column is so marked, height at Boston should be multiplied by this ratio.

** Varies widely; accurate only within 1½ hours. Consult local tide tables for precise times and heights.

Example: The conversion of the times and heights of the tides at Boston to those of Coney Island, New York, is given below:

Sample tide calculation July 1, 2000:

High tide Boston (p. 76)	11:30 A.M., EDT	
Correction for Coney Island	−3:33 hrs.	
High tide Coney Island	7:57 A.M., EDT	
Tide height Boston (p. 77)	10.3 ft.	
Correction for Coney Island	−4.9 ft.	
Tide height Coney Island	5.4 ft.	

The **Old Farmer's**
General Store

A special section featuring unique mail order products for all our readers who shop by mail.

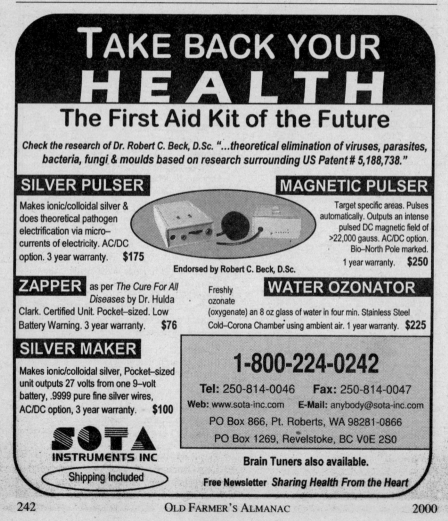

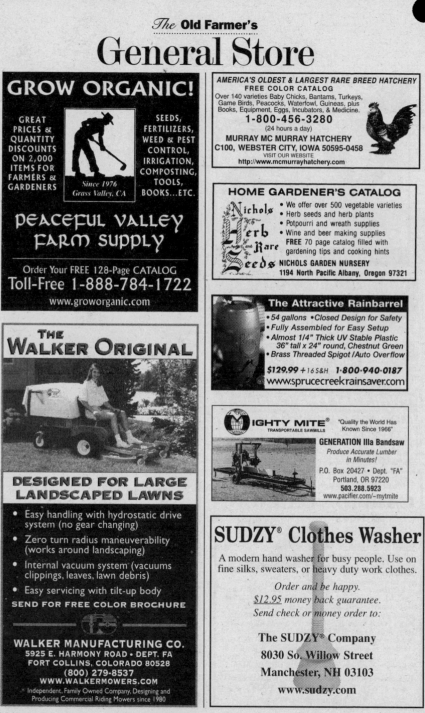

The Old Farmer's
General Store

Classified Advertising

ALTERNATIVE ENERGY

SOLAR-, WIND-, WATER-powered appliances. 30 plans. Details $3. MCOD, 3203 Bordero, Thousand Oaks CA 91362.

YOUR OWN ELECTRIC COMPANY. Costs 60% less than grid power. Use anywhere. Imperial Diesel generators, Trace inverters. Auto-start panels. Complete systems. Specialists in remote and alternative power generation since 1987. Free brochures. Imperial-A, 8569 Ward North Rd., Kinsman OH 44428-9536. 800-830-0498/330-876-8709.

"SHRED NEWSPAPERS for cash." Fun home business. Details $4. To: Barens By-Products, 14780 Lehman, Portland MI 48875.

APPAREL

DON'T GET BURNED! Legionnaires-type cap. Large bill and drape protects neck and ears from sun and bugs. Fits all adults. Colors: oyster or khaki. $23.50 ea. Check or money order: JCM, PO Box 249, Alto NM 88312.

ASTROLOGY/OCCULT

FREE OCCULT CATALOG! Over 5,000 books, jewelry, ritual items, incense, music, etc. AzureGreen, PO Box 48-OFA, Middlefield MA 01243. 413-623-2155.

BIORHYTHMS — Your physical, emotional, intellectual cycles charted in color. Interpretation guide. Six months ($14). Twelve months ($20). Send name, birth date. CYCLES, Dept. FAB, 2251 Berkely Ave., Schenectady NY 12309.

MRS. KING SPIRITUAL READER and advisor will help where all others failed in love, marriage, and health. Call 912-283-0635.

FREE METAPHYSICAL CATALOG. Feng Shui, incense, oils, tarot, and candles. Moonrise Magic; 505-332-2665; www.moonrisebooks.com.

POWERFUL SPELLS PERFORMED by Gabrielle. Specializing in reuniting lovers. Guaranteed in two hours. 504-471-2693.

ASTROLOGY — Personalized, comprehensive natal chart ($14). Progressed chart for current year ($14). Both ($20). Send name, birth date, birth time, birthplace. CYCLES, Dept. FAA, 2251 Berkely Ave., Schenectady NY 12309.

FREE MINI READINGS. Psychic Diana has the ability to solve all problems. Removes spells and reunites loved ones. Toronto, Ontario; 416-226-5418.

PSYCHIC COUNSELOR. Helps all problems of life. Money back guaranteed. Help for those who need it. Call or write Madam Sylvia, 1416 S. Main St., Ste. 220-275, Adrian MI 49221. 517-264-1895.

REVEREND SAVANNAH GOD-GIFTED. Specializing in all problems. 100% guaranteed immediate results. 504-651-3479.

EGYPTIAN PSYCHIC HELENA unlocks the secrets of your future. Love, career, health, matters of the heart. Readings $25 Visa/MC/Amex. 415-460-1985.

999 EMERGENCY. God-gifted Vanessa Jackson helps in all problems. Reunites lovers immediately. Guaranteed. Call anytime 817-498-9718.

WITCHCRAFT: FREE PROTECTIVE PENTACLE! World's foremost teachers now accepting students. Gavin and Yvonne, Box 297-OP, Hinton WV 25951-0297.

OCCULT CATALOG: COMPLETE NEEDS. Herbs, oils, incense, books, etc. $3. Power Products, Box 442 F, Mars Hill NC 28754.

FREE! ONE BLACK OR WHITE MAGIC SPELL! Tell me what you need! EKSES, PO Box 9315(B), San Bernardino CA 92427-9315.

MISS LISA, astrology reader, extraordinary powers; call for help for love or money. 3810 Memorial Dr., Waycross GA 31501. 912-283-3206.

GET WHAT YOU WANT! Results, answers; reap life's bountiful harvest. Powerful formulas for success! NSOG, Inc., PO Box 12108, Gainesville FL 32604. Web site: www.angelfire.com/ns/natural sys/.

ACCURATE, INCREDIBLE telephone psychic readings with Stephen & Tasha Halpert. Visa/MC 508-839-0111. http://members.aol.com/PeaceNow4u/.

THE MOST COMPLETE metaphysical, magical, psychic-power correspondence course ever. Become a recognized professional. Earn unlimited income with our university doctoral degree program. Reasonable rates. Priesthood, PO Box 1447, Redondo Beach CA 90278-0447.

WICCA/MAGIC — Seminary of Wicca offers home-study course and degree programs. PO Box 1366, Nashua NH 03061.

FREE LUCKY NUMBERS! Send birth date, self-addressed stamped envelope. Mystic, Box 2009-R, Jamestown NC 27282.

PSYCHIC SAMPLES. Unlimited calling. 800-647-7813. Adults over 18 only.

AMAZING OCCULT DISCOVERIES develop supernatural powers safely, easily! Free experiments. Williamsburg, Box 3483-JZ, New York NY 10008.

WITCH WORKS™ empowered moon-cultivated herbal potions, essences. Box 1839A, Royal Oak MI 48068-1839. 248-542-3113. Web site: www.witchworks.com.

RESULTS IMMEDIATELY! SISTER CROSS helps in all problems. Call for one free reading. Guaranteed. 504-651-5851.

INTERNATIONALLY KNOWN PSYCHIC John Russell. 25 years providing accurate, personal, confidential readings that utilize the Tarot as well as many other psychic/spiritual talents. MC/Visa/Discover. 914-258-8357. http://members.tripod.com/~atdaylong/index.html.

120 SECRET ASTROLOGICAL RECIPES for only $5. Send to Good Taste, PO Box 1202A, Antioch TN 37011-1202.

BEER & WINE MAKING

WINEMAKERS-BEERMAKERS. Free illustrated catalog. Fast service. Since 1967. Kraus, Box 7850-YB, Independence MO 64054. 800-841-7404.

BIRDHOUSES

PURPLE MARTIN BIRDHOUSES only $29.95. Free catalog. 800-764-8688. www.purplemartin.net.

BOOKS/MAGAZINES/CATALOGS

GIANT PUMPKINS. Grow your biggest ever with help from books and competition-strain seeds. For information, write to: Giant Pumpkins, Box 247-OFA, Norton MA 02766, or call 800-985-7878.

AMAZING SECRETS AND AMAZING PRODUCTS. You must see. Hurry. Now. Free information. Toll-free: 888-840-1942.

GRACE LIVINGSTON HILL BOOK COLLECTORS! We stock them all! Phone 800-854-8571 for free lists.

HAWAIIAN LUAU of taste treats. Kona Confections Original Macadamia Nut Korn Krunch, 100% Kona Coffee and new 100% Hawaiian Coffee, scrumptious gourmet chocolates, Hawaiian macadamia nuts; factory-direct prices. Free catalog. 800-437-7477. www.konaconfections.com.

FREE BOOKLETS: Life, death, soul, resurrection, pollution crisis, hell, Judgment Day, restitution. Bible Standard(OF), PO Box 67, Chester Springs PA 19425-0067.

MANUSCRIPTS WANTED, ALL TYPES. Publisher with 75-year tradition. "Author's Guide to Subsidy Publishing." 800-695-9599.

OVER 10 PROVEN BUSINESSES. Kit includes money-saving guidebooks, examples, mailing lists, etc. Free information 800-653-8688.

BUSINESS OPPORTUNITIES

$10,000 MONTHLY POSSIBLE! Paychecks mailed weekly. Call daily 8 A.M.-10 P.M. (CST), 800-811-2141, Code: 46824.

EXPLOSION OF INCOME! In your mailbox. Send two (2) first-class stamps to: M. A. James, PMB #233, 4354-A Old Shell Rd., Mobile AL 36608-2000.

$400 WEEKLY ASSEMBLING PRODUCTS from home. For free information, send SASE to Home Assembly-FA, PO Box 216, New Britain CT 06050-0216.

MAILERS WANTED! Make $575 weekly mailing our "List Letters" from home. Send SASE: Superior (#FA-20), Box 7, Bedford Park IL 60499.

LET THE GOVERNMENT FINANCE your small business. Grants/loans to $800,000. Free recorded message: 707-448-0270. (KE1).

PIANO TUNING PAYS: Learn at home. American School correspondence course. 800-497-9793. www.piano-tuning.com.

HUNDREDS OF INCOME OPPORTUNITIES! Receive three free issues! Spare Time Magazine, 2400 S. Commerce Dr., Dept. FA00, New Berlin WI 53151. USA only.

RECORD VIDEOTAPES AT HOME! Easy $1,800 weekly income! Free start-up information kit! CMSVIDEO, Dept. 174, 210 Lorna Square, Birmingham AL 35216-5439. 205-663-9888.

LET THE GOVERNMENT START YOUR BUSINESS. Grants, loans; HUD Tracer, $800/week; free incorporation; free merchant account for accepting credit cards. 202-298-0526. www.capitalpublications.com.

NATIONAL DIRECTORY: Home workers wanted by over 100 companies. Good pay. Free newsletter. Gulf Books, Box 263484, Tampa FL 33683-3484.

CASINO MANIA! Win consistently. Slot machines, blackjack, craps, roulette bingo, and more. Free info package! Your name and address to: JSA Publications, Box 7038, North Arlington NJ 07031.

GET PAID $268/roll taking easy snapshots at home! Film supplied. Phototek, Box 3706-FO, Idyllwild CA 92549. 909-659-9757. Web site: www.phototek.net.

MAKE MONEY ON 1/20 ACRE or less growing small landscape plants. I'll show you how. Mine earn thousands. Plantsman, 4390-F Middleridge, Perry OH 44081. Web site: www.freeplants.com.

EARN SUBSTANTIAL INCOME LOCATING DISTRESSED PROPERTY. Use our money. No financial risk to you. Split big profits. No experience needed. Complete training provided. Unlimited earnings potential. Call for free information package. 800-331-4555 ext. 7830.

BUY IT WHOLESALE

WHOLESALE DIRECTORIES. Worldwide factory-direct sources revealed. Savings to 900%. Free report. Recorded information. 415-456-5663 ext. 310.

49,457 PRODUCTS, FACTORY-DIRECT. Taiwan, Hong Kong, Mexico! Save 500%-900%. Echomark, Box 739-FA9, Shalimar FL 32579-0739.

BUY WHOLESALE! 4,000 gifts, jewelry, collectibles, tons more at true wholesale prices. Free catalog. 888-840-0385.

CARNIVOROUS PLANTS

CARNIVOROUS (insect-eating) plants, seeds, supplies, and books. Peter Paul's Nurseries, Canandaigua NY 14424-8713. www.peterpauls.com.

CRAFTS

HISTORIC STENCILS for walls and floors. For catalog, cost refunded with order. MB HISTORIC DECO. 888-649-1790. www.communityinfo.com/stencils.

DEER CONTROL

DEER PROBLEMS? We can help! Free catalog. Call Deerbusters, 800-248-DEER (3337). Web site: www.deerbusters.com.

EDUCATION/INSTRUCTION

COMPLETE HIGH SCHOOL AT HOME. Diploma awarded. Low tuition. Est. 1897 — Accredited. Telephone 800-531-9268 for free information, or write to AMERICAN SCHOOL, Dept. #348, 220 E. 170th St., Lansing IL 60438.

BECOME A MEDICAL TRANSCRIPTIONIST. Home study. Free career literature. P.C.D.I., Atlanta, Georgia. 800-362-7070. Dept. YYK554.

LEARN COMPUTERS! Improve your efficiency, learn valuable skills, use the Internet, and more! Lifetime Career Schools, Dept. OB1010, 101 Harrison St., Archbald PA 18403. 800-326-9221.

BECOME A HOME INSPECTOR. Approved home study. Free literature. P.C.D.I., Atlanta, Georgia. 800-362-7070. Dept. PPK554.

HIGH SCHOOL DIPLOMA! Graduate in four weeks. Free brochure. Call now! 800-532-6546 ext. 75.

BECOME A MEDICAL BILLING/ CLAIMS SPECIALIST. Home study. P.C.D.I., Atlanta, Georgia. Free literature. 800-362-7070. Dept. MCK554.

LEARN TO RESOLVE YOUR IRS problems (liens, garnishments, returns). SASE. Preferred $ervices, 203 Argonne B209, Long Beach CA 90803. www.preferredservices.org.

BECOME A PRIVATE INVESTIGATOR. Approved home study. Free literature. P.C.D.I., Atlanta, Georgia. 800-362-7070. Dept. JRK554.

LEARN SMALL-BUSINESS MANAGEMENT at home. Free information. Call 800-326-9221 or write Lifetime Career Schools, Dept. OB0910, 101 Harrison St., Archbald PA 18403.

BECOME A CARPENTER. Approved home study. Free career literature. P.C.D.I., Atlanta, Georgia. 800-362-7070. Dept. JCK554.

BECOME A BRIDAL CONSULTANT. Home study. Free literature. P.C.D.I., Atlanta, Georgia. 800-362-7070. Dept. MRK554.

ALTERNATIVE MEDICINE. Aromatherapy home studies, certification. Learn to make healing oils, skin care products, massage products, etc. 610-394-8655. E-mail cece2152@aol.com.

LEARN HOW TO START AND RUN A SMALL BUSINESS. Home study. Free literature. P.C.D.I., Atlanta, Georgia. 800-362-7070. Dept. RKK554.

BECOME A PHARMACY TECHNICIAN. Home study. Free career literature. P.C.D.I., Atlanta, Georgia. 800-362-7070. Dept. PTK554.

LEARN LANDSCAPING at home. Free brochure. Call 800-326-9221 or write Lifetime Career Schools, Dept. OB0120, 101 Harrison St., Archbald PA 18403.

EARN YOUR HIGH SCHOOL DIPLOMA. Home study. Free literature. P.C.D.I., Atlanta, Georgia. 800-362-7070. Dept. JMK554.

WILDERNESS WAY primitive skills, tracking, nature awareness school. Free catalog. 744A Glenmary Dr., Owego NY 13827. Web site: www.tier.net/wildernessway.com.

BECOME A VETERINARY ASSISTANT/animal science specialist. Home study. Exciting careers for animal lovers. Free literature package. 800-362-7070. Dept. CCK554.

FARM & GARDEN

TROY-BILT® OWNERS. Discount parts catalog, send stamp. Replacement tines $64. Kelley's, Manilla IN 46150. 317-398-9042. Web site: www.svs.net/kelley/index.htm.

NEPTUNE'S HARVEST ORGANIC FERTILIZERS. Extremely effective. Commercially proven. Outperforms chemicals. Wholesale/retail/farm/catalog. 800-259-4769.

FINANCIAL/LOANS BY MAIL

FREE CASH! Wealthy families unloading millions to help minimize their taxes. Fortune, PM B 249A, 1626 N. Wilcox Ave., Hollywood CA 90028.

FLAGS

FLAGS! American, state, MIA/POW, Confederate, historical. Color catalog send $2. Flags & Things, PO Box 356, Dillsburg PA 17019.

FLOWERING PLANTS

BEAUTIFUL BEARDED IRIS. Top-quality rhizomes. Free flyer: Brook Lomond Iris Farm, 10310 California Dr., Ben Lomond CA 95005.

FOR THE HOME

REPLACEMENT GLASS LAMP SHADES, including chimneys, student shades, and hurricanes. Send $1 for catalog. Lamp Glass, PO Box 400791, Cambridge MA 02140. www.lampglass.nu.

AFFORDABLE NATIVE BLANKETS, RUGS. Warm, colorful home furnishings. Blankets start at $18.47, rugs $30.95. 610-394-8655. E-mail cece2152@aol.com.

AWNINGS/UMBRELLAS. Sunbrella® fabric. Discount prices. Guaranteed and warranted. Free shipping. Free catalog. 888-417-7700. Web site: www.pycawnings.com.

FAMILY EMERGENCY preparedness — valuable resource, checklists, tips for every budget. $7. E. Barrios, PO Box 877, Tuolumne CA 95379.

FULLER BRUSH, AMERICA'S HOME-CARE EXPERTS. Superior products. Free catalog. Independent distributor. 3721 Reynolds St., Fort Wayne IN 46803. 219-426-2322.

FUND-RAISING

MAKE GOOD MONEY for your school, group, or organization selling The Old Farmer's Almanac publications and calendars to friends and neighbors. Great products sell themselves! Great prices! Great opportunity! Call today 800-424-6906. The Old Farmer's Almanac Fund-Raising, 220 South St., Bernardston MA 01337. www.gbimkt.com.

GIFTS

"REMEMBER ME" TEDDY BEARS. Lovingly handcrafted from your child's outgrown clothing. SASE. Alaska Custom Memorables, PO Box 233555, Anchorage AK 99523.

AMAZING GIFTS FOR SPECIAL OCCASIONS. Angels, sports/collectibles. Save money and time! Get the best! Send $2 for catalog. ARMU, 8322-P Dalesford, Baltimore MD 21234-5010. Web site: www.armuproducts.com.

CUSTOM WOOD SIGNS and wood gifts by Good News Carvers of Gatlinburg, Tennessee. Catalog $1. 651 Parkway, Gatlinburg TN 37738. 423-430-9595.

GINSENG

WANT GREATEST CASH CROP WORKING FOR YOU? Send $1 to: Ginseng, OFAG, Flag Pond TN 37657.

GREENHOUSES

CATCH THE SUNSHINE! Beautiful greenhouse kits. Send $1 for brochure. Gothic Arch Greenhouses, Box 1564-OLD, Mobile AL 36633-1564.

GROW VEGETABLES YEAR-ROUND! Build your own 12x20-foot greenhouse for under $200 using common materials and tools. For detailed plans, send $5 plus SASE to: Sugar Creek Farm, PO Box 1688, Leicester NC 28748.

HEALTH

SAFE MEDICINE FOR INCONTINENCE, headaches, rheumatism, backache. Faster healing . . . just call 800-HOMEOPATHY (800-466-3672). Free catalog.

THE COUMADIN COOKBOOK. A complete guide to healthy meals when taking Coumadin. To order or to request flyer describing book, call 410-749-1989 or write to Marsh Publishing Co., PO Box 1597, Salisbury MD 21802-1597. Cost $20.95 including shipping and handling. www.coumadincookbook.com.

DEATH BEGINS IN THE COLON. Headaches, indigestion, constipation, diarrhea, heartburn, fatigue, irritable bowel, gas, and big stomach all have been directly attributed to toxic colon. Raw dietary fiber and enzymes are the answer. Call 800-JUST-ASK (587-8275) to reclaim your health.

IS PRID DRAWING SALVE missing from your pharmacy? Just call 800-HOMEOPATHY — that's 800-466-3672. Free catalog.

HELP WANTED

$800 WEEKLY POTENTIAL processing government refunds at home! No experience necessary. 800-945-6880 ext. 1743.

EASY WORK! EXCELLENT PAY! Assemble products at home. Call toll-free, 800-467-5566 ext. 1126.

HERBS

FREE GRANDMA'S HOME REMEDIES BOOKLET. Collection of recipes, herbs, and folklore. Send long, stamped envelope. Champion's RX-Herb Store, 2369 Elvis Presley, Memphis TN 38106.

INTERNET

FREE INTERNET HOME PAGE. We market your business, products, and inventions. No computer needed. Call for details. 610-394-8655. E-mail cece2152@aol.com.

INVENTIONS/PATENTS

INVENTIONS, IDEAS, NEW PRODUCTS! Presentation to industry/exhibition at national innovation exposition. Patent services. 888-439-IDEA (4332).

MUSIC/RECORDS/TAPES

ACCORDIONS, CONCERTINAS, button boxes. New, used, buy, sell, trade, repair. Hohners, Martin guitars. Catalog $5. Castiglione, Box 40-A, Warren MI 48090. 810-755-6050.

ESCAPE TO THE HILLS OF SOUTH-CENTRAL KENTUCKY. Secluded country properties. Inexpensive homes. Call Century 21, Vibbert Realty, 800-267-2600 for free brochure.

ARKANSAS LAND. Free lists! Recreational, investment, retirement homes, acreages. Gatlin Farm Agency, Box 790, Waldron AR 72958. Toll-free 800-562-9078 ext. OFA.

RECIPES

MAGDALIA'S GYPSY FISH STEW. Easy and scrumptious! Plus two recipes/stories. $3 plus SASE. KREATIVE KAOS, PO Box 20443, New York NY 10021.

FESTIVE EGGNOG PIE — celebrate with this recipe. $2. Z Blue Kitchen, PO Box 67137, Northland Village P.O., Calgary AB T2L 2L2, Canada.

SCOTTISH OATCAKES everyone raves about! For recipe $3 U.S. or $5 Canadian to PO Box 93, St. George ON N0E 1N0, Canada.

RELIGION

WHAT IS THE WORLD COMING TO? What Bible prophecies predict for the future. Free booklet. Clearwater Bible Students, PO Box 8216, Clearwater FL 33758.

BIBLICAL ANSWERS to questions pastors hate. SASE. Ja-dam, PO Box 259, Avenel NJ 07001-0259.

SEEDS

TOBACCO SEEDS AND SUPPLIES. Grow tobacco anywhere in the USA for cigarettes, cigars, and chew! Kits, rolling machines, and more. Free catalog. 800-793-8186. www.tobaccosupply.com.

GOURDS. More than 15 different shapes and sizes! The Gourd Garden and Curiosity Shop, 4808 E. C-30A, Santa Rosa Beach FL 32459. 850-231-2007.

HEIRLOOM TOMATO SEEDS, 400 varieties! Catalog $1. Pomodori Di Marianna, 1955 CCC Rd., Dickson TN 37055.

RARE HILARIOUS peter, female, and squash pepper seeds. $3 per package. Any two $5, all three $7.50, and many new ones. SEEDS, Rt. 2 Box 246, Atmore AL 36502.

GROW YOUR OWN pesticide-free tobacco and healing plants. Also seeds for hot peppers, houseplants, vines, specialty vegetables. Free catalog. EONS/FA, PO Box 4604, Hallandale FL 33008. 954-455-0229. www.eonseed.com.

FREE CATALOG. Top-quality vegetable, flower, and herb seeds since 1900. Burrell, Box 150-OFA, Rocky Ford CO 81067.

WANTED

STEAM WHISTLES WANTED, any size or condition, from locomotives, ships, tractors, factories, sawmills, etc. 606-248-6260.

MAGIC! I PAY CASH for old magic posters and memorabilia, especially Houdini. 800-673-8158. E-mail: trombly@erols.com.

WANTED: AUTOGRAPHS, signed photos, letters, documents of famous people. Gray, 300 Boylston St. #510, Boston MA 02116. 617-426-4912.

WEATHER VANES

WEATHER VANES AND CUPOLAS. 50% off sale. America's largest selection. Free catalog. 800-724-2548. www.weathervanesandcupola.com.

MISCELLANEOUS

TYPING. $8 page, postal money order. 23 years experience. Free spelling and grammar corrections. Mrs. Lantz, Box 2103-FA, Claremore OK 74018.

INCREDIBLE MOSQUITO REPELLENT. For information, send SASE to: D. Langford, PO Box 404, Spruce Home SK S0J 2N0, Canada. www.incredibleproductsmall.com/penthouselevel/suite1591989.

JEHOVAH'S WITNESSES, friends, family, find out facts the society doesn't want you to know. Free and confidential. JW FACTS, Box 454, Metaline Falls WA 99153. Web site: www.macgregorministries.org.

FREE DEGREES! Counseling, metaphysics, hypnotherapy, parapsychology! Ministerial license! P.U.L.C., Box 276265-FR, Sacramento CA 95827.

Y2K SURVIVAL MANUAL. Send $10 plus SASE. Millennium Laboratories, Box 274, Prince Albert SK S6V 5R5, Canada.

The Old Farmer's Almanac accepts classified ads for products and services we feel will be of interest to our readers. However, we cannot verify the quality or reliability of the products or services offered.

THINKING A LITTLE TOO BIG: FOUR IDEAS THAT DIDN'T CHANGE THE WORLD

A man's reach, it's said,
should exceed his grasp. It's advice
worth following, up to a point.
(We might add that it also applies to
women.) But trying to extend one's
reach too far can lead to ... well,
to enterprises like these.

The Great Eastern

An idea ahead of — and behind — its time

Until the mid-1830s, it was widely believed that steam-powered ships would never replace sailing vessels for long-distance travel. The problem, the experts agreed, was that no steamship would ever be able to carry enough coal to go more than 2,500 miles.

Like so many predictions of its kind, this one was proven wrong with embarrassing promptness. Before the end of the decade, steamships were crossing the Atlantic regularly and profitably, largely as a result of a key insight by the great British engineer Isambard Kingdom Brunel. The way to make space for additional coal, he realized — while leaving room for profitable cargo and passengers — was simply to build bigger ships.

The success of transatlantic steamships led Brunel, in 1852, to propose an even bolder plan: to build a steamship large enough to travel from England to Australia and back without recoaling (a practical necessity, because there were few recoaling stations en route).

The result was the *Great Eastern,* an almost unimaginably huge ship for its time, measuring nearly 700 feet long and displacing 32,000 tons — fully twice as long as any ship then in existence, and with six times the cargo capacity.

But the great ship was dogged by misfortune from the beginning. Its hull stuck to the launching ways, and instead of sliding into the Thames with a dramatic splash, it had to be forced down the incline with enormous jacks, a painfully public process that took almost three months. Costs ran high, and by the time the ship had been fitted out and had undergone sea trials, her owners were at the end of their financial tether.

Lacking the money to finance a trip to the Far East, they put the *Great Eastern* on the relatively short transatlantic route to New York — a task for which she was never intended — and lost a fortune on almost every trip. Soon they were bankrupt.

The ship was put onto the auction block — but the imminent completion of the Suez Canal (which the *Great Eastern* was too large to use) made the old route to Australia obsolete, and the ship was eventually sold for less than 3 percent of her original cost. She was put to work laying the first undersea telegraph cables between Europe and North America — a task that no other vessel afloat had the cargo space to undertake.

In 1888, with the telegraph project complete, the *Great Eastern* was dismantled for scrap metal — which her final owner sold, not surprisingly, at a heavy loss. No larger ship was launched until the *Lusitania,* early in the 20th century, best remembered as the vessel whose sinking by a German U-boat helped bring the United States into World War I.

— photos courtesy George Eastman House

Above: *This 1857 photograph by Robert Howlett shows engineer Isambard Kingdom Brunel next to the chain that held the* Great Eastern *to the launch runway. Left: The* Great Eastern *under construction, 1857.*

Improving the Mediterranean
Engineering la dolce vita

How high is sea level? All the world's interconnected oceans — and their partly enclosed seas, such as the Mediterranean and Red Seas — share a common level, but the surfaces of some landlocked seas, such as the Caspian and Dead Seas, lie far above or below sea level. Moreover, sea level can change dramatically over time. During the last ice age, when much of the world's water was tied up in continental ice sheets, world sea level was hundreds of feet lower than it is today.

In the late 1920s, those facts inspired

The Atlantropa Plan featured a dam at the Strait of Gibraltar. Once landlocked, the Mediterranean Sea would shrink through evaporation.

power production exponentially and reclaiming 90,000 square miles of potentially productive land from the sea.

At that point, the second phase of the Atlantropa Plan would go into effect. Additional dams between Sicily and Tunisia and between Sicily and the Italian mainland would divide the diminished Mediterranean into eastern and western halves. The eastern part would be permitted to shrink for another century, reclaiming an additional 130,000 square miles of land.

Sörgel's 1929 plan (which never considered the cultural and ecological devastation it would bring) dissolved to nothing in the face of worldwide economic depression in the 1930s and looming world war. Ironically, in the late 1990s, a University of Minnesota professor suggested damming the Strait of Gibraltar for a different reason — to keep the warm, saline Mediterranean from spilling into the Atlantic and changing global currents and weather patterns enough to trigger an ice age. This theory met with a storm of protest, and so far, the Mediterranean seems to be safe from being dammed.

a German architect named Herman Sörgel to outline a far-reaching engineering project. Sörgel's idea — which came to be known as the Atlantropa Plan — was to isolate the Mediterranean Sea by erecting a massive, 18-mile-long dam at the Strait of Gibraltar, with a second dam at the Dardanelles, between the Mediterranean and the Black Sea.

After project completion, Sörgel calculated, natural evaporation would lower the level of the artificially landlocked Mediterranean by about 40 inches per year. A decade later, the level of the new, improved Mediterranean would have fallen more than 30 feet, enough to begin producing hydroelectric power by letting controlled amounts of Atlantic seawater flow downhill into the basin. After 100 years, the water level would have fallen an estimated 330 feet, increasing

Rain Follows the Plow
An Adventure in Wishful Thinking

It's axiomatic that everyone talks about the weather but no one does anything about it. For a good part of the late 1800s, however, millions of Americans believed in a theory that held that you *could* do something about the weather — and believed it so strongly they bet their futures on it.

With the end of the Civil War, America was poised to expand into the vast open spaces of the Great Plains, although it had long been assumed that much of the land there was much too dry to be farmed. Early explorers, in fact, had labeled it the Great American Desert.

But something surprising happened. As the first settlers planted crops on the eastern edge of the Plains, the weather took a turn for the better. Rainfall increased and the new farms flourished. The phenomenon was so pronounced that it soon evolved into a quasiscientific slogan: "Rain follows the plow." The theory was that breaking the tough layer of sod that covered much of the Plains enabled the exposed soil to better absorb moisture. The moisture in the soil, in turn, would foster the formation of clouds, producing still more rain and altering the climate.

The theory quickly attracted many prominent supporters, including Ferdinand V. Hayden, director of the United States Geological and Geophysical Survey in the Territories, who gave it wide currency in official publications.

The concept also came to the attention of the western railroads, which had been given huge land grants along their rights-of-way. The railroads stood to profit handsomely by transporting eager settlers westward, then selling them land when they arrived. The eastern states and much of Europe were soon flooded with brochures and pamphlets presenting the western plains as a new Garden of Eden, and promising that increased settlement would push the "rain line" west at a scientific-sounding 18 miles per year. By the early 1880s, at least 2 million new emigrants were busily busting sod on the Great Plains.

It seemed too good to be true, and of course it was. Within the decade, drought returned. Rain, it was found, didn't follow the plow after all but came and went in an irregular cycle that defied prediction, let alone control. The influx of new settlers dried up as well, and a wholesale retreat from the western plains followed, allowing untold thousands of new farms to revert to grassland. The entire venture still serves as a matchless example of the power of wishful thinking.

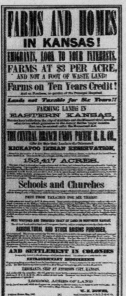

Western railroads invited easterners to settle in places like Kansas, enticing them with low land prices and easy terms, as shown in this 1867 poster.

Nuclear Excavation
Mike Mulligan, Meet the A-Bomb

In the aftermath of World War II — which, in addition to its other horrors, introduced the world to the awesome destructive power of the atomic bomb — the federal government invested heavily in experimental projects aimed at harnessing the atom for peaceful ends. It was a well-intentioned

Fired on July 6, 1962, the Sedan test left the largest crater in the Plowshare program.

1,280 feet wide and more than 300 feet deep.

No cost-conscious civil engineer could look upon the test data unmoved: Nuclear earth-moving cost a mere 5 cents per cubic yard, as compared with a dollar or so for conventional means. Proposals for some real-world projects soon followed. One called for setting off a 24-kiloton explosion 3,300 feet beneath a state forest in northern Pennsylvania, and using the ensuing underground cavity as a storage reservoir for natural gas. More ambitious was a proposal to use a long string of blasts to gouge a new, sea-level Panama Canal.

In the end, none of this took place, for reasons that seem obvious in retrospect — most notably the radioactive fallout that accompanies any nuclear explosion. As the 1960s wound down — and the mood of the American public grew steadily less radiation-tolerant — the program's days were clearly numbered. Although the project's last explosion occurred as late as 1973, with Plowshare's public relations people continuing to turn out upbeat promotional films until then, the only memorial to the project is a huge mass of paperwork — now gradually being declassified — and a scattering of large holes on the floor of the Nevada desert. □□

effort that produced some clear successes (e.g., the use of radiation in medical treatments) as well as applications that are still controversial (e.g., irradiated food and nuclear power). And inevitably, there were some projects that never lived up to their early promise.

Among the latter group was Project Plowshare, established in 1957 to look for ways of putting nuclear explosives to practical engineering and industrial use. It was hoped, for example, that deep underground explosions might be used to liquefy oil-shale deposits or to create pockets of superheated steam that might drive turbines. Surface blasts might be used for mining, improving harbors, constructing dams and canals, and aiding other earth-moving projects.

Within a few years, the Plowshare researchers were busily setting off nuclear and nonnuclear explosions at test sites, mostly in Nevada. Many of the efforts were named after vehicles or ships, including Buggy, Cabriolet, and Schooner. In the 1962 Sedan test, for example, a 104-kiloton nuclear blast displaced 12 million tons of earth, leaving a crater

HORSESHOEING:

Still a Ringer of a Career

by Anne Dingus

"No foot, no horse," they say in the farrier's trade. Every year, hundreds of would-be horseshoers apply to special schools to learn all about the business end of the country's nearly 7 million horses, the original four-wheel-drive vehicles. At four hooves per horse, trimming and shoeing all those horses is a big job.

Like the school-marm and the circuit rider, the horseshoer practices a profession that recalls a saner, simpler time. But unlike that teacher and preacher, the horseshoer is more in demand than ever before. With the number of horses in the United States at an all-time modern high, the business has hit full gallop, and for the estimated 7,000 such professionals in North America, the horseshoe has become an especially appropriate good-luck charm.

"Since I started shoeing, the business has grown a hundredfold," says Mike Chambers, whose Hill Country Horseshoeing School in Kerrville, Texas, is one of about 60 in the United States and Canada. "There's a great demand, mostly because of pleasure horses." Much of Chambers's work comes from nearby dude ranches and summer camps. Other clients ride in rodeos or merely keep their animals as pets. Texans have always been horse-happy. At over 1.6 million, the equine population of the Lone Star State is tops in the nation.

Chambers is a big, genial man with a bristling red mustache. In his barn, he supervises two students clad in jeans, boots, and leather aprons. Both are intent on fitting their four-legged friends with brand-new hoofwear — a sizable job, since each foot is different and must be measured precisely. Soft whinnies and loud clangs fill the air, and the sharp smell of manure and hot steel stings the nostrils.

Twenty-one-year-old Jerel Brandenburg, of Pasadena, Texas, holds the foreleg of a hoary gray between his knees, paring off new hoof growth under his instructor's watchful eye. Next to him is a toolbox loaded with rasps, nippers, and his own homemade measuring tool. Currently an apprentice, Brandenburg hopes to strike out on his own someday.

Fellow student Thomas T. Shaw III, 30, of San Antonio, who previously worked in a lumberyard, places a glowing

Mike Chambers (right) teaches the farrier's art at his Hill Country Horseshoeing School in Kerrville, Texas.

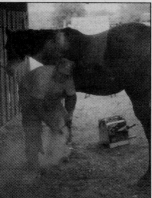

– photos courtesy Mike Chambers

red horseshoe on his anvil, pounding it with a hammer to thin the sides. A glossy bay waits patiently for the new shoe. Shaw holds up his creation for Chambers's appraisal. "Why did those nails come out low on that side?" Chambers asks. "Too much flare. Let me draw you a picture."

They move to Chambers's barn office, a plain room whose walls are covered with scores of horseshoes — rusty old ones, shiny new ones, Frisbee-size ones for draft animals, and curiously shaped devices for corrective or therapeutic wear. At half a ton or so apiece, horses are particularly subject to foot woes. That's why there are several hundred different types of shoes (for racehorses, cutting horses, hunter-jumpers, and so on) — thousands if you count all the brand names. A horseshoer must be able to diagnose and treat any equine podiatry problem, from fungus to frostbite. Chambers's office includes anatomical aids such as a freeze-dried hoof, which is split and hinged so that it can be opened for inspection. It sits near the chalkboard where Chambers and Shaw confer. "I have to keep that stored way up high," Chambers says over his shoulder. "My dog likes to chew on it."

On the shelf are modern and vintage texts for farriers, as horseshoers are also called (from the Latin word *ferrum,* meaning "iron"), as well as a copy of the *American Farrier's Journal,* published by the American Farrier's Association. Chambers credits the association with "bringing horseshoers together. Thirty years ago, it was a cutthroat business. Now we help each other out."

Horseshoeing Schools

All these schools offer courses for the greenest novice to the most experienced professional.

ALABAMA: Lookout Mountain School of Horseshoeing, 400 Lewis Rd., Gadsden, AL 35901; 205-546-2036.

CALIFORNIA: Pacific Coast Horseshoeing School, 9625 Florin Rd., Sacramento, CA 95829; 916-366-6064.

Chambers is a born horseshoer. "When I was five or six," he says, "I watched an old gray-haired fellow shoe my mama's horse. From then on, I knew that's what I wanted to be." Now 48, he passes on his 31 years of experience at Hill Country Horseshoeing School, established in 1995. "We crawled the first year; now we're walking. We're gonna break into a trot real soon," he says.

His students are guaranteed plenty of attention: Chambers prefers to teach only two at a time. The various courses of study — eight hours a day for two to eight weeks — include written exams as well as hands-on work. (Sample test question: Define the following and give shoes and methods of trimming to correct them: stumbling, interfering, forging, overreaching, brushing.) The $1,800 monthly tuition covers accommodations in a small bunkhouse surrounded by cacti and wagon wheels. Inside, horseshoes serve as cup racks and towel hooks in the kitchenette.

In addition to teaching, Chambers nails on as many as 40 shoes a week for regular clients, charging $50 per horse. In big cities where dressage is popular, a good shoer can easily fetch twice that much.

Pioneers rode their horses to the village smithy, but today's shoer makes stable calls. In addition to supplies and tools, Chambers hauls a portable gas-powered forge for on-site customizing. He also keeps a large coal forge in the barn. "It's dirtier and hotter" than the portable forge, he says. "It will actually melt a shoe if you leave it in too long."

Burns are an occupational hazard, and bruises and nicks are common, too. "Band-Aids are one of my highest costs," Chambers says with a grin. More dangerous but far rarer — because most modern horses are wholly accustomed to humans — are crushing kicks from the animals' powerful legs.

To Chambers, though, the good far outweighs the bad. Once, he recalls, as he was returning home in his horseshoeing rig, a highway patrolman pulled him over. "The trooper came over to my window and said, 'Sir, did you know your trailer license is expired? And your inspection sticker is expired, too?' I'm thinking, 'Uh-oh . . .'

"But then the trooper said, 'That's not why I stopped you, though. I need a new horseshoer.'"

GEORGIA: Casey & Son Horseshoeing School, 14013 East Highway 136, LaFayette, GA 30728; 706-397-8909.

ILLINOIS: Midwest Horseshoeing School, 2312 South Maple Ave., Macomb, IL 61455; 309-833-4063.

KENTUCKY: Kentucky Horseshoeing School, P.O. Box 120, Mount Eden, KY 40046; 800-626-5359.

MINNESOTA: Minnesota School of Horseshoeing, 6250 Riverdale Dr. NW, Ramsey, MN 55303; 612-421-5750.

MISSOURI: Heartland Horseshoeing School, 327 Southwest First Lane, Lamar, MO 64759; 417-682-6896.

NEW JERSEY: Far Hills Forge, P.O. Box 703, 98 Spring Hollow Rd., Far Hills, NJ 07931; 908-766-5384.

OKLAHOMA: Oklahoma Horseshoeing School, Rte. 1 Box 281, Purcell, OK 73080; 800-538-1383.

TENNESSEE: Tennessee State Blacksmith and Farrier School, 3780 Shepardsville Hwy., Bloomington Springs, TN 38545; 931-653-4341.

TEXAS: Hill Country Horseshoeing School, 278 Camino Real, Kerrville, TX 78028; 830-896-3682.

CANADA

Canadian School of Horseshoeing, RR 2, Guelph, ON N1H 6H8, Canada; 519-824-5484.

For a more complete listing, contact the American Farrier's Association, 4059 Iron Works Pkwy. Ste. 2, Lexington, KY 40511; 606-233-7411; fax 606-231-7862; Web site www.amfarriers.com. □□

Spinning the Web: Go to www.almanac.com and click on **Article Links 2000** for Web sites related to this article. — *The Editors*

Anecdotes
AND
Pleasantries

A sampling from the hundreds of letters, clippings, and E-mails sent to us by Almanac readers from all over the United States and Canada during the final year of the 1900s.

What It's Like to Have a Mouse Run up Your Pants

This is a true story from V. W. of Hampton, Connecticut, which she originally wrote for her home-town newsletter, The Hampton Gazette.

Like most everyone who lives in the country, I try to prepare well each season. So, one weekend last spring, when *Earthcare* said it was time to "put the mice out of the bluebird houses," I set out to do just that. Using a small hand

cultivator to claw out the debris, a jug of water to slosh it out, and a long-handled brush for scrubbing, I started my spring mouse cleaning.

Things were going well until a panic-stricken mouse leaped out, landed at my feet, and bolted for the nearest cover — the long, dark tunnel of my pants leg!

The term "went ballistic" comes to mind, but it doesn't begin to describe the scene. It took a lot of flapping and yelling and an update of the Macarena, alternating between fast-forward and reverse, to dislodge it.

Once I thought I had that accomplished, it took some time to quit shaking and re-gain a regular heartbeat. Then I continued on my rounds. Because we have several widely spaced bluebird boxes, it took quite some time to finish the job.

Back at the house, I had settled down with a hot cup of tea, when I felt a sudden motion at my beltline. I thought the dog had nudged me and I turned to speak sharply to him for begging. To my horror, he was lying quietly some distance away.

Quickly clapping one hand over the struggling "lump" and tearing wildly at my zipper with the other, I headed outside at a dead run with my dungarees at half-mast. The mouse popped out running in midair in the direction of the state forest, while I ran in exactly the opposite direction.

A lesson to share: When cleaning out bluebird houses, wear elastic bands around the bottoms of your pants.

■ ■ ■

Why You Should Never Underestimate a Little Old Lady

We received the following from Captain C.R.T., an airline pilot from a town near Chicago. We won't include the name of the airline — and we don't know the name of the lady.

On one flight a few months ago, there was a tough crosswind during a landing and I hammered the ship onto the runway pretty hard. Like most airlines, mine has a policy that requires the first officer to stand at the door while passengers exit. The idea is to smile at each person and say "thanks for flying with us today" or some such. I must say that on this particular occasion, in light of my bad landing, I had a difficult time looking each passenger in the

eye. I thought surely a few would have some sort of smart comment. But none did.

Finally, everyone had gotten off except for a tiny, very elderly lady who was walking slowly with the help of a cane. As she reached the exit door, she stopped, looked up at me, and said, "Sonny, mind if I ask you a question?"

"Why, of course not, Ma'am," I replied cordially. "What is it?"

"Tell me," she said. "Did we land or were we shot down?"

Questions Today's Scientists Want Answered During the Next Century

The following are just a few of the questions recently asked by some of today's prominent scientists, collected from various sources, including the Internet, and sent to us by M.E.M. of Sheboygan, Wisconsin.

■ **"What is the crucial distinction between inanimate matter and an entity that can act as an 'agent,' manipulating the world on its own behalf; and how does that change happen?"**
Philip W. Anderson, Nobel laureate physicist at Princeton University

■ **"Exactly how much of nature can we trash and burn and get away with?"**
Natalie Angier, science writer for The New York Times *and author of* The Beauty of the Beastly

■ **"What is information and where does it ultimately originate?"**
Paul Davies, professor of physics (retired) at The University of Adelaide, Australia; author of The Mind of God

■ **"What are the powers, and the limits, of human intuition?"**
David G. Myers, professor of psychology at Hope College; author of The Pursuit of Happiness

■ **"Is justice real?"**
Thomas de Zengotita, anthropologist; teaches philosophy and anthropology at The Dalton School and is an adjunct professor at the Draper Graduate Program at New York University

■ **"What makes a soul?"**
Esther Dyson, president, EDventures Holdings, Inc.; publisher of Release 1.0 Newsletter; *author of* Release 2.0: Design for Living in the Digital Age

■ **"What question should I ask?"**
George C. Williams, evolutionary biologist (professor emeritus) at SUNY-Stony Brook; author of Adaptation and Natural Selection

(continued)

Creating a Musical Instrument from Your Oven Rack

After reader J. V. of Marshfield, Vermont, sent us these directions, we tried it. It's cool.

An oven harp may not be a *real* musical instrument, but it's an unbeatable party trick. Go to the kitchen and remove one of the wire racks from your oven, then find some string or lightweight twine, like the kind used for tying up packages. Cut off a three-foot length of string and tie one end to a corner of the rack, then cut and tie another length to an adjacent corner.

Now have a volunteer wrap the last few inches of each string around the tips of his or her little fingers — like a strand of dental floss — before inserting one string-wrapped finger into each ear and bending forward from the waist, so the rack hangs free of his or her body. Pause for a moment to allow the suspense to build, then strum lightly on the bars of the dangling oven rack with the handle of a wooden spoon. You'll only hear some faint plinks, but your volunteer will experience an astonishing series of echoing, bell-like tones.

The music of the oven harp is so astonishing, in fact, that onlookers are almost always treated to music of another sort: the delighted laughter of the volunteer. Trade places and you'll both be entertained all over again.

■ ■ ■

— Eldon Doty

Yes, Virginia, It Does Rain More On Saturdays

(at least on the East Coast)

S. L. from Iowa City, Iowa, found the following in one of Roland Sweet's newspaper columns, "Newsquirks."

■ Weekends on the East Coast are wetter than weekdays, according to climatologists at Arizona State University, who analyzed weather data going back to 1946. They reported that Saturdays are 22 percent rainier than Mondays. The likely culprit is air pollution caused by factories and commuters' cars. The pollution builds toward the weekend, increasing the chances of rain, then clears after a two-day respite, signaling fairer weather.

An Amazing New Discovery About Birdies

Our thanks to L.R.G. of Terre Haute, Indiana.

■ You might be interested to know that, apart from flying, birds have yet another enviable ability — and this one has just recently been discovered. They can sleep with one eye open *and* with one half of their brain awake while the other eye is closed and the other half of their brain is asleep. This phenomenon is called "unihemispheric slow-wave sleep" or USWS. The capability allows birds to detect approaching predators while still getting a bit of shut-eye.

Niels Rattenborg, a behavioral neurophysiologist at Indiana State University, and his colleagues Steven Lima and Charles Amlaner believe their research, published in the science journal *Nature,* is the first evidence that a living creature can control sleep and wakefulness simultaneously in different parts of its brain.

Can You Guess Why You Feel Smarter After Drinking a Few Beers?

G. P. of Toronto, Canada, E-mailed us his sensible-sounding explanation. But, of course, if you believe it, the majority of your brain cells are already dead and gone.

A herd of buffalo can move only as fast as the slowest buffalo. When the herd is hunted, the slowest and weakest ones at the back are killed first. This natural selection is good, because the general speed and health of the whole group is improved by the weeding out of the weakest members.

In much the same way, the human brain can operate only as fast as the slowest brain cells. Excessive intake of alcohol, we all know, kills brain cells, but naturally, it attacks the slowest and weakest brain cells first. In this way, regular consumption of beer eliminates the

weaker brain cells, making the brain a faster and more efficient machine. *That's* why you always feel smarter after a few beers.

■ ■ ■

How Much the 1793 Edition of This Almanac Would Cost If It Were On Sale Today

Credit goes to R. M. of Alstead, New Hampshire, for the financial calculations . . .

According to a copy of the 1793 edition I saw on display at your office in Dublin, N.H., last summer, the first *Old Farmer's Almanac,* which came out in the fall of 1792, cost sixpence. So, just for the heck of it, I've figured out what that would be in today's money.

Currency at that time was still denominated in pounds, with one pound consisting of 20 shillings, and each shilling comprising 12 pence (240 pence per pound). It is possible to determine the cost of the 1793 Almanac

[Nº 1.]

THE

FARMER's ALMANAC,

CALCULATED ON A NEW AND IMPROVED PLAN,

FOR THE YEAR OF OUR LORD
1793:

Being the first after Leap Year, and (eventual) of the Independence of America.

Fitted to the town of Boston, but will serve for any of the adjoining States.

Containing, besides the large number of Astronomical Calculations and Farmer's Calendar for every month in the year, as great a variety as are to be found in any other Almanac, Of NEW, USEFUL, and ENTERTAINING MATTER.

by ROBERT B. THOMAS.

"While the bright redient sun in center glows,
The earth, in annual out-set round it goes;
At the same time on its own axil reels,
And gives at change of feasons as it wheel."

Published according to Act of Congress.

PRINTED AT THE Apollo Press, IN BOSTON,
by BELKNAP AND HALL,
Sold at their Office, State Street; also, by the Author and M. Smith, Sterling.
[Sixpence single, 4s. per dozen, 40s. per groce.]

in today's money by using a composite consumer price index developed by economists.

First, we must convert 1792 pounds to 1792 dollars in order to compare dollar amounts between 1792 and 1998. I used John J. McCusker's book, *How Much Is That in Real Money?*, put out in 1992 by the American Antiquarian Society. Between 1782 and 1796, one hundred pounds was equivalent to $333.33, or $3.33 per pound. One pence thus equaled $.013875 ($3.33 ÷ 240). The Almanac price of sixpence works out to $.08325, or about 8 cents, the cost of the Almanac in 1792 dollars.

To account for more than two centuries of inflation, I used McCusker again and Consumer Price Index (CPI) figures from the U.S. Bureau of Labor Statistics through 1998, to determine the ratio that compares today's CPI to the 1792 CPI. That ratio works out to

16.95. Multiplying $.08325 times 16.95 gives an adjusted cost of $1.41.

So, in today's money, each copy of the Almanac in the fall of 1792 sold for $1.41. You must remember, however, that the first edition consisted of only 48 pages, or about 2.9 cents per page in today's currency. When you calculate that number for the Almanac's 2000 edition, both newsstand and bookstore editions work out to about 1.8 cents per page. It makes you realize that over the years, technology has worked to offset the tremendous accumulated effects of inflation. The Almanac today is bigger . . . and costs *less*.

■ ■ ■

How to Stay Awake on Long-Distance Drives

The following tips are courtesy of B. J. of Nelson, New Hampshire.

As a long-distance truck driver, I've had to come up with ways to fight the "drowsies" on long runs. For truck drivers, who can legally put in no more than ten hours at a stretch, two o'clock in the morning and two o'clock in the afternoon (particularly on a sunny day after a big lunch) are the sleepiest times. Here's what I do to stay awake. It's worked so far!

1 At a truck stop, I buy a bag of sunflower seeds in the shells, a cup of coffee, and a soda. First, I drink the coffee. Then, one by one, I crack open the sunflower seeds with my teeth as I drive along. The shells go into the empty coffee cup. When I am thirsty from the salty sunflower seeds, I open the soda. All of this gives my mouth and my hands something to do. One bag of sunflower seeds will get you many miles down the road.

2 Every truck stop sells ginseng tablets for mental energy. I take a tablet with a spoonful of honey for a pick-me-up.

3 Caffeine works, up to a point. Truckers drink coffee, of course, but they also drink a lot of Mountain Dew and Jolt.

4 Talking on the CB radio really helps me, especially late at night. When you see a number of trucks running close together, you can bet the drivers are talking up a storm on their CBs. During the day, truckers love to report to each other on odd things they see people doing in cars. [*Editor's note:* B. J. did not elaborate on this point. Probably all for the best.]

5 Sometimes nothing works except to pull over and take a nap. Short naps — 10 to 20 minutes — work best for me.

Six Things No One Knows About Yawning

After a lot of research on the subject, S.C.B. of Lewistown, Montana, shared with us the following findings (or lack thereof) . . .

1 Although they suspect the mesencephalon (midbrain), scientists still aren't sure what part of the nervous system governs yawning.

2 We all know that yawns are contagious — but we don't know why. We *do* know that if 360 people individually watch a videotape of someone yawning, more than half of them will yawn within five minutes, and *all* of them will be *tempted* to yawn.

3 We have not as yet determined the precise physical trigger for yawning. No, it is *not* caused by a buildup of carbon dioxide or a shortage of oxygen.

4 We know that bored people yawn more than alert people — but we don't know why. Anxiety and nervousness are also associated with yawning (paratroopers about to jump from a plane yawn a lot), but we don't know why.

5 We can't figure out why we yawn *and* stretch simultaneously in the morning (an action called pandiculation), but we usually just yawn at night.

6 For the life of us, we cannot figure out why the above five facts are, essentially, not really much more than a big yawn.

□ □

Table of Measures

Apothecaries'

1 scruple = 20 grains
1 dram = 3 scruples
1 ounce = 8 drams
1 pound = 12 ounces

Avoirdupois

1 ounce = 16 drams
1 pound = 16 ounces
1 hundredweight = 100 pounds
1 ton = 2,000 pounds
1 long ton = 2,240 pounds

Cubic Measure

1 cubic foot = 1,728 cubic inches
1 cubic yard = 27 cubic feet
1 cord = 128 cubic feet
1 U.S. liquid gallon = 4 quarts = 231 cubic inches
1 Imperial gallon = 1.20 U.S. gallons = 0.16 cubic feet
1 board foot = 144 cubic inches

Dry Measure

2 pints = 1 quart
4 quarts = 1 gallon
2 gallons = 1 peck
4 pecks = 1 bushel

Liquid Measure

4 gills = 1 pint
2 pints = 1 quart
4 quarts = 1 gallon
63 gallons = 1 hogshead
2 hogsheads = 1 pipe or butt
2 pipes = 1 tun

Linear Measure

1 foot = 12 inches
1 yard = 3 feet
1 rod = 5½ yards
1 mile = 320 rods = 1,760 yards = 5,280 feet
1 Int. nautical mile = 6,076.1155 feet
1 knot = 1 nautical mile per hour

1 furlong = ⅛ mile = 660 feet = 220 yards
1 league = 3 miles = 24 furlongs
1 fathom = 2 yards = 6 feet
1 chain = 100 links = 22 yards
1 link = 7.92 inches
1 hand = 4 inches
1 span = 9 inches

Square Measure

1 square foot = 144 square inches
1 square yard = 9 square feet
1 square rod = 30¼ square yards = 272¼ square feet
1 acre = 160 square rods = 43,560 square feet
1 square mile = 640 acres = 102,400 square rods
1 square rod = 625 square links
1 square chain = 16 square rods
1 acre = 10 square chains

Household Measures

120 drops of water = 1 teaspoon
60 drops thick fluid = 1 teaspoon
2 teaspoons = 1 dessertspoon
3 teaspoons = 1 tablespoon
16 tablespoons = 1 cup
1 cup = 8 ounces
2 cups = 1 pint
2 pints = 1 quart
4 quarts = 1 gallon
3 tablespoons flour = 1 ounce
2 tablespoons butter = 1 ounce
2 cups granulated sugar = 1 pound

3¾ cups confectioners' sugar = 1 pound
3½ cups wheat flour = 1 pound
5⅓ cups dry coffee = 1 pound
6½ cups dry tea = 1 pound
2 cups shortening = 1 pound
1 stick butter = ½ cup
2 cups cornmeal = 1 pound
2¾ cups brown sugar = 1 pound
2⅜ cups raisins = 1 pound
9 eggs = 1 pound
1 ounce yeast = 1 scant tablespoon

Metric

1 inch = 2.54 centimeters
1 centimeter = 0.39 inch
1 meter = 39.37 inches
1 yard = 0.914 meters
1 mile = 1,609.344 meters = 1.61 kilometers
1 kilometer = .62 mile
1 square inch = 6.45 square centimeters
1 square yard = 0.84 square meter
1 square mile = 2.59 square kilometers
1 square kilometer = 0.386 square mile
1 acre = 0.40 hectare
1 hectare = 2.47 acres
1 cubic yard = 0.76 cubic meter
1 cubic meter = 1.31 cubic yards
1 liter = 1.057 U.S. liquid quarts
1 U.S. liquid quart = 0.946 liter
1 U.S. liquid gallon = 3.78 liters
1 gram = 0.035 ounce
1 ounce = 28.349 grams
1 kilogram = 2.2 pounds
1 pound avoirdupois = 0.45 kilogram

Gestation and Mating Table

	Proper Age for First Mating	Period of Fertility (years)	Number of Females for One Male	Period of Gestation (days) AVERAGE	RANGE
Ewe	90 lb. or 1 yr.	6		147 / 151[8]	142-154
Ram	12-14 mo., well matured	7	50-75[2] / 35-40[3]		
Mare	3 yr.	10-12		336	310-370
Stallion	3 yr.	12-15	40-45[4] / Record 252[5]		
Cow	15-18 mo.[1]	10-14		283	279-290[6] 262-300[7]
Bull	1 yr., well matured	10-12	50[4] / Thousands[5]		
Sow	5-6 mo. or 250 lb.	6		115	110-120
Boar	250-300 lb.	6	50[2] / 35-40[3]		
Doe goat	10 mo. or 85-90 lb.	6		150	145-155
Buck goat	Well matured	5	30		
Bitch	16-18 mo.	8		63	58-67
Male dog	12-16 mo.	8			
She cat	12 mo.	6		63	60-68
Doe rabbit	6 mo.	5-6		31	30-32
Buck rabbit	6 mo.	5-6	30		

[1]Holstein and beef: 750 lb.; Jersey: 500 lb. [2]Hand-mated. [3]Pasture. [4]Natural. [5]Artificial. [6]Beef; 8-10 days shorter for Angus. [7]Dairy. [8]For fine wool breeds.

Incubation Periods of Birds and Poultry (days)

Canary ..14-15	Goose.......30-34	Pheasant 22-24
Chicken......21	Guinea ...26-28	Swan...............42
Duck 26-32	Parakeet...18-20	Turkey.............28

Gestation Periods of Wild Animals (days)

Black bear 210	Seal.....................330	
Hippopotamus 225-250	Squirrel, gray 44	
Moose 240-250	Whale, sperm.........480	
Otter....................270-300	Wolf.................60-63	
Reindeer.............210-240		

Maximum Life Spans of Animals in Captivity (years)

Ant (queen) .... 18+	Duck (domestic) ... 23	Mouse (house).......... 6
Badger 26	Eagle.................... 55	Mussel
Beaver .... 15+	Elephant................. 75	(freshwater) 70-80
Box turtle	Giraffe 36	Octopus 2-3
(Eastern) 138	Goat (domestic) ... 20	Quahog 150
Camel .... 35+	Goldfish 41	Rabbit .... 18+
Cat (domestic) 34	Goose (domestic) ... 20	Squirrel, gray 23
Chicken	Gorilla .... 50+	Tiger..................... 26
(domestic)............ 25	Horse 62	Toad....................... 40
Chimpanzee........... 51	Housefly .... 17 days	Tortoise
Coyote .... 21+	Kangaroo 30	(Marion's) .... 152+
Dog (domestic)....... 29	Lion 29	Turkey (domestic)... 16
Dolphin................. 25	Monarch butterfly . 1+	

	Estral (estrous) Cycle Including Heat Period		Length of Heat (estrus)		Usual Time of Ovulation	When Cycle Recurs if Not Bred
	AVERAGE	RANGE	AVERAGE	RANGE		
Mare	21 days	10-37 days	5-6 days	2-11 days	24-48 hours before end of estrus	21 days
Sow	21 days	18-24 days	2-3 days	1-5 days	30-36 hours after start of estrus	21 days
Ewe	16½ days	14-19 days	30 hours	24-32 hours	12-24 hours before end of estrus	16½ days
Goat	21 days	18-24 days	2-3 days	1-4 days	Near end of estrus	21 days
Cow	21 days	18-24 days	18 hours	10-24 hours	10-12 hours after end of estrus	21 days
Bitch	24 days		7 days	5-9 days	1-3 days after first acceptance	Pseudo-pregnancy
Cat		15-21 days	3-4 days, if mated	9-10 days, in absence of male	24-56 hours after coitus	Pseudo-pregnancy

Are you over 55?

"Look What Seniors Can Get Free!"

by Murry L Broach - Staff Writer

Washington DC (Special) An amazing new book reveals thousands of little-known Government giveaways for people over 55.

Each year, lots of these benefits are NOT given away simply because people don't know they're available... and the government doesn't advertise them.

Many of these fabulous freebies can be yours regardless of your income or assets. Entitled "Free for Seniors", the book tells you all about such goodies as how you can:

■ Get free prescription drugs. (This one alone could save you thousands of dollars!)

■ Get free dental care... for yourself AND for your grandkids.

■ Get up to $800 for food.

■ How you can get free legal help.

■ How to get some help in paying your rent, wherever you live.

■ How to get up to $15,000 free money to spruce up your home!

■ Here's where to get $1,800 to keep you warm this winter.

■ Access the very best research on our planet on how you can live longer.

■ Are you becoming more forgetful? Here's valuable free information you should get now.

■ Stop high blood pressure and cholesterol worries from ruling your life

■ Free help if you have arthritis of any type.

■ Incontinence is not inevitable. These free facts could help you.

■ Free eye treatment.

■ Depression: Being down in the dumps is common, but it doesn't have to be a normal part of growing old.

■ Free medical care from some of the very best doctors in the world for Alzheimer's, cataracts, or heart disease.

■ New Cancer Cure? Maybe! Here's how to find out what's known about it to this point.

■ Promising new developments for prostate cancer.

■ Get paid $100 a day plus expenses to travel overseas!

■ Up to $5,000 free to help you pay your bills.

■ Free and confidential help with your sex life.

■ Impotence? Get confidential help... Free therapies, treatments, implants, and much more.

■ Hot Flashes? This new research could help you now!

■ Find out if a medicine you're taking could be affecting your sex life.

There's more! Much, much more, and "Free for Seniors" comes with a solid no-nonsense guarantee. Send for your copy today and examine it at your leisure. Unless it makes or saves you AT LEAST ten times it's cost, simply return it for a full refund within 90 days.

To get your copy of "Free for Seniors", send your name and address along with a check or money-order for only $12.95 plus $2 postage and handling (total of $14.95) to:

FREE FOR SENIORS
Dept. FS8131
718 - 12th St. N.W., Box 24500
Canton, Ohio 44701

To charge to your VISA or MasterCard, include your card number, expiration date, and signature. For even faster service, have your credit card handy and call toll-free 1-800-772-7285, Ext. FS8131.

Want to save even more? Do a favor for a friend or relative and order 2 books for only $20 postpaid. ©1997 TCO FS0131S04

http://www.trescoinc.com

1999

January
S	M	T	W	T	F	S
					1	2
3	4	5	6	7	8	9
10	11	12	13	14	15	16
17	18	19	20	21	22	23
24	25	26	27	28	29	30
31						

February
S	M	T	W	T	F	S
	1	2	3	4	5	6
7	8	9	10	11	12	13
14	15	16	17	18	19	20
21	22	23	24	25	26	27
28						

March
S	M	T	W	T	F	S
	1	2	3	4	5	6
7	8	9	10	11	12	13
14	15	16	17	18	19	20
21	22	23	24	25	26	27
28	29	30	31			

April
S	M	T	W	T	F	S
				1	2	3
4	5	6	7	8	9	10
11	12	13	14	15	16	17
18	19	20	21	22	23	24
25	26	27	28	29	30	

May
S	M	T	W	T	F	S
						1
2	3	4	5	6	7	8
9	10	11	12	13	14	15
16	17	18	19	20	21	22
23	24	25	26	27	28	29
30	31					

June
S	M	T	W	T	F	S
		1	2	3	4	5
6	7	8	9	10	11	12
13	14	15	16	17	18	19
20	21	22	23	24	25	26
27	28	29	30			

July
S	M	T	W	T	F	S
				1	2	3
4	5	6	7	8	9	10
11	12	13	14	15	16	17
18	19	20	21	22	23	24
25	26	27	28	29	30	31

August
S	M	T	W	T	F	S
1	2	3	4	5	6	7
8	9	10	11	12	13	14
15	16	17	18	19	20	21
22	23	24	25	26	27	28
29	30	31				

September
S	M	T	W	T	F	S
			1	2	3	4
5	6	7	8	9	10	11
12	13	14	15	16	17	18
19	20	21	22	23	24	25
26	27	28	29	30		

October
S	M	T	W	T	F	S
					1	2
3	4	5	6	7	8	9
10	11	12	13	14	15	16
17	18	19	20	21	22	23
24	25	26	27	28	29	30
31						

November
S	M	T	W	T	F	S
	1	2	3	4	5	6
7	8	9	10	11	12	13
14	15	16	17	18	19	20
21	22	23	24	25	26	27
28	29	30				

December
S	M	T	W	T	F	S
			1	2	3	4
5	6	7	8	9	10	11
12	13	14	15	16	17	18
19	20	21	22	23	24	25
26	27	28	29	30	31	

2000

January
S	M	T	W	T	F	S
						1
2	3	4	5	6	7	8
9	10	11	12	13	14	15
16	17	18	19	20	21	22
23	24	25	26	27	28	29
30	31					

February
S	M	T	W	T	F	S
		1	2	3	4	5
6	7	8	9	10	11	12
13	14	15	16	17	18	19
20	21	22	23	24	25	26
27	28	29				

March
S	M	T	W	T	F	S
			1	2	3	4
5	6	7	8	9	10	11
12	13	14	15	16	17	18
19	20	21	22	23	24	25
26	27	28	29	30	31	

April
S	M	T	W	T	F	S
						1
2	3	4	5	6	7	8
9	10	11	12	13	14	15
16	17	18	19	20	21	22
23	24	25	26	27	28	29
30						

May
S	M	T	W	T	F	S
	1	2	3	4	5	6
7	8	9	10	11	12	13
14	15	16	17	18	19	20
21	22	23	24	25	26	27
28	29	30	31			

June
S	M	T	W	T	F	S
				1	2	3
4	5	6	7	8	9	10
11	12	13	14	15	16	17
18	19	20	21	22	23	24
25	26	27	28	29	30	

July
S	M	T	W	T	F	S
						1
2	3	4	5	6	7	8
9	10	11	12	13	14	15
16	17	18	19	20	21	22
23	24	25	26	27	28	29
30	31					

August
S	M	T	W	T	F	S
		1	2	3	4	5
6	7	8	9	10	11	12
13	14	15	16	17	18	19
20	21	22	23	24	25	26
27	28	29	30	31		

September
S	M	T	W	T	F	S
					1	2
3	4	5	6	7	8	9
10	11	12	13	14	15	16
17	18	19	20	21	22	23
24	25	26	27	28	29	30

October
S	M	T	W	T	F	S
1	2	3	4	5	6	7
8	9	10	11	12	13	14
15	16	17	18	19	20	21
22	23	24	25	26	27	28
29	30	31				

November
S	M	T	W	T	F	S
			1	2	3	4
5	6	7	8	9	10	11
12	13	14	15	16	17	18
19	20	21	22	23	24	25
26	27	28	29	30		

December
S	M	T	W	T	F	S
					1	2
3	4	5	6	7	8	9
10	11	12	13	14	15	16
17	18	19	20	21	22	23
24	25	26	27	28	29	30
31						

2001

January
S	M	T	W	T	F	S
	1	2	3	4	5	6
7	8	9	10	11	12	13
14	15	16	17	18	19	20
21	22	23	24	25	26	27
28	29	30	31			

February
S	M	T	W	T	F	S
				1	2	3
4	5	6	7	8	9	10
11	12	13	14	15	16	17
18	19	20	21	22	23	24
25	26	27	28			

March
S	M	T	W	T	F	S
				1	2	3
4	5	6	7	8	9	10
11	12	13	14	15	16	17
18	19	20	21	22	23	24
25	26	27	28	29	30	31

April
S	M	T	W	T	F	S
1	2	3	4	5	6	7
8	9	10	11	12	13	14
15	16	17	18	19	20	21
22	23	24	25	26	27	28
29	30					

May
S	M	T	W	T	F	S
		1	2	3	4	5
6	7	8	9	10	11	12
13	14	15	16	17	18	19
20	21	22	23	24	25	26
27	28	29	30	31		

June
S	M	T	W	T	F	S
					1	2
3	4	5	6	7	8	9
10	11	12	13	14	15	16
17	18	19	20	21	22	23
24	25	26	27	28	29	30

July
S	M	T	W	T	F	S
1	2	3	4	5	6	7
8	9	10	11	12	13	14
15	16	17	18	19	20	21
22	23	24	25	26	27	28
29	30	31				

August
S	M	T	W	T	F	S
			1	2	3	4
5	6	7	8	9	10	11
12	13	14	15	16	17	18
19	20	21	22	23	24	25
26	27	28	29	30	31	

September
S	M	T	W	T	F	S
						1
2	3	4	5	6	7	8
9	10	11	12	13	14	15
16	17	18	19	20	21	22
23	24	25	26	27	28	29
30						

October
S	M	T	W	T	F	S
	1	2	3	4	5	6
7	8	9	10	11	12	13
14	15	16	17	18	19	20
21	22	23	24	25	26	27
28	29	30	31			

November
S	M	T	W	T	F	S
				1	2	3
4	5	6	7	8	9	10
11	12	13	14	15	16	17
18	19	20	21	22	23	24
25	26	27	28	29	30	

December
S	M	T	W	T	F	S
						1
2	3	4	5	6	7	8
9	10	11	12	13	14	15
16	17	18	19	20	21	22
23	24	25	26	27	28	29
30	31					

A Reference Compendium

compiled by Mare-Anne Jarvela

Calendar

Total Solar Eclipses (2000-2025) 274
Easter Sunday (2000-2004) .. 274
Triskaidekaphobia 274
Leap Years 274
Glossary of Almanac Oddities 275
Phases of the Moon 276
Month Names 277
Dining by the Calendar 277
Full-Moon Names 280
Day Names 280
Chinese Zodiac............ 281

Weather

Clouds 282
Snowflakes 282
Windchill Table 283
Heat Index................ 283
Is It Raining, Drizzling, or
    Misting?.............. 284
A Table Foretelling the Weather
    Through All the Lunations of
    Each Year (Forever) 284
Beaufort Wind Force Scale .. 285
Atlantic Hurricane Names ... 285
East-Pacific Hurricane Names 286
Retired Atlantic Hurricane
    Names 286
Fujita Scale (or F Scale) for
    Tornadoes 286
Richter Scale for Measuring
    Earthquakes........... 286
Winter Weather Terms...... 287
Safe Ice Thickness 287

The Garden

A Beginner Garden 288
Plants with Interesting
    Foliage............... 288
Perennials for Cutting
    Gardens 288
Herb Gardening 289
Herbs to Plant in Lawns..... 289
Herbs That Attract Butterflies 289

Heat-Loving Wildflowers ... 289
Flowers That Attract
    Butterflies 290
Flowers That Attract
    Hummingbirds 290
Forcing Blooms Indoors 290
Fall-Planted Bulbs 291
Spring-Planted Bulbs....... 291
Forcing Bulbs Indoors 292
Planning Your Garden 292
Vegetable Seeds Best Sown in
    the Ground............ 292
Vegetables and Herbs Best
    Started Indoors 293
Minimum Soil Temperature for
    Seeds to Germinate 293
The Healthiest Vegetables... 293
Critical Low Temperatures for
    Frost Damage to Vegetables
    293
When Is a Good Time to Fertilize
    Your Vegetables? 294
Manure Guide............. 294
General Rules for Pruning... 295
Soil Fixes 295
Soil Amendments.......... 295
Lawn Tips................ 296
Vegetable Gardening in
    Containers 296
Fall Palette 296

Food

Food We Love to Brag About 297
How to Order Two Bun Halves
    Filled with Cheese, Meat,
    Onions, Peppers, and Other
    Stuff 303
Pan Sizes and Equivalents ... 304
Food for Thought 304
Don't Freeze These 304
Appetizing Amounts 304
The Party Planner.......... 305
Substitutions for Common
    Ingredients 306
Measuring Vegetables 306
Measuring Fruits 307

Substitutions for Uncommon
    Ingredients............ 308

Household

American Farmland and Life
    in 1900 and 2000: a
    Comparison 309
Hand Thermometer for Outdoor
    Cooking 310
Life Expectancy by Current
    Age................... 310
Is It a Cold or the Flu? 310
Are You Skinny, Just Right, or
    Overweight? 311
Calorie Burning 311
How Much Paint Will You
    Need?................. 312
How Much Wallpaper Will You
    Need?................. 313
Guide to Lumber and Nails .. 314
Firewood Heat Values 315
How Many Trees in a Cord of
    Wood? 315
Heat Values of Fuels 315
How to Find the Number of
    Bricks in a Wall or
    Building.............. 315

Animals

Animal Terminology 316
More Animal Collectives.... 317
Dogs: Gentle, Fierce, Smart,
    Popular............... 318
Don't Poison Your Pussycat!.. 318
Ten Most Intelligent Animals 318
Nutritional Value of Various
    Insects per 100 Grams... 318

Last Words

The Songs We Sang: The Greatest
    Tunes of the Decades ... 319
Famous Last Words of Real
    People 319
"New Years Rulins"........ 319
Know Your Angels......... 320
Animals in the Bible (KJV).. 320
The Golden Rule 320

Total Solar Eclipses (2000-2025)

Date		Regions with Visible Totality
2001	June 21	Atlantic Ocean, southern Africa
2002	Dec. 4	southern Africa, Indian Ocean, Australia
2003	Nov. 23	Antarctica
2005	Apr. 8	S. Pacific Ocean
2006	Mar. 29	Africa, Turkey, Soviet Union
2008	Aug. 1	Greenland, Siberia, China
2009	July 22	India, China, S. Pacific Ocean
2010	July 11	S. Pacific Ocean, southern South America
2012	Nov. 13	Australia, S. Pacific Ocean
2013	Nov. 3	Atlantic Ocean, Central Africa
2015	Mar. 20	N. Atlantic Ocean, Arctic
2016	Mar. 9	Southeast Asia, N. Pacific Ocean
2017	Aug. 17	United States
2019	July 2	S. Pacific Ocean, South America
2020	Dec. 14	S. Pacific Ocean, South America
2021	Dec. 4	Antarctica
2023	Apr. 20	Indonesia
2024	Apr. 8	Mexico, United States, Canada

Easter Sunday (2000-2004)

■ Christian churches that follow the Gregorian calendar (Eastern Orthodox churches follow the Julian calendar) celebrate Easter on the first Sunday after the full Moon that occurs on or just after the vernal equinox.

In	Easter will fall on
2000	April 23
2001	April 15
2002	March 31
2003	April 20
2004	April 11

Triskaidekaphobia

Here are a few conclusions on Friday the 13th:

Of the 14 possible configurations for the annual calendar (see any perpetual calendar), the occurrence of Friday the 13th is this:

■ 6 of 14 years have one Friday the 13th.
6 of 14 years have two Fridays the 13th.
2 of 14 years have three Fridays the 13th.
There is no year without one Friday the 13th, and no year with more than three.

■ There is only one Friday the 13th in 2000. The next year to have three Fridays the 13th is 2009.

■ The reason we say "Fridays the 13th" is that no one can pronounce "Friday the 13ths."

Leap Years

■ The actual length of a year (the rotation of Earth around the Sun) is 365.2422 days. If we didn't have leap years, the seasons would shift about a quarter of a day every year. But adding one day every four years would create a surplus of about three days in 400 years. We correct this by dropping three leap years in that span; any year evenly divisible by 4 is a leap year, except for the century years, which must be evenly divisible by 400 to be a leap year. So the years 1700, 1800, and 1900 were not leap years, but 2000 is a leap year, the first century leap year since 1600.

Glossary of Almanac Oddities

■ Many readers have expressed puzzlement over the rather obscure notations that appear on our Right-Hand Calendar Pages (pages 61-87). These "oddities" have long been fixtures in the Almanac, and we are pleased to provide some definitions. (Once explained, it may seem that they are not so odd after all!)

■ Ember Days (Movable)

The *Almanac* traditionally marks the four periods formerly observed by the Roman Catholic and Anglican churches for prayer, fasting, and the ordination of clergy. These Ember Days are the Wednesdays, Fridays, and Saturdays that follow in succession after 1) the First Sunday in Lent; 2) Pentecost (Whitsunday); 3) the Feast of the Holy Cross (September 14); and 4) the Feast of St. Lucy (December 13). (The word *ember* is perhaps a corruption of the Latin *quatuor tempora,* "four times.")

Folklore has it that the weather on each of the three days foretells weather for three successive months — that is, in September Ember Days, Wednesday forecasts weather for October, Friday for November, and Saturday for December.

■ Plough Monday (January)

The first Monday after the Epiphany; so called because it was the end of the Christmas holidays, when men returned to their plough — or daily work. It was customary for farm laborers to draw a plough through the village, soliciting money for a "plough-light," which was kept burning in the parish church all year. In some areas, the custom of blessing the plough is maintained.

■ Three Chilly Saints (May)

Mammertius, Pancratius, and Gervatius, three early Christian saints, whose feast days occur on May 11, 12, and 13, respectively. Because these days are traditionally cold (an old French saying goes: "St. Mammertius, St. Pancras, and St. Gervais do not pass without a frost"), they have come to be known as the Three Chilly Saints.

■ Midsummer Day (June 24)

Although it occurs near the summer solstice, to the farmer it is the midpoint of the growing season, halfway between planting and harvest and an occasion for festivity. The English church considered it a "Quarter Day," one of the four major divisions of the liturgical year. It also marks the feast day of St. John the Baptist.

■ Cornscateous Air (July)

A term first used by the old almanac makers to signify warm, damp air. While it signals ideal climatic conditions for growing corn, it also poses a danger to those affected by asthma, pneumonia, and other respiratory problems.

■ Dog Days (July-August)

The hottest and most unhealthy days of the year. Also known as "Canicular Days," the name derives from the Dog Star, Sirius. The Almanac lists the traditional timing of Dog Days: The 40 days beginning July 3 and ending August 11, coinciding with the heliacal (at sunrise) rising of Sirius.

■ Cat Nights Begin (August)

The term harks back to the days when people believed in witches. An old Irish legend has it that a witch could turn herself into a cat eight times and

then regain herself, but on the ninth time — August 17 — she couldn't change back. Hence the saying, "A cat has nine lives." Since August is a "yowly" time for cats, this may have prompted the speculation about witches on the prowl in the first place.

■ Harvest Home (September)

In both Europe and Britain, the conclusion of the harvest each autumn was once marked by great festivals of fun, feasting, and thanksgiving known as "Harvest Home." It was also a time to hold elections, pay workers, and collect rents. These festivals usually took place around the time of the autumnal equinox. Certain ethnic groups in this country, particularly the Pennsylvania Dutch, have kept the tradition alive.

■ St. Luke's Little Summer (October)

A spell of warm weather occurring about the time of the saint's feast day, October 18. This period is sometimes referred to as "Indian Summer."

■ Indian Summer (November)

A period of warm weather following a cold spell or a hard frost. While there are differing dates for the time of occurrence, for more than 200 years the Almanac has adhered to the saying, "If All Saints brings out winter, St. Martin's brings out Indian Summer." Accordingly, Indian Summer can occur between St. Martin's Day (November 11) and November 20. As for the origin of the term, some say it comes from the early Indians, who believed the condition was caused by a warm wind sent from the court of their southwestern God, Cautantowwit.

■ Halcyon Days (December)

A period (about 14 days) of calm weather, following the blustery winds of autumn's end. The ancient Greeks and Romans believed them to occur around the time of the winter solstice when the halcyon, or kingfisher, was brooding. In a nest floating on the sea, the bird was said to have charmed the wind and waves so the waters were especially calm during this period.

■ Beware the Pogonip (December)

The word *pogonip* is a meteorological term used to describe an uncommon occurrence — frozen fog. The word was coined by American Indians to describe the frozen fogs of fine ice needles that occur in the mountain valleys of the western United States. According to Indian tradition, breathing the fog is injurious to the lungs.

Phases of the Moon

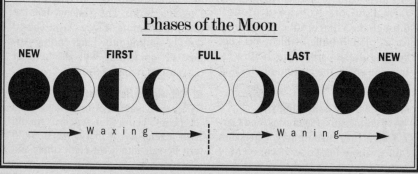

NEW   FIRST   FULL   LAST   NEW

Waxing ———→ | ———→ Waning ———→

Month Names

January   Named for the Roman god Janus, protector of gates and doorways. Janus is depicted with two faces, one looking into the past, the other into the future.

February   From the Latin word *februa,* "to cleanse." The Roman Februalia was a month of purification and atonement.

March   Named for the Roman god of war, Mars. This was the time of year to resume military campaigns that had been interrupted by winter.

April   From the Latin word *aperio,* "to open (bud)," because plants begin to grow in this month.

May   Named for the Roman goddess Maia, who oversaw the growth of plants. Also from the Latin word *maiores,* meaning "elders," who were celebrated during this month.

June   Named for the Roman goddess Juno, patroness of marriage and the well-being of women. Also from the Latin word *juvenis,* "young people."

July   Named to honor Roman dictator Julius Caesar (100 B.C.- 44 B.C.). In 46 B.C., Julius Caesar made one of his greatest contributions to history: With the help of Sosigenes, he developed the Julian calendar, the precursor to the Gregorian calendar we use today.

August   Named to honor the first Roman emperor (and grandnephew of Julius Caesar), Augustus Caesar (63 B.C.-A.D. 14).

September   From the Latin word *septem,* "seven," because this had been the seventh month of the early Roman calendar.

October   From the Latin word *octo,* "eight," because this had been the eighth month of the early Roman calendar.

November   From the Latin word *novem,* "nine," because this had been the ninth month of the early Roman calendar.

December   From the Latin word *decem,* "ten," because this had been the tenth month of the early Roman calendar.

Dining by the Calendar
Traditional Foods for Feasts and Fasts

■ **January**

Feast of the Circumcision: Black-eyed peas and pork (United States); oat-husk gruel or oatmeal porridge (Scotland).

Epiphany: Cake with a lucky bean baked in it; the one who finds the bean is the king or queen of the feast, in memory of the three wise men (France).

Robert Burns Day: Haggis — sheep's stomach stuffed with suet, chopped organ meat (heart, lungs, liver), onions, oatmeal, and seasonings (Scotland). Haggis is a traditional Scottish delicacy served on all holidays of national importance.

(continued)

■ February

Candlemas Day: Pancakes eaten today will prevent hemorrhoids for a full year (French American).

St. Agatha: Round loaves of bread blessed by a priest (southern Europe).

Shrove Tuesday: Pancakes (England); oatcakes (Scotland); rabbit (Ireland). Rich foods are eaten to usher in the Lenten fast; pancakes use up the last of the eggs and butter.

Lent: Simnel, a large fruitcake baked so hard it has sometimes been mistaken by recipients for a hassock or footstool (Great Britain).

■ March

St. David: Leeks, to be worn (Wales) or eaten raw (England). Recalls a Welsh victory over the Saxons in A.D. 640; the Welsh wore leeks in their hats to distinguish them from the enemy.

St. Benedict: Nettle soup (ancient monastic practice). Picking nettles, which irritate the skin, was a penance in keeping with the spirit of the monastic rule of St. Benedict.

Purim: Strong drink and three-cornered cookies flavored with poppy seed (Jewish). These cookies, called hamantaschen, are said to represent the three-cornered hat of Haman, the enemy of the Jewish people, whose downfall is celebrated on this holiday.

Maundy Thursday: Green foods or foods colored green (southern Europe). The medieval liturgical observance called for green vestments; in some parts of Europe, it is still called Green Thursday.

Good Friday: Hot cross buns. If made properly on this day, they will never get moldy (England).

■ April

Easter: Lamb as symbol of sacrifice; ham.

Beltane, May Day Eve: Strong ale (England); oatcakes with nine knobs to be broken off one by one and offered to each of nine supernatural protectors of domestic animals (Scotland).

■ May

Ascension Day: Fowl, or pastries molded in the shape of birds, to commemorate the taking of Jesus into the skies (medieval Europe).

Whitsunday (Pentecost): Dove or pigeon in honor of the Holy Spirit (southern Europe); strong ale (England).

St. Dunstan: Beer. Cider pressed today will go bad (England).

Corpus Christi: Orange peel dipped in chocolate, chicken stuffed with sauerkraut (Basque Provinces).

■ June

St. Anthony of Padua: Liver, possibly based on the pre-Christian custom of eating liver on the summer solstice.

Feast of St. John the Baptist: First fruits of spring harvest eaten.

■ July

St. Swithin: Eggs, because the saint miraculously restored intact a basket of eggs that had been broken by a poor woman taking them to market; he also looks after apples (medieval England).

St. James: Oysters, because James was a fisherman (England).

■ August

Lammas Day: Oatcakes (Scotland); loaves made from new grain of the season (England); toffee; seaweed pudding. Blueberries in baskets as an offering to a sweetheart are the last vestige of this holiday as a pagan fertility festival (Ireland).

St. Lawrence of Rome: Because the saint was roasted to death on a gridiron, it is courteous to serve only cold meat today (southern Europe).

Feast of the Assumption: Onions, possibly because they have always been considered wholesome and potent against evil (Polish American).

■ September

St. Giles: Tea loaf with raisins (Scotland).

Nativity of Mary: Blackberries, possibly because the color is reminiscent of the depiction of the Virgin's blue cloak (Brittany).

Michaelmas Day: New wine (Europe); goose, originally a sacrifice to the saint (Great Britain); cake of oats, barley, and rye (Scotland); carrots (Ireland).

■ October

Rosh Hashanah: Sweet foods; honey; foods colored orange or yellow to represent a bright, joyous, and sweet new year (Jewish).

Yom Kippur: Fast day; the day before, eat kreplach (filled noodles), considered by generations of mothers to be good and filling (Jewish).

St. Luke: Oatcakes flavored with anise and cinnamon (Scotland).

Sts. Simon and Jude: Dirge cakes, simple fried buns made for distribution to the poor. Also apples or potatoes, for divination (Scotland and England). Divination with apples is accomplished by peeling the fruit in one long strip and tossing the peel over one's shoulder. The letter formed by the peel is then interpreted.

All Hallows Eve: Apples and nuts for divination (England); buttered oat-husk gruel (Scotland); bosty, a mixture of potatoes, cabbage, and onions (Ireland).

■ November

All Saints Day: Chestnuts (Italy); gingerbread and oatcakes (Scotland); milk (central Europe); doughnuts, whose round shape indicates eternity (Tyrol).

All Souls Day: Skull-shaped candy (Mexico); beans, peas, and lentils, considered food of the poor, as penance for souls in purgatory (southern Europe).

St. Martin: Last religious feast day before the beginning of the Advent fast. Goose, last of fresh-killed meat before winter; blood pudding (Great Britain).

St. Andrew: Haggis — stuffed sheep's stomach (Scotland).

■ December

St. Nicholas: Fruit, nuts, candy for children (Germany). Commemorates, in part, the miracle by which the saint restored to life three young boys who had been murdered by a greedy innkeeper.

St. Lucy: Headcheese; cakes flavored with saffron or cardamom, raisins, and almonds (Sweden). The saffron imparts a yellow color to the cakes, representing sunlight, whose return is celebrated at the solstice.

Christmas: Boar's head or goose, plum pudding, nuts, oranges (England); turkey (United States); spiced beef (Ireland).

St. John the Evangelist: Small loaves of bread made with blessed wine (medieval Europe). This is a feast on which wine is ritually blessed in memory of the saint, who drank poisoned wine and miraculously survived.

Chanukah: Latkes — potato pancakes (Jewish).

Holy Innocents Day: Baby food, pablum, Cream of Wheat, in honor of the children killed by King Herod of Judea (monastic observance).

St. Sylvester: Strong drink (United States); haggis, oatcakes and cheese, oat-husk gruel or porridge (Scotland).

– E. Brady

Full-Moon Names

■ Historically, the Indians of what are now the northern and eastern United States kept track of the seasons by giving a distinctive name to each recurring full Moon, this name being applied to the entire month in which it occurred. With some variations, the same Moon names were used throughout the Algonquin tribes from New England to Lake Superior.

Name	Month	Other Names Used
Full Wolf Moon	January	Full Old Moon
Full Snow Moon	February	Full Hunger Moon
Full Worm Moon	March	Full Crow Moon, Full Crust Moon, Full Sugar Moon, Full Sap Moon
Full Pink Moon	April	Full Sprouting Grass Moon, Full Egg Moon, Full Fish Moon
Full Flower Moon	May	Full Corn Planting Moon, Full Milk Moon
Full Strawberry Moon	June	Full Rose Moon, Full Hot Moon
Full Buck Moon	July	Full Thunder Moon, Full Hay Moon
Full Sturgeon Moon	August	Full Red Moon, Full Green Corn Moon
Full Harvest Moon*	September	Full Corn Moon, Full Barley Moon
Full Hunter's Moon	October	Full Travel Moon, Full Dying Grass Moon
Full Beaver Moon	November	Full Frost Moon
Full Cold Moon	December	Full Long Nights Moon

* The Harvest Moon is always the full Moon closest to the autumnal equinox. If the Harvest Moon occurs in October, the September full Moon is usually called the Corn Moon.

Day Names

■ The Romans named the days of the week after the Sun, the Moon, and the five known planets. These names have survived in European languages, but English names also reflect an Anglo-Saxon influence.

LATIN	FRENCH	ITALIAN	SPANISH	SAXON	ENGLISH
Solis (Sun)	dimanche	domenica	domingo	Sun	Sunday
Lunae (Moon)	lundi	lunedì	lunes	Moon	Monday
Martis (Mars)	mardi	martedì	martes	Tiw (the Anglo-Saxon god of war, the equivalent of the Norse Tyr or the Roman Mars)	Tuesday
Mercurii (Mercury)	mercredi	mercoledì	miércoles	Woden (the Anglo-Saxon equivalent of the Norse Odin or the Roman Mercury)	Wednesday
Jovis (Jupiter)	jeudi	giovedì	jueves	Thor (the Norse god of thunder, the equivalent of the Roman Jupiter)	Thursday
Veneris (Venus)	vendredi	venerdì	viernes	Frigg (the Norse god of love and fertility, the equivalent of the Roman Venus)	Friday
Saturni (Saturn)	samedi	sabato	sábado	Saterne (Saturn, the Roman god of agriculture)	Saturday

Chinese Zodiac

■ The animal designations of the Chinese zodiac follow a 12-year cycle and are always used in the same sequence. The Chinese year of 354 days begins three to seven weeks into the western 365-day year, so the animal designation changes at that time, rather than on January 1.

Rat

Ambitious and sincere, you can be generous with your financial resources. Compatible with the dragon and the monkey. Your opposite is the horse.

1900	1960
1912	1972
1924	1984
1936	1996
1948	2008

Rabbit (Hare)

Talented and affectionate, you are a seeker of tranquility. Compatible with the sheep and the pig. Your opposite is the rooster.

1903	1963
1915	1975
1927	1987
1939	1999
1951	2011

Horse

Physically attractive and popular, you like the company of others. Compatible with the tiger and the dog. Your opposite is the rat.

1906	1966
1918	1978
1930	1990
1942	2002
1954	2014

Rooster (Cock)

Seeking wisdom and truth, you have a pioneering spirit. Compatible with the snake and the ox. Your opposite is the rabbit.

1909	1969
1921	1981
1933	1993
1945	2005
1957	2017

Ox (Buffalo)

A leader, you are bright and cheerful. Compatible with the snake and the rooster. Your opposite is the sheep.

1901	1961
1913	1973
1925	1985
1937	1997
1949	2009

Dragon

Robust and passionate, your life is filled with complexity. Compatible with the monkey and the rat. Your opposite is the dog.

1904	1964
1916	1976
1928	1988
1940	2000
1952	2012

Sheep (Goat)

Aesthetic and stylish, you enjoy being a private person. Compatible with the pig and the rabbit. Your opposite is the ox.

1907	1967
1919	1979
1931	1991
1943	2003
1955	2015

Dog

Generous and loyal, you have the ability to work well with others. Compatible with the horse and the tiger. Your opposite is the dragon.

1910	1970
1922	1982
1934	1994
1946	2006
1958	2018

Tiger

Forthright and sensitive, you possess great courage. Compatible with the horse and the dog. Your opposite is the monkey.

1902	1962
1914	1974
1926	1986
1938	1998
1950	2010

Snake

Strong-willed and intense, you display great wisdom. Compatible with the rooster and the ox. Your opposite is the pig.

1905	1965
1917	1977
1929	1989
1941	2001
1953	2013

Monkey

Persuasive and intelligent, you strive to excel. Compatible with the dragon and the rat. Your opposite is the tiger.

1908	1968
1920	1980
1932	1992
1944	2004
1956	2016

Pig (Boar)

Gallant and noble, your friends will remain at your side. Compatible with the rabbit and the sheep. Your opposite is the snake.

1911	1971
1923	1983
1935	1995
1947	2007
1959	2019

Clouds

1. High clouds (bases starting at an average of 20,000 feet)

Cirrus: thin feather-like crystal clouds.
Cirrostratus: thin white clouds that resemble veils.
Cirrocumulus: thin clouds that appear as small "cotton patches."

2. Middle clouds (bases starting at about 10,000 feet)

Altostratus: grayish or bluish layer of clouds that can obscure the Sun.
Altocumulus: gray or white layer or patches of solid clouds with rounded shapes.

3. Low clouds (bases starting near Earth's surface to 6,500 feet)

Stratus: thin, gray sheet-like clouds with low base; may bring drizzle and snow.
Stratocumulus: rounded cloud masses that form on top of a layer.
Nimbostratus: dark, gray shapeless cloud layers containing rain, snow, and ice pellets.

4. Clouds with vertical development (high clouds that form at almost any altitude and that reach up to 14,000 feet)

Cumulus: fair-weather clouds with flat bases and domeshaped tops.
Cumulonimbus: large, dark, vertical clouds with bulging tops that bring showers, thunder, and lightning.

Snowflakes

■ Snowflakes are made up of six-sided crystals. If you look carefully at the snowflakes during the next snowstorm, you might be able to find some of the crystal types below. The temperature at which a crystal forms mainly determines the basic shape. Sometimes a snowflake is a combination of more than one type of crystal.

Capped columns (also called tsuzumi crystals) occur when colder than 12° F.

Columns (dense crystals, act like prisms) occur when colder than 12° F.

Needles (long and thin but still six-sided) occur at warmer temperatures, 21° to 25° F.

Plates (mirror-like crystals) occur under special weather conditions.

Spatial dendrites (irregular and feathery) occur in high-moisture clouds, 3° to 10° F.

Stellar crystals (beautiful, delicate crystals) occur under special weather conditions.

Windchill Table

■ As wind speed increases, the air temperature against your body falls. The combination of cold temperature and high wind creates a cooling effect so severe that exposed flesh can freeze. (Inanimate objects, such as cars, do not experience windchill.)

To gauge wind speed: At 10 miles per hour, you can feel wind on your face; at 20, small branches move and dust or snow is raised; at 30, large branches move and wires whistle; at 40, whole trees bend. – courtesy Mount Washington Observatory

Wind Velocity (mph)	Temperature (° F)												
	50	41	32	23	14	5	–4	–13	–22	–31	–40	–49	–58
	Equivalent Temperature (° F) (Equivalent in cooling power on exposed flesh under calm conditions)												
5	48	39	28	19	10	1	–9	–18	–27	–36	–51	–56	–65
10	41	30	18	7	–4	–15	–26	–36	–49	–60	–71	–81	–92
20	32	19	7	–6	–18	–31	–44	–58	–71	–83	–96	–108	–121
30	28	14	1	–13	–27	–40	–54	–69	–81	–96	–108	–123	–137
40	27	12	–2	–17	–31	–45	–60	–74	–89	–103	–116	–130	–144
50	25	10	–4	–18	–33	–47	–62	–76	–90	–105	–119	–134	–148
	Little Danger			**Increasing Danger**				**Great Danger**					
	Danger from freezing of exposed flesh (for properly clothed person)												

Heat Index

■ As humidity increases, the air temperature feels hotter to your skin. The combination of hot temperature and high humidity reduces your body's ability to cool itself. For example, the heat you feel when the actual temperature is 90 degrees Fahrenheit with a relative humidity of 70 percent is 106 degrees.

	Temperature (° F)										
	70	75	80	85	90	95	100	105	110	115	120
Humidity (%)	Equivalent Temperature (° F)										
0	64	69	73	78	83	87	91	95	99	103	107
10	65	70	75	80	85	90	95	100	105	111	116
20	66	72	77	82	87	93	99	105	112	120	130
30	67	73	78	84	90	96	104	113	123	120	148
40	68	74	79	86	93	101	110	123	137	135	
50	69	75	81	88	96	107	120	135	150		
60	70	76	82	90	100	114	132	149			
70	70	77	85	93	106	124	144				
80	71	78	86	97	113	136					
90	71	79	88	102	122						
100	72	80	91	108							

Is It Raining, Drizzling, or Misting?

	Drops (per sq. ft. per sec.)	Diameter of Drops (mm)	Intensity (in. per hr.)
Cloudburst	113	2.85	4.00
Excessive rain	76	2.40	1.60
Heavy rain	46	2.05	.60
Moderate rain	46	1.60	.15
Light rain	26	1.24	.04
Drizzle	14	.96	.01
Mist	2,510	.10	.002
Fog	6,264,000	.01	.005

A Table Foretelling the Weather Through All the Lunations of Each Year (Forever)

■ This table is the result of many years of actual observation and shows what sort of weather will probably follow the Moon's entrance into any of its quarters. For example, the table shows that the week following February 19, 2000, will be cold with high winds because the Moon becomes full that day at 11:27 A.M., EST. (See Left-Hand Calendar Pages 60-86 for 2000 Moon phases.)

Editor's note: While the data in this table is taken into consideration in the yearlong process of compiling the annual long-range weather forecasts for The Old Farmer's Almanac, we rely far more on our projections of solar activity.

Time of Change	Summer	Winter
Midnight to 2 A.M.	Fair	Hard frost, unless wind is south or west
2 A.M. to 4 A.M.	Cold, with frequent showers	Snow and stormy
4 A.M. to 6 A.M.	Rain	Rain
6 A.M. to 8 A.M.	Wind and rain	Stormy
8 A.M. to 10 A.M.	Changeable	Cold rain if wind is west; snow if east
10 A.M. to noon	Frequent showers	Cold with high winds
Noon to 2 P.M.	Very rainy	Snow or rain
2 P.M. to 4 P.M.	Changeable	Fair and mild
4 P.M. to 6 P.M.	Fair	Fair
6 P.M. to 10 P.M.	Fair if wind is northwest; rain if wind is south or southwest	Fair and frosty if wind is north or northeast; rain or snow if wind is south or southwest
10 P.M. to midnight	Fair	Fair and frosty

This table was created more than 160 years ago by Dr. Herschell for the Boston Courier; *it first appeared in* The Old Farmer's Almanac *in 1834.*

Beaufort Wind Force Scale

"Used Mostly at Sea but of Help to All Who Are Interested in the Weather"

■ A scale of wind velocity was devised by Admiral Sir Francis Beaufort of the British Navy in 1805. The numbers 0 to 12 were arranged by Beaufort to indicate the strength of the wind from a calm, force 0, to a hurricane, force 12. Here's a scale adapted to land.

Beaufort Force	Description	When You See This	mph	km/h
0	Calm	Smoke goes straight up. No wind.	less than 1	less than 2
1	Light air	Direction of wind is shown by smoke drift but not by wind vane.	1-3	2-5
2	Light breeze	Wind felt on face. Leaves rustle. Wind vane moves.	4-7	6-11
3	Gentle breeze	Leaves and small twigs move steadily. Wind extends small flag straight out.	8-12	12-19
4	Moderate breeze	Wind raises dust and loose paper. Small branches move.	13-18	20-29
5	Fresh breeze	Small trees sway. Waves form on lakes.	19-24	30-39
6	Strong breeze	Large branches move. Wires whistle. Umbrellas are hard to use.	25-31	40-50
7	Moderate gale	Whole trees are in motion. Hard to walk against the wind.	32-38	51-61
8	Fresh gale	Twigs break from trees. Very hard to walk against wind.	39-46	62-74
9	Strong gale	Small damage to buildings. Roof shingles are removed.	47-54	75-87
10	Whole gale	Trees are uprooted.	55-63	88-101
11	Violent storm	Widespread damage from wind.	64-72	102-116
12	Hurricane	Widespread destruction from wind.	73+	117+

Atlantic Hurricane Names for 2000

Alberto	Ernesto	Joyce	Nadine	Tony
Beryl	Florence	Keith	Oscar	Valerie
Chris	Gordon	Leslie	Patty	William
Debby	Helene	Michael	Rafael	
	Isaac		Sandy	

East-Pacific Hurricane Names for 2000

Aletta	Fabio	Kristy	Paul	Willa
Bud	Gilma	Lane	Rosa	Xavier
Carlotta	Hector	Miriam	Sergio	Yolanda
Daniel	Ileana	Norman	Tara	Zeke
Emilia	John	Olivia	Vicente	

Retired Atlantic Hurricane Names

■ These are some of the most destructive and costly storms whose names have been retired from the six-year rotating hurricane list.

Year Retired	Name	Year Retired	Name	Year Retired	Name	Year Retired	Name
1970	Celia	1979	David	1985	Gloria	1990	Klaus
1972	Agnes	1979	Frederic	1988	Gilbert	1991	Bob
1974	Carmen	1980	Allen	1988	Joan	1992	Andrew
1975	Eloise	1983	Alicia	1989	Hugo	1995	Opal
1977	Anita	1985	Elena	1990	Diana	1995	Roxanne

Fujita Scale (or F Scale) for Tornadoes

■ This is a system developed by Dr. Theodore Fujita to classify tornadoes based on wind damage. All tornadoes, and most other severe local windstorms, are assigned a single number from this scale according to the most intense damage caused by the storm.

F0 (weak) . . . . . . 40-72 mph, light damage
F1 (weak). . 73-112 mph, moderate damage
F2 (strong) . . . . 113-157 mph, considerable damage
F3 (strong) . . 158-206 mph, severe damage
F4 (violent). . . . . 207-260 mph, devastating damage
F5 (violent) . . . . 261-318 mph, (rare) incredible damage

Richter Scale for Measuring Earthquakes

Magnitude	Possible Effects
1	Detectable only by instruments
2	Barely detectable, even near the epicenter
3	Felt indoors
4	Felt by most people; slight damage
5	Felt by all; damage minor to moderate
6	Moderately destructive
7	Major damage
8	Total and major damage

Devised by American geologist Charles W. Richter in 1935 to measure the magnitude of an earthquake.

Winter Weather Terms

Winter Storm Watch
■ Possibility of a winter storm. Be alert to changing weather conditions. Avoid unnecessary travel.

Winter Storm Warning
■ A severe winter storm has started or is about to begin in the forecast area. You should stay indoors during the storm. If you must go outdoors, wear several layers of lightweight clothing, which will keep you warmer than a single heavy coat. In addition, wear gloves or mittens and a hat to prevent loss of body heat. Cover your mouth to protect your lungs.

Heavy Snow Warning
■ Snow accumulations are expected to approach or exceed six inches in 12 hours but will not be accompanied by significant wind. This warning could also be issued if eight inches or more of snow accumulation is expected in a 24-hour period. During a heavy snow warning, freezing rain and sleet are not expected.

Blizzard Warning
■ Sustained winds or frequent gusts of 35 miles per hour or greater will occur in combination with considerable falling and/or blowing snow for a period of at least three hours. Visibility will often be reduced to less than ¼ mile in a blizzard.

Ice Storm Warning
■ A significant coating of ice, ½ inch thick or more, is expected.

Windchill Warning
■ Windchills reach life-threatening levels of minus 50 degrees Fahrenheit or lower.

Windchill Advisory
■ Windchill factors fall between minus 35 and minus 50 degrees Fahrenheit.

Sleet
■ Frozen or partially frozen rain in the form of ice pellets hit the ground so fast they bounce off with a sharp click.

Freezing Rain
■ Rain falls as a liquid but turns to ice on contact with a frozen surface to form a smooth ice coating called glaze.

Safe Ice Thickness *

Ice Thickness	Permissible Load
2 inches	One person on foot
3 inches	Group in single file
7-1/2 inches	Passenger car (2-ton gross)
8 inches	Light truck (2-1/2-ton gross)
10 inches	Medium truck (3-1/2-ton gross)
12 inches	Heavy truck (8-ton gross)
15 inches	10 tons
20 inches	25 tons
30 inches	70 tons
36 inches	110 tons

* **Solid clear blue/black pond and lake ice**

■ Slush ice has only half the strength of blue ice.

■ Strength value of river ice is 15 percent less.

Source: American Pulpwood Association

A Beginner Garden

■ A good size for a beginner vegetable garden is 10x16 feet and features crops that are easy to grow. A plot this size, planted as suggested below, can feed a family of four for one summer, with a little extra for canning and freezing (or giving away).

Make your garden 11 rows of ten feet each of the following:

ROW	
1	Zucchini (4 plants)
2	Tomatoes (5 plants, staked)
3	Peppers (6 plants)
4	Cabbage
5	Bush beans
6	Lettuce
7	Beets
8	Carrots
9	Chard
10	Radish
11	Marigolds (to discourage rabbits!)

Ideally the rows should run north and south to take full advantage of the Sun.

Plants with Interesting Foliage

■ **Airy/fine foliage**
Barrenwort, *Epimedium* spp.
Maidenhair fern, *Adiantum pedatum*
Meadow rue, *Thalictrum* spp.
Silver mound, *Artemisia schmidtiana*

■ **Linear foliage**
Blazing star, *Liatris* spp.
Daylily, *Hemerocallis* spp.
Iris, *Iris* spp.
Yucca, *Yucca* spp.

■ **Textured foliage**
Lamb's-ear, *Stachys byzantina*
Sea holly, *Eryngium* spp.
Silver sage, *Salvia argentea*
Woolly thyme, *Thymus pseudolanuginosus*

■ **Foliage with attractive shapes**
Cranesbill, *Geranium* spp.
Foamflower, *Tiarella cordifolia*
Hybrid lupine, *Lupinus* x *rus selianus*
Lady's-mantle, *Alchemilla vulgaris*

Perennials for Cutting Gardens

Aster *(Aster)*	False sunflower *(Heliopsis)*	Peony *(Paeonia)*
Baby's-breath *(Gypsophila)*	Flowering onion *(Allium)*	Phlox *(Phlox)*
Bellflower *(Campanula)*	Foxglove *(Digitalis)*	Purple coneflower *(Echinacea)*
Black-eyed Susan *(Rudbeckia)*	Gay-feather *(Liatris)*	Sea holly *(Eryngium)*
Blanket flower *(Gaillardia)*	Globe thistle *(Echinops)*	Speedwell *(Veronica)*
Chrysanthemum *(Chrysanthemum)*	Goldenrod *(Solidago)*	Tickseed *(Coreopsis)*
Delphinium *(Delphinium)*	Iris *(Iris)*	Yarrow *(Achillea)*
	Lavender *(Lavandula)*	
	Meadow rue *(Thalictrum)*	

Herb Gardening

Name	Height (inches)	Part Used	Name	Height (inches)	Part Used
Anise	18	Seeds	Hyssop	14	Leaves
Basil	20	Leaves	Lemonbalm	20	Leaves
Borage	18	Leaves, flowers	Marjoram	18	Leaves
Caraway	18	Seeds	Mint	24	Leaves
Catnip	24	Leaves	Rosemary	18	Leaves
Chamomile	10	Flowers	Sage	16	Leaves
Chevril	15	Leaves	Savory	16	Leaves
Chive	12	Leaves	Tarragon	20	Leaves
Coriander	20	Leaves, seeds	Thyme	7	Leaves
Dill	36	Leaves, seeds			

Herbs to Plant in Lawns

■ Choose plants that suit your soil and your climate. All these can withstand mowing and considerable foot traffic.

- Ajuga or bugleweed *(Ajuga reptans)*
- Corsican mint *(Mentha requienii)*
- Dwarf cinquefoil *(Potentilla tabernaemontani)*
- English pennyroyal *(Mentha pulegium)*
- Green Irish moss *(Sagiona subulata)*
- Pearly everlasting *(Anaphalis margaritacea)*
- Roman chamomile *(Chamaemelum nobile)*
- Rupturewort *(Herniaria glabra)*
- Speedwell *(Veronica officinalis)*
- Stonecrop *(Sedum ternatum)*
- Sweet violets *(Viola odorata* or *tricolor)*
- Thyme *(Thymus serpyllum)*
- White clover *(Trifolium repens)*
- Wild strawberries *(Fragaria virginiana)*
- Wintergreen or partridgeberry *(Mitchella repens)*

Herbs That Attract Butterflies

Catmint	*Nepeta*
Creeping thyme	*Thymus serpyllum*
Dill	*Anethum graveolens*
Mealy-cup sage	*Salvia farinacea*
Mint	*Mentha*
Oregano	*Origanum vulgare*
Parsley	*Petroselinum crispum*
Sweet marjoram	*Origanum majorana*

Heat-Loving Wildflowers

Bee balm *(Monarda)*

Black-eyed Susan *(Rudbeckia)*

Blazing star *(Liatris)*

Butterfly weed *(Asclepias tuberosa)*

Four-o'clock *(Mirabilis)*

Prairie coneflower *(Ratibida pinnata)*

Purple coneflower *(Echinacea purpurea)*

Wild indigo *(Baptisia)*

Flowers That Attract Butterflies

Allium . . . . *Allium*	Helen's flower *Helenium*	Purple coneflower
Aster . . . . *Aster*	Hollyhock . . . . *Alcea*	. . . . *Echinacea purpurea*
Bee balm . . . . . . *Monarda*	Honeysuckle . . . *Lonicera*	Purple loosestrife . . *Lythrum*
Butterfly bush . . *Buddleia*	Lavender . . . . . *Lavendula*	Rock cress . . . . *Arabis*
Clove pink . . . . . *Dianthus*	Lilac . . . . *Syringa*	Sea holly . . . . . . *Eryngium*
Cornflower . . . . *Centaurea*	Lupine . . . . *Lupinus*	Shasta daisy *Chrysanthemum*
Daylily . . . . *Hemerocallis*	Lychnis . . . . *Lychnis*	Snapdragon . . *Antirrhinum*
False indigo . . . . *Baptisia*	Mallow . . . . *Malva*	Stonecrop . . . . *Sedum*
Fleabane . . . . *Erigeron*	Milkweed . . . . . *Asclepias*	Sweet alyssum . . *Lobularia*
Floss flower . . . *Ageratum*	Pansy . . . . *Viola*	Sweet rocket . . . . . *Hesperis*
Globe thistle . . . . *Echinops*	Phlox . . . . *Phlox*	Tickseed . . . . *Coreopsis*
Goldenrod . . . . . . *Solidago*	Privet . . . . *Ligustrum*	Zinnia . . . . *Zinnia*

Flowers That Attract Hummingbirds

Beard tongue . . . . *Penstemon*	Lily . . . . *Lilium*
Bee balm . . . . *Monarda*	Lupine . . . . *Lupinus*
Butterfly bush . . . . *Buddleia*	Petunia . . . . *Petunia*
Catmint . . . . *Nepeta*	Pincushion flower . . . . *Scabiosa*
Clove pink . . . . *Dianthus*	Red-hot poker . . . . *Kniphofia*
Columbine . . . . *Aquilegia*	Scarlet sage . . . . *Salvia splendens*
Coral bells . . . . *Heuchera*	Soapwort . . . . *Saponaria*
Daylily . . . . *Hemerocallis*	Summer phlox . . . . *Phlox paniculata*
Desert candle . . . . *Yucca*	Trumpet honeysuckle . . . . *Lonicera*
Flag . . . . *Iris*	*sempervirens*
Flowering tobacco . . . . . . *Nicotiana alata*	Verbena . . . . *Verbena*
Foxglove . . . . *Digitalis*	Weigela . . . . *Weigela*
Larkspur . . . . *Delphinium*	**Note: Choose varieties in red and orange shades.**

Forcing Blooms Indoors

◾ Here is a list of some shrubs and trees that can be forced to flower indoors. (The trees tend to be stubborn and their blossoms may not be as rewarding as those of the shrubs.) The numbers indicate the approximate number of weeks they will take to flower.

Buckeye 5	Flowering quince 4	Red maple 2
Cherry 4	Forsythia 1	Redbud 2
Cornelian dogwood 2	Honeysuckle 3	Red-twig dogwood 5
Crab apple 4	Horse chestnut 5	Spicebush 2
Deutzia 3	Lilac 4	Spirea 4
Flowering almond 3	Magnolia 3	Wisteria 3
Flowering dogwood 5	Pussy willow 2	Source: Purdue University Cooperative Extension Service

Fall-Planted Bulbs

	Planting Depth (inches)	Spacing (inches)	Flower Height (inches)
Early-Spring Blooms			
Crocus	3	2-3	4-6
Glory-of-the-snow	3	2-3	6-10
Grape hyacinth	3-4	3	8-10
Snowdrop	4	2-3	6
Mid-Spring Blooms			
Daffodil	7	3-4	6-18
Squill	2	4-6	8
Tulip	8	3-6	6-28
Windflower	2	3-4	3-18
Late-Spring Blooms			
Dutch iris	4	3-6	15-24
Hyacinth	6	6-8	4-12
Ornamental onion	6	4-6	6-24
Spanish bluebell	3	3-6	15-20

Spring-Planted Bulbs

	Planting Depth (inches)	Spacing (inches)	Flower Height (inches)
Summer Blooms			
Begonia	2	12	8-18
Blazing star	3-4	6	18
Caladium	2	8-12	12-24
Canna lily	5	16	18-72
Dahlia	4-6	16	12-60
Freesia	2	2-4	12-24
Gladiolus	5	4	24-34
Gloxinia	4	15	12-24
Lily	6-8	12	24-72

Forcing Bulbs Indoors

■ The technique is simple. Plant bulbs in pots of rich soil so tips are just even with pot rims. Store in a cold frame, cellar, or refrigerator at a cold temperature for two to several months. Water bulbs just enough to keep them from drying out. When roots can be seen poking out through bottoms of pots, bring them into a lighted room to flower.

The table below shows estimated times for rooting and ideal temperatures for flowering for some of the most common spring bulbs.

Name of Bulb	Time for Rooting	Temperature for Flowering
Crocus *(Crocus)*	8-12 weeks	55-60° F
Daffodil *(Narcissus)*	10-12 weeks	50-60° F
Freesia *(Freesia)*	8-12 weeks	50-55° F
Glory-of-the-snow *(Chionodoxa)*	10-14 weeks	55-60° F
Grape hyacinth *(Muscari)*	10-12 weeks	55-60° F
Hyacinth *(Hyacinthus)*	8-10 weeks	55-60° F
Lily-of-the-valley *(Convallaria)*	10-12 weeks	60-65° F
Netted iris *(Iris reticulata)*	10-14 weeks	55-60° F
Snowdrop *(Galanthus)*	9-12 weeks	55-60° F
Squill *(Scilla)*	12-16 weeks	55-60° F
Striped squill *(Puschkinia)*	8-12 weeks	50-55° F
Tulip *(Tulipa)*	12-16 weeks	55-60° F

Planning Your Garden

Sow or plant in cool weather	Beets/chard, broccoli, brussels sprouts, cabbage, lettuce, onions, parsley, peas, radishes, spinach, turnips
Sow or plant in warm weather	Beans, carrots, corn, cucumbers, eggplant, melons, okra, peppers, squash tomatoes
One crop per season	Corn, eggplant, leeks, melons, peppers, potatoes, spinach (New Zealand), squash, tomatoes
Resow for additional crops	Beans, beets, cabbage family, carrots, kohlrabi, lettuce, radishes, rutabagas, spinach, turnips

Vegetable Seeds Best Sown in the Ground

Beans, bush and pole
Beets
Carrots
Collards
Corn
Cucumbers
Endive
Kale
Kohlrabi
Mustard greens
Parsnips
Peas
Potatoes
Radishes
Spinach
Squash, summer and winter
Swiss chard
Turnips

Vegetables and Herbs Best Started Indoors

Seeds	Weeks Before Last Frost in Spring
Basil	6
Broccoli	6-8
Brussels sprouts	4-8
Cabbage	6-8
Cauliflower	6-8
Celeriac	6-8
Celery	6-8
Chives	8-12
Eggplant	8-10
Leeks	8-12
Lettuce	4-6
Onions	10-12
Parsley	8
Peppers	8-10
Sweet marjoram	8
Tomatoes	6-8

Minimum Soil Temperature for Seeds to Germinate

Vegetable	Minimum Soil Temperature (°F)
Beans	48-50
Beets	39-41
Cabbage	38-40
Carrots	39-41
Corn	46-50
Melons	55-60
Onions	34-36
Peas	34-36
Radishes	39-41
Squash	55-60
Tomatoes	50-55

The Healthiest Vegetables

■ These results come from adding up the percent of the USRDA for six nutrients (vitamin A, vitamin C, folate, iron, copper, calcium) plus fiber for each vegetable.

1	Sweet potato	6	Kale
2	Carrot	7	Dandelion greens
3	Spinach	8	Broccoli
4	Collard greens	9	Brussels sprouts
5	Red pepper	10	Potato

Critical Low Temperatures for Frost Damage to Vegetables

Vegetable	Temperature (°F)
Artichoke	31-32
Asparagus	30-31
Beans	31-32
Beets (roots)	29-30
Beets (tops)	31-32
Broccoli	29-30
Cabbage	26-28
Carrots	28-30
Cauliflower	27-29
Celery	31-32
Cucumbers	30-32
Kale	27-29
Muskmelon	33-34
Okra	29-30
Peas	28-30
Potato tubers	28-30
Pumpkins	31-32
Radishes	30-32
Spinach	30-32
Squash (summer)	31-33
Squash (winter)	30-32
Sweet corn	32-33
Sweet potatoes	32-33
Tomatoes	32-34
Watermelon	32-33

When Is a Good Time to Fertilize Your Vegetables?

Crop	Time of Application
Asparagus	Before growth starts in spring.
Beans	After heavy blossom and set of pods.
Broccoli	Three weeks after transplanting.
Cabbage	Three weeks after transplanting.
Cauliflower	Three weeks after transplanting.
Corn	When eight to ten inches tall and again when silk first appears.
Cucumber	One week after blossoming and again three weeks later.
Eggplant	After first fruit-set.
Kale	When plants are one-third grown.
Lettuce, Head	Two to three weeks after transplanting.
Muskmelon	One week after blossoming and again three weeks later.
Onions	When bulbs begin to swell and again when plants are one foot tall.
Peas	After heavy bloom and set of pods.
Peppers	After first fruit-set.
Potatoes	At blossom time or time of second hilling.
Spinach	When plants are one-third grown.
Squash	Just before vines start to run, when plants are about one foot tall.
Tomatoes	One to two weeks before first picking and again two weeks after first picking.
Watermelon	Just before vines start to run, when plants are about one foot tall.

Manure Guide

Type of Manure	Water Content	Primary Nutrients (pounds per ton)		
		Nitrogen	Phosphate	Potash
Cow, horse	60%-80%	12-14	5-9	9-12
Sheep, pig, goat	65%-75%	10-21	7	13-19
Chicken: Wet, sticky, and caked	75%	30	20	10
Moist, crumbly to sticky	50%	40	40	20
Crumbly	30%	60	55	30
Dry	15%	90	70	40
Ashed	None	None	135	100

Type of Garden	Best Type of Manure	Best Time to Apply
Flower	Cow, horse	Early spring
Vegetable	Chicken, cow, horse	Fall, spring
Potato or root crop	Cow, horse	Fall
Acid-loving plants (blueberries, azaleas, mountain laurels, rhododendrons)	Cow, horse	Early fall or not at all

General Rules for Pruning

What	When	How
Apple	Early spring	Prune moderately. Keep tree open with main branches well spaced. Avoid sharp V-shaped crotches.
Cherry	Early spring	Prune the most vigorous shoots moderately.
Clematis	Spring	Cut weak growth. Save as much old wood as possible.
Flowering dogwood	After flowering	Remove dead wood only.
Forsythia	After flowering	Remove old branches at ground. Trim new growth.
Lilac	After flowering	Remove diseased, scaly growth, flower heads, and suckers.
Peach	Early spring	Remove half of last year's growth. Keep tree headed low.
Plum	Early spring	Cut dead, diseased branches; trim rank growth moderately.
Rhododendron	After flowering	Prune judiciously. Snip branches from weak, leggy plants to induce growth from roots.
Roses (except climbers)	Spring, after frosts	Cut dead and weak growth; cut branches or canes to four or five eyes.
Roses, climbers	After flowering	Cut half of old growth; retain new shoots for next year.
Rose of Sharon	When buds begin	Cut all winter-killed wood to swell growth back to live wood.
Trumpet vine	Early spring	Prune side branches severely to main stem.
Virginia creeper	Spring	Clip young plants freely. Thin old plants and remove dead growth.
Wisteria	Spring, summer	Cut new growth to spurs at axils of leaves.

Soil Fixes

■ **CLAY SOIL:** Add coarse sand (not beach sand), compost, and peat moss.

■ **SILT SOIL:** Add coarse sand (not beach sand) or gravel and compost, or well-rotted horse manure mixed with fresh straw.

■ **SANDY SOIL:** Add humus or aged manure, peat moss, or sawdust with some extra nitrogen. Heavy, clay-rich soil can also be added to improve the soil.

Soil Amendments

■ **Bark, ground:** Made from various tree barks. Improves soil structure.

■ **Compost:** Excellent conditioner.

■ **Leaf mold:** Decomposed leaves that add nutrients and structure to soil.

■ **Lime:** Raises the pH of acid soil and helps loosen clay soil.

■ **Manure:** Best if composted. Good conditioner.

■ **Peat moss:** Conditioner that helps soil retain water.

■ **Sand:** Improves drainage in clay soil.

■ **Topsoil:** Usually used with another amendment. Replaces existing soil.

Lawn Tips

■ Moss and sorrel in lawns usually means poor soil, poor aeration or drainage, or excessive acidity.

■ During a drought, let the grass grow longer between mowings, and reduce fertilizer.

■ Raise the level of your lawn-mower blades during the hot summer days. Taller grass better resists drought.

■ Water your lawn early in the morning or in the evening.

■ The best time to apply fertilizer is just before it rains.

■ You can reduce mowing time by redesigning your lawn, reducing sharp corners and adding sweeping curves.

■ Any feeding of lawns in the fall should be done with a low-nitrogen, slow-acting fertilizer.

■ In areas of your lawn where tree roots compete with the grass, apply some extra fertilizer to benefit both.

Vegetable Gardening in Containers

■ Lack of yard space is no excuse for not gardening, since many vegetables can be readily grown in containers. In addition to providing five hours or more of full sun, attention must be given to choosing the proper container, using a good soil mix, planting and spacing requirements, fertilizing, watering, and variety selection.

Vegetable	Type of Container	Recommended Varieties
Beans, snap	5-gallon window box	Bush 'Romano', Bush 'Blue Lake', 'Tender Crop'
Broccoli	1 plant/5-gallon pot 3 plants/15-gallon tub	'Green Comet', 'DeCicco'
Carrot	5-gallon window box at least 12 inches deep	'Short 'n Sweet', 'Danvers Half Long', 'Tiny Sweet'
Cucumber	1 plant/1-gallon pot	'Patio Pik', 'Spacemaster', 'Pot Luck'
Eggplant	5-gallon pot	'Slim Jim', 'Ichiban', 'Black Beauty'
Lettuce	5-gallon window box	'Salad Bowl', 'Ruby'
Onion	5-gallon window box	'White Sweet Spanish', 'Yellow Sweet Spanish'
Pepper	1 plant/2-gallon pot 5 plants/15-gallon tub	'Sweet Banana', 'Yolo', 'Wonder', 'Long Red', 'Cayenne'
Radish	5-gallon window box	'Cherry Belle', 'Icicle'
Tomatoes	Bushel basket	'Tiny Tim', 'Small Fry', 'Early Girl', 'Sweet 100', 'Patio'

– courtesy North Carolina Cooperative Extension Service

Fall Palette

Tree	Color
Sugar maple and sumac	Flame red and orange
Red maple, dogwood, sassafras, and scarlet oak	Dark red
Poplar, birch, tulip tree, willow	Yellow
Ash	Plum purple
Oak, beech, larch, elm, hickory, and sycamore	Tan or brown
Locust	Stays green (until leaves drop)
Black walnut and butternut	Drops leaves before turning color

Food We Love to Brag About

■ Every state has bragging rights to a regional specialty, an important crop, a culinary oddity. Can you guess where chocolate gravy is popular, or how many BLT sandwiches can be made from Illinois hogs, or which state is experimenting with blueberry wine?

by Robin Bloksberg

ALABAMA	■ The leaves of the wild **sassafras** trees that grow near the Gulf of Mexico are used to make filé powder, which is used to thicken gumbo.	■ In 1896, George Washington Carver was hired to head the agriculture department at the Tuskegee Institute, where he helped develop hundreds of uses for peanuts and sweet potatoes.
ALASKA	■ The tender Alaskan abalone, also known as the **pinto abalone,** is the only species of Pacific abalone that is found exclusively in Alaska.	■ During the Alaskan Gold Rush, prospectors traveled with sourdough starter pots so they could make fresh bread.
ARIZONA	■ Thanks to irrigation, farmers now cultivate the arid land in southern Arizona to produce oranges, grapefruit, and market vegetables.	■ **Piki,** a thin toasted bread made of blue cornmeal, is a specialty of the Hopi of northeastern Arizona.
ARKANSAS	■ In 1985, a world-record watermelon was grown on the Bright Farm in Hope. The melon weighed in at 260 pounds.	■ A regional breakfast favorite in the Arkansas Ozarks is **chocolate gravy,** made with butter, flour, sugar, cocoa, and milk. Aficionados like to sop up the gravy with hot biscuits.
CALIFORNIA	■ Virtually all the artichokes grown commercially in the United States come from California.	■ **Hangtown Fry,** a dish of fried oysters cooked with eggs and bacon, is said to have originated in a settlement known as Hangtown because of the many hangings carried out there.
COLORADO	■ More than $1 billion in agricultural products are exported annually from Colorado, most destined for Japan, South Korea, Canada, and Mexico.	■ **Sonora wheat** was the first variety of wheat planted in Colorado.
CONNECTICUT	■ The **Eastern Oyster** is the designated state shellfish of Connecticut.	■ Perhaps inspired by the bucolic New England countryside, Connecticut cows produce more milk per animal than cows in any state east of Michigan.

(continued)

DELAWARE	■ Delaware's chicken broiler industry produces the state's top agricultural commodity. Other important products include soybeans, corn, and milk.	■ The **weakfish** — also known as sea trout, gray trout, yellow mouth, yellow fin trout, squeteague, and tiderunner — is Delaware's state fish.
DISTRICT OF COLUMBIA	■ Abraham Lincoln's inaugural luncheon menu in 1861 was composed of **mock turtle soup,** corned beef and cabbage, parsley potatoes, and blackberry pie.	■ Corn and tobacco once grew on the land that now makes up Washington, D.C. Near 15th Street in the District, a granite marker, known as the Settlers' Memorial, pays homage to those who once farmed where today people govern.
FLORIDA	■ While known for its citrus industry, Florida also produces nearly three quarters of another agricultural commodity: eggplant.	■ **Swamp cabbage** sounds more uptown when it goes by the name of hearts of palm, but no matter what you call it, this indigenous delicacy is an ideal accompaniment to alligator. Check it out in February at the annual Swamp Cabbage Festival in the town of LaBelle.
GEORGIA	■ Producing more than $2.4 billion in revenues annually, Georgia's poultry industry makes up the largest percentage of the state's agribusiness.	■ It's so sweet you can eat it like an apple, and it can be grown only in a designated area of southern Georgia. It's the **Vidalia onion** — and in 1990, it became Georgia's official state vegetable.
HAWAII	■ When it comes to **Kona coffee,** connoisseurs prize the rare, round Peaberry beans, which have a high content of oil and minerals.	■ Hawaiians lead the nation in per capita consumption of Spam luncheon meat. Every year, more than 4.3 million cans are sold in the islands — more than four cans for every Hawaiian.
IDAHO	■ Idaho is the nation's top producer of **trout,** particularly the prized rainbow.	■ Rich soil and good water for irrigation make Idaho a top producer of small red beans and pink beans.
ILLINOIS	■ Soybeans, corn, and swine are famous state crops, but Illinois farmers also grow and raise **horseradish,** ostriches, and sorghum, among other commodities.	■ Close to 4½ million hogs are kept on Illinois farms; that's enough to make 190 million bacon, lettuce, and tomato sandwiches.
INDIANA	■ Pass the butter and salt — Indiana is the country's top producer of **popcorn.**	■ Native American persimmons are rare, but not in Mitchell, which hosts a Persimmon Festival every fall.

IOWA	■ Iowa's Amana Colonies have roots going back to 1855, when a group of West German, Swiss, and Alsatian people made their way west in search of religious freedom. The colonies became famous for their wine, bread, and smoked meats.	■ Initially known as an "I-Scream-Bar," the frozen, chocolate-covered treat invented in an ice cream shop in Onawa in 1920, is what we call an **Eskimo Pie.**
KANSAS	■ In the 19th century, Mennonite immigrants from southern Russia brought seed for a hard, red winter wheat, which became known as **Turkey Red.** Kansas wheat farmers today produce several hundred million bushels of this wheat every year.	■ Charlie and Arthur Bryant, George Gates, Otis Boyd — they all helped create Kansas City–style barbecue, for which the city is now famous.
KENTUCKY	■ Approximate number of **mint juleps** sold at Churchill Downs during Kentucky Derby week: 90,000.	■ A favorite regional specialty is burgoo, a stew thick with a hodge-podge of vegetables (lima beans, potatoes, corn, okra, and more) and meats (most authentic are rabbit and squirrel).
LOUISIANA	■ Louisiana produces approximately 90 percent of the country's commercially harvested crawfish. Most of the 50,000 tons sold on the market are red swamp or white river crawfish.	■ More than 130 years ago, Edmund McIlhenny got hold of some hot red-pepper seeds from Central America and planted them on Avery Island. They still grow them there for McIlhenny's **Tabasco** Sauce.
MAINE	■ Close to 250 years ago, Scotch-Irish immigrants found the state's rich soil, warm days, and cool nights ideal for growing potatoes.	■ Every year in late July, thousands of people journey to Pittsfield to enjoy **eggs and omelets** made in the world's largest frying pan at the Central Maine Egg Festival.
MARYLAND	■ A bushel of Maryland-steamed crabs — that's 60 to 70 crabs — will feed 10 to 12 people.	■ Those who live along Chesapeake Bay are fond of **croaker,** a sweet-flavored local fish. A member of the drum family, croakers do in fact make a croaking noise.
MASSACHUSETTS	■ True to its name, the **Concord grape** was first planted in Concord in 1849. Its grower: Ephraim W. Bull.	■ John Chapman was born in Massachusetts in 1774. We know him as Johnny Appleseed, and some of the trees he planted in the Midwest still bear apples.

(continued)

MICHIGAN	■ The number of asparagus growers in Michigan: approximately 500. Pounds of asparagus they produce every year: 25 million.	■ Michigan produces about 20 percent of the sweet cherries grown in the United States every year. Many of them become **maraschino** cherries.
MINNESOTA	■ The Chippewa and Sioux Indians have long feasted on **wild rice** (which is actually a grass seed, not rice). By law, wild rice in Minnesota must be harvested from a canoe according to traditional Native American methods.	■ In 1888, the Minneapolis Grain Exchange opened, boosting the city into prominence as a center for grain and flour.
MISSISSIPPI	■ You'll find approximately 500 **catfish** producers here, in a $265 million a year industry.	■ If researchers at Mississippi State University have their way, southern Mississippi blueberries will soon be made into wine.
MISSOURI	■ Before Prohibition, St. Louis was the nation's winemaking center. Although California took over, today Missouri claims more than 30 wineries.	■ In 1904, the **ice cream cone** debuted at the St. Louis World's Fair.
MONTANA	■ Sixty-two percent of the state of Montana — 59.7 million acres — is given over to farmland. The average size of Montana's 22,000 farms: 2,714 acres.	■ Although wheat and hay dominate, the state's other crops include **lentils,** garlic, sunflowers, grapes, mint, mustard, and cherries.
NEBRASKA	■ Almost a quarter of all the corn grown in Nebraska is exported to other countries.	■ First created in the burg of Hastings, **Kool-Aid** is Nebraska's official state soft drink.
NEVADA	■ There may not be many of them, but Nevada's ranches are the third largest in the country, averaging 3,500 acres each.	■ **Alfalfa** hay makes up more than half of the value of crops grown in Nevada. The state's high desert climate is ideally suited to growing the alfalfa.
NEW HAMPSHIRE	■ In a typical year, New Hampshire's apple orchards yield a million bushels of the fruit.	■ It was at New Hampshire's Londonderry Common Field in 1719 that the first **potato** was planted in the United States.
NEW JERSEY	■ Tomatoes — approximately 60 million pounds a year — are New Jersey's leading cash crop.	■ Englishman Richard Bache (Ben Franklin's son-in-law) was the first person to raise **pheasants** in the United States, on his New Jersey estate.

NEW MEXICO	■ As far back as 4000 B.C., Native Americans were planting and harvesting corn in what is now New Mexico.	■ When New Mexicans eat atole for breakfast, they're feasting on **roasted blue cornmeal,** cooked and combined with milk and sugar.
NEW YORK	■ The city's first restaurant that was not part of a hotel opened in 1831, when Swiss immigrants John and Peter Delmonico opened Delmonico and Brother, Confectioners and Restaurant Français (later famous simply as Delmonico's Restaurant).	■ When you eat an **apple muffin** in New York State, you're biting into the official state muffin.
NORTH CAROLINA	■ Agriculture is the top industry in North Carolina, adding more than $46 billion annually to the state's economy.	■ Before Europeans colonized North America, Native Americans grew **sweet potatoes** here. Today, the sweet potato is the official state vegetable.
NORTH DAKOTA	■ More than 25 percent of North Dakotans work in agriculture or related businesses.	■ North Dakota is the top state in production of durum wheat, spring wheat, barley, dry edible beans, pinto beans, oats, **sunflower seeds,** and flaxseed.
OHIO	■ Ohio produces more **tomato juice** than any other state. Since 1965, it's been the official state beverage.	■ Per capita, Ohioans consume more eggs than people from any other state.
OKLAHOMA	■ Oklahoma wheat growers produce an average of 3,000 pounds of wheat per year for each Oklahoma resident.	■ The official state meal of Oklahoma includes **fried okra,** squash, corn bread, barbecued pork, biscuits, sausage and gravy, grits, corn, strawberries, chicken fried steak, pecan pie, and black-eyed peas.
OREGON	■ The **Marionberry,** a variety of blackberry known for its intense, sweet flavor, is grown exclusively in Oregon.	■ The great American culinarian James Beard was born in Portland on May 5, 1903.
PENNSYLVANIA	■ Pennsylvania leads the nation in the production of potato chips, **pretzels,** and processed chocolate and cocoa.	■ Milton Hershey failed as a candymaker in New York and Philadelphia. But he started a wildly successful chocolate industry in the company town of Hershey, near where he was born.

(continued)

RHODE ISLAND	■ Johnson and Wales University's Culinary Archives and Museum feature half a million food-related artifacts, including antique cooking tools and culinary curios associated with U.S. presidents.	■ **Coffee milk** is the official state drink of Rhode Island.
SOUTH CAROLINA	■ In 1984, the **peach** was declared the official state fruit of South Carolina.	■ The only black tea grown in North America is cultivated at the Charleston Tea Plantation on Wadmalaw Island.
SOUTH DAKOTA	■ Honey production is so important here that in 1978, the honeybee was named the state insect.	■ One of America's great roadside attractions is the **Corn Palace** in Mitchell. The building is decorated with 3,000 bushels of corn, and is adorned with Moorish-style minarets.
TENNESSEE	■ The Tennessee Agricultural Museum just south of Nashville features more than 2,600 artifacts from 19th-century homes and farms.	■ Known for their peculiarly strong odor, **ramps** — sweet wild leeks native to Tennessee — are savored raw or fried with eggs. Ramps are exalted at the annual Cosby Ramp Festival, the first Sunday in May.
TEXAS	■ In 1919, the Texas state legislature adopted the pecan as the state tree. Texas leads the nation in the production of native pecans.	■ Czech settlers around Caldwell brought their recipes for **kolache,** a pastry filled with poppy seeds, prunes, apricots, or other fruits. The pastry is celebrated in the annual Kolache Festival held every September.
UTAH	■ Two-thirds of Utah's agribusiness is based on production of cattle, milk, and hay.	■ In the mid-19th century, Mormon settlers began irrigating the land around Salt Lake City. **Irrigation** continues to be essential to Utah agriculture.
VERMONT	■ Maple syrup is produced in every county in the state, which leads the nation in maple syrup production.	■ In the 19th century, Vermont farmers would herd large flocks of **turkeys** to Boston every fall in what was known as the great turkey drives. The state is still known as a premium turkey producer.

VIRGINIA	■ Approximately 92,000 acres are devoted to growing **peanuts.** Average production is 3,000 pounds per acre.	■ To carry the official "Smithfield" designation, hams must be cured and processed near Smithfield. These coveted hams are dry-cured, seasoned, smoked, and aged for a minimum of 12 months.
WASHINGTON	■ The state produces more apples than any other state but is also acclaimed for its pears, cherries, plums, and other fruit.	■ The tiny **Olympia oyster** is native to the waters around Puget Sound. Prized for its superior flavor, this shellfish is becoming increasingly hard to find.
WEST VIRGINIA	■ In the early 19th century, **salt** deposits discovered outside Charleston gave an economic boost to the region.	■ The L. Norman Dillon Farm Museum in Hedgesville boasts a fine collection of historic farm equipment.
WISCONSIN	■ Wisconsin may be America's Dairyland, but it's also the top producer of cranberries, with approximately 5,000 acres devoted to growing the fruit.	■ In Wisconsin's Door County, residents still enjoy a traditional **fish boil,** a culinary custom dating back to the region's Scandinavian settlers. Whitefish steaks, onions, and potatoes are layered in a large pot and boiled in salted water over an open fire.
WYOMING	■ Wyoming ranks second in the nation when it comes to the size of its farms and ranches.	■ With 15,846 miles of fishing streams, Wyoming is a prime destination for serious anglers.

How to Order Two Bun Halves Filled with Cheese, Meat, Onions, Peppers, and Other Stuff

Place	Name	Place	Name
Norfolk, VA	Submarine	Norristown, PA	Zeppelin
Akron, OH	"	Mobile, AL	Poor boy
Jacksonville, FL	"	Sacramento, CA	"
Los Angeles, CA	"	Houston, TX	"
Philadelphia, PA	Hoagie	Montgomery, AL	"
Ann Arbor, MI	"	New Orleans, LA	Poor boy or musalatta
Knoxville, TN	"	Gary, IN	Submarine or torpedo
Newark, NJ	"	Allentown, PA	Hoagie or Italian sandwich
Providence, RI	"	Cheyenne, WY	Hoagie, submarine, or rocket
Des Moines, IA	Grinder	Cincinnati, OH	Hoagie, submarine, or rocket
Hartford, CT	"	Buffalo, NY	Hoagie, submarine, or bomber
Chester, PA	"	Dublin, NH	Two bun halves filled with
Cleveland, OH	"		cheese, meat, onions,
Madison, WI	Garibaldi		peppers, and other stuff

Pan Sizes and Equivalents

■ In the midst of cooking but don't have the right pan? You can substitute one size for another, keeping in mind that when you change the pan size, you must sometimes change the cooking time. For example, if a recipe calls for using an 8-inch round cake pan and baking for 25 minutes, and you substitute a 9-inch pan, the cake may bake in only 20 minutes, since the batter forms a thinner layer in the larger pan. (Use a toothpick inserted into the center of the cake to test for doneness. If it comes out clean, the cake has finished baking.) Also, specialty pans such as tube and Bundt pans distribute heat differently; you may not get the same results if you substitute a regular cake pan for a specialty one, even if the volume is the same.

Pan Size	Volume	Substitute
9-inch pie pan	4 cups	■ 8-inch round cake pan
8x4x2-1/2-inch loaf pan	6 cups	■ Three 5x2-inch loaf pans ■ Two 3x1-1/4-inch muffin tins ■ 12x8x2-inch cake pan
9x5x3-inch loaf pan	8 cups	■ 8-inch square cake pan ■ 9-inch round cake pan
15x10x1-inch jelly roll pan	10 cups	■ 9-inch square cake pan ■ Two 8-inch round cake pans ■ 8x3-inch springform pan
10x3-inch Bundt pan	12 cups	■ Two 8x4x2-1/2-inch loaf pans ■ 9x3-inch angel food cake pan ■ 9x3-inch springform pan
13x9x2-inch cake pan	14-15 cups	■ Two 9-inch round cake pans ■ Two 8-inch square cake pans

■ If you are cooking a casserole and don't have the correct size dish, here are some baking-pan substitutions. Again, think about the depth of the ingredients in the dish and lengthen or shorten the baking time accordingly.

CASSEROLE SIZE	BAKING-PAN SUBSTITUTE
1-1/2 quarts	9x5x3-inch loaf pan
2 quarts	8-inch square cake pan
2-1/2 quarts	9-inch square cake pan
3 quarts	13x9x2-inch cake pan
4 quarts	14x10x2-inch cake pan

Food for Thought

Food	Calories
Piece of pecan pie	580
Grilled cheese sandwich	440
Chocolate shake	364
Bagel with cream cheese	361
20 potato chips	228
10 french fries	214
Half a cantaloupe	94
Corn on the cob (no butter)	70
Carrot	30

Don't Freeze These

Bananas
Canned hams
Cooked eggs
Cooked potatoes
Cream fillings and puddings
Custards
Fried foods
Gelatin dishes
Mayonnaise
Raw vegetables, such as cabbage, celery, green onions, radishes, and salad greens
Soft cheeses, cottage cheese
Sour cream
Yogurt

Appetizing Amounts

Occasion	Number of Bites per Person
Hors d'oeuvres (with meal following)	4
Cocktail party	10
Grand affair, no dinner following (e.g., wedding reception)	10-15

The Party Planner

How much do you need when you're cooking for a crowd?

■ If you're planning a big meal, these estimates can help you determine how much food you should buy. They're based on "average" servings; adjust quantities upward for extra-big eaters and downward if children are included.

Food	To Serve 25	To Serve 50	To Serve 100
MEATS			
Chicken or turkey breast	12-1/2 pounds	25 pounds	50 pounds
Fish (fillets or steaks)	7-1/2 pounds	15 pounds	30 pounds
Hamburgers	8 to 9 pounds	15 to 18 pounds	30 to 36 pounds
Ham or roast beef	10 pounds	20 pounds	40 pounds
Hot dogs	6 pounds	12-1/2 pounds	25 pounds
Meat loaf	6 pounds	12 pounds	24 pounds
Oysters	1 gallon	2 gallons	4 gallons
Pork	10 pounds	20 pounds	40 pounds
MISCELLANEOUS			
Bread (loaves)	3	5	10
Butter	3/4 pound	1-1/2 pounds	3 pounds
Cheese	3/4 pound	1-1/2 pounds	3 pounds
Coffee	3/4 pound	1-1/2 pounds	3 pounds
Milk	1-1/2 gallons	3 gallons	6 gallons
Nuts	3/4 pound	1-1/2 pounds	3 pounds
Olives	1/2 pound	1 pound	2 pounds
Pickles	1/2 quart	1 quart	2 quarts
Rolls	50	100	200
Soup	5 quarts	2-1/2 gallons	5 gallons
SIDE DISHES			
Baked beans	5 quarts	2-1/2 gallons	5 gallons
Beets	7-1/2 pounds	15 pounds	30 pounds
Cabbage for cole slaw	5 pounds	10 pounds	20 pounds
Carrots	7-1/2 pounds	15 pounds	30 pounds
Lettuce for salad (heads)	5	10	20
Peas (fresh)	12 pounds	25 pounds	50 pounds
Potatoes	9 pounds	18 pounds	36 pounds
Potato salad	3 quarts	1-1/2 gallons	3 gallons
Salad dressing	3 cups	1-1/2 quarts	3 quarts
DESSERTS			
Cakes	2	4	8
Ice cream	1 gallon	2 gallons	4 gallons
Pies	4	9	18
Whipping cream	1 pint	2 pints	4 pints

Substitutions for Common Ingredients

ITEM	QUANTITY	SUBSTITUTION
Allspice	1 teaspoon	½ teaspoon cinnamon plus ⅛ teaspoon ground cloves
Arrowroot, as thickener	1½ teaspoons	1 tablespoon flour
Baking powder	1 teaspoon	¼ teaspoon baking soda plus ⅝ teaspoon cream of tartar
Bread crumbs, dry	¼ cup	1 slice bread
Bread crumbs, soft	½ cup	1 slice bread
Buttermilk	1 cup	1 cup plain yogurt
Chocolate, unsweetened	1 ounce	3 tablespoons cocoa plus 1 tablespoon butter or fat
Cracker crumbs	¾ cup	1 cup dry bread crumbs
Cream, heavy	1 cup	¾ cup milk plus ⅓ cup melted butter (this will not whip)
Cream, light	1 cup	⅞ cup milk plus 3 tablespoons melted butter
Cream, sour	1 cup	⅞ cup buttermilk or plain yogurt plus 3 tablespoons melted butter
Cream, whipping	1 cup	⅔ cup well-chilled evaporated milk, whipped; **or** 1 cup nonfat dry milk powder whipped with 1 cup ice water
Egg	1 whole	2 yolks
Flour, all-purpose	1 cup	1⅛ cups cake flour; **or** ⅝ cup potato flour; **or** 1¼ cups rye or coarsely ground whole grain flour; **or** 1 cup cornmeal
Flour, cake	1 cup	1 cup minus 2 tablespoons sifted all-purpose flour
Flour, self-rising	1 cup	1 cup all-purpose flour plus 1¼ teaspoons baking powder plus ¼ teaspoon salt
Garlic	1 small clove	⅛ teaspoon garlic powder; **or** ½ teaspoon instant minced garlic
Herbs, dried	½ to 1 teaspoon	1 tablespoon fresh, minced and packed
Honey	1 cup	1¼ cups sugar plus ½ cup liquid

Measuring Vegetables

Asparagus: 1 pound = 3 cups chopped

Beans (string): 1 pound = 4 cups chopped

Beets: 1 pound (5 medium) = 2-1/2 cups chopped

Broccoli: 1/2 pound = 6 cups chopped

Cabbage: 1 pound = 4-1/2 cups shredded

Carrots: 1 pound = 3-1/2 cups sliced or grated

Celery: 1 pound = 4 cups chopped

Cucumbers: 1 pound (2 medium) = 4 cups sliced

Eggplant: 1 pound = 4 cups chopped (6 cups raw, cubed = 3 cups cooked)

Garlic: 1 clove = 1 teaspoon chopped

Leeks: 1 pound = 4 cups chopped (2 cups cooked)

Mushrooms: 1 pound = 5 to 6 cups sliced = 2 cups cooked

Onions: 1 pound = 4 cups sliced = 2 cups cooked

Parsnips: 1 pound unpeeled = 1-1/2 cups cooked, pureed

Peas: 1 pound whole = 1 to 1-1/2 cups shelled

Potatoes: 1 pound (3 medium) sliced = 2 cups mashed

Pumpkin: 1 pound = 4 cups chopped = 2 cups cooked and drained

Spinach: 1 pound = 3/4 to 1 cup cooked

ITEM	QUANTITY	SUBSTITUTION
Lemon	1	1 to 3 tablespoons juice, 1 to 1½ teaspoons grated rind
Lemon juice	1 teaspoon	½ teaspoon vinegar
Lemon rind, grated	1 teaspoon	½ teaspoon lemon extract
Milk, skim	1 cup	⅓ cup instant nonfat dry milk plus about ¾ cup water
Milk, to sour	1 cup	Add 1 tablespoon vinegar or lemon juice to 1 cup milk minus 1 tablespoon. Stir and let stand 5 minutes.
Milk, whole	1 cup	½ cup evaporated milk plus ½ cup water; **or** 1 cup skim milk plus 2 teaspoons melted butter
Molasses	1 cup	1 cup honey
Mustard, prepared	1 tablespoon	1 teaspoon dry or powdered mustard
Onion, chopped	1 small	1 tablespoon instant minced onion; **or** 1 teaspoon onion powder; **or** ¼ cup frozen chopped onion
Sugar, granulated	1 cup	1 cup firmly packed brown sugar; **or** 1¾ cups confectioners' sugar (do not substitute in baking); **or** 2 cups corn syrup; **or** 1 cup superfine sugar
Tomatoes, canned	1 cup	½ cup tomato sauce plus ½ cup water; **or** 1⅓ cups chopped fresh tomatoes, simmered
Tomato juice	1 cup	½ cup tomato sauce plus ½ cup water plus dash each salt and sugar; **or** ¼ cup tomato paste plus ¾ cup water plus salt and sugar
Tomato ketchup	½ cup	½ cup tomato sauce plus 2 tablespoons sugar, 1 tablespoon vinegar, and ⅛ teaspoon ground cloves
Tomato puree	1 cup	½ cup tomato paste plus ½ cup water
Tomato soup	1 can (10¾ oz.)	1 cup tomato sauce plus ¼ cup water
Vanilla	1-inch bean	1 teaspoon vanilla extract
Yeast	1 cake (⅗ oz.)	1 package active dried yeast (1 scant tablespoon)
Yogurt, plain	1 cup	1 cup buttermilk

Squash (summer): 1 pound = 4 cups grated = 2 cups salted and drained

Squash (winter): 2 pounds = 2-1/2 cups cooked, pureed

Sweet Potatoes: 1 pound = 4 cups grated = 1 cup cooked, pureed

Swiss Chard: 1 pound = 5 to 6 cups packed leaves = 1 to 1-1/2 cups cooked

Tomatoes: 1 pound (3 or 4 medium) = 1-1/2 cups seeded pulp

Turnips: 1 pound = 4 cups chopped = 2 cups cooked, mashed

Measuring Fruits

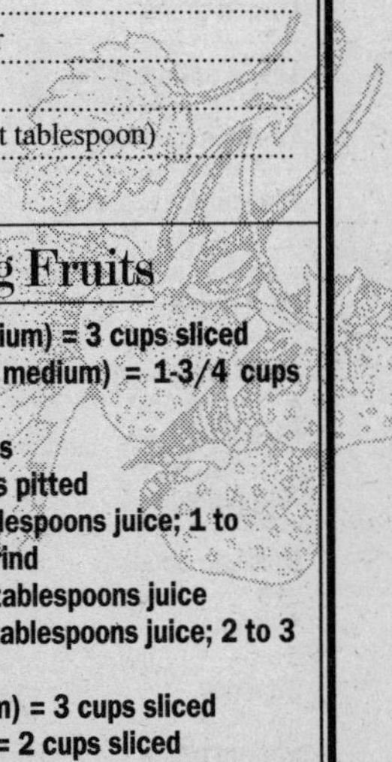

Apples: 1 pound (3 or 4 medium) = 3 cups sliced

Bananas: 1 pound (3 or 4 medium) = 1-3/4 cups mashed

Berries: 1 quart = 3-1/2 cups

Dates: 1 pound = 2-1/2 cups pitted

Lemon: 1 whole = 1 to 3 tablespoons juice; 1 to 1-1/2 teaspoons grated rind

Lime: 1 whole = 1-1/2 to 2 tablespoons juice

Orange: 1 medium = 6 to 8 tablespoons juice; 2 to 3 tablespoons grated rind

Peaches: 1 pound (4 medium) = 3 cups sliced

Pears: 1 pound (4 medium) = 2 cups sliced

Rhubarb: 1 pound = 2 cups cooked

Strawberries: 1 quart = 4 cups sliced

Substitutions for Uncommon Ingredients

Cooking an ethnic dish but can't find a special ingredient?
Here are a few ideas for alternatives.

ITEM	SUBSTITUTION
Balsamic vinegar, 1 tablespoon	1 tablespoon red wine vinegar plus ½ teaspoon sugar
Bamboo shoots	Asparagus (in fried dishes)
Bergamot	Mint
Chayotes	Yellow summer squash **or** zucchini
Cilantro	Parsley (for color only; flavor cannot be duplicated)
Coconut milk	2½ cups water plus 2 cups shredded, unsweetened coconut. Combine and bring to a boil. Remove from heat; cool. Mix in a blender for 2 minutes; strain. Makes about 2 cups.
Delicata squash	Butternut squash **or** sweet potato
Green mangoes	Sour, green cooking apples
Habanero peppers	5 jalapeño peppers **or** serrano peppers
Italian seasoning	Equal parts basil, marjoram, oregano, rosemary, sage, and thyme
Lemon grass	Lemon zest (zest from 1 lemon equals 2 stalks lemon grass)
Limes or lime juice	Lemons or lemon juice
Lo Mein noodles	Egg noodles
Mascarpone, 1 cup	3 tablespoons heavy cream plus ¾ cup cream cheese plus 4 tablespoons butter
Neufchâtel	Cream cheese **or** Boursin
Palm sugar	Light brown sugar
Rice wine	Pale, dry sherry **or** white vermouth
Red peppers	Equal amount pimientos
Romano cheese	Parmesan cheese
Saffron	Turmeric (for color; flavor is different)
Shallots	Red onions **or** Spanish onions
Shrimp paste	Anchovy paste
Tamarind juice	5 parts ketchup to 1 part vinegar

American Farmland and Life in 1900 and 2000:
a Comparison

	1900	2000
Farms		
Average size of farms	147 acres	470 acres
Number of farms	4,564,641	2,058,000
U.S. population	76,094,000	265,283,783
Percent of population working on farms	41.90%	1.90%
Water used for irrigation	20.19 billion gallons/day	153 billion gallons/day
Farm Animals		
Number of cattle	67,719,000	99,501,000
Number of milk cows	16,544,000	9,191,000
Number of hogs	51,055,000	61,600,000
Number of sheep	48,105,000	7,616,000
Number of working horses	13,537,534	Too insignificant to measure
Number of working oxen	27,610,054	Too insignificant to measure
Beef value	$25/head	$653/head
Hog value	$6/head	$85/head
Sheep value	$3/head	$66/head
Food Consumption per Capita (annual)		
Butter	20.1 pounds	4.4 pounds
Margarine	1.3 pounds	10.9 pounds
Cheese	3.8 pounds	24.7 pounds
Milk and cream	343 gallons	233.2 gallons
Ice cream	1.6 gallons	15.7 gallons
Eggs	293	233
Chicken and turkey	14.7 pounds	63.6 pounds
Beef and veal	72.3 pounds	64.9 pounds
Pork	71.9 pounds	46.3 pounds
Potatoes	187 pounds	127.2 pounds
Fresh fruit	135 pounds	92.3 pounds
Wheat flour	217 pounds	137.8 pounds

– compiled by Clare Innes

Hand Thermometer for Outdoor Cooking

■ Hold your palm close to where the food will be cooking: over the coals or in front of a reflector oven. Count "one-and-one, two-and-two," and so on, for as many seconds as you can hold your hand still.

Seconds Counted	Heat	Temperature
6-8	Slow	250-350° F
4-5	Moderate	350-400° F
2-3	Hot	400-450° F
1 or less	Very hot	450-500° F

Life Expectancy by Current Age

If your age now is . . .   **You can expect to live to age . . .**

	Men	Women
0	72	79
20	74	80
25	74	80
30	75	80
35	75	81
40	76	81
45	76	81
50	77	82
55	78	82
60	79	83
65	80	84
70	82	86
75	85	87
80	87	89
85	90	92

Source: U.S. Department of Health and Human Services, 1995

Is It a Cold or the Flu?

Symptoms	Flu	Cold	Allergy	Sinusitis
Headache	Always	Occasionally	Occasionally	Always
Muscle aches	Always	Usually	Rarely	Rarely
Fatigue, weakness	Always	Usually	Rarely	Rarely
Fever	Always	Occasionally	Never	Occasionally
Cough	Usually	Occasionally	Occasionally	Usually
Runny, stuffy nose	Occasionally	Usually	Usually	Always
Nasal discharge	Occasionally	Usually	Usually	Always
Sneezing	Rarely	Occasionally	Usually	Rarely
Sore throat	Rarely	Usually	Occasionally	Rarely
Itchy eyes, nose, throat	Rarely	Rarely	Usually	Never

Are You Skinny, Just Right, or Overweight?

■ Here's an easy formula to figure your Body Mass Index (BMI), now thought to be a more accurate indicator of relative body size than the old insurance charts. **W** is your weight in pounds and **H** is your height in inches.

$$BMI = \frac{(W \times 705) \div H}{H}$$

■ If the result is 25 or less, you are within a healthy weight range.

■ If it's 19 or below, you are too skinny.

■ Between 25 and 27, you are as much as 8 percent over your healthy weight.

■ Between 27 and 30, you are at increased risk for health problems.

■ Above 30, you are more than 20 percent over your healthy weight. It puts you at a dramatically increased risk for serious health problems.

There are a couple of exceptions to the above. Very muscular people with a high BMI generally have nothing to worry about, and extreme skinniness is generally a symptom of some other health problem, not the cause.

Here's another way to see if you are dangerously overweight. Measure your waistline. A waist measurement of 35 inches or more in women and 41 inches or more in men, regardless of height, suggests a serious risk of weight-related health problems.

Calorie Burning

■ If you hustle through your chores to get to the fitness center, relax. You're getting a great workout already. The left-hand column lists "chore" exercises, the middle column shows number of calories you burn per minute per pound of your body weight, the right-hand column lists comparable "recreational" exercises. For example, a 150-pound person forking straw bales burns 9.45 calories per minute, the same workout he/she would get playing basketball.

Chore	Calories	Recreational
Chopping with an ax, fast	0.135	Skiing, cross country, uphill
Climbing hills, with 44-pound load	0.066	Swimming, crawl, fast
Digging trenches	0.065	Skiing, cross country, steady walk
Forking straw bales	0.063	Basketball
Chopping down trees	0.060	Football
Climbing hills, with 9-pound load	0.058	Swimming, crawl, slow
Sawing by hand	0.055	Skiing, cross country, moderate
Mowing lawns	0.051	Horseback riding, trotting
Scrubbing floors	0.049	Tennis
Shoveling coal	0.049	Aerobic dance, medium
Hoeing	0.041	Weight training, circuit training
Stacking firewood	0.040	Weight lifting, free weights
Shoveling grain	0.038	Golf
Painting houses	0.035	Walking, normal pace, asphalt road
Weeding	0.033	Table tennis
Shopping for food	0.028	Cycling, 5.5 mph
Mopping floors	0.028	Fishing
Washing windows	0.026	Croquet
Raking	0.025	Dancing, ballroom
Driving a tractor	0.016	Drawing, standing position

How Much Paint Will You Need?

■ Estimate your room size and paint needs before you go to the store. Running out of a custom color halfway through the job could mean disaster. For the sake of the following exercise, assume you have a 10x15-foot room with an 8-foot ceiling. The room has two doors and two windows.

For Walls

■ Measure the total distance (perimeter) around the room:
(10 ft. + 15 ft.) x 2 = 50 ft.

■ Multiply the perimeter by the ceiling height to get the total wall area:
50 ft. x 8 ft. = 400 sq. ft.

■ Doors are usually 21 square feet (there are two in this exercise):
21 sq. ft. x 2 = 42 sq. ft.

■ Windows average 15 square feet (there are two in this exercise):
15 sq. ft. x 2 = 30 sq. ft.

■ Take the total wall area and subtract the area for the doors and windows to get the wall surface to be painted:

400 sq. ft. (wall area)
– 42 sq. ft. (doors)
– 30 sq. ft. (windows)
_____
328 sq. ft.

■ As a rule of thumb, one gallon of quality paint will usually cover 400 square feet. One quart will cover 100 square feet. Since you need to cover 328 square feet in this example, one gallon will be adequate to give one coat of paint to the walls. (Coverage will be affected by the porosity and texture of the surface. In addition, bright colors may require a minimum of two coats.)

For Ceilings

■ Using the rule of thumb for coverage above, you can calculate the quantity of paint needed for the ceiling by multiplying the width by the length:

10 ft. x 15 ft. = 150 sq. ft.

This ceiling will require approximately two quarts of paint. (A flat finish is recommended to minimize surface imperfections.)

For Doors, Windows, and Trim

■ The area for the doors and windows has been calculated above. Determine the baseboard trim by taking the perimeter of the room, less 3 feet per door (3 ft. x 2 = 6 ft.), and multiplying this by the average trim width of your baseboard, which in this example is 6 inches (or 0.5 feet).

50 ft. (perimeter) - 6 ft. = 44 ft.
44 ft. x 0.5 ft. = 22 sq. ft.

■ Add the area for doors, windows, and baseboard trim.

42 sq. ft. (doors)
+30 sq. ft. (windows)
+22 sq. ft. (baseboard trim)
_____
94 sq. ft.

One quart will probably be sufficient to cover the doors, windows, and trim in this example.

– courtesy M.A.B. Paints

Exterior Paint

■ Here's how to estimate the number of gallons needed for one-coat coverage of a home that is 20 feet wide by 40 feet long, has walls that rise 16 feet to the eaves on the 40-foot sides, and has full-width gables on the 20-foot sides rising 10 feet to the peaks.

■ First, find the area of the walls. Add the width to the length:

20 ft. + 40 ft. = 60 ft.

Double it for four sides:

60 ft. x 2 = 120 ft.

Multiply that by the height of the walls:

120 ft. x 16 ft. = 1,920 sq. ft.

The area of the walls is 1,920 square feet.

■ Next, find the area of the gables. Take half the width of one gable at its base:

20 ft. ÷ 2 = 10 ft.

Multiply that by the height of the gable:

10 ft. x 10 ft. = 100 sq. ft.

Multiply that by the number of gables:

100 sq. ft. x 2 = 200 sq. ft.

The area of the gables is 200 square feet.

■ Add the two figures together for the total area:

1,920 sq. ft. + 200 sq. ft. = 2,120 sq. ft.

■ Finally, divide the total area by the area covered by a gallon of paint (400 square feet) to find the number of gallons needed:

2,120 sq. ft. ÷ 400 sq. ft./gal. = 5.3 gal.

Buy five gallons of paint to start with. The sixth gallon might not be necessary.

How Much Wallpaper Will You Need?

■ Measure the length of each wall, add these figures together, and multiply by the height of the walls to get the area (square footage) of the room.

■ Calculate the square footage of each door, window, or other opening in the room. Add these figures together and subtract the total from the area of the room.

■ Take that figure and multiply by 1.15, to account for a waste rate of about 15 percent in your wallpaper project.

■ Wallpaper is sold in single, double, and triple rolls. (Average coverage for a double roll, for example, is 56 square feet.) Divide the coverage figure (from the label) into the total square footage of the room you're papering. Round the answer up to the nearest whole number. This is the number of rolls you need to buy.

■ Save leftover wallpaper rolls, carefully wrapped to keep them clean.

Guide to Lumber and Nails

Lumber Width and Thickness in Inches

NOMINAL SIZE	ACTUAL SIZE Dry or Seasoned
1 x 3	¾ x 2½
1 x 4	¾ x 3½
1 x 6	¾ x 5½
1 x 8	¾ x 7¼
1 x 10	¾ x 9¼
1 x 12	¾ x 11¼
2 x 3	1½ x 2½
2 x 4	1½ x 3½
2 x 6	1½ x 5½
2 x 8	1½ x 7¼
2 x 10	1½ x 9¼
2 x 12	1½ x 11¼

Nail Sizes

The nail on the left is a 5d (penny) finish nail; on the right, 20d common. The numerals below the nail sizes indicate the approximate number of common nails per pound.

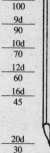
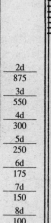

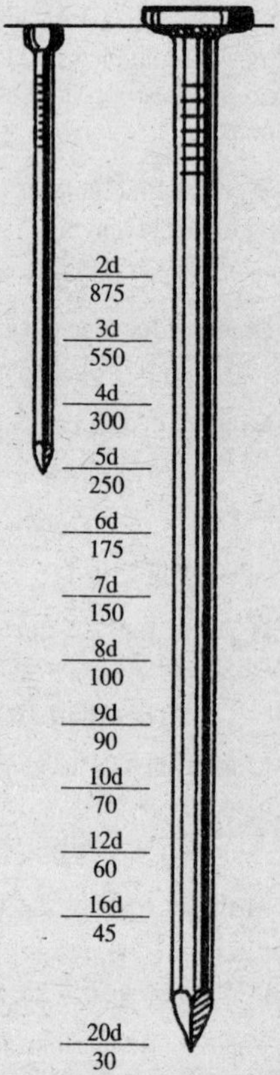

Size	Per lb.
2d	875
3d	550
4d	300
5d	250
6d	175
7d	150
8d	100
9d	90
10d	70
12d	60
16d	45
20d	30

Lumber Measure in Board Feet

Size in Inches	12 ft.	14 ft.	16 ft.	18 ft.	20 ft.
1 x 4	4	4⅔	5⅓	6	6⅔
1 x 6	6	7	8	9	10
1 x 8	8	9⅓	10⅔	12	13⅓
1 x 10	10	11⅔	13⅓	15	16⅔
1 x 12	12	14	16	18	20
2 x 3	6	7	8	9	10
2 x 4	8	9⅓	10⅔	12	13⅓
2 x 6	12	14	16	18	20
2 x 8	16	18⅔	21⅓	24	26⅔
2 x 10	20	23⅓	26⅔	30	33⅓
2 x 12	24	28	32	36	40
4 x 4	16	18⅔	21⅓	24	26⅔
6 x 6	36	42	48	54	60
8 x 8	64	74⅔	85⅓	96	106⅔
10 x 10	100	116⅔	133⅓	150	166⅔
12 x 12	144	168	192	216	240

Firewood Heat Values

High Heat Value

1 CORD = 200-250 GALLONS OF FUEL OIL

American beech
Apple
Ironwood
Red oak
Shagbark hickory
Sugar maple
White ash
White oak
Yellow birch

Medium Heat Value

1 CORD = 150-200 GALLONS OF FUEL OIL

American elm
Black cherry
Douglas fir
Red maple
Silver maple
Tamarack
White birch

Low Heat Value

1 CORD = 100-150 GALLONS OF FUEL OIL

Aspen
Cottonwood
Hemlock
Lodgepole pine
Red alder
Redwood
Sitka spruce
Western red cedar
White pine

How Many Trees in a Cord of Wood?

Diameter of Tree (breast high, in inches)	Number of Trees (per cord)
4	50
6	20
8	10
10	6
12	4
14	3

Heat Values of Fuels
(approximate)

Fuel	BTU	Unit of Measure
Oil	141,000	Gallon
Coal	31,000	Pound
Natural gas	1,000	Cubic foot
Steam	1,000	Cubic foot
Electricity	3,413	Kilowatt-hour
Gasoline	124,000	Gallon

How to Find the Number of Bricks in a Wall or Building

(or how to estimate how many bricks will be needed for a project)

Rule

■ Multiply the length of the wall in feet by its height in feet, and that by its thickness in feet, and then multiply that result by 20. The answer will be the number of bricks in the wall.

Example

■ 30 feet (length) x 20 feet (height) x 1½ feet (thickness) = 900 x 20 = 18,000 bricks

Animal Terminology

Animal	Male	Female	Young
Ant	Male-ant (reproductive)	Queen (reproductive), worker (nonreproductive)	Antling
Antelope	Ram	Ewe	Calf, fawn, kid, yearling
Ass	Jack, jackass	Jenny	Foal
Bear	Boar, he-bear	Sow, she-bear	Cub
Beaver	Boar	Sow	Kit, kitten
Bee	Drone	Queen or queen bee, worker (nonreproductive)	Larva
Buffalo	Bull	Cow	Calf, yearling, spike-bull
Camel	Bull	Cow	Calf, colt
Caribou	Bull, stag, hart	Cow, doe	Calf, fawn
Cat	Tom, tomcat, gib, gibcat, boarcat, ramcat	Tabby, grimalkin, malkin, pussy, queen	Kitten, kit, kitling, kitty, pussy
Cattle	Bull	Cow	Calf, stot, yearling, bullcalf, heifer
Chicken	Rooster, cock, stag, chanticleer	Hen, partlet, biddy	Chick, chicken, poult, cockerel, pullet
Deer	Buck, stag	Doe	Fawn
Dog	Dog	Bitch	Whelp
Duck	Drake, stag	Duck	Duckling, flapper
Elephant	Bull	Cow	Calf
Fox	Dog	Vixen	Kit, pup, cub
Giraffe	Bull	Cow	Calf
Goat	Buck, billy, billie, billie-goat, he-goat	She-goat, nanny, nannie, nannie-goat	Kid
Goose	Gander, stag	Goose, dame	Gosling
Horse	Stallion, stag, horse, stud	Mare, dam	Colt, foal, stot, stag, filly, hog-colt, hogget
Kangaroo	Buck	Doe	Joey
Leopard	Leopard	Leopardess	Cub
Lion	Lion, tom	Lioness, she-lion	Shelp, cub, lionet
Moose	Bull	Cow	Calf
Partridge	Cock	Hen	Cheeper
Quail	Cock	Hen	Cheeper, chick, squealer
Reindeer	Buck	Doe	Fawn
Seal	Bull	Cow	Whelp, pup, cub, bachelor
Sheep	Buck, ram, male-sheep, mutton	Ewe, dam	Lamb, lambkin, shearling, yearling, cosset, hog
Swan	Cob	Pen	Cygnet
Swine	Boar	Sow	Shoat, trotter, pig, piglet, farrow, suckling
Termite	King	Queen	Nymph
Walrus	Bull	Cow	Cub
Whale	Bull	Cow	Calf
Zebra	Stallion	Mare	Colt, foal

Collective

Collective
Colony, nest, army, state, swarm
Herd
Pace, drove, herd
Sleuth, sloth
Family, colony
Swarm, grist, cluster, nest, hive, erst
Troop, herd, gang
Flock, train, caravan
Herd
Clowder, clutter (kindle or kendle of kittens)
Drove, herd
Flock, run, brood, clutch, peep
Herd, leash
Pack (cry or mute of hounds, leash of greyhounds)
Brace, team, paddling, raft, bed, flock, flight
Herd
Leash, skulk, cloud, troop
Herd, corps, troop
Tribe, trip, flock, herd
Flock (on land), gaggle, skein (in flight), gaggle or plump (on water)
Haras, stable, remuda, herd, string, field, set, pair, team
Mob, troop, herd
Leap
Pride, troop, flock, sawt, souse
Herd
Covey
Bevy, covey
Herd
Pod, herd, trip, rookery, harem
Flock, drove, hirsel, trip, pack
Herd, team, bank, wege, bevy
Drift, sounder, herd, trip (litter of pigs)
Colony, nest, swarm, brood
Pod, herd
Gam, pod, school, herd
Herd

More Animal Collectives

army of caterpillars, frogs
bale of turtles
band of gorillas
bed of clams, oysters
brood of jellyfish
business of flies
cartload of monkeys
cast of hawks
cete of badgers
charm of goldfinches
chatter of budgerigars
cloud of gnats, flies, grasshoppers, locusts
colony of penguins
congregation of plovers
convocation of eagles
crash of rhinoceri
descent of woodpeckers
dole of turtles
down of hares
dray of squirrels
dule of turtle doves
exaltation of larks
family of sardines
flight of birds
flock of lice
gang of elks
hatch of flies
horde of gnats
host of sparrows

hover of trout
husk of hares
knab of toads
knot of toads, snakes
murder of crows
murmuration of starlings
mustering of storks
nest of vipers
nest or nide of pheasants
pack of weasels
pladge of wasps
plague of locusts
scattering of herons
sedge or siege of cranes
smuck of jellyfish
span of mules
spring of teals
steam of minnows
tittering of magpies
troop of monkeys
troubling of goldfish
volery of birds
watch of nightingales
wing of plovers
yoke of oxen

Dogs: Gentle, Fierce, Smart, Popular

Gentlest Breeds	Fiercest Breeds	Smartest Breeds	Most Popular Breeds
Golden retriever	Pit bull	Border collie	Labrador retriever
Labrador retriever	German shepherd	Poodle	Rottweiler
Shetland sheepdog	Husky	German shepherd	Cocker spaniel
Old English sheepdog	Malamute	(Alsatian)	German shepherd
Welsh terrier	Doberman pinscher	Golden retriever	Poodle
Yorkshire terrier	Rottweiler	Doberman pinscher	Golden retriever
Beagle	Great Dane	Shetland sheepdog	Beagle
Dalmatian	Saint Bernard	Labrador retriever	Dachshund
Pointer		Papillon	Shetland sheepdog
		Rottweiler	Chow chow
		Australian cattle dog	

Don't Poison Your Pussycat!

■ Certain common houseplants are poisonous to cats. They should not be allowed to eat the following:

➤ Azalea *(Rhododendron)*

➤ Common or cherry laurel *(Prunus laurocerasus)*

➤ Dumb cane *(Dieffenbachia)*

➤ Elephant's ears *(Caladium)*

➤ Mistletoe *(Ficus deltoidea)*

➤ Oleander *(Nerium oleander)*

➤ Philodendron *(Philodendron)*

➤ True ivy *(Hedera)*

➤ Winter or false Jerusalem cherry
(Solanum capiscastrum)

Ten Most Intelligent Animals

(besides humans)

■ According to Edward O. Wilson, behavioral biologist, professor of zoology, Harvard University, they are:

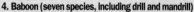

1. Chimpanzee (two species)
2. Gorilla
3. Orangutan
4. Baboon (seven species, including drill and mandrill)
5. Gibbon (seven species)
6. Monkey (many species, especially the macaques, the patas, and the Celebes black ape)
7. Smaller toothed whale (several species, especially killer whale)
8. Dolphin (many of the approximately 80 species)
9. Elephant (two species)
10. Pig

Nutritional Value of Various Insects per 100 Grams

Insect	Protein (g)	Fat (g)	Carbohydrate (g)	Calcium (mg)	Iron (mg)
Giant water beetle	19.8	8.3	2.1	43.5	13.6
Red ant	13.9	3.5	2.9	47.8	5.7
Silkworm pupa	9.6	5.6	2.3	41.7	1.8
Dung beetle	17.2	4.3	0.2	30.9	7.7
Cricket	12.9	5.5	5.1	75.8	9.5
Small grasshopper	20.6	6.1	3.9	35.2	5.0
Large grasshopper	14.3	3.3	2.2	27.5	3.0
June beetle	13.4	1.4	2.9	22.6	6.0
Termite	14.2	—	—	—	35.5
Weevil	6.7	—	—	—	13.1
Compared with:					
Beef (lean ground)	27.4	—	—	—	3.5
Fish (broiled cod)	28.5	—	—	—	1.0

– courtesy Department of Entomology, Iowa State University

The Songs We Sang:
The Greatest Tunes of the Decades

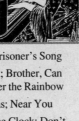

1900-1909   Let Me Call You Sweetheart; Down by the Old Mill Stream; The Preacher and the Bear

1910-1919   Alexander's Ragtime Band; Casey Jones

1920-1929   Sonny Boy; My Blue Heaven; The Prisoner's Song

1930-1939   Cheek to Cheek; Brother, Can You Spare a Dime?; Over the Rainbow

1940-1949   White Christmas; Near You

1950-1959   Rock Around the Clock; Don't Be Cruel

1960-1969   Hey Jude; Yesterday

1970-1979   You Light Up My Life; Tie a Yellow Ribbon 'Round the Old Oak Tree

1980-1989   Thriller; Physical

1990-1999   Candle in the Wind; My Heart Will Go On; I Will Always Love You

– compiled by Kenneth Sheldon

Famous Last Words of Real People

"My exit is the result of too many entrees."
– Richard Monckton Milnes (Victorian politician)

"I'm dying, as I have lived, beyond my means."
– Oscar Wilde

"I am going to the great perhaps."
– Rabelais (writer, priest, physician)

"Well, if this is dying, there is nothing unpleasant about it."
– Maria Mitchell (professor of astronomy)

"Just pull my legs straight, and place me as a dead man; it will save trouble for you shortly."
– Dr. Fidge

"I am about to — or I am going to — die: either expression is used."
– Dominique Bouhours (philosopher and grammarian)

". . . the fog is rising."
– Emily Dickinson

"New Years Rulins"
Resolutions written by Woody Guthrie

1. Work more and better
2. Work by a schedule
3. Wash teeth if any
4. Shave
5. Take bath
6. Eat good — fruit - vegetables - milk
7. Drink very scant if any
8. Write a song a day
9. Wear clean clothes — look good
10. Shine shoes
11. Change socks
12. Change bed clothes often
13. Read lots of good books
14. Listen to radio a lot
15. Learn people better
16. Keep rancho clean
17. Don't get lonesome
18. Stay glad
19. Keep hoping machine running
20. Dream good
21. Bank all extra money
22. Save dough
23. Have company but don't waste time
24. Send Mary and kids money
25. Play and sing good
26. Dance better
27. Help win war — beat fascism
28. Love Mama
29. Love Papa
30. Love Pete
31. Love everybody
32. Make up your mind
33. Wake up and fight

– courtesy the Woody Guthrie Archives

Know Your Angels

I.	**First Group — nearest to God**	Seraphim Cherubim Thrones
II.	**Second Group — receives the reflection of Divine Presence from the first group**	Dominions Virtues Powers
III.	**Angelic Group — ministers directly to human beings**	Principalities Archangels Angels

Animals in the Bible (KJV)

■ In addition to the following list of references to specific animals, there are numerous general references: beast (337), cattle (153), fowl (90), fish (56), bird (54), and serpent (53).

Animal	Old Testament	New Testament	Total
Sheep	155	45	200
Lamb	153	35	188
Ox	156	10	166
Ram	165	0	165
Lion	145	9	154
Horse	137	16	153
Bullock	152	0	152
Ass	142	9	151
Goat	127	7	134
Camel	56	6	62

The Golden Rule

(It's true in all faiths.)

Brahmanism:
This is the sum of duty: Do naught unto others which would cause you pain if done to you.
Mahabharata 5:1517

Buddhism:
Hurt not others in ways that you yourself would find hurtful.
Udana-Varga 5:18

Confucianism:
Surely it is the maxim of loving-kindness: Do not unto others what you would not have them do unto you.   *Analects 15:23*

Taoism:
Regard your neighbor's gain as your own gain and your neighbor's loss as your own loss.
T'ai Shang Kan Ying P'ien

Zoroastrianism:
That nature alone is good which refrains from doing unto another whatsoever is not good for itself.
Dadistan-i-dinik 94:5

Judaism:
What is hateful to you, do not to your fellowman. That is the entire Law; all the rest is commentary.
Talmud, Shabbat 31a

Christianity:
All things whatsoever ye would that men should do to you, do ye even so to them; for this is the law and the prophets.
Matthew 7:12

Islam:
No one of you is a believer until he desires for his brother that which he desires for himself.
Sunnah

– courtesy Elizabeth Pool